Evolutionary Multi-Criteria Optimization: Methods and Applications

Evolutionary Multi-Criteria Optimization: Methods and Applications

Guest Editors

Rui Wang
Shi Cheng

MDPI

Basel • Beijing • Wuhan • Barcelona • Belgrade • Novi Sad • Cluj • Manchester

Guest Editors

Rui Wang
College of System
Engineering
National University of
Defense Technology
Changsha
China

Shi Cheng
School of Artificial
Intelligence and Computer
Science
Shaanxi Normal University
Xi'an
China

Editorial Office
MDPI AG
Grosspeteranlage 5
4052 Basel, Switzerland

This is a reprint of the Special Issue, published open access by the journal *Mathematics* (ISSN 2227-7390), freely accessible at: https://www.mdpi.com/journal/mathematics/special_issues/Evol_Multi_Criteria_Optim.

For citation purposes, cite each article independently as indicated on the article page online and as indicated below:

Lastname, A.A.; Lastname, B.B. Article Title. *Journal Name* **Year**, *Volume Number*, Page Range.

ISBN 978-3-7258-5509-4 (Hbk)
ISBN 978-3-7258-5510-0 (PDF)
https://doi.org/10.3390/books978-3-7258-5510-0

Contents

About the Editors

Rui Wang

Rui Wang received his B.S. degree from the National University of Defense Technology (NUDT), China, in July 2008, and his Ph.D. degree from the University of Sheffield, UK, in January 2014. Currently, he works as a Professor with the National University of Defense Technology. His current research interests include multi-objective optimization and the development of algorithms applicable in practice. He has authored more than 40 peer-reviewed papers including those published in *IEEE Transactions on Evolutionary Computation* and *IEEE Transactions on Cybernetics*. Dr. Wang serves as an Associate Editor of many journals, including *IEEE Transactions on Evolutionary Computation*, *Swarm and Evolutionary Computation*, and *Expert System with Applications*. He was awarded the Operational Research (OR) Society Doctoral Award in 2014, the Funds for Distinguished Young Scientists from the Natural Science Foundation of Hunan Province in 2016, the Wu Wen-Jun Artificial Intelligence Outstanding Young Scholar in 2017, and the National Science Fund for Outstanding Young Scholars in 2021.

Shi Cheng

Shi Cheng received his bachelor's degree in Mechanical and Electrical Engineering from Xiamen University, Xiamen, China, his master's degree in Software Engineering from Beihang University (BUAA), Beijing, China, and his Ph.D. degree in Electrical Engineering and Electronics from the University of Liverpool, Liverpool, UK, in 2005, 2008, and 2013, respectively. He is currently an Associate Professor at the School of Artificial Intelligence and Computer Science, Shaanxi Normal University, Xi'an, China. His current research interests include swarm intelligence, automated planning, and big data mining techniques, as well as their applications. He has authored more than 40 peer-reviewed papers, including those published in *IEEE Transactions on Evolutionary Computation* and *IEEE Transactions on Cybernetics*. Dr. Cheng serves as an Associate Editor for *Expert Systems with Applications*, *Computers & Industrial Engineering*, and other publications.

mathematics

MDPI

Editorial

Evolutionary Multi-Criteria Optimization: Methods and Applications

Shi Cheng [1] and Rui Wang [2,*]

[1] School of Artificial Intelligence and Computer Science, Shaanxi Normal University, Xi'an 710119, China; cheng@snnu.edu.cn
[2] College of Systems Engineering, National University of Defense Technology, Changsha 410073, China
* Correspondence: rui_wang@nudt.edu.cn

Complex problems usually require the simultaneous consideration of multiple performance criteria within multidisciplinary environments. Since the mid-1990s, population-based heuristic approaches have been widely used by researchers in the field of evolutionary multi-criteria/multi-objective optimization (EMO) to address such problems. The EMO research is supported by the rapidly growing number of research publications and the availability of numerous related software tools [see the journal *IEEE Transactions on Evolutionary Computation*]. Recently, EMO researchers have recognized the need to develop and integrate decision-making into EMO, and the need for cross-fertilization between EMO and the multiple-criteria decision-making (MCDM) communities has become apparent.

This Special Issue aims to bring together both experts and newcomers to discuss new and existing issues in these areas, in particular to continue the integration and blending of ideas between EMO and MCDM researchers, thereby stimulating engagement with the user community. Ten papers from five countries (China, Contributions 1–7; the UK, Contribution 8; Kazakhstan, Contribution 9; Republic of Korea, Contribution 10; and Canada, Contribution 10) have been accepted for publication in this Special Issue.

Theory analysis and new algorithms are practical approaches for solving EMO problems. Combining the evolutionary algorithm with the reinforcement learning algorithm is an efficient approach for solving multi-objective optimization problems. The advantages of evolutionary algorithms and machine learning algorithms could be integrated through combining learning and optimization. A hybrid improved arithmetic optimization algorithm was proposed for solving global and engineering optimization problems in Contribution 6.

Real-world applications are vital for EMO research. A multi-objective evolutionary algorithm was proposed for optimizing standalone hybrid renewable energy system (HRES) configuration problems (Contribution 1). An improved intelligent auction mechanism was utilized to solve a multi-trip, time-dependent, dynamic vehicle routing problem with split delivery (Contribution 2). A multi-kernel learning algorithm with a multi-strategy grey wolf optimizer based on time series (MSGWO-MKL-SVM) was utilized in UAV swarm network reconstruction (Contribution 3). A bilevel optimal sizing and operation method was proposed for solving fuel cell/battery hybrid all-electric ship problems (Contribution 8). Heuristic methods for fuzzy multi-criteria decision-making were proposed to solve the problems of controlling the operating modes of the stabilization column in the primary oil-refining unit (Contribution 9). An equivalent load-based method was proposed to solve time-of-use pricing optimization problems (Contribution 4). An energy–logistics collaborative optimization method was proposed to fully tap the potential of port-integrated energy systems (Contribution 5). An improved Pareto local search-based evolutionary algorithm was proposed for solving the multi-objective shortest-path network counter-interdiction problem (Contribution 7). A multi-modal convolutional neural network integrated with an evolutionary optimization method was proposed to solve the determination of sequential well placement problems (Contribution 10). The EMO methods could be more useful with more applications.

We would like to thank several Academic Editors and the Managing Editor, Ms. Helene Hu, for their excellent assistance with this Special Issue during the entire process. We are equally grateful to all the authors for their valuable contributions and to the reviewers for their constructive suggestions that have greatly helped to improve the quality of the papers presented here. We hope that the reader finds the papers collected in this thematic Special Issue interesting and helpful.

Funding: The authors gratefully acknowledge the financial support provided by the Open Project of Xiangjiang Laboratory (No. 22XJ02003), the National Natural Science Foundation of China (72421002), the Science & Technology Project for Young and Middle-aged Talents of Hunan (2023TJ-Z03), the University Fundamental Research Fund (23-ZZCX-JDZ-28), the Natural Science Basic Research Plan In Shaanxi Province of China (No. 2024JC-YBMS-516), and the Fundamental Research Funds for the Central Universities (No. GK202507001).

Conflicts of Interest: The authors declare no conflicts of interest.

List of Contributions:

1. Li, K.; Song, Y.; Wang, R. Multi-Objective Optimal Sizing of HRES under Multiple Scenarios with Undetermined Probability. *Mathematics* **2022**, *10*, 1508. https://doi.org/10.3390/math10091508.
2. Zhang, J.; Zhu, Y.; Wang, T.; Wang, W.; Wang, R.; Li, X. An Improved Intelligent Auction Mechanism for Emergency Material Delivery. *Mathematics* **2022**, *10*, 2184. https://doi.org/10.3390/math10132184.
3. Nan, M.; Zhu, Y.; Zhang, J.; Wang, T.; Zhou, X. MSGWO-MKL-SVM: A Missing Link Prediction Method for UAV Swarm Network Based on Time Series. *Mathematics* **2022**, *10*, 2535. https://doi.org/10.3390/math10142535.
4. Zeng, X.; He, Z.; Wang, Y.; Wu, Y.; Liu, A. An Effective Method of Equivalent Load-Based Time of Use Electricity Pricing to Promote Renewable Energy Consumption. *Mathematics* **2024**, *12*, 1408. https://doi.org/10.3390/math12091408.
5. Mo, A.; Zhang, Y.; Xiong, Y.; Ma, F.; Sun, L. Energy–Logistics Cooperative Optimization for a Port-Integrated Energy System. *Mathematics* **2024**, *12*, 1917. https://doi.org/10.3390/math12121917.
6. Zhang, Y.; Xing, L. A New Hybrid Improved Arithmetic Optimization Algorithm for Solving Global and Engineering Optimization Problems. *Mathematics* **2024**, *12*, 3221. https://doi.org/10.3390/math12203221.
7. Mao, C.; Gao, R.; Luo, Q.; Wu, G. An Improved Pareto Local Search-Based Evolutionary Algorithm for Multi-Objective Shortest-Path Network Counter-Interdiction Problem. *Mathematics* **2025**, *13*, 2683. https://doi.org/10.3390/math13162683.
8. Jin, H.; Yang, X. Bilevel Optimal Sizing and Operation Method of Fuel Cell/Battery Hybrid All-Electric Shipboard Microgrid. *Mathematics* **2023**, *11*, 2728. https://doi.org/10.3390/math11122728.
9. Orazbayev, B.; Ospanov, Y.; Makhatova, V.; Salybek, L.; Abdugulova, Z.; Kulmagambetova, Z.; Suleimenova, S.; Orazbayeva, K. Methods of Fuzzy Multi-Criteria Decision Making for Controlling the Operating Modes of the Stabilization Column of the Primary Oil-Refining Unit. *Mathematics* **2023**, *11*, 2820. https://doi.org/10.3390/math11132820.
10. Kwon, S.; Ji, M.; Kim, M.; Leung, J.Y.; Min, B. Determination of Sequential Well Placements Using a Multi-Modal Convolutional Neural Network Integrated with Evolutionary Optimization. *Mathematics* **2025**, *13*, 36. https://doi.org/10.3390/math13010036.

mathematics

MDPI

Article

Multi-Objective Optimal Sizing of HRES under Multiple Scenarios with Undetermined Probability

Kaiwen Li, Yuanming Song * and Rui Wang

College of Systems Engineering, National University of Defense Technology, Changsha 410073, China; likaiwen@nudt.edu.cn (K.L.); rui_wang@nudt.edu.cn (R.W.)
* Correspondence: ysong9701@sina.com

Abstract: In recent years, technologies for renewable energy utilization have been booming. Hybrid renewable energy systems (HRESs), integrating multiple energy sources to mitigate the unstable, unpredictable, and intermittent characteristics of a single renewable energy source, have become increasingly popular. However, due to the inherent intermittency and uncertainty of renewable energies, the impact of uncertain factors on the capacity optimization of HRESs needs to be considered. In the traditional scenario-based planning method, when dealing with uncertain factors, the probability corresponding to the scenario is difficult to determine. Furthermore, when applying the robust optimization method, it is difficult to fully use existing data to describe uncertain parameters in the form of intervals. To tackle these difficulties, this study proposes a probability undetermined scenario-based sizing model (PUSS model) for stand-alone HRES configuration optimization and a multi-objective evolutionary algorithm as the problem solver. The solution set obtained by the method covers multiple possible values of scenario probability combinations and can provide decision-makers with an overview of alternatives for HRES sizing under different power supply pressures. Based on the real environment data and load data of a certain place, the proposed model and algorithm are applied to sizing a typical HRES comprising wind generators, solar photovoltaic panels, energy-storage devices, and diesel generators. The experimental results show that the proposed PUSS method is both effective and efficient.

Keywords: HRES; microgrid; multiple scenarios; multi-objective optimization; evolutionary algorithms; decision-making

MSC: 90C29

1. Introduction

As countries continue to focus on energy security and the need to achieve low-carbon development, more and more hybrid renewable energy systems (HRESs) have been built and put into practice. Because of its multi-energy complementarity and its ability to operate off-grid, a self-sufficient, independent hybrid renewable energy system is often used for power supply on remote islands and in high mountain residential areas. Simultaneously, the structure of microgrids can be adjusted to meet specific local needs.

Till now, researchers have conducted a series of relevant research for the optimal design of microgrids [1–3]. The data, e.g., solar radiation intensity or wind speed, is often taken from historical records [1,2] or is predicated based on historical data [3]. Even if different types of neural networks are used for prediction, the application scenarios are different [4–6], and the predicted results still reflect the characteristics of historical data. However, due to the inherent intermittency and uncertainty of the output of renewable energies, even if multi-energy complementarity [1–3] is achieved, its energy supply still has many unstable factors than traditional hydropower and thermal power plants. When climate anomalies or natural disasters occur, this intermittency and uncertainty can even become extremely deadly. Therefore, in the capacity optimization of HRESs, the influence of uncertain factors needs to be considered.

Using the existing methods considering uncertainty [7–17] to perform microgrid planning can only obtain a set of solutions with a certain degree of environmental uncertainty. Hence, decision-makers can only choose among the solutions with this degree of uncertainty. To solve these problems, this paper proposes a probability undetermined scenario-based sizing model (PUSS model) for HRES configuration optimization. We incorporate the occurrence probability of the scenario into the optimization objectives. A set of configuration schemes that can cope with various environmental uncertainties can be obtained by conducting the proposed multi-objective evolutionary algorithm. This solution set allows decision-makers to intuitively understand the relationship between the maximum environmental uncertainty that the microgrid can bear and the objectives (for example, economic costs, lost probability of power supply, etc.) of configuration optimization. The PUSS model does not rely on the probability distribution of various uncertain factors and does not need to obtain the probability of each uncertain scenario. Multiple solutions that are used to deal with different environmental data uncertainties can be obtained in a single run.

The contributions of this paper are summarized as follows:

(i) A probability undetermined scenario-based HRES sizing (PUSS) model is proposed. This model can solve the issue that traditional scenario-based HRES configuration optimization relies heavily on actual data or cannot make full use of existing data.

(ii) The effectiveness of the PUSS model is demonstrated by comparing its results with those obtained by repeatedly solving the scenario-based dual-objective HRES optimization with preset scenario probability combinations. PUSS obtains a comparable solution quality, but with significantly less calculation cost.

The remainder of this paper is organized as follows: Section 2 reviews related studies for microgrid planning considering uncertainty. Section 3 introduces the structure, main energy supply unit model, and operation strategy of HRESs. Section 4 elaborates the principles of the PUSS model and its application. In Section 5, the solution of the PUSS model is performed based on NSGA-II, whose results are compared with the results of a scenario-based dual-objective HRES optimization method using the same algorithm, NSGA-II. Section 6 concludes this study.

2. Literature Review

In the literature, there are mainly two classes of methods to deal with uncertainties in HRES configuration optimization. These are robust optimization methods and stochastic programming.

HERS configuration optimization based on robust optimization generally uses the interval form to describe uncertain factors such as wind speed and illumination intensity. The authors in [10] adopted a robust optimization method to perform energy system design and found that the obtained results exhibit better performance than those obtained by a deterministic model. The study [11] considered the trade-off between expected costs in the nominal scenario and costs in the worst case while guaranteeing the security of energy supply. A two-stage robustness trade-off approach was proposed to design energy supply systems.

Robust optimization methods based on uncertain parameters described in the form of intervals require fewer characteristics of the uncertain parameters. Only the fluctuation interval instead of the accurate probability distribution is required, which makes the robust optimization method widely used in engineering problems [10,11,13,15]. However, at the same time, it brings about the problem that too little information is needed and the existing information cannot be effectively used when using a robust optimization method to perform HRES configuration optimization. This makes robust optimization methods bring large additional costs while ensuring energy supply security.

In terms of stochastic programming, a typical way is to use multiple scenarios to represent the relevant uncertainty and set each scenario with a corresponding probability. The work [7] presented a model for optimal distributed energy system design under uncertainty, which was formulated as a two-stage stochastic mixed-integer linear program, and probabilistic scenarios were used to describe the uncertainty. In [8], a stochastic model was proposed for coordinated scheduling of renewable and thermal units. Uncertainties of wind speed, solar irradiation, and market prices were considered in this scenario-based model. In [9], a scenario-based method was used for modeling the uncertainties of electrical market price, wind speed, and solar irradiation, and the multi-objective firefly algorithm was used to solve the stochastic nonlinear programming model.

The description of uncertainty in stochastic programming methods is often based on scenarios. The scenarios and the corresponding probability of each scenario should reflect the future operation of HRESs. However, the scenario structure and the determination of the scenario probability under this requirement is quite difficult. There are many uncertain factors in the microgrid system, and the probability distribution function is complex, which is difficult to obtain accurately. Correspondingly, the reliability of the optimization results obtained by the stochastic optimization method is weakened.

Besides, there is also a class of scenario-based robust optimal design methods [16,17], which have been developed from the minimax regret criterion (MMR) method [18] and derived minimax expected criterion (MER) [19] and other methods. In [12], a new method was proposed to solve the upper bound of the maximum regret optimal value and revise the robust optimization design method of the energy supply system under uncertain energy demand. Since such methods also perform optimization calculations based on energy use scenarios and their corresponding probabilities, they all face the same issue of determining a proper probability of each scenario.

In summary, when sufficient information is available, the optimization results obtained by stochastic programming or scenario-based robust optimization methods are often better than those obtained by robust optimization methods that describe uncertain parameters in the form of intervals. However, it is not easy to construct the scenario needed for optimization and determine its corresponding probability. The above-mentioned methods used to deal with uncertain factors in HRESs have their shortcomings. For example, they can only perform optimization based on a certain degree of environmental uncertainty (indicated by uncertain intervals or scenarios with their corresponding probabilities). In this way, the optimization results are only able to deal with a specific maximum environmental uncertainty and cannot reflect the relationship between environmental uncertainty and the goals of microgrid optimization.

Compared with the traditional stochastic programming method, the PUSS model proposed in this study does not need to pre-determine the probability of each scenario. Furthermore, a variety of configuration schemes, corresponding to various maximum environmental uncertainties, can be obtained in one solution set. As for the scenario-based robust optimization method, since the PUSS model uses the same probabilistic way as the stochastic programming method in describing scenarios, rather than describing the uncertainty by uncertainty intervals, and the use of the PUSS model would generally lead to better results than interval-number-based robust optimization methods.

3. HRES Model

3.1. The Structure of the HRES

The case study in this study is based on an off-grid HRES using a DC bus structure simplified from [20], consisting of photovoltaic panels, wind turbines, diesel generators, batteries, and other accessories, as shown in Figure 1. The unit models of the system are shown in [20]. The HRES sizing involves the combinatorial optimization of multiple devices. For a certain probability combination of the scenario set, the optimal solution needs to be weighed under multiple goals to satisfy the requirements of reliable power supply, low cost, and environmental friendliness. This study, therefore, proposes a method to find an optimal solution under different probability combinations of the scenario set.

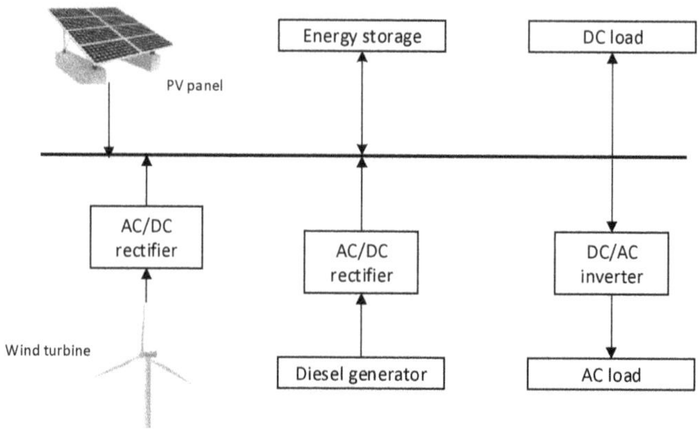

Figure 1. Off-grid HRES structure.

3.2. HRES Operating Strategies

Since the off-grid HRES model in this paper uses a DC bus, the electrical energy output by photovoltaic arrays and wind turbines will be directly supplied to the DC loads, and it will be converted by the inverter when supplying AC loads. If the power generated by renewable energies exceeds the total demand (DC loads plus AC loads), the excess power would be stored in the battery packs after all loads are met. Conversely, if the amount of power generated by renewable energies cannot meet the load demand, the battery pack would be discharged based on the state of charge, that is the state of charge cannot be lower than the minimum.

If the battery packs can meet all loads, they will meet the DC loads and the AC loads in order; if they still cannot meet the load demand, the diesel generators start to fill the power shortage. Because the electricity generated by the diesel generators is alternating current, the electricity used to provide the DC loads will be converted into direct current by the rectifier. If the diesel generators are all running at full power output, but the microgrid system still has a power shortage, this situation will be included in the statistics of the lack of power supply.

4. PUSS Model

4.1. Principle of the Model

4.1.1. Microgrid Operating Scenario and Its Power Supply Pressure

Before introducing the PUSS model, the microgrid operating scenario (hereinafter referred to as simply the scenario) and the power supply pressure are defined. The scenario used in microgrid optimization is essentially a microgrid operating state determined by environmental conditions and load demand. Scenarios are generally generated based on actual data, and a small number of representative scenarios are obtained for microgrid optimization through clustering and some scenario reduction methods.

For a specific scenario, environmental conditions such as solar irradiation and wind speed in the scenario affect the power supply capacity of the microgrid. Whether the power supply capacity matches the load demand determines the power supply pressure of the microgrid in this scenario. Specifically, the power supply pressure of a scenario refers to the difficulty for the HRES to meet the power demand of all loads in this scenario. The more difficult it is to meet the power demand of all loads, the larger the pressure on the power supply is.

4.1.2. The Occurrence Probability of the Scenario

In the traditional scenario-based method, the occurrence probability of each scenario needs to be determined when constructing the scenario set required for optimization; the sum of the probabilities of all scenarios in the set is 1. In the PUSS model, the occurrence probabilities of the scenarios used for optimization need not be determined in advance.

The scenario set required by the PUSS model can be expressed as: $S = \{S_1, S_2, \ldots, S_n\}$. The occurrence probability corresponding to the scenario S_i is denoted as $P_s^i, i = 1, 2, \cdots, n$. Here, the label i of S_i is determined according to the power supply pressure of the microgrid in each scenario. The smaller the power supply pressure, the smaller the label. Then, we have:

$$PRES(S_1) \leq PRES(S_2) \leq \ldots \leq PRES(S_{n-1}) < PRES(S_n) \tag{1}$$

$PRES(S_i)$ indicates the power supply pressure in scenario S_i. The maximum power supply pressure $PRES(S_n)$ must be strictly greater than the power supply pressure of other scenarios.

In this paper, P_s^i, which corresponds to element S_i in the scenario set, constitutes probability set P. For the set P, there are:

$$\begin{array}{l} P = \{P_s^1, P_s^2, \ldots, P_s^n\}, \\ \sum_{i=1}^{n} P_s^i = 1, P_s^i \geq 0. \end{array} \tag{2}$$

Here, the set obtained by assigning values to all the elements in P is defined as a scenario probability combination.

4.1.3. Optimization Objectives

This paper proposes a probability undetermined scenario-based sizing model (PUSS model) and algorithm for off-grid HRES configuration optimization. In general, objectives in a multi-objective problem conflict with one another. Figure 2 illustrates the solution set of the inverted two-objective MOP2 problem obtained by NSGA-II.

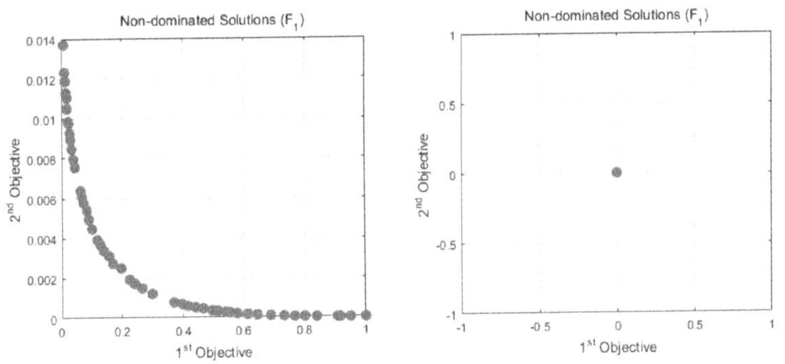

Figure 2. Example of a two-objective minimization problem solution set. (**a**) Mutually constrained dual-target Pareto front. (**b**) Unconstrained two-objective optimization results.

Taking the dual-target capacity optimization of the HRES as an example, the annualized cost of the system (*ACS*) and the loss probability of power supply (*LPSP*) are selected as the optimization goals. The objective function should be:

$$\text{Min } F_{obj}^{origin} = (ACS, LPSP). \tag{3}$$

Minimizing the *LPSP* requires a higher power supply capacity of the microgrid, which naturally leads to an increase in the annual cost of the microgrid. Therefore, there is a restrictive relationship between the *ACS* and *LPSP*.

The *ACS* and *LPSP* are computed according to the PV power, wind power, diesel power, load power, battery charging, and discharging power. Specifically, the output power of PV panels is computed by [20]:

$$\begin{aligned} &T_C(t) = T_A(t) + \tfrac{\text{NCOT}-20}{800} S_P(t,\beta) \\ &I_{SC}(t) = [I_{SC,STC} + K_I(T_C(t) - 25)] \tfrac{S_P(t,\beta)}{1000} \\ &V_{OC}(t) = V_{OC,STC} - K_V \cdot T_C(t) \\ &P_M(t,\beta) = N_S \cdot N_P \cdot V_{OC}(t) \cdot I_{SC}(t,\beta) \cdot FF(t) \end{aligned} \tag{4}$$

where N_P, β are decision variables that indicate the number of PV modules and the PV panel slope angle. Refer to [20] for the details of other parameters. The output power of wind turbine is computed by [20]:

$$P_{WG}(v,t) = \begin{cases} 0, & v < V_c \\ \frac{1}{2} C_P \rho A_{WG} v^3, & V_c \leqslant v < V_r \\ P_{WGR}, & V_r \leqslant v < V_f \\ 0, & v \geqslant V_f \end{cases}, v = v_r \left(\frac{H_{wg}}{H_r} \right)^{\gamma} \tag{5}$$

where H_{wg} is the decision variable that indicates the wind turbine height. v_r is the wind speed at the reference height H_r. V_c, V_f, V_r are the cut-in, cut-off, and rated wind speed. In addition, the battery model is constructed as:

$$\text{SOC}(t+1) = \text{SOC}(t) + \frac{(P_{bat}(t)/V_{bus}) \cdot \Delta t \cdot \eta_{bat}}{C_n} \tag{6}$$

where $P_{bat} < 0$ represents the charging power and $P_{bat} > 0$ represents the discharging power. C_n is the total capacity of the energy storage determined by the number of batteries N_{bat}, which is to be optimized. V_{bus} and η_{bat} are the DC bus voltage and the round-trip efficiency.

Accordingly, the objective of the LPSP is computed as:

$$\text{LPSP} = \frac{\sum_{t=0}^{T} \left(P_{dg}(t) + P_{pv}(t) + P_{wg}(t) + P_{es}(t) < P_{load}(t) \right)}{T} \tag{7}$$

where $P_{dg}(t), P_{pv}(t), P_{wg}(t), P_{es}(t)$ are the output power of diesel generators, PV panels, wind turbines, and batteries, as calculated above.

The ACS is computed as:

$$\begin{aligned} \text{ACS} = &C_{ainv}(\text{PV} + \text{WG} + \text{ Tower } + \text{BAT} + \text{DG}) \\ &+ C_{aom}(\text{PV} + \text{WG} + \text{ Tower } + \text{BAT} + \text{DG}) \end{aligned} \tag{8}$$

where C_{ainv} represents the annualized cost of initial investment, which is determined by the number of diesel generators, PV panels, wind turbines, and batteries. C_{aom} is the operation and maintenance cost, which is calculated by the number/time of operations and fuel consumption. The fuel consumption of the diesel generator is computed as:

$$F_{cons} = A_{dg} P_{rdg} + B_{dg} P_{dg} \tag{9}$$

where A_{dg}, B_{dg} are fuel consumption coefficients and P_{rdg} represents the rated power of the generator.

The PUSS model adds all the elements in the probability set P, except P_s^n (the amount of elements in P is n), to the original objective function F_{obj}^{origin} and hopes to minimize the new objective function F_{obj}:

$$\text{Min}\, F_{obj} = \left(ACS, LPSP, P_s^1, P_s^2, \cdots, P_s^{n-1} \right). \tag{10}$$

For the microgrid, the new objective function minimizes the occurrence probability of scenarios with low power supply pressure. In other words, the occurrence probability of the scenario with the highest power supply pressure is maximized. This requires that the microgrid has a higher power supply capacity; there is also a restrictive relationship between the ACS and the scenario probabilities in F_{obj}. Therefore, solving the PUSS model, we can obtain the required Pareto front.

At this front, each solution (configuration scheme) corresponds to a scenario probability combination. This scenario probability combination reflects the maximum environmental uncertainty that the microgrid constructed with its corresponding scheme can withstand. In the combination of scenario probabilities, the greater the occurrence probability of scenarios with high power supply pressure, the greater the maximum environmental uncertainty that the corresponding configuration scheme can withstand.

Through this Pareto front, decision-makers can intuitively understand the relationship between the maximum environmental uncertainty that the microgrid can bear and other objectives in F_{obj}.

4.1.4. Encoding Individuals

At the same time, the encoding of population individuals in evolutionary computation must be adjusted accordingly. The PUSS model encodes decision variables of optimization and a randomly generated scenario probability combination into an individual. Thus, the scenario probability combinations of individuals change in the crossover and mutation process. Individual chromosome composition is shown in Figure 3. Among them, $DV_1 \sim DV_m$ are decision variables in the optimization and $P_s^1 \sim P_s^n$ are all elements in the scenario probability combination.

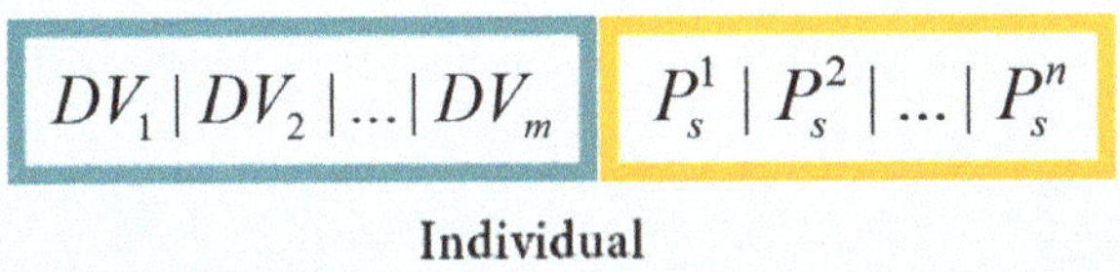

Figure 3. Individual chromosome composition.

The advantage of this method is that the optimal decision variable sets corresponding to similar scenario probability combinations are often similar, and the information of the optimal solution under similar scenario probability combinations can be effectively used when searching for optimal solutions under different scenario probability combinations. In this way, the optimal solution set under a variety of different scenario probability combinations can be obtained quickly.

4.2. Solving Procedure

In past studies, several multi-objective evolutionary algorithms have been proposed, e.g., NSGA-II [21], SPEA2 [22], IBEA [23], MOEA/D [24], and RVEA [25]. Among them, NSGA-II [21] perhaps is the most popular one, which has been applied in many disciplines [26,27]; its characteristics are also suitable for the experiments in this study.

All the solving process in the experimental part of this paper are based on NSGA-II. When using NSGA-II, the procedure of solving the PUSS model is as shown in Figure 4.

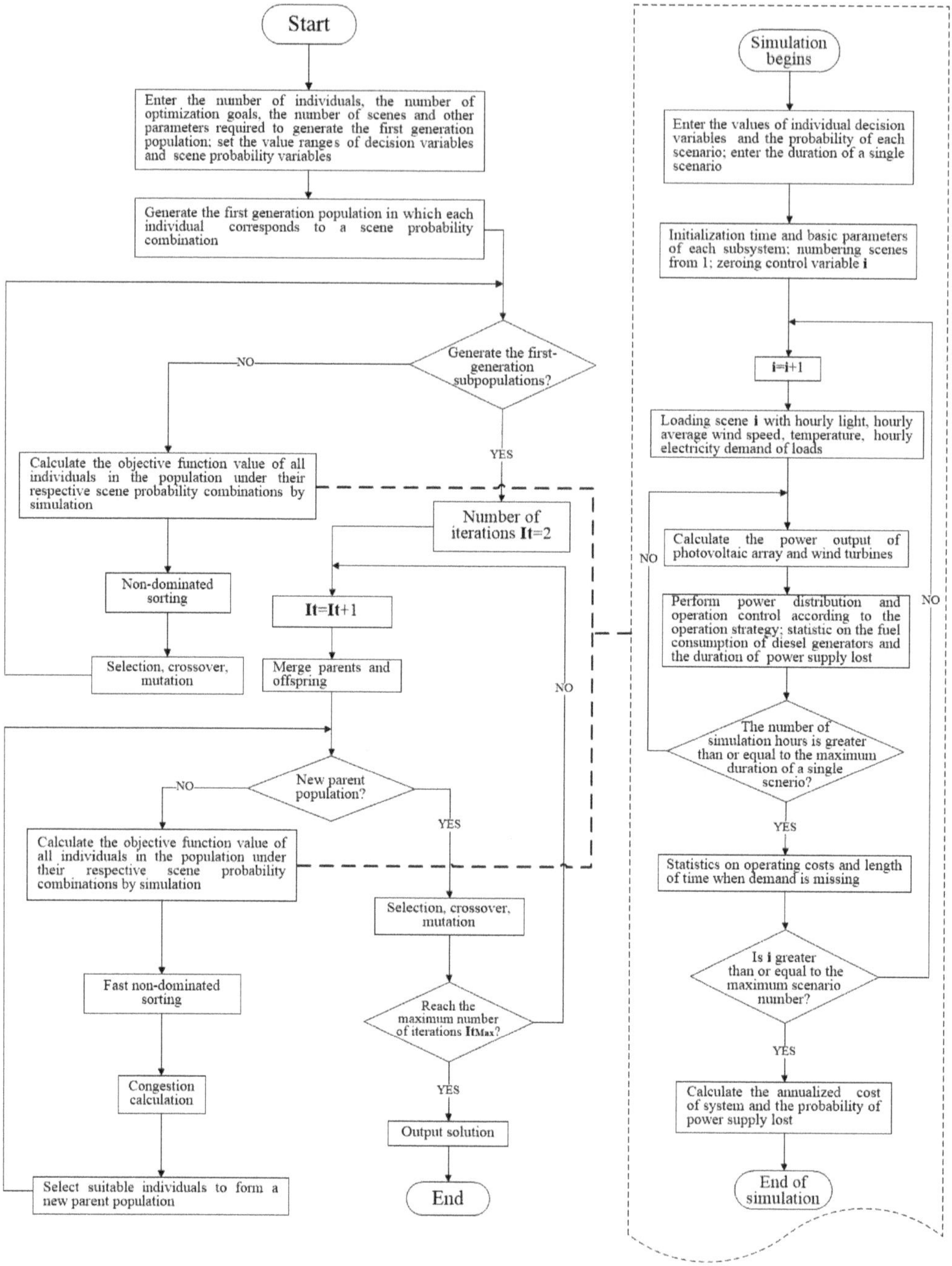

Figure 4. Flowchart of the PUSS model based on NSGA-II.

The input variables include the population size, the number of objectives, the total number of scenarios, the range of the decision variables, and the probability variables of the scenarios. Then, we generate the initial population and start the evolutionary computation. The objective function value is calculated by the simulation of the HRES.

Since the probability combinations of the scenarios corresponding to each individual in the population are different, the probability of each scenario is used as the proportion of the total simulation duration (8760 h) in the simulation calculation. After fast non-dominated sorting, congestion calculation, selection, crossover, and mutation operations, a new generation of the population is obtained. When the evolution reaches the maximum generation, the loop is terminated and the final Pareto front is output.

5. Case Study

5.1. Data Preparation

For the purposes of validating the PUSS method, a remote region (41.65 degrees north latitude) in Spain was selected as the background to carry out the case study. The distribution of the data including load consumption, solar irradiation, temperature, and wind speed is shown in Figure 5, with a total duration of 8760 h.

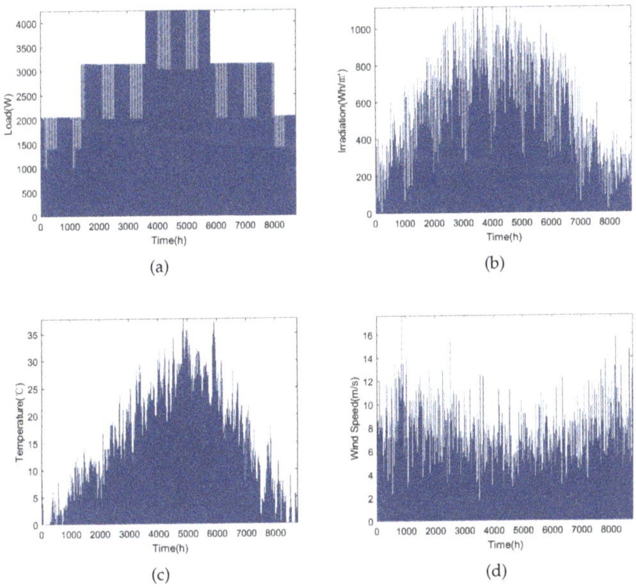

Figure 5. Distribution of load data and environmental data. (**a**) Load. (**b**) Solar irradiation. (**c**) Temperature. (**d**) Wind speed.

5.2. Typical Scenario Construction

When using the PUSS model for HRES planning, the construction of a typical energy consumption scenario must first be performed, and the scenario duration and scenario data step size need to be preset. Generally speaking, the scenario duration is determined according to the planning needs and the richness of the collected data. Typical scenarios can be a typical day, a typical week, or a typical month; the step size of the scenario data should be the same as the simulation step size of the microgrid system. This study set the total scenario duration to 168 h (one week), and the scenario data step size was 1 h; the data required for the scenario were extracted from the existing data set. Because this study needed to compare the performance of multiple evolutionary algorithms in solving the PUSS problem, to quickly obtain the result data, the total number of scenarios here was temporarily set to 2; at this time, the two typical scenarios are the normal power consumption scenario and the peak power consumption scenario. See Figures 6 and 7 for the specific data distribution of a typical week of normal power consumption and a typical week of peak power consumption used in the experiment.

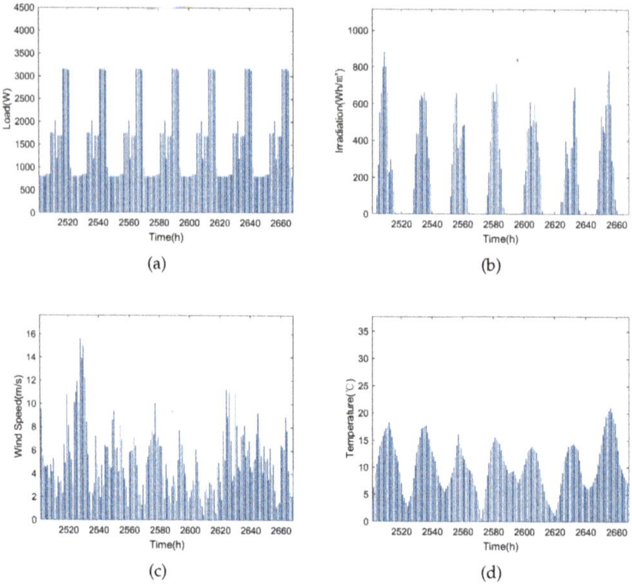

Figure 6. Typical week of normal power consumption. (**a**) Load. (**b**) Solar irradiation. (**c**) Temperature. (**d**) Wind speed.

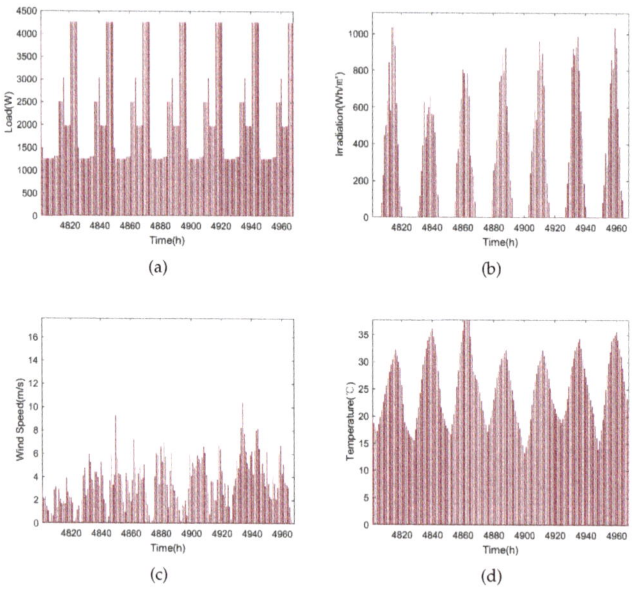

Figure 7. Typical week of peak power consumption. (**a**) Load. (**b**) Solar irradiation. (**c**) Temperature. (**d**) Wind speed.

Among them, the typical week of peak power consumption is taken from the period when the weekly average load reaches its peak within one year; the average load of the selected typical week is about equal to the average load of the whole year. Comparing

Figures 6 and 7, it can be seen that the power demand, temperature, and daily solar irradiation during the typical week of peak power consumption are significantly higher than those of the typical week of normal power consumption; the daily wind speed data of the typical week of peak power consumption are lower than those of the typical week normal power consumption. For typical weekly peak power usage scenarios, higher power demand and lower wind energy resources bring greater pressure on the power supply. Although stronger solar radiation increases the amount of photovoltaic power generation, and to a certain extent alleviates the pressure of the microgrid power supply, it was not enough to offset the pressure on the microgrid power supply caused by the sharply increasing power demand in summer.

Comparing the year-round load and environmental data in Figure 5, the two types of typical weeks constructed can reflect the HRES operating conditions at ordinary times and during peak power consumption. Taking into account the environmental conditions and load data, the power supply pressure during the typical week of peak power consumption is significantly greater than the typical week of normal power consumption. Therefore, the typical week of normal power consumption was set to $S_1$and the typical week of peak power consumption was set to S_2. At this time, $PRES(S_1) \le PRES(S_2)$.

5.3. Parameter Settings

The parameters used in subsequent experiments are set here:

(1) Algorithm running times: the maximum generation number of evolution was $It = 1000$;

(2) Population and individuals: the population size was set to $N = 200$. The dimension of the decision variable for each individual in the population was $D = 6$, and the number of scenarios considered was $S = 2$. The individual coding form is:

$$\left[N_{pv} \middle| N_{wg} \middle| N_{bat} \middle| N_{dg} \middle| H_{wg} | \beta | P_s^1\right]. \tag{11}$$

The above variables represent the number of photovoltaic panels, wind turbines, batteries, and diesel generators, the height of the wind turbine tower, the tilt angle of the photovoltaic panels, and the occurrence probability of a typical week.

(3) The goals of the optimization are:

$$\text{Min}\, F_{obj} = \left(ACS, LPSP, P_s^1\right) \tag{12}$$

(4) Model constraints: For the amount of each microgrid component ($N_{pv}/N_{wg}/N_{bat}/N_{dg}$), the height of wind turbine tower H_{wg}, and the inclination of the photovoltaic panel β, the relevant constraints of the model in [20] were adopted; for the scenario probability P_s^1, $P_s^1 \in [0, 1]$ needs to be met in the optimization. For other parameters of the HRES, refer to [20].

(5) Simulated binary crossover (SBX) and polynomial mutation (PM) were used as the genetic operators. Given parents $\mathbf{x}^1(x_1^1, \cdots, x_n^1)$ and $\mathbf{x}^2(x_1^2, \cdots, x_n^2)$, the offspring $\mathbf{c}^1(c_1^1, \cdots, c_n^1)$ and $\mathbf{c}^2(c_1^2, \cdots, c_n^2)$ can be obtained by SBX as:

$$\begin{cases} c_i^1 = 0.5 \times \left[(1+\beta) \cdot x_i^1 + (1-\beta) \cdot x_i^2\right] \\ c_i^2 = 0.5 \times \left[(1-\beta) \cdot x_i^1 + (1+\beta) \cdot x_i^2\right] \end{cases} \tag{13}$$

where β is calculated according to η by:

$$\beta = \begin{cases} (\text{rand } \times 2)^{1/(1+\eta)} & \text{rand } \le 0.5 \\ (1/(2- \text{ rand } \times 2))^{1/(1+\eta)} & \text{otherwise.} \end{cases} \tag{14}$$

PM uses a polynomial probability distribution to make the current value of a continuous variable change to a neighboring value [28]. The crossover probability pc, mutation probability pm, and distribution index settings are shown in Table 1.

Table 1. Settings of the algorithm parameters.

pc (SBX)	ηc (SBX)	pm (PM)	ηm (PM)
1	20	1	20
It	N	D	S
1000	200	6	2

All solutions were performed based on the PlatEMO [29] platform, a well-known evolutionary multi-objective optimization platform in MATLAB. The algorithms uses the same processor for single-core single-thread calculations.

5.4. *Optimization Results and Performance Evaluation*

Solutions similar to that of the PUSS model can be obtained based on multiple times of solving using any scenario-based multi-objective sizing method; in the multiple times of solving, different preset combinations of scenario probabilities are used, and the final solution sets are merged, while dominated solutions are eliminated.

Therefore, in this section, based on the model and input data described in Section 2, a scenario-based dual-objective HRES optimization method using preset scenario probability combinations was selected. NSGA-II was used to perform multiple iterations and eliminate the dominated solution in the final merged solution set. It was compared with the PF obtained by the PUSS model to evaluate the performance of the PUSS model. Both methods use the same optimization goals and parameter settings.

In order to make the results of the two methods have better comparability and credibility, when the scenario-based dual-objective HRES optimization method was used to solve, the occurrence probability of the scenario was increased or decreased by 2% for each solution. To obtain the final solution set, a total of 51 times of solving was performed; when using the PUSS model to solve, the possible value of the scenario probability was also discretized in units of 2%.

As a comparison method, the scenario-based dual-objective HRES optimization method uses NSGA-II to solve the problem after presetting the scenario probability. The obtained PF quality and the solving speed are both current advanced levels [30]; when comparing the results of the PUSS model based on NSGA-II, the solution performance can be better reflected.

5.4.1. Comparison of Time Consumption

When using NSGA-II to solve the PUSS model, the population number was set to 1020 and the number of iterations was set to 200. The HV curve during the solution is shown in Figure 8; the solution took 9683.0 s and only needs to be solved once. When using NSGA-II to solve the scenario-based dual-objective HRES optimization, we set the number of population to 10 and the number of iterations to 1000. The HV curve in a single solution is shown in Figure 9; 51 iterations were needed to obtain the required solution set. In Figures 8 and 9, the horizontal axis represents the times of evaluations and the ordinate is the HV value. For Figure 8, the population evolves every 1020 times of evaluation; for Figure 9, the population evolves every 10 times of evaluation.

It can be seen that using the PUSS model to perform the optimization, its solution set converged in the 70th generation (after 71,400 times of evaluations); when performing dual-objective HRES optimization, because the required population is small, the HV indicator fluctuates to a certain extent; the solution set converged in the 500th generation (after 5000 times of evaluation). The statistics are shown in Table 2.

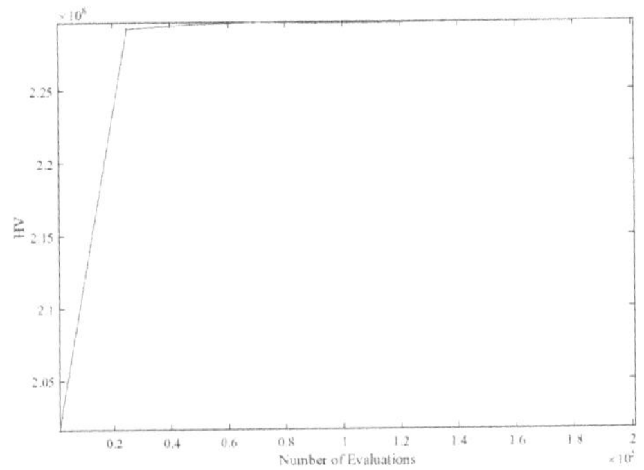

Figure 8. HV curve of the PUSS model.

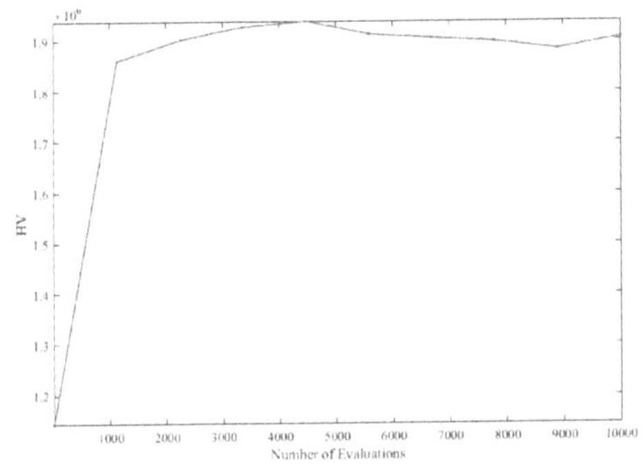

Figure 9. HV curve of dual-objective HRES optimization.

Table 2. Time cost data of methods.

Method	N_{sov} [1]	T_c [2]	G_{conv} [3]	G_{total} [4]	t_c [5]
PUSS	1	9683.0 s	70	200	3389.05 s
Dual-objective HRES optimization	51	402.13 s	500	1000	10,254.315 s

[1] Required solving times; [2] Time-consuming for single solution; [3] Number of iterations required for convergence; [4] Total number of iterations of single solution; [5] Time consumption of solving method.

Taking the time from the beginning of the calculation to the convergence of the solution as the time consumption t_c of the solving method, then:

$$t_c = N_{sov} \cdot T_c \cdot G_{conv} / G_{total} \tag{15}$$

Among them, N_{sov} is the number of times to obtain the required PF, T_c is the time required for a single solution, G_{conv} is the number of iterations required for convergence, and G_{total} is the total number of iterations. As shown in Table 2, the time cost of obtaining the PF by the PUSS model was 3389.05 s; the time cost of obtaining the required solution set by the two-objective HRES optimization solution was 10,254.315 s. It can be seen that the PUSS model has significant advantages in solving time.

If the results of multiple solving using the dual-objective HRES optimization method are directly merged, the solutions in the obtained solution set may dominate each other. Therefore, in addition to the time consumed by multiple iterations, additional non-dominated sorting operations need to be performed on the solution to eliminate dominated solutions. The calculation time (6.690769 s) here should also be included in the algorithm time cost. Hence, the time consumption to obtain the Pareto front by using the dual-objective HRES optimization method multiple times was 10,261.005769 s. Furthermore, removing the dominated solution reduces the number of solutions in the solution set. Therefore, if the two-objective HRES optimization method is used to obtain the same number of solutions as the PUSS model, the actual time consumption will be slightly longer than 10,261.005769 s.

In summary, using the NSGA-II-based PUSS model for optimization, the calculation time of PF was 3389.05 s; using the dual-target HRES optimization method to obtain a solution set of the same quality required more than 10,261.005769 s. In comparison, using the PUSS model for optimization can save at least 66.97% of the time compared with the two-objective HRES optimization method; the PUSS model has a great advantage in the calculation time.

5.4.2. Performance Comparison of Solutions

Firstly, the PUSS method based on NSGA-II was used to optimize the microgrid system. To ensure the coverage of the final solution set, the number of populations was set to 1020. According to the analysis of the convergence of the previous experiments, the number of iterations was set to 125. Then, the solution set obtained by merging the solutions of 51 times of iterations using the scenario-based dual-objective HRES optimization method (based on NSGA-II) was used as a comparison; the scenario probability in the solving process started from 0% and gradually changed to 100% in 2% increments.

Three-dimensional PF including 1020 solutions was obtained by using the PUSS model to perform 125 iterations. After combining the 51 two-dimensional PFs obtained by solving the dual-objective HRES optimization multiple times, a solution set (also including 1020 elements), which contains mutually dominating solutions, was obtained. After ruling out the dominated solution, a three-dimensional PF with 851 solutions was obtained. The final comparison of the two PFs is shown in Figures 10 and 11.

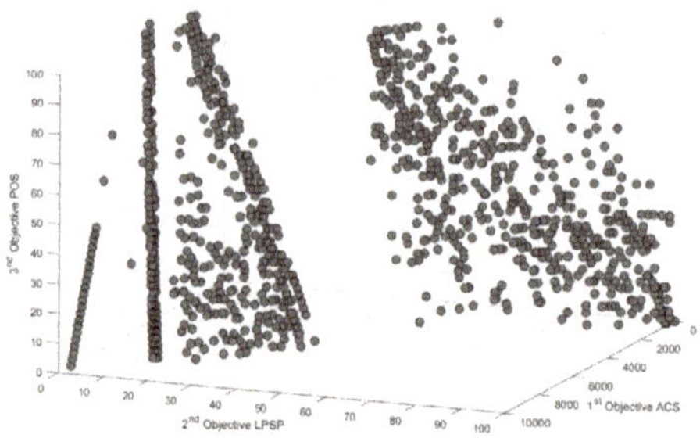

Figure 10. PF obtained by the PUSS model.

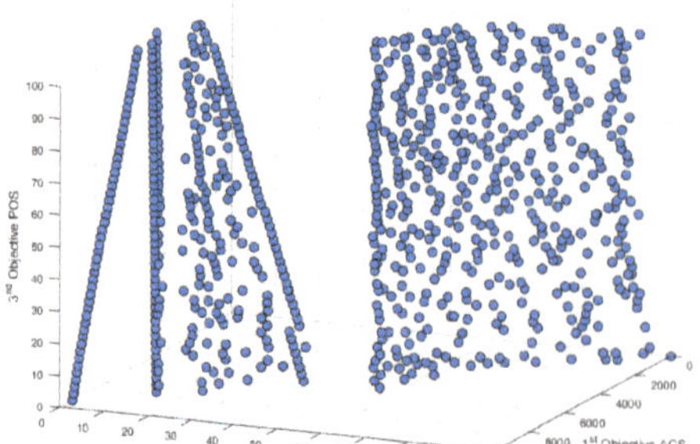

Figure 11. The PF obtained after 51 times of algorithm running.

For the PF shown in Figure 11, because there are many related results about using NSGA-II to solve the scenario-based dual-objective HRES optimization problem [23,24], this method is relatively mature. Therefore, it can be considered that this front can basically represent the real front.

Comparing Figures 10 and 11, it can be seen that the PF obtained by the PUSS model can reflect the basic distribution of real frontiers. Due to the limitation of NSGA-II's performance, the solution in some areas is relatively sparse; the algorithm still needs to be improved on this point. Figure 12 compares the distribution of the two fronts projected onto the X-Y(ACS-LPSP) plane, X-Z(ACS-POS) plane, and Y-Z (LPSP-POS) planes; grey is the projection of the PF obtained by the PUSS model, and blue is the projection of the PF obtained after the merged solution results are processed. It can be seen that the distribution of the PF solution obtained by the PUSS model on the X-Y plane is close to the true front; the distribution of the solutions on the X-Z and Y-Z planes forms a situation of clustering along a certain centerline, and the solution is very sparse in the area far from the centerline. In later work, the PUSS model can be further adjusted and improved to address this problem.

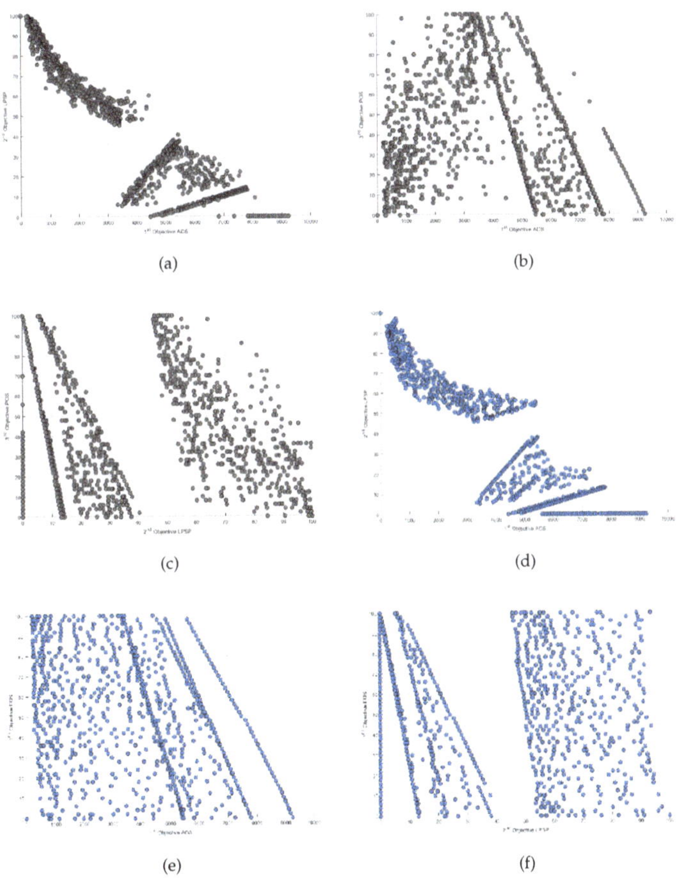

Figure 12. Contrast of 2D PF projections. (**a**) PF obtained by the PUSS method projected onto the X-Y(ACS-LPSP) plane. (**b**) PF obtained by the PUSS projected onto the X-Z(ACS-POS) plane. (**c**) PF obtained by the PUSS method projected onto the and Y-Z (LPSP-POS) planes. (**d**) PF obtained by the compared method projected onto the X-Y(ACS-LPSP) plane. (**e**) PF obtained by the compared projected onto the X-Z(ACS-POS) plane. (**f**) PF obtained by the compared method projected onto the and Y-Z (LPSP-POS) planes.

Figure 13 gives the statistics of the distribution of the number of solutions of the Pareto front obtained by the PUSS model under different scenario probabilities (P_s^1). It can be seen from the figure that the 51 possible values of P_s^1 are all covered. In the PF with a total of 1020 solutions, there should be an average of 20 solutions for each value of P_s^1. In the actual solution results, there are at least 10 solutions and a maximum of 40 solutions for each value of P_s^1. When the value of P_s^1 is small, the corresponding number of solutions is relatively large, and vice versa; although the number of solutions changes according to this trend, there is a certain fluctuation in the specific number.

In summary, there is no need to obtain a PF including a very large amount of solutions. Without a very large number of solutions in the PF, the results of the PUSS model can cover all possible values of P_s^1. When the expectation of the number of solutions corresponding to each P_s^1 being 20, at least 10 solutions can be guaranteed for all possible P_s^1 values. The solution results of the PUSS model can reflect the overall situation of the configuration scheme under different scenario probability combinations and provide sufficient alternatives under each scenario probability combination.

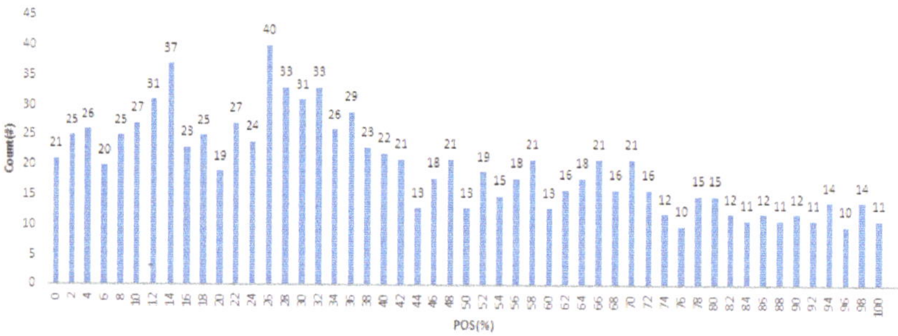

Figure 13. Distribution of solutions obtained by the PUSS model under different scenario probabilities.

To compare the quality of the solutions in the two PFs, the solutions in the two PFs are labeled separately and then combined into a set for non-dominated sorting. Then, we calculate the number of remaining non-dominated solutions separately. The results are shown in Table 3. By statistics, after merging the PF into a set and excluding the dominated solution, the remaining non-dominated solutions accounted for 80.29% (PF obtained by PUSS) and 84.61% (3D PF obtained by excluding the dominated solution after merging 2D PF) of the original PF. It can be seen that the optimality of the solutions in the two PFs is basically the same.

Table 3. Settings of algorithm parameters.

Objects	Solution Set Obtained by PUSS Model	Solution Set Obtained by Solving Multiple Times
Number of solutions	1020	1020
Number of undominated solutions	1020	851
Number of undominated solutions after merging PFs	819	720
The proportion of undominated solutions in the origin PF	80.29%	84.61%

6. Conclusions

Because the traditional HRES configuration optimization considering the influence of uncertainty has a large dependence on actual data, or it cannot effectively utilize the existing data information in the application, this paper proposed a probability undetermined scenario-based sizing model (PUSS model) to solve the above problems and provide a set of configuration schemes that can cope with various maximum environmental uncertainties.

In this study, the optimization results obtained by the PUSS model (based on NSGA-II) were compared with the configuration schemes obtained by using the scenario-based dual-objective HRES optimization method (also based on NSGA-II) multiple times. This comparison showed that the solution of the PUSS model only took about 33% of the time of the other method, and the performance of the PF obtained by the two methods was basically equivalent in terms of the optimality of the solutions; the solution results of the PUSS model can cover all scenario probability combinations and provide no less than half the mathematical expectation of the number of solutions for each possible scenario probability combination.

When comparing the results of these two methods, the dominated solutions in the solution set obtained by using the dual-objective HRES optimization method multiple times were first eliminated. Based on multiple times of solving, solutions similar to that of the PUSS model can be obtained using any scenario-based multi-objective sizing method. In this solving process, different preset combinations of scenario probabilities were used, and the final solution sets need to be merged to obtain the solution set. It must be pointed out that this solution set is essentially different from the results obtained by the PUSS model. In the solution set of the PUSS model, the individuals do not dominate each other. That is, each solution is optimal in this solution set. For the results obtained by solving the traditional scenario-based method multiple times, although there must be no Pareto dominance between the solutions under a certain combination of scenario probabilities, the solutions between different scenario probability combinations may dominate each other. In other words, the result obtained by solving multiple times and merging is not a Pareto set and cannot be directly used by decision-makers.

In comparison, the solution set obtained by the PUSS model is sparse in some regions and too dense in other regions. Further research is needed to address this problem: improve NSGA-II's adaptively or select more appropriate algorithms and perform adjustments accordingly. Though the PUSS model describes the uncertainty caused by renewable energy fluctuations in HRES planning in the form of scenarios and their occurrence probabilities, it is not required to determine the corresponding occurrence probability of each scenario before the optimization. In this way, the PUSS model solves the problem to a certain extent as the probability corresponding to a scenario is difficult to determine when using the traditional method to deal with uncertain factors; the PUSS model also avoids the problem of it being difficult to fully use the existing information to describe uncertain parameters in the form of intervals. Besides, solving the PUSS model, we can obtain the optimal set under a variety of scenario probability combinations, which can deal with multiple degrees of maximum environmental uncertainty and reflect the relationship between the microgrid optimization objective values of the configuration scheme and the maximum environmental uncertainty that the configuration scheme can withstand. In the case where the optimality of the optimization results of the two methods is equivalent, the calculation speed of the PUSS model has obvious advantages over the alternative method.

If the number of scenarios to be considered is high, the number of objectives will also be high. In this case, more Pareto solutions are needed to characterize the Pareto front, which will lead to high computational cost. Future works can investigate more efficient many-objective optimization algorithms for the cases with a large number of scenarios. Moreover, the long execution time of the algorithms mainly results from the large computational burden of the simulation process that is used to compute the objectives. Future works can investigate efficient proxy model to estimate the objectives, which can improve the efficiency of the optimization algorithms significantly.

Author Contributions: Conceptualization, R.W.; methodology, K.L. and Y.S.; validation, K.L.; investigation, K.L.; resources, Y.S.; data curation, Y.S.; writing—original draft preparation, K.L.; writing—review and editing, K.L.; visualization, K.L. All authors have read and agreed to the published version of the manuscript.

Funding: This research was funded by the Hunan Youth elite program (2018RS3081) and the key project of National University of Defense Technology (ZK18-02-09). This paper is partially supported by the National Natural Science Foundation of China (No. 72071205 and No. 61773390).

Institutional Review Board Statement: Not applicable.

Informed Consent Statement: Not applicable.

Data Availability Statement: Not applicable.

Conflicts of Interest: The authors declare no conflict of interest. The funders had no role in the design of the study; in the collection, analyses, or interpretation of the data; in the writing of the manuscript; nor in the decision to publish the results.

References

1. Alsmadi, Y.M.; Abdel-hamed, A.M.; Ellissy, A.E.; El-Wakeel, A.S.; Abdelaziz, A.Y.; Utkin, V.; Uppal, A.A. Optimal configuration and energy management scheme of an isolated micro-grid using Cuckoo search optimization algorithm. *J. Frankl. Inst.* **2019**, *356*, 4191–4214. [CrossRef]
2. Rubio-Maya, C.; Uche-Marcuello, J.; Martínez-Gracia, A.; Bayod-Rújula, A.A. Design optimization of a polygeneration plant fuelled by natural gas and renewable energy sources. *Appl. Energy* **2011**, *88*, 449–457. [CrossRef]
3. Zhang, J.; Lei, Y.; Liu, N.; Rui, X. Capacity Configuration Optimization for Island Microgrid with Wind/Photovoltaic/Diesel/Storage and Seawater Desalination Load. *Trans. China Electrotech. Soc.* **2014**, *29*, 102–112.
4. Guelpa, E.; Marincioni, L.; Capone, M.; Deputato, S.; Verda, V. Thermal load prediction in district heating systems. *Energy* **2019**, *176*, 693–703. [CrossRef]
5. Fan, C.; Xiao, F.; Zhao, Y. A short-term building cooling load prediction method using deep learning algorithms. *Appl. Energy* **2017**, *195*, 222–233. [CrossRef]
6. Li, K.; Wang, R.; Lei, H.; Zhang, T.; Liu, Y.; Zheng, X. Interval prediction of solar power using an Improved Bootstrap method. *Sol. Energy* **2018**, *159*, 97–112. [CrossRef]
7. Mavromatidis, G.; Orehounig, K.; Carmeliet, J. Design of distributed energy systems under uncertainty: A two-stage stochastic programming approach. *Appl. Energy* **2018**, *222*, 932–950. [CrossRef]
8. Bornapour, M.; Hooshmand, R.A.; Parastegari, M. An efficient scenario-based stochastic programming method for optimal scheduling of CHP-PEMFC, WT, PV and hydrogen storage units in micro grids. *Renew. Energy* **2019**, *130*, 1049–1066. [CrossRef]
9. Bornapour, M.; Hooshmand, R.A.; Khodabakhshian, A.; Parastegari, M. Optimal stochastic scheduling of CHP-PEMFC, WT, PV units and hydrogen storage in reconfigurable micro grids considering reliability enhancement. *Energy Convers. Manag.* **2017**, *150*, 725–741. [CrossRef]
10. Akbari, K.; Nasiri, M.M.; Jolai, F.; Ghaderi, S.F. Optimal investment and unit sizing of distributed energy systems under uncertainty: A robust optimization approach. *Energy Build.* **2014**, *85*, 275–286. [CrossRef]
11. Majewski, D.E.; Lampe, M.; Voll, P.; Bardow, A. TRusT: A Two-stage Robustness Trade-off approach for the design of decentralized energy supply systems. *Energy* **2017**, *118*, 590–599. [CrossRef]
12. Yokoyama, R.; Fujiwara, K.; Ohkura, M.; Wakui, T. A revised method for robust optimal design of energy supply systems based on minimax regret criterion. *Energy Convers. Manag.* **2014**, *84*, 196–208. [CrossRef]
13. Moret, S.; Bierlaire, M.; Maréchal, F. Robust optimization for strategic energy planning. *Informatica* **2016**, *27*, 625–648. [CrossRef]
14. Bertsimas, D.; Litvinov, E.; Sun, X.A.; Zhao, J.; Zheng, T. Adaptive robust optimization for the security constrained unit commitment problem. *IEEE Trans. Power Syst.* **2012**, *28*, 52–63. [CrossRef]
15. Dong, C.; Huang, G.H.; Cai, Y.P.; Liu, Y. Robust planning of energy management systems with environmental and constraint-conservative considerations under multiple uncertainties. *Energy Convers. Manag.* **2013**, *65*, 471–486. [CrossRef]
16. Liu, Y.; Lei, H.; Zhang, D.; Wu, Z. Robust optimization for relief logistics planning under uncertainties in demand and transportation time. *Appl. Math. Model.* **2018**, *55*, 262–280. [CrossRef]
17. Gulpinar, N.; Pachamanova, D.; Çanakoğlu, E. Robust strategies for facility location under uncertainty. *Eur. J. Oper. Res.* **2013**, *225*, 21–35. [CrossRef]
18. Kouvelis, P.; Yu, G. *Robust Discrete Optimization and Its Applications*; Springer Science & Business Media: Berlin/Heidelberg, Germany, 2013; Volume 14.
19. Halpern, J.Y.; Leung, S. Weighted sets of probabilities and minimax weighted expected regret: A new approach for representing uncertainty and making decisions. *Theory Decis.* **2015**, *79*, 415–450. [CrossRef]
20. Song, Y.; Liu, Y.; Wang, R.; Ming, M. Multi-Objective Configuration Optimization for Isolated Microgrid with Shiftable Loads and Mobile Energy Storage. *IEEE Access* **2019**, *7*, 95248–95263. [CrossRef]
21. Deb, K.; Pratap, A.; Agarwal, S.; Meyarivan, T. A fast and elitist multiobjective genetic algorithm: NSGA-II. *IEEE Trans. Evol. Comput.* **2002**, *6*, 182–197. [CrossRef]
22. Zitzler, E.; Laumanns, M.; Thiele, L. *SPEA2: Improving the Strength Pareto Evolutionary Algorithm*; TIK-Report 103; ETH Zurich: Zurich, Switzerland, 2001.

23. Zitzler, E.; Künzli, S. Indicator-based selection in multiobjective search. In *International Conference on Parallel Problem Solving from Nature*; Springer: Berlin/Heidelberg, Germany, 2004; pp. 832–842.
24. Zhang, Q.; Li, H. MOEA/D: A multiobjective evolutionary algorithm based on decomposition. *IEEE Trans. Evol. Comput.* **2007**, *11*, 712–731. [CrossRef]
25. Cheng, R.; Jin, Y.; Olhofer, M.; Sendhoff, B. A reference vector guided evolutionary algorithm for many-objective optimization. *IEEE Trans. Evol. Comput.* **2016**, *20*, 773–791. [CrossRef]
26. Buayai, K.; Ongsakul, W.; Mithulananthan, N. Multi-objective micro-grid planning by NSGA-II in primary distribution system. *Eur. Trans. Electr. Power* **2012**, *22*, 170–187. [CrossRef]
27. Lu, X.Y.; Huang, Y.Q.; Liu, N.; Zhang, J.H.; Huang, L.Z. A Study of Optimal Capacity Configuration with multi-Objective for Islanded Micro-grid. *Appl. Mech. Mater. Trans. Tech. Publ.* **2014**, *521*, 464–468. [CrossRef]
28. Deb, K.; Agrawal, R.B. Simulated binary crossover for continuous search space. *Complex Syst.* **1995**, *9*, 115–148.
29. Tian, Y.; Cheng, R.; Zhang, X.; Jin, Y. PlatEMO: A MATLAB platform for evolutionary multi-objective optimization [educational forum]. *IEEE Comput. Intell. Mag.* **2017**, *12*, 73–87. [CrossRef]
30. Zhichao, S. Research on Hybrid Renewable Energy System Planning Based on Multi-Objective Evolutionary Algorithm. Ph.D. Thesis, National University of Defense Technology, Changsha, China, 2016.

mathematics

Article

An Improved Intelligent Auction Mechanism for Emergency Material Delivery

Jie Zhang, Yifan Zhu, Tao Wang, Weiping Wang, Rui Wang and Xiaobo Li *

School of Systems Engineering, National University of Defense Technology, Changsha 410000, China; zhangjie@nudt.edu.cn (J.Z.); zhuyf@nudt.edu.cn (Y.Z.); wangtao1976@nudt.edu.cn (T.W.); wangwp@nudt.edu.cn (W.W.); rui_wang@nudt.edu.cn (R.W.)

* Correspondence: lixiaobo@nudt.edu.cn

Abstract: Emergency material delivery is vital to disaster emergency rescue. Herein, the framework of the emergency material delivery system (EMDS) with the unmanned aerial vehicle (UAV) as the vehicle is proposed, and the problem is modeled into a multi-trip time-dependent dynamic vehicle routing problem with split-delivery (MTTDDVRP-SD) in combination with the rescue reality, which provides decision support for planning disaster relief material. Due to the universality of dynamic interference in the process of material delivery, an optimization algorithm based on the traditional intelligent auction mechanism is proposed to avoid system performance degradation or even collapse. The algorithm adds pre-authorization and sequential auction mechanisms to the traditional auction mechanism, where the pre-authorization mechanism improves the capability performance of the system when there is no interference during the rescue process and the sequential auction mechanism improves the resilience performance of the system when it faces interferences. Finally, considering three types of interference comprehensively, which includes *new task generations*, *task unexpected changes* and *UAV's number decreases*, the proposed algorithm is compared with DTAP (DTA based on sequential single item auctions) and CBBA-PR (consensus-based bundle algorithms-partial replanning) algorithms under different dynamic interference intensity scenarios for simulation experimental from two perspectives of the capability performance and resilience performance. The results of Friedman's test with 99% confidence interval indicate that the proposed algorithm can effectively improve the capability performance and resilience performance of EMDS.

Keywords: emergency material delivery; MTVRP; DVRP; SDVRP; pre-authorization mechanism; sequential auction mechanism; resilience

MSC: 90C39

1. Introduction

Earthquakes, floods and other large-scale natural disasters occur frequently, causing serious damage and far-reaching impacts on modern society. How to deal with natural disasters and their consequences can benefit the maintenance of social stability, and this is an emerging topic that has garnered increasing attention from both practitioners and academics in recent years. According to relevant research reports [1], the Wenchuan earthquake in 2008 caused 69,277 deaths, 374,643 injuries, 17,923 people missing, and direct economic losses of more than 800 billion US dollars and the 2015 earthquake in Nepal caused at least 8786 deaths, 22,303 injuries, and economic losses of about 113 billion yuan. The way to reduce the impact of natural disasters on human life, the economy and the environment requires not only to be prepared for detection and early warning before disasters occur [2], but also rapid post-disaster relief supplies and post-disaster recovery work, which led to the emergence of an EMDS. Due to the destruction of ground communication facilities, road traffic, and increased environmental hazards, the selection of vehicles in EMDS presents challenges. While the use of UAVs as vehicles in EMDS can weaken the impact of ground traffic on rescue work more than manned aircraft and unmanned vehicles and avoid the loss of rescue equipment and personnel, UAVs as temporary communication relay technology are also very mature, which can replace communication base stations to restore certain communication capabilities in disaster areas [3].

The impact of the complex post-disaster environment is the urgent demand for materials by the disaster victims. Moreover, with the delay of time, the deterioration of the health of the disaster victims will further aggravate the urgency of the relief materials in the disaster area, resulting in greater casualties [4]. Song et al. [5] proposed an emergency material scheduling model with multiple disaster points and multiple rescue points, but the model is mainly aimed at the emergency material scheduling of disaster points with the same emergency indicator of material demand. Based on the weight-TOPSIS method, Guan et al. [6] determined the emergency indicator of the tasks in the disaster area, considered the penalty cost of unmet needs in the disaster area, and they established a collaborative disaster relief material scheduling model, but did not consider the change of the emergency indicator of the tasks. At the same time, due to the aftershocks after the earthquake and the crash of the UAVs, some other situations have brought great dynamics to the post-disaster rescue. On the other hand, considering the loading capacity constraints of UAVs and battery life constraints, UAVs are often required to be reused, and the material needs of a single disaster area may not be satisfied by a single UAV at one time. These are all issues that EMDS should consider when completing disaster relief, so we modeled it as a multi-trip time-dependent dynamic vehicle routing problem with split-delivery (MTTDDVRP-SD), based on the classic multi-trip vehicle routing problem (MTVRP) [7], which also takes into account the following characteristics: multi-trip per UAV, time-dependent emergency indicator, dynamics of the environment, split-delivery, and trip duration limit.

MTTDDVRP-SD takes into account various practical situations in the delivery of emergency materials, which makes it unique and difficult. From the perspective of models, MTTDDVRP-SD can be seen as a combination of MTTDVRP, DVRP and SDVRP, although these three models are more in line with the real problem, but the relevant research is not sufficient, especially the combination of the three is less.

- In the delivery of emergency materials, it is common to allow vehicles to make multiple trips, and it is also widely used in logistics [8], public transportation scheduling [9] and other fields. Cattaruzza et al. [10] emphasized that allowing vehicles to make multiple trips can significantly improve vehicle utilization and reduce the number of vehicles required, thereby further reducing fixed costs and overall costs, and the application in life is more realistic. Moreover, they theoretically proved that the MTVRP problem was NP-hard. Dorling et al. [11] argued that existing VRPs are insufficient for planning UAV deliveries, that is because multiple trips to the depot are not permitted, resulting in too many UAV solutions, so they proposed two multi-trip VRPs for UAV deliveries to address both problems. Sun et al. [12] proposed a time-dependent multi-trip vehicle routing problem (TDMTVRP) with an improved travel speed model, arguing that speed is time-dependent. Moreover, the experimental results indicated that compared with the capacitated vehicle routing problem with the time windows model (CVRPTW), the TDMTVRP model proposed can both decrease the vehicle utilized times dramatically and shorten the vehicle travel distances slightly in dealing with the vehicle routing problem (VRP).
- Dynamic VRP (DVRP) [13] emerged as a new variant of VRP and attracted more and more attention. Li et al. [14] investigated the emergency material dispatching problem under uncertainty and built a multi-objective optimization model to minimize the total cost and maximize the affected rate of demand, but without considering the case of multiple trips of vehicles. Nan et al. [15] investigated the dynamic demand VRP with time windows for the model of mixed distribution of electric and fuel

logistics vehicles, i.e., the demand of the task changes randomly or a new task is generated randomly during the execution of the task. Sabar et al. [16] considered the DVRP problem under vehicle speed uncertainty caused by traffic congestion, but this uncertainty has regularity. Ouaddi et al. [17] proposed the MTDVRP problem with a combination of MTVRP and DVRP and recognized the complexity of such problems. Their work considered the problem of vehicle overloadable transportation and distribution, with dynamics reflected in the cancellation and modification of user orders and changes in vehicle speed due to congestion, but without considering the problem of delivery splitting at a task.

- The split-delivery vehicle routing problem (SDVRP) is a variant of the Capacitated Vehicle Routing Problem (CVRP) in which a customer can be served by more than one vehicle, i.e., the requirement of a customer can be split among vehicles. Casazza et al. [18] addressed a single commodity Pickup and Delivery Vehicle Routing Problem and assumed that the requirements of both pickup and delivery nodes can be split, and each node can be visited more than once. An extensive experimental analysis showed their method to offer simultaneously more modeling flexibility and more computational effectiveness. Hartomo et al. [19] investigated the problem of distribution of relief materials from a logistics center to a network of demand points, and their assumptions included that the requirement for materials at a node would be served by several trucks or over multiple trips. However, their work does not take into account the dynamic changes in the environment and emergency indicator over time. Zhang et al. [20] considered the case of a customer requiring multiple vehicles for service, but without considering the change in capability due to the change in external information during the working process, and the case of multiple trips.

Currently, to solve these kinds of problems, the exact algorithm [21] and memetic algorithm [17] are commonly used, but they are only suitable for solving small-scale arithmetic cases. On the other hand, most of the processing methods of DVRP are dividing time slices and decomposing into a series of static VRP problems [22,23], and then using heuristic algorithms to solve them, but under the conditions of multi-trip and delivery splittable, the solution search space is huge and the time complexity is very high, so much so that it is not suitable for emergency material delivery scenarios under environmental uncertainty. For this purpose, this paper considers an intelligent auction algorithm based on the market mechanism, such as Guo et al. [24] who proposed an auction algorithm that introduces the idea of "blockchain" to realize the task allocation problem in the "last mile" logistics distribution. Auction algorithms have been improved in the literature, Choi et al. [25] proposed a consensus-based auction algorithm (CBBA), which uses both auction and consensus mechanisms for task selection and conflict resolution, thus reducing the computational resource consumption of the algorithm and accelerating the convergence. The performance improvement of CBBA algorithm over the initial auction algorithm was experimentally verified, but the research does not address the dynamic change of task information. In a later study, Buckman et al. [26] proposed the CBBA-PR algorithm for partial replanning based on the CBBA algorithm in order to cope with dynamic changes in the environment by mixing a subset of unfinished tasks with new tasks to achieve fast reallocation. CBBA-PR ensures optimality in dynamic assignment and improves the fast response of the algorithm to dynamic situations, but the algorithm is not effective in some cases where real-time performance is required or the problem size is large. Chen et al. [27] argued for the better applicability of online algorithms for the uncertain arrival of dynamic tasks and proposed that tasks should be assigned one by one rather than in batches to ensure the efficiency of UAV execution. Farinelli et al. [28] converted multi-robot patrol into a task assignment problem, considered online decision making techniques, proposed the DTAP algorithm based on sequential single auction, and verified the performance of the algorithm on a real robot platform. However, they relied only on the task information at the current moment, without considering more global known information. Of course, centralized algorithms such as the genetic algorithm (GA) and particle swarm optimization

(PSO) can also solve VRP, but they are less adaptable to the dynamic situation of changing environment in the disaster area. For example, Luo et al. [29] pointed out that when the global information of the task changes dynamically over time, the centralized algorithm tends to decompose and re-iterate the constraint solution, which is less flexible than the auction algorithm.

When EMDS is implemented to start the emergency material delivery task, it is still necessary to pay attention to two aspects, i.e., not only to ensure the capability performance to avoid secondary damage to the disaster area due to untimely rescue, but also to ensure the resilience performance to have the ability to continue the task. In fact, accurate and timely information about the disaster area can be obtained through efficient reconnaissance detection [30]. However, the uncertainty of the environment in a disaster is common and may cause the system to collapse, thus requiring the EMDS to adapt effectively to interferences, i.e., to have a good resilience performance. While resilience was first introduced to engineering systems in 1995 [31], defined as, "Resilience is the probability of a system's recovery from failures", in 2009, Woods [32] argued that the focus should be on the adaptability of a system facing more complex situations, thus giving the definition, "Resilience, as a form of adaptive capacity, is a system's potential for adaptive action in the future when information varies, conditions change, or new kinds of events occur, any of which challenge the viability of previous adaptations, models, or assumptions". As to how to quantitatively evaluate resilience, summarizing the research results over the years, it can be broadly divided into two categories: time-dependent and time-independent models.

The core of time-dependent models is that the performance of systems (e.g., power transmission systems [33] and communication systems [34]) is time-dependent and can be expressed quantitatively, and such models usually describe the resilience of the system in terms of performance change curves. In contrast, time-independent models are mostly used to describe the system capability performance only calculated after the completion of the task, such as air defense systems [35]. The integral resilience model is commonly used for quantitative description of resilience, which describes the system resilience by comparing the cumulative distributional impact of system performance over time with and without interference, and can be found in the literature [36]. Dessavre et al. [37] studied the resilience of offensive and defensive countermeasures based on the integral resilience metric, using the number of OODA cycles as a performance indicator, but without considering the multi-interference situation, so some improvements are needed in emergency material delivery.

Motivated both by the adaption of new technologies and delivering vehicle (UAV) in practical transportation industry and the theoretical gap existing in the current literature, we investigate a problem model (MTTDDVRP-SD) that is more adapted to the emergency material delivery scenario in disaster areas. On this basis, due to the existence of two layers of optimization of UAV routing and delivery quantity, which leads to a huge solution search space of the traditional evolutionary algorithm and does not adapt to the objective demand of the dynamics of the disaster area. So, we try to design a new algorithm based on the intelligent auction mechanism and propose a resilience evaluation indicator under dynamic multiple interferences. Specifically, the main contributions of this paper can be summarized as follows.

- To meet the performance requirements of emergency material delivery, an overall framework of EMDS with UAV as the vehicle is proposed, and the emergency material delivery problem is described as a new variant of VRP (MTTDDVRP-SD);
- Based on the traditional intelligent auction algorithm, pre-authorization and sequential auction mechanisms are added, and sequential auction algorithm based on pre-authorization (SAABoPA) is proposed to solve MTTDDVRP-SD to optimize the system performance.
- Based on the integral resilience model, a multi-interference resilience evaluation indicator suitable for emergency material delivery scenarios is proposed;
- The experiments are carried out under different dynamic interference intensities through the post-earthquake emergency material delivery scenario and compared

with the comparative algorithms from two perspectives of capability performance and resilience performance to verify the effectiveness of the algorithm in this paper.

The problem MTTDDVRP-SD will be deeply analyzed and defined in the next section, while in Section 3, the proposed method of SAABoPA for solving it is presented. The experimental results are reported in Section 4. Section 5 concludes this study and discusses future research directions.

2. Problem Definition and Formulation

2.1. Problem Definition

UAVs with loading capacity were considered to deliver relief materials to the earthquake-affected areas, and information about the danger in the affected areas was obtained by satellite remote sensing technology, UAV reconnaissance technology, and ground rescue teams [38]. The relief materials are concentrated in the distribution center at the border of the disaster area, and the UAV makes task assignment according to the disaster area danger information, determines the task target, loads the materials at the distribution center, and then carries out the delivery to the disaster area target. The specific EMDS framework is shown in Figure 1, which describes the interaction between the system and the outside. The EMDS includes *information processing subsystem (IPSys)*, *command and control subsystem (CCSys)*, and *loading and transportation subsystem (LTSys)*.

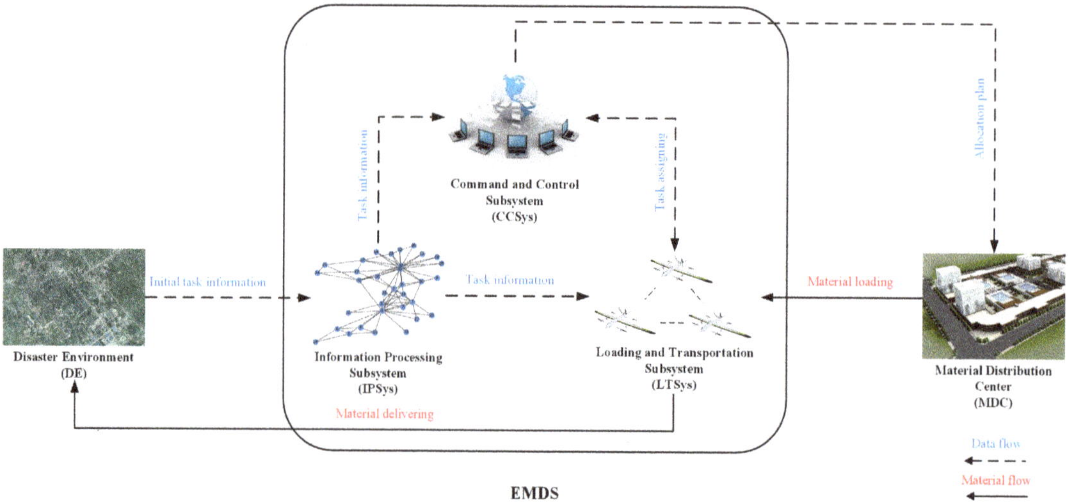

Figure 1. EMDS interaction framework chart.

The subsystem functions can be described as follows:

1. *IPSys*: Responsible for filtering, standardizing and sharing task information. Task information provided by the *disaster environment (DE)* is filtered, standardized, and shared with *CCSys* and *LTSys*. The sharing of task information is discontinuous and will only be re-shared when there is a sudden change in the information.
2. *CCSys*: Responsible for task assignment and solution sharing. Based on the task information shared by *IPSys*, the task assignment is executed by combining the status and capability of each *LTSys* component. Due to the dynamic change of task information, task assignment is not executed at once. After the allocation plan is formed, it is shared to the *material distribution center (MDC)*.

3. *LTSys*: Responsible for task assignment and material delivery. Based on the task information shared by *IPSys*, the task assignment is completed with the unified scheduling of *CCSys*. After the assignment plan is determined, the UAVs in *LTSys* load the materials stored in the *MDC* and execute the material delivery process.

The relevant assumptions of this paper are as follows:

1. The material requirements of the task may not be met by one UAV at a time;
2. A single deployment of a UAV may execute multiple tasks;
3. When the UAV is empty, it needs to be returned to the *MDC* and reloaded to be able to execute the next task;
4. Obstacle avoidance among UAVs and against obstacles (e.g., mountains and forests) is not considered. Obstacle avoidance can be accomplished by adjusting the height of the UAV under certain conditions [39], and the increase in range due to height change can be ignored because the height difference is small relative to the range;
5. In the case of emergency rescue, the UAV always maintains the maximum capacity, i.e., the UAV always maintains the maximum power during the task. The UAV endurance can be considered as fixed for a certain battery capacity;
6. Ignoring the deceleration of the UAV during the delivery of the material, as well as the change in direction, the time variation from this is insignificant in comparison. Theoretically, this variation could be integrated into the velocity and loading relationship, but we do not consider it in order to simplify the problem. Moreover, the kinematic model of the UAV is not investigated in depth in this paper;
7. Consider using a single base, i.e., an *MDC*. For a general multi-base VRP, it can be divided into sub-blocks by clustering methods, and within the sub-blocks still remains a single base VRP;
8. The material in the MDC meets the material needs of all affected areas and only one type of material is considered. The current national reserve of emergency resources is sufficient, and the amount of emergency resources available can be considered adequate in the face of a catastrophic event in a local area. In fact, many types of materials are needed in disaster relief situations, including food, water, medicine, etc. However, in order to facilitate the emergency and effective implementation of relief, in many cases we do not count the requirements of various types of materials too much and make a precise delivery, and the more general practice is to synthesize various materials into a rescue kit [40].

2.2. Problem Formulation

In this section, the mathematical model proposed to solve the above problem is introduced. However, before that we need a formal description of the disaster area environment and dynamic interferences.

2.2.1. *DE* Formulation

Here, we first formalize spatio-temporal characteristics and dynamic properties of *DE* based on task information of the disaster area.

Definition 1. *Task environment G. The task environment is modeled as an undirected graph $G = (V, E)$, where V denotes the set of vertices in Euclidean space, E denotes the set of edges.*

In G, V includes the task node T and the *MDC* node V_B. The edge $E \subset V \times V$ indicates that two neighboring vertices are reachable between them and are paths for the UAV to move. A task node represents a delivery task, and the set of all tasks is $T = \{T_1, T_2, \ldots, T_j, \ldots, T_{|T|}\}$.

Definition 2. *Time t. Time is represented by a set of discrete sequences, $t \in \{0, 1, 2, \ldots\}$.*

Take the time of the first UAV taking off for the task as the base time 0.

Definition 3. *Coordinates* (x, y). *The node position is represented by the two-dimensional coordinates* (x, y).

The node coordinates considered in this paper include the task coordinates and *MDC* coordinates, and the task coordinates are used to characterize the nearby affected areas that need relief materials.

Definition 4. *Quantity required* $R(t)$. *At t moments, the quantity of material required by the task* $T_j \in T$ *is denoted by* $R_j(t)$.

To simplify the problem, the quantity required is unitized, e.g., $R_j(t) = 3$ means that the quantity of material required for the task T_j at time t is 3 units.

Definition 5. *Emergency indicator* $E(t)$. *At t moments, the emergency of the task* $T_j \in T$ *on the material is denoted by* $E_j(t)$.

The emergency indicator [6] indicates the urgency of the requirement for materials at the task, which varies with time and the delivery of materials. When the upper threshold is reached, it will cause secondary damage to the disaster area due to the lack of replenishment of materials for a long time [41]. This is similar to a time window constraint, but the difference is that the emergency indicator can describe the range of time constraints, the value of the task is varying, i.e., the sooner the task is completed the higher the value. The formula is expressed as follows.

$$E_j(t) = \begin{cases} 0, & R_j(t) \leq 0, \\ 1, & E_j(t) \geq 1, \\ E_j(t_0) + a \cdot (t - t_0) - \frac{E_j(t_0)}{R_j(t_0)} \cdot MD_{ij}(t), & \text{others}. \end{cases} \tag{1}$$

where t_0 denotes the moment of the last *IPSys* shared information. Equation (1) indicates that the emergency indicator $E_j(t)$ of a task gradually increases with time t, but the material replenishment decreases the value of $E_j(t)$. In fact, the task emergency indicator formula is a fit to the actual indicator, and *IPSys* shares the information every time the task information changes, i.e., the task emergency indicator can be corrected at the t_0 moment.

2.2.2. Dynamic Interference Formulation

The dynamic scenarios in this paper consider three possible types of interferences in which their occurrence is unpredictable, and are therefore described in terms of stochastic processes and defined as follows.

Definition 6. *Dynamic interference type 1: new task generations. This means that during the delivery of emergency materials, new tasks will emerge as the disaster continues.*

Taking the stochastic process $\left\{\widetilde{\mathbf{X}}(n^1), n^1 \in \{1, 2, \ldots, |DIS^1|\}\right\}$ denotes the occurrence of dynamic interference events of the type *new task generations*, where $\widetilde{\mathbf{X}}(n^1) = (\widetilde{t}(n^1), \widetilde{x}(n^1), \widetilde{y}(n^1), \widetilde{R}(n^1), \widetilde{E}(n^1))$, and each random variable $\widetilde{t}(n^1), \widetilde{x}(n^1), \widetilde{y}(n^1), \widetilde{R}(n^1), \widetilde{E}(n^1)$ satisfies a certain probability distribution, respectively, $\widetilde{t}(n^1) \sim DiscreteU(0, T_{end})$, $\widetilde{x}(n^1) \sim U(\underline{x}, \overline{x})$, $\widetilde{y}(n^1) \sim U(\underline{y}, \overline{y})$, $\widetilde{R}(n^1) \sim DiscreteU(\underline{R}, \overline{R})$, $\widetilde{E}(n^1) \sim U(\underline{E}, \overline{E})$. The result of the occurrence of dynamic interference events of this type causes the task T to be expanded, and the information of the new task is all generated randomly in the random vector $\widetilde{\mathbf{X}}(n^1)$, which is represented by the following equation.

$$T = T \cup \{T_{|T|+n^1}\}, \ t = \widetilde{t}(n^1) \tag{2}$$

Definition 7. *Dynamic interference type 2: task unexpected changes. This means that during the delivery of emergency materials, information on the material requirements and emergency indicator of currently known tasks will deteriorate as the disaster continues and disaster information is reevaluated.*

Taking the stochastic process $\left\{\widetilde{\mathbf{Y}}(n^2), n^2 \in \{1,2,\ldots,|DIS^2|\}\right\}$ denotes the occurrence of dynamic interference events of the type *task unexpected changes*, where $\widetilde{\mathbf{Y}}(n^2) = (\widetilde{t}(n^2), \widetilde{j}(n^2), \widetilde{\Delta R}(n^2), \widetilde{\Delta E}(n^2))$, and each random variable $\widetilde{t}(n^2), \widetilde{j}(n^2), \widetilde{\Delta R}(n^2)$, $\widetilde{\Delta E}(n^2)$ satisfies a certain probability distribution, respectively, $\widetilde{t}(n^2) \sim DiscreteU(0, T_{end})$, $\widetilde{j}(n^2) \sim DiscreteU(1, |T|)$, $\widetilde{\Delta R}(n^2) \sim DiscreteU(0, \overline{R}/2)$, $\widetilde{\Delta E}(n^2) \sim U(0, \overline{E}/2)$. The result of the occurrence of dynamic interference events of this type causes changes in the information about the material requirements and emergency indicator in the current task T, and the amount of changes in the information are generated randomly in the random vector $\widetilde{\mathbf{Y}}(n^2)$, which is represented by the following equation.

$$R_{\widetilde{j}(n^2)}(t) = R_{\widetilde{j}(n^2)}(t) + \widetilde{R}(n^2), \ t = \widetilde{t}(n^2) \tag{3}$$

$$E_{\widetilde{j}(n^2)}(t) = E_{\widetilde{j}(n^2)}(t) + \widetilde{E}(n^2), \ t = \widetilde{t}(n^2) \tag{4}$$

Definition 8. *Dynamic interference type 3: UAV's number decreases. This means that during the delivery of emergency materials, the number of available UAVs will be reduced due to failure and other circumstances.*

Taking the stochastic process $\left\{\widetilde{\mathbf{Z}}(n^3), n^3 \in \{1,\ldots,|DIS^3|\}\right\}$ denotes the occurrence of dynamic interference events of the type *UAV's number decreases*, where $\widetilde{\mathbf{Z}}(n^3) = (\widetilde{t}(n^3), \widetilde{i}(n^3))$, and each random variable $\widetilde{t}(n^1) \sim DiscreteU(0, T_{end}), \widetilde{i}(n^3) \sim DiscreteU(1, |U|)$. The result of the occurrence of dynamic interference events of this type causes the number of currently available drones is reduced, which is represented by the following equation.

$$U = U - \{U_{\widetilde{i}(n^3)}\}, \ t = \widetilde{t}(n^3) \tag{5}$$

2.2.3. MTTDDVRP-SD

In summary, The MTTDDVRP-SD is formulated as follows.

$$f = \min \sum\nolimits_1^{N_T} E_j(T_{end}) \tag{6}$$

$$0 \le L_i^k(t) < L_i^{\max} \tag{7}$$

$$L_i^k(t) = L_i^k(sT_i^k) - \sum\nolimits_{j=1}^{|T|} x_{ij}^k \times MD_{ij}(t) \tag{8}$$

$$L_i^k(sT_i^k) > 0 \tag{9}$$

$$0 \le MD_{ij}(t) \le L_i^k(t) \tag{10}$$

$$aT_i^k - sT_i^k \le T_i^{duration} \tag{11}$$

$$v_i(t) = v_i^{unload} - \delta_i \times L_i^k(t) \tag{12}$$

$$1 \le Ex_i \tag{13}$$

$$\sum_{k=1}^{Ex_i} x_{ij}^k \in \{0, 1\} \tag{14}$$

$$\sum_{j=1}^{|T|} x_{ij}^k \geq 1 \tag{15}$$

$$\sum_{i=1}^{|U|} \sum_{k=1}^{Ex_i} x_{ij}^k \geq 1 \tag{16}$$

$$0 \leq MD_{ij}(\mathrm{t}) \leq R_j(t) \tag{17}$$

$$x_{ij}^k \in \{0, 1\} \tag{18}$$

Equation (6) aims to minimize the number of tasks whose emergency indicator reaches the threshold 1 at the end of the emergency material delivery. Different from the general objective function of the VRP and its variants problem, which considers minimizing transportation and inventory costs or maximizing transportation and inventory rewards [42,43]. In the disaster area emergency material delivery problem, this paper considers, based on the rescue work after the earthquake disaster, to ensure the safety of victims' lives and avoid more secondary injuries. Equation (7) indicates that the loading of any UAV at any time is less than the maximum loading and is non-negative. Equation (8) represents the change in the current UAV loading. Equation (9) represents the loading capacity of the UAV U_i when it is deployed from the MDC is strictly large 0. Equation (10) indicates that the quantity delivered by the UAV U_i to the task T_j is less than the current loading capacity of the UAV i. Equation (11) represents the flight time constraint for a single UAV trip. Equation (12) represents the relationship between the UAV speed and the loading capacity [44]. Equation (13) indicates the constraint on the number of trips of a single UAV. Equation (14) indicates the entire emergency material delivery process, the UAV U_i to the task T_j at most once. Equation (15) indicates that a single UAV executes at least one task in a single trip. Equation (16) indicates that the entire emergency material delivery process, task j is executed at least once. Equation (17) indicates that the quantity of UAV U_i to task T_j delivery is less than the current requirement of task T_j. Equation (18) represents the decision variables.

3. Method: SAABoPA

3.1. Overall Framework

In the EMDS framework, *CCSys* and *LTSys* use the SAABoPA algorithm for task assignment based on the task information shared by *IPSys*. The tasks shared by *IPSys* are equivalent to *auction items*. *CCSys* acts as the *auctioneer* and sends the task information to the UAVs in the corresponding *LTSys*. The UAV acts as a *bidder*, calculates the net benefit for each task with the task price stated by *CCSys*, and sends the bid price of the task back to *CCSys*. *CCSys* decides the pre-authorization and authorization of the task based on the bid price, and sends the task to the authorized UAV and the overall framework of SAABoPA is shown in Figure 2.

The SAABoPA algorithm requires the UAV to obtain at most one task authorization and one task pre-authorization in one auction. The algorithm is based on pre-authorization to ensure the system capability performance, and based on sequential auctions to effectively improve the system resilience performance and avoid the frequent occurrence of interference that causes the system performance degradation by reallocation or adjustment of the assignment results. It should be noted that since the published task is executed in the future time and has no effect on the current execution process, the UAV can participate in the auction during the execution of the task [27], but it can only obtain the pre-authorization of the task instead of the authorization.

There are two possibilities for starting an auction:

1. *CCSys* active start: in case of interference.
   - In EMDS, when the task information changes abruptly (due to new task T_{new} generation, unexpected changes in task information and completion of one delivery), *IPSys* shares the current task information with *CCSys*. Based on the shared information and the set of previous authorization information Y, *CCSys* can determine the cause of the task information mutation. If a task is completed, the auction is not started; if a new task T_{new} is created and the task information changes unexpectedly, the auction is started and the previous set of preauthorization information X is deleted and the task price vector $\mathbf{P}(t)$ is updated;
   - In the case that the UAV U_i is lost, the UAV U_i task completion time is known from the elements in the previous set of authorization information from *CCSys* (expected arrival time t_i^1). If *IPSys* shares the information with *CCSys* at this point and it matches the expected change, the task is successfully executed and the auction is not started; otherwise, it means that the UAV is malfunctioning and there is one less bidder in the next auction, so ask *IPSys* to share the task information at this moment, start a new auction, and delete the previous set of pre-authorization information X and reset the task price vector $\mathbf{P}(t)$.
2. CCSys passive start: in case of no interference.
   After the UAV U_i arrives at the *MDC* V_0, it sends an auction asking to *CCSys*. If U_i has been pre-authorized, it is directly converted to authorization and sent to U_i. Meanwhile, what needs to be achieved is to add the pre-authorization quintuple relation related to U_i to the authorization set Y and remove it from the pre-authorization set X; conversely, start the auction and *CCSys* sends the task information set *TASK* to all UAVs that are not pre-authorized.

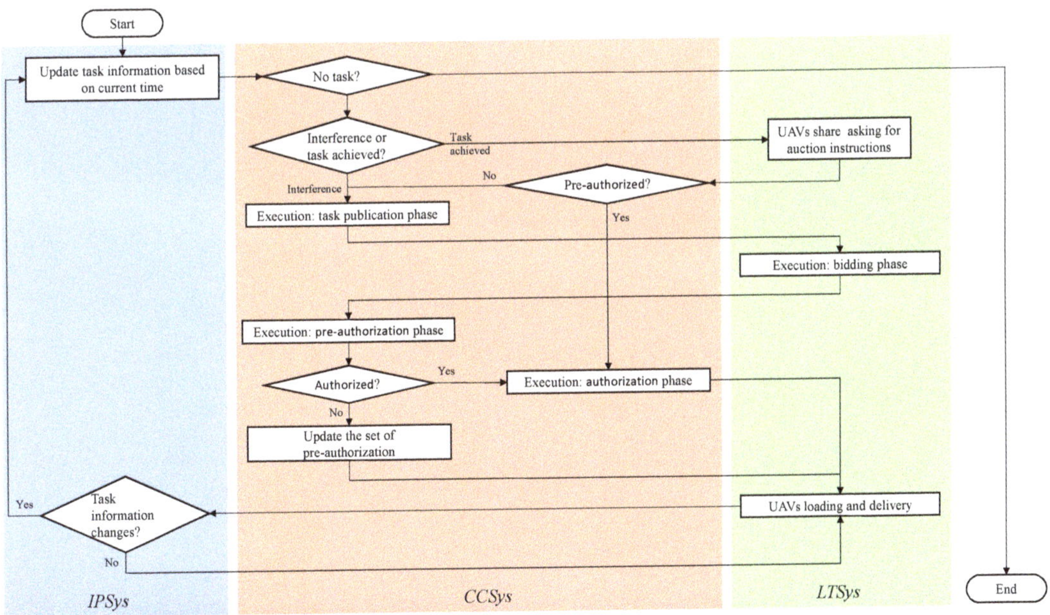

Figure 2. Overall framework of SAABoPA.

3.2. Mechanism Design

In MTTDDVRP-SD, after a task is executed once, if it is not completely completed, it is considered as a new task and the gain obtained from the execution is recalculated. In a dynamic environment, interference *new tasks generations* and *task unexpected changes* occur without burden to the proposed algorithm. This is because newly generated tasks or tasks with unintended changes in information are treated the same as tasks after one execution. Moreover, in the auction mechanism, UAVs lose their capabilities due to failures, which is equivalent to a reduction in the number of *auctioneers*. Due to the loose coupling between UAVs, no additional burden is imposed on the algorithm of this paper.

The SAABoPA mechanism consists of four phases: (1) Task Publication Phase, (2) Bidding Phase, (3) Pre-authorization Phase and (4) Authorization Phase. The *CCSys* performs the task publication, pre-authorization and authorization phases, and the UAV in the *LTSys* performs the bidding phase.

3.2.1. Task Publication Phase

At the beginning of an auction, *CCSys* releases to *LTSys* the estimated set of task information $TASK = \{T, (x, y), R', E', \mathbf{P}(\tau)\}$, where T denotes the set of uncompleted tasks at the current τ moment. When task T_j is partially completed, T_j will not be deleted from T, but the information of material requirements and emergency indicator will be updated; when task T_j is fully completed, T_j will be deleted, $T = T - \{T_j\}$; when a new task T_{new} appears, the set of tasks T is expanded, $T = T \bigcup \{T_{new}\}$. N_T denotes the number of elements in the set T. $(x, y) = \{(x_j, y_j) | T_j \in T\}$ denotes the position information of the uncompleted tasks. $R' = \{R_j^{'}(\tau) | T_j \in T\}$ denotes the estimated material requirement of the uncompleted tasks. $E' = \{E_j^{'}(\tau) | T_j \in T\}$ denotes the estimated value of the emergency indicator of the uncompleted tasks. $\mathbf{P}(t)$ is the price vector consisting of the prices of all current outstanding tasks, and the initial moment price vector $\mathbf{P}(0) = 0$.

In the r-th auction, there are some tasks that have been authorized but not executed in the $r-1$-th auction. In order to accurately calculate the rewards of the UAV for the tasks in the r-th auction, we introduce the material requirement information prediction $R_j^{'}(\tau)$ and the emergency indicator information prediction $E_j^{'}(\tau)$. The $R_j^{'}(\tau)$ and $E_j^{'}(\tau)$ of the task T_j are calculated based on the $R_j(\tau)$ and $E_j(\tau)$ true values and the authorized UAV U_{i_j} in the $r-1$ auction delivery $MD_{i_j j}(\tau)$, expressed as follows.

$$R_j^{'}(\tau) = R_j(\tau) - MD_{i_j j}(\tau) \tag{19}$$

$$E_j^{'}(\tau) = \begin{cases} E_j(\tau) - \frac{E_j(\tau)}{R_j(\tau)} \cdot MD_{i_j j}(\tau), & R_j^{'}(\tau) \neq 0, \\ 0, & \text{others.} \end{cases} \tag{20}$$

3.2.2. Bidding Phase

Different loadings of UAVs lead to different speeds, so that UAVs may obtain different rewards for the same task. Accordingly, while completing the task assignment in EMDS, the loading and delivery of UAVs can be determined. The pseudo-code is shown in Algorithm 1.

Before bidding, the UAVs in *LTSys* calculate the income values based on their own computational resources based on the set of task information shared by *CCSys*, and form the income matrix:

$$INCOME_{i,T}(t) = \begin{bmatrix} Income_{i,1}^{1}(t) & \cdots & Income_{i,1}^{L_i}(t) \\ \vdots & \ddots & \vdots \\ Income_{i,|T|}^{1}(t) & \cdots & Income_{i,|T|}^{L_i}(t) \end{bmatrix}_{|T| \times L_i} \tag{21}$$

where, $INCOME_{i,T}(t)$ denotes the income matrix of the UAV U_i for the current set of outstanding tasks T at t moments. The matrix elements are calculated as:

$$Income_{ij}^{L_i}(t) = Value_{ij}^{L_i}(t) - Cost_{ij}^{L_i}(t) \tag{22}$$

$$Value_{ij}^{L_i}(t) = \begin{cases} E_j(t_0) + a \cdot (\frac{D_{ij}}{v_i(t)} + t - t_0) + \frac{E_j(t_0)}{R_j(t_0)} \cdot \max(MD_{ij}, L_i), & E_j(t) + \frac{a \cdot D_{ij}}{v_i(t)} < 1, \\ 0, & \text{others.} \end{cases} \quad (23)$$

$$Cost_{ij}^{L_i}(t) = \begin{cases} \frac{s \cdot (t_i^1 - t_i^0 + -\frac{d_{j,V_0}}{v_i(t_i^1)})}{T_i^{duration} - T_i^{fly}}, & t_i^1 - t_i^0 + -\frac{d_{j,V_0}}{v_i(t_i^1)} + T_i^{fly} \leq T_i^{duration}, \\ \infty, & \text{others.} \end{cases} \quad (24)$$

where, $Income_{ij}^{L_i}(t)$ denotes the reward value that a UAV U_i with loading L_i of materials can obtain by executing a task T_j at time t, which is determined by the value of the task $Value_{ij}^{L_i}(t)$ and cost $Cost_{ij}^{L_i}(t)$; s is the scaling factor; t_i^0 denotes the expected time to start the task T_i; t_i^1 denotes the expected time to complete the task T_j, satisfying $D_{ij} = \int_t^{t_i^1} v_i(\tau)d\tau$; T_i^{fly} denotes the time that the UAV U_i has flown; MD_{ij} denotes the time that the UAV U_i has performed the task T_j of material delivery, satisfying $MD_{ij} = \min\{L_i, R_j(t)\}$; D_{ij} denotes the actual flight distance of the UAV U_i from the current position to the task T_j.

Algorithm 1: Bidding phase (Part of *LTSys*, take U_i as an example).

Input : set of task information $TASK$;
Output: Set of bidding BID_i.

```
calculate INCOME_{i,T}(t);
calculate NET_{i,T}(t);
if all(NET_{i,T}(t)(:) < 0) then
    P'_i(t) ← (−∞, −∞, ..., −∞)^T;
    BID_i ← {U_i, ∅, P'_i, 0, 0, 0};
    NODE_i ← NODE_i ∪ {V_0} and go to V_0;
else
    net^max_{i,T}(t) ← max NET_{i,T}(t);
    (T_{ji}, L_i) ← index(net^max_{i,T}(t));
    MD_{iji} ← min{L_i, R_{ji}(t)};
    t^1_i ← f(D_{iji}, t, v_i(τ));
    net^max_{i,T−{T_ji}}(t) ← max NET_{i,T−{T_ji}}(t);
    calculate P'_i(t);
send BID_i ← {U_i, T_{ji}, P'_i, L_i, MD_{ij}, t^1_i} to CCSys;
```

In Equation (23), under the constraint of $\frac{E_j(t)}{a} + \frac{D_{ij}}{v_i(t)} < 1$, the first two terms of the right-hand side of the $Value_{ij}^{L_i}(t)$ calculation equation indicate the emergency indicator at the moment before the task is executed, which reflects the basic value of the UAV to execute the task; the third term of the equation reflecting the additional value of the UAV U_i executing task T_j, i.e., the UAV loads as much materials as possible under the condition that the material is obtained before the emergency indicator of the task T_j reaches 1.

The UAV U_i based on the price vector $\mathbf{P}(t)$ of the uncompleted tasks, combined with the income matrix can be calculated to obtain the net income matrix $NET_{i,T}(t)$ as:

$$NET_{i,T}(t) = INCOME_{i,T}(t) - [\mathbf{P}_T(t); \mathbf{P}_T(t); ...; \mathbf{P}_T(t)]_{N_T \times L_i} \quad (25)$$

The maximum net income $net_{i,T}^{\max}(t)$ is:

$$net_{i,T}^{\max}(t) = \max NET_{i,T}(t) \quad (26)$$

Then, the tasks T_{j^i} bid by the UAV U_i, the material load L_i and the delivery MD_{ij^i} to the task T_{j^i} are:

$$(m,n) = index(net_{i,T}^{\max}(t)) \tag{27}$$

$$T_{j^i} = T(m) \tag{28}$$

$$L_i = n \tag{29}$$

$$MD_{ij^i} = \min\{L_i, R_{j^i}(t)\} \tag{30}$$

where the function $(m,n) = index(a)$ in Equation (27) means to obtain the values of the ranks of a in the matrix A, and if there are multiple values of a in the matrix A, then a randomly selected rank value.

To further determine the bidding of the UAV U_i to the task T_{j^i}, the maximum net income value $net_{i,T-\{T_{j^i}\}}^{\max}(t)$ in the net income matrix of the UAV U_i other than the task T_{j^i} is also needed, expressed as follows:

$$net_{i,T-\{T_{j^i}\}}^{\max}(t) = \max NET_{i,T-\{T_{j^i}\}}(t) \tag{31}$$

where $T - \{T_{j^i}\}$ denotes the deletion of elements of the set T_{j^i} from the set of tasks T.

Combining Equations (21)~(31), the bidding vector $\mathbf{P_i}'(t)$ of the UAV U_i for all tasks is determined as follows.

$$\mathbf{P}_i'(t) = (p_{i,1}'(t), p_{i,2}'(t), \ldots, p_{ij}'(t), \ldots, p_{i,N_T}'(t))^T \tag{32}$$

$$p_{ij}'(t) = \begin{cases} Income_{i,j^i}^{L_i}(t) - net_{i,T-\{T_{j^i}\}}^{\max}(t) + \varepsilon, & j = j^i, \\ -\infty, & j \neq j^i. \end{cases} \tag{33}$$

where $\varepsilon > 0$ is a slack parameter [42] that ensures that the algorithm does not enter a dead loop when multiple UAVs compete for the same task because the bids do not improve; $P_{ij}'(t)$ denotes the bidding of the UAV U_i for the task T_j at time t.

If the elements of the net income matrix $NET_{i,T}(t)$ are all non-positive, which means that the UAV U_i will not profit from bidding on any task at the current price, then the UAV U_i abandons further bidding in this auction and sets $\mathbf{P}_i'(t) = (-\infty, -\infty, \ldots, -\infty)^T$, as shown in lines 3~6 of Algorithm 1; lines 7~13 show that if there are positive values of the elements in the net income matrix, the UAV U_i participates in the bid, and the task, loading and bid price of the bid are determined by Equations (26)~(33).

After the UAV U_i in *LTSys* completes the bidding phase, it sends the set of bid information $BID_i = \{U_i, T_{j^i}, \mathbf{P}_i', L_i, MD_{ij}, t_i^1\}$. The elements in the set BID_i denote the UAV order number, the bid task, the bid vector to the task, the material loading, the delivery to the task, and the expected arrival time, respectively.

3.2.3. Pre-Authorization Phase

The *CCSys* receives the bid information from the UAV and starts the pre-authorization phase, the pseudo-code is shown in Algorithm 2.

As in lines 1~3 of Algorithm 2, *CCSys* waits to receive the bid information BID_i and then updates its own stored bidding matrix $P'(t)$ based on the bidding vector in the bid information, expressed as follows.

$$P'(t) = \begin{bmatrix} P'_{1,1}(t) & \cdots & P'_{|U|,1}(t) \\ \vdots & \ddots & \vdots \\ P'_{1,|T|}(t) & \cdots & P'_{|U|,|T|}(t) \end{bmatrix}_{|T|\times|U|} \tag{34}$$

Pre-authorize the task T_j to the UAV with the highest bid U_{ij},

$$U_{ij} = \arg\max_{U_i \in U} \left\{ P'_{1,j}(t), P'_{2,j}(t), \ldots, P'_{|U|,j}(t), \right\} \tag{35}$$

We consider removing the quintet of relations $(U_i, L_i, MD_{ij}, t_i^1, T_j)$ associated with the task T_j from the set of pre-authorized information X, and adding new quintet of relations $(U_{ij}, L_{ij}, MD_{ij\,j}, t_{ij}^1, T_j)$, as shown in lines 4∼8.

Where line 7 indicates that once the task T_j is pre-authorized to the UAV U_{ij} at moment t, the price vector $\mathbf{P}(t)$ of all uncompleted tasks is updated, i.e., the price of the task T_j is updated to the bidding price of the UAV U_{ij},

$$p_j(t) = P'_{ij,j}(t) \tag{36}$$

As in lines 9∼13 of Algorithm 2, at the end of an auction round, *CCSys* sends a rebid command to the UAVs U_i that have not abandoned their bids and are not pre-authorized, and sends a set of current information about all tasks *TASK*. The UAVs that receive the rebidding command start a new round of the auction process, while the other UAVs enter the waiting phase. Lines 14∼15 indicate that the iterative process terminates with the condition that all UAVs that have not abandoned their bids during the auction process are pre-authorized for the task.

Algorithm 2: Pre-authorization phase (*CCSys* part).

Input : Bid vector BID_i;
Output: Set of task *TASK*.

```
1  BID ← BID_i;
2  wait;
3  P'(t) ← BID;
4  for T_j ← T_1 to T_|T| do
5      U_ij ← argmax_{U_i∈U}{P'_{1,j}(t), P'_{2,j}(t), ..., P'_{|U|,j}(t)};
6      if U_ij ≠ 0 then
7          p_j(t) ← P'_{ij,j}(t);
8          X ← X − {x_i} and X ← X ∪ {x_ij};        // Update the set of
            pre-authorization
9  flag ← 0;
10 for U_i ← U_1 to U_|U| do
11     if P'_i(t) ≠ (−∞, −∞, ..., −∞)^T and x_i == ∅ then  // Indicate that U_i has
        not abandoned the bid and is not pre-authorized
12         send TASK to U_i and flag ← 1;
13         Execution: bidding phase;
14 if flag ≠ 1 then // Indicates the end of the pre-authorization phase of
    an auction
15     Execution: authorization phase;
```

3.2.4. Authorization Phase

CCSys updates the set of authorization information Y based on the set of pre-authorization information X, adds the pre-authorization quintet relation to Y for UAVs U_i that are pre-authorized but not authorized, and removes it in X, while resetting the task price vector. $CCSys$ sends the authorization quintet y_i to the UAVs authorized in this auction, sends the loading information U_i, L_i to the MDC, and saves the set of pre-authorization information and the set of authorization information Y as the initial state for the next auction.

3.3. *Algorithm Analysis*

The algorithm involves internal system interaction and inevitably has communication problems. On the one hand, in the disaster area environment, ground communication base stations are damaged, and it is necessary to restore communication, and UAVs are mature and widely used as temporary communication relays [3]; on the other hand, the bidding process is performed by UAVs, which greatly reduces the state information interacted between $CCSys$ and UAVs, and can be used in a limited bandwidth environment [27].

The computation time of one auction in the SAABoPA algorithm is much less than that of the traditional auction algorithm [25], although the former requires multiple executions of the algorithm during the completion of all tasks, resulting in a longer cumulative execution time. However, considering the case of excessive interference, the traditional auction algorithm needs to reset or partially reset the previous allocation results and reallocate them. If we consider the case of poor communication, the conventional auction algorithm may cause excessive waiting time due to waiting for communication in a single execution, which may affect the timely departure of UAVs [28], and thus affect the capability performance and resilience performance of EMDS. In the EMDS framework, a single auction execution can be performed during the UAV's return trip or by using another gap time. As argued in the literature [45], real-time does not mean that the faster the computation time is, the more real-time it is, but that the solution to the problem is found within a limited time.

Specifically, we analyze the time complexity and space complexity of one auction round in a single auction of SAABoPA. As mentioned above, an auction is divided into the task publication phase, bidding phase, pre-authorization phase, and authorization phase, and the main complexity is concentrated in the bidding phase and pre-authorization phase. However, in the task publication phase and authorization phase, the main work is to complete the packaging, sending, and assignment of data processing operations. In the bidding phase, see (Algorithm 1), the main work is to complete the computation of the $INCOME_{i,T}(t)$ matrix, and the sorting operation to find the maximum element of the matrix. Assuming that the time complexity of computing a single matrix element is I and the space complexity is J, then the average time complexity is $O(|T| * L_i * I)$, and the space complexity is $O(|T| * L_i * J)$. On the other hand, the sorting algorithms are heap sorting, bubble sorting, and shell sorting, whose time complexity is $O(\log(|T| * L_i))$, $O((|T| * L_i)^2)$, and $O((|T| * L_i)^{1.3})$, respectively, and the space complexity is is $O(1)$. In the Pre-authorization Phase (Algorithm 2), the main work is to complete the sorting operation to find the maximum element of the bidding vector BID for each task, similarly using heap sorting, bubble sorting, shell sorting, their time complexity is $O(|T| * \log(L_i))$, $O(|T| * (L_i)^2)$ and $O(|T| * (L_i)^{1.3})$, respectively, and the space complexity is $O(1)$.

4. Computational Experiment

In this section, the effectiveness of the proposed method is verified by experiments. The simulation experiments were performed using Visual Studio 2022 platform, C++ programming language, CPU is Intel(R) Core(TM) i9-10885H CPU @ 2.40GHz 2.40GHz, OS is Windows 10.

4.1. *Experimental Settings*

4.1.1. Case Scenario

The relevant data for the computational case were chosen using a combination of real and hypothetical data, since some disaster data is not published or could not be obtained through official reports [46,47]. The data of the UAVs are derived from some public sources and scaled accordingly to fit the case scenario. Meanwhile, in order to verify the performance of the algorithm, large sample experiments are required in this section, and the data for the experimental scenarios are randomly generated on the basis of known partial data.

The earthquake disaster in a city in southwest China is simulated as a scenario, and the affected area C is a rectangular area of 4000 × 4000 m, with $|T|$ tasks uniformly distributed in the area, and the quantity of material required for the tasks $R(0)$ and the emergency indicator $E(0)$ also obey uniform distribution. The outside of the rectangular area is secure, and a well-stocked *MDC* is deployed on the boundary of the disaster area with a total of $|U|$ UAVs involved in the task execution. The number of the three dynamic interference types considered during the task execution is determined in advance as $|DIS^1|$, $|DIS^2|$, and $|DIS^3|$, but the time of occurrence of the dynamic interference types is random and uncertain, and the values of the changed information obey a uniform distribution. The specific parameters are shown in Table 1.

Table 1. Scenario parameters instructions.

Parameters	Value	Parameters	Value
x, y	$U(0, 4000)$	(x_0, y_0)	Boundary of C
$R(0)$	$DiscreteU(6, 10)$	L^{max}	$U(11, 15)$
$E(0)$	$U(0.1, 0.8)$	V^{unload}	$U(15, 20)$
ΔR	$DiscreteU(0, 5)$	$T^{duration}$	$U(400, 500)$
ΔE	$U(0, 0.4)$	δ	0.5

In order to investigate the effects of different dynamic interference intensities on the performance of the algorithm, this paper designs experiments with seven different control variables at different scenario scales, as shown in Table 2.

Table 2. Scenario scale instructions.

Name of Scenario	$\|T\| \times \|U\| \times \|DIS^1\| \times \|DIS^2\| \times \|DIS^3\|$ [1]
Scenario 1	50 × 5 × 10 × 10 × 2
Scenario 2	50 × 5 × 20 × 10 × 2
Scenario 3	50 × 5 × 30 × 10 × 2
Scenario 4	50 × 5 × 20 × 20 × 2
Scenario 5	50 × 5 × 20 × 30 × 2
Scenario 6	50 × 5 × 20 × 10 × 3
Scenario 7	50 × 5 × 20 × 10 × 4

[1] Taking Scenario 2 as an example, 50 × 5 × 20 × 10 × 2 means that there are 50 tasks in the scenario, 5 UAVs, and the number of three dynamic disturbances *new task generations*, *task unexpected changes* and *UAV 's number decreases* are 20, 10 and 2, respectively.

4.1.2. Comparison Algorithms

The experiments with 1000 random samples are conducted for each scenario, respectively, considering all three interference types, and the SAABoPA algorithm under the EMDS framework is compared with the DTAP (DTA based on sequential single item auctions) [28] and CBBA-PR (consensus-based bundle algorithms-partial replanning) [26] algorithms to verify and compare the capability performance and resilience performance of EMDS under the three algorithms.

Numbered lists can be added as follows:

1. DTAP: Dynamic task assignment algorithm based on sequential single-item auctions is an online algorithm that differs from the algorithm in this paper in that there is no pre-authorization phase, and the DTAP algorithm starts once the auction timing is the current target task completion.

2. CBBA-PR: Dynamic task assignment based on the consistent consent bundle algorithm is an offline algorithm where one auction UAV gets one task sequence, i.e., one task bundle. When interference occurs, a certain percentage of unexecuted tasks with low revenue are selected for authorization reset and the auction is restarted.

4.2. *Performance Indicators*

To verify the performance of EMDS based on the SAABoPA algorithm, the performance metrics fully consider the trade-off between efficiency and resilience [48]. In this paper, two main types of performance metrics are used: (a) capability performance, i.e., the completion of the rescue mission; and (b) resilience performance, i.e., the change of the system capability performance in the case of dynamic interference.

4.2.1. Capability Performance (CP)

In Definition 5, it is considered that when the emergency indicator reaches 1, the task will not be completed for a long time and the actual rescue will not be timely and cause secondary injuries. In this paper, the system capability performance is described as the proportion of tasks that are not subject to secondary injuries, i.e., the proportion of tasks whose emergency indicator fails to reach 1, which, combined with Equation (6), is expressed as follows.

$$CP = \frac{N - f}{N} \times 100\% \tag{37}$$

where N denotes the total number of tasks that occur during the entire EMDS emergency material delivery.

4.2.2. Resilience Performance (RP)

The EMDS capability performance metric proposed in this paper is time-invariant, not computable at any moment, and is obtained only at the end of the whole working process. In order to describe the calculation of the resilience performance metric, this paper considers the system capability performance as time-invariant and represents the in-process capability performance by the calculated value CP. When an interference situation occurs, for example, DIS^1 occurs at t_1^s, the system capability performance after t_1^s moment is denoted by the computed value CP; the computed value CP in the same initial situation, under the condition that DIS^1 does not occur at t_1^s moment denotes the system capacity performance before t_1^s moments. The same is true for the case of multiple interferences. The resulting EMDS capability performance metric is converted to time-dependent and the system capability performance changes as shown in Figure 3.

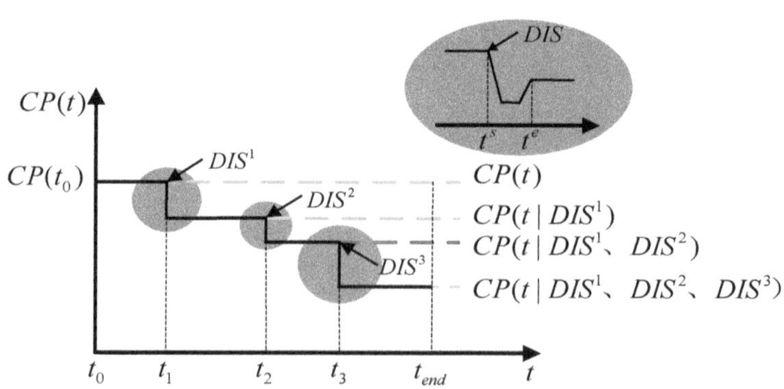

Figure 3. The change of system capability performance.

Since the capability performance at any moment of the whole working process is expressed by the calculated value CP, this paper does not describe too much the change of the system capability performance in a short time after the interference occurs, as Figure 3 incorporates the capability degradation, maintenance and recovery phases of the system after suffering from the interference [49].

Combined with the integral elasticity model, this paper defines the resilience performance of the system expressed as follows.

$$RP(\tau|DIS) = \frac{\int_{t_0}^{t_{end}} CP(\tau|DIS)d\tau}{\int_{t_0}^{t_{end}} CP(\tau)d\tau} \tag{38}$$

where $RP(\tau|DIS)$ denotes the system resilience performance with interference DIS occurring, $CP(\tau)$ denotes the system baseline capability performance when τ without interference, and $CP(\tau|DIS)$ denotes the system capability performance when τ with interference.

4.3. Algorithm Results of Hypothesis Testing: Friedman Test

Based on the experimental design of 1000 random instances of 7 scenarios in the previous paper, the three algorithms can obtain 7 sets of experimental results. We compare the computational results of the three algorithms pair-wisely for each group of results, from three perspectives of no interference capability performance, interference capability performance, and resilience performance, to test the performance of the SAABoPA algorithm proposed in this paper by whether there are significant differences. Current experiments on comparing the average performance of multiple algorithms on multiple problem instances are widely and well-known by methods such as Complete Block Design (CBD) ANOVA or Friedman's test [50]. In this paper, Friedman's test is used, but the Friedman's test can only test whether the average performance indicator value of at least one algorithm has a significant difference from the average performance indicator value of at least one algorithm, and cannot specifically determine which two algorithms have a significant difference between them, so Multcompare is also required. The results are shown in Figure A1. As an additional note, the confidence interval of Friedman's test in this paper is 99%.

From the results, in the seven scenarios, there are no significant differences in the capability performance of the system without interference under the SAABoPA and CBBA-PR algorithms, but there are significant differences with the DTAP algorithm. However, there are significant differences in the capability performance of the system with interferences under the three algorithms. It indicates that the SAABoPA and CBBA-PR algorithms have similar capability performance in the no interference case and are significantly better than the DTAP algorithm. However, in the case of interferences, the capability performance of the system under the CBBA-PR algorithm degrades more and is significantly worse than SAABoPA and DTAP algorithms. Analyzing Figure A1c,f,i,l,o,r,u together, it can be found that there are significant differences in the resilience performance of the system under the three algorithms. The exception is that in Figure A1f,i (scenarios 2 and 3), there is no significant difference between SAABoPA and DTAP algorithms regarding the system resilience performance, which may be because the resilience performance of them gradually approaches as the number of new tasks generation and the intensity of interference faced by the system increases. However, compared to scenarios 4 and 5, 6 and 7, the system is not yet facing the maximum intensity of interference, but the type of interference has changed, which reflects the greater adaptability of the SAABoPA algorithm to *new task generations* type of dynamic interferences. On the other hand, the specific performance gap also needs to be analyzed in terms of average, standard deviation, CDF, etc.

4.4. Algorithm Comparison Analysis: Scenario 2 as an Example

At the scale of Scenario 2, 1000 random sample experiments were conducted. The results of the simulation experiments are studied from the mean and variance of the metrics, as shown in Tables 3 and 4. The SAABoPA has a slightly lower capability performance than the CBBA-PR and roughly 6% higher than the DTAP in the static case where no interference occurs, because the DTAP, as an online algorithm, considers only the current deterministic information when making decisions, while the SAABoPA adds a pre-authorization process that considers the current information along with the next task estimation information, and achieved better results. However, it is obvious that the CBBA-PR, as an offline algorithm, considers all the information of the whole system working process, so the derived allocation scheme is better. It should be noticed that this algorithm requires higher accuracy of information, and in the presence of errors in the model, the errors in the offline solution will gradually accumulate causing the degradation of the solution quality.The resilience performance of SAABoPA and DTAP is similar, which is more than 5% higher than that of CBBA-PR, reflecting that the former two have better adaptability to the dynamic environment and resistance to interference situations are stronger. After analysis, the reason is that when there is an interference situation, the CBBA-PR needs to reallocate some of the uncompleted tasks with the interference in a comprehensive consideration, and considering the trade-off between algorithm execution time and optimality, it often cannot handle the interference situation in time, and it causes a significant decrease in the system capability performance, which reflects the lack of system resilience performance. Analyzing the mean value of system capability performance and the mean value of resilience performance under the three algorithms, although the mean value of resilience performance is above 0.85, the resilience indicator integrally considers the time of occurrence of multiple interferences, so the change of the calculated value of the indicator is relatively insignificant, but the capability performance after corresponding to multiple interferences will have a large reduction, for example, the highest resilient performance DTAP with multiple interferences and the ability to perform without interference differ by about 14%.

Analyzing the system performance variance, it is found that the variance of both metrics is around 0.01, which reflects the stability of the capacity performance and resilience performance of EMDS under the three algorithms in the scale of Scenario 2, and the experimental results are effective.

Table 3. Average of system performance with different algorithms for 1000 sample experiments.

Algorithm	$CP(\tau)$	$CP(\tau\|DIS)$	$RP(t\|DIS)$
SAABoPA	0.9491	0.7992	0.9443
DTAP	0.8867	0.7506	0.9459
CBBA-PR	0.9497	0.6663	0.8916

Table 4. Variance of system performance with different algorithms for 1000 sample experiments.

Algorithm	$CP(\tau)$	$CP(\tau\|DIS)$	$RP(t\|DIS)$
SAABoPA	0.0032	0.0102	0.0009
DTAP	0.0055	0.0115	0.0005
CBBA-PR	0.0031	0.0132	0.0013

A comparative analysis of the cumulative distribution functions (CDF) of the capability performance and resilience performance of SAABoPA, DTAP and CBBA-PR (Figure 4) shows that: (a) the CDF curves of the capability performance of the SAABoPA and CBBA-PR almost overlap in the initial case where no interference occurs, and the percentage of capability performance greater than 0.9 is 80% much higher than the 44% of the DTAP; (b) the capability performance of all three algorithms decreases in the presence of multiple disturbances. However, the SAABoPA maintains the best capability performance with 50% of capability performance greater than 0.8 higher than 31% of DTAP and 10% of CBBA-PR; (c) the CDF curves of the resilience performance of SAABoPA and DTAP are close, and the percentage of resilience performance greater than 0.9 is over 90% much higher than 41% of CBBA-PR algorithm. Moreover, the lower limit of the resilience performance of SAABoPA and DTAP still exceeds 0.8, which indicates that SAABoPA and DTAP have stronger resilience performance and better adaptability in the face of interference situations.

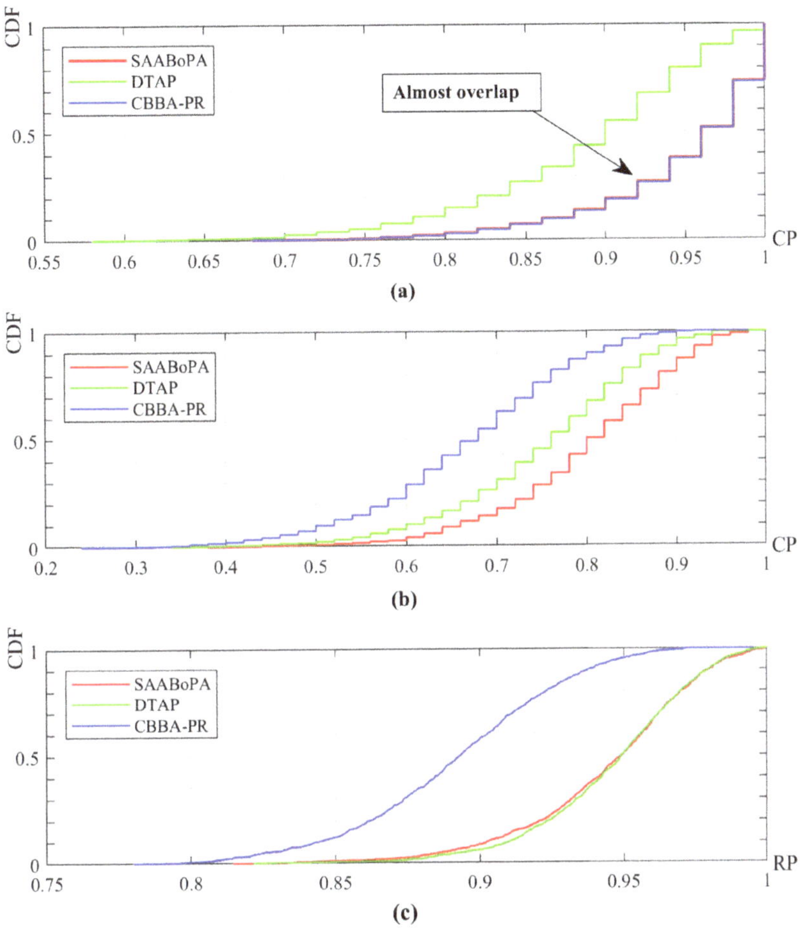

Figure 4. Comparison of CDF of system performance under different algorithms: (**a**) Capability performance without dynamic interference; (**b**) Capability performance with dynamic interference; (**c**) Resilient performance.

For further analysis, the performance metrics of each sample were compared as shown in Figure 5. To facilitate the observation of the experimental results, we adjusted the sample serial numbers and reordered the samples in the lowest to highest order of SAABoPA's metrics. We found that although the experimental parameters are the same, the disaster area environment and UAV parameters (e.g., mission coordinates, UAV speed, etc.) are different for different samples, resulting in different performance metrics for different samples by different algorithms, which we believe is reasonable, and there is a certain applicability of different algorithms to different scenarios themselves, which is why we consider large sample experiments.

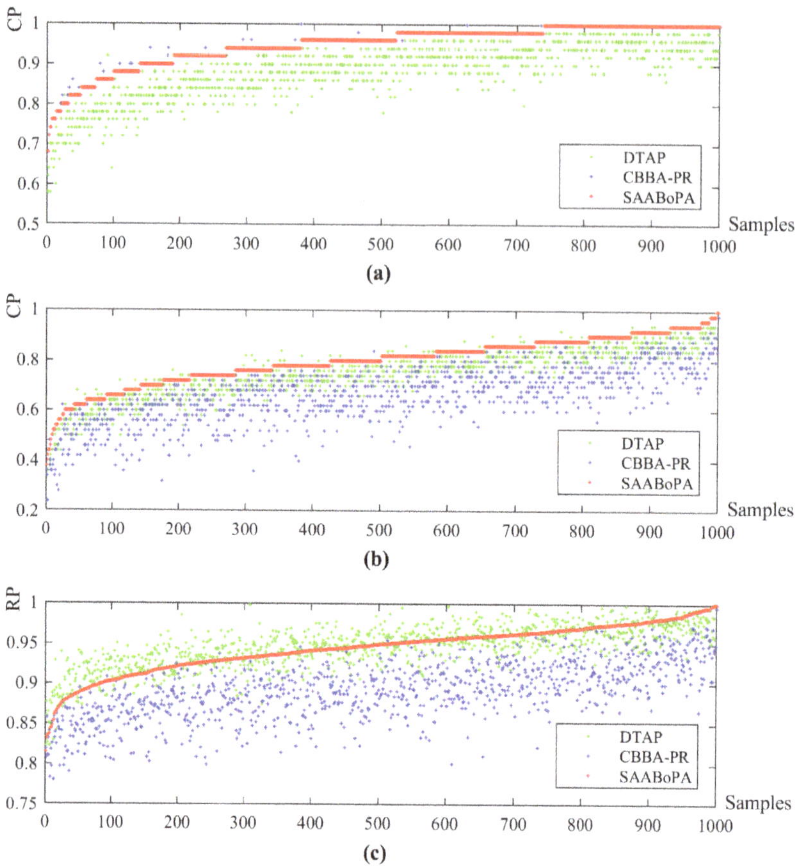

Figure 5. Comparison of system performance under different algorithms in each sample scenario: (**a**) Capability performance without dynamic interference; (**b**) Capability performance with dynamic interference; (**c**) Resilient performance.

4.5. Analysis of the Results under Different Dynamic Interference Intensity

As for the seven scenarios shown in Table 2, they are divided into three groups (scenario 1, 2, 3, scenario 2, 4, 5 and scenario 2, 6, 7) according to the principle of controlled variable method in this paper to study the effects of *new task generations*, *task unexpected changes* and *UAV 's number decreases* at different intensities on the performance of EMDS, as shown in Figures 6–8. From the experimental results, the more *new task generations* type of dynamic interferences have a certain degradation on the capability performance and resilience performance of all three algorithms. The capability performance of the SAABoPA proposed in this paper is optimal under different intensities of dynamic interference. On the other hand, when the number of new tasks increases from 10 to 30 (from Scenario 1 to Scenario 3), the capability performance of SAABoPA and DTAP decreases by about 10% and the resilience performance decreases by about 4%, but the CBBA-PA decreases by about 22% and 8%, respectively, which reflects the importance of the resilience performance indicator in the scenario with dynamic interference, which can better describe the performance of EMDS. *task unexpected changes* and *UAV's number decreases* type of dynamic interference at different intensities can still obtain the same conclusion as *new task generations*.

In the vertical comparison, compared with Scenario 2, the number of *new tasks generations* and *task unexpected changes* increases by 10 in Scenario 3 and Scenario 4, respectively, but the capability performance of the three algorithms decreases by approximately 7%, 7% and 13% in Scenario 3, and the resilience performance decreases by 3%, 3% and 5%, respectively; then the capability performance of the three algorithms decreases by approximately 4%, 2% and 7% in Scenario 4, and the resilience performance decreases by 1%, 1% and 4%, respectively. In Scenario 4, the capability performance of the three algorithms decreases by about 4%, 2% and 7%, and the resilience performance decreases by 1%, 1% and 4%, respectively. This reflects the fact that dynamic interference of the *new tasks generations* type has a greater impact on the system capability performance and resilience performance than *task unexpected changes*, which is reasonable. However, since *UAV's number decreases* type of dynamic interference is the reduction in task execution vehicles, it is not comparable to *new tasks generations* and *task unexpected changes*.

To analyze the dynamic interference of *UAV's number decreases* type individually, from scenario 2 to scenario 6 to scenario 7, the UAVs are reduced by 1 in turn, which means that the transport delivery capacity is reduced by 20% in turn (total number = 5), while the capability performance reductions of the three algorithms become larger from 8%, 7%, and 9%, respectively, with reductions of 13%, 19%, 12%; on the other hand, the reduction in resilience performance becomes 4%, 4%, 4% from 3%, 2%, 3%, respectively. This indicates that the smaller the number of available UAVs, the worse the system performance, and this gap is increasing as the number of UAVs decreases. It can also be found that the DTAP has a more drastic performance degradation compared to the SAABoPA and CBBA-PA algorithms in scenario 7 (loss of 4 UAVs), and the reason for this analysis is that the capability performance of EMDS under the DTAP is not high when no such interference occurs, and the more UAVs are lost to the DTAP brings about a further degradation of the task planning capability.

Comparing the standard deviations of the experimental results under each experimental scenario, it can be found that the resilience indicator *RP* is smaller compared to *CP* under no interference and *CP* under multiple interferences, reflecting that the resilience indicator of multiple interferences proposed in this paper is more stable under large sample experiments, and it is robust and convincing to describe the system resilience performance by *RP*.

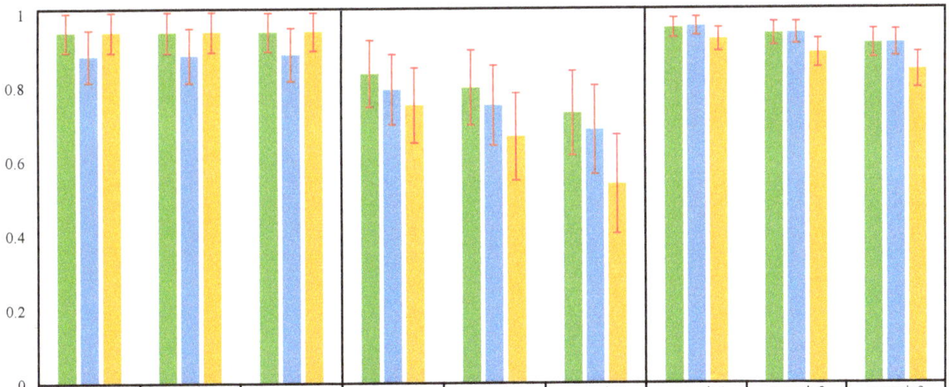

	scenario1	scenario2	scenario3	scenario1	scenario2	scenario3	scenario1	scenario2	scenario3
SAABoPA	0.9490	0.9491	0.9501	0.8373	0.7992	0.7301	0.9597	0.9443	0.9173
DTAP	0.8854	0.8867	0.8894	0.7935	0.7506	0.6848	0.9641	0.9459	0.9184
CBBA-PR	0.9495	0.9497	0.9507	0.7511	0.6663	0.5376	0.9288	0.8916	0.8456
	$CP(\tau)$			$CP(\tau \mid DIS)$			$RP(\tau \mid DIS)$		

Figure 6. Comparison of system performance of each algorithm at different dynamic strengths (different number of *new task generations*).

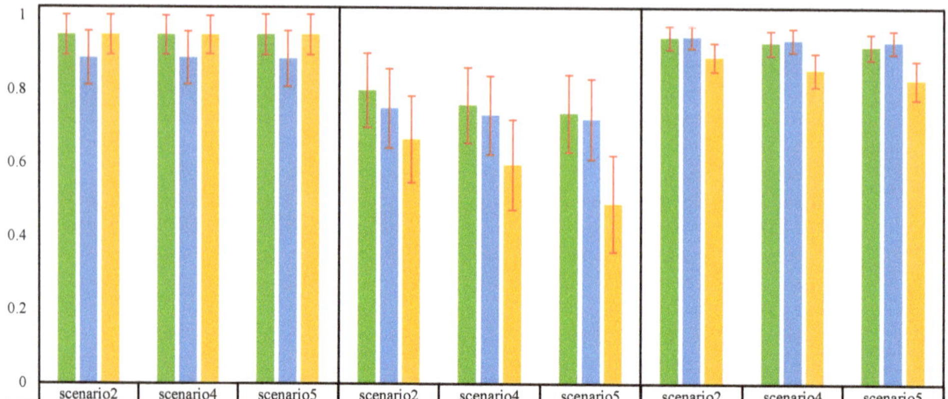

	scenario2	scenario4	scenario5	scenario2	scenario4	scenario5	scenario2	scenario4	scenario5
SAABoPA	0.9491	0.9490	0.9503	0.7992	0.7593	0.7373	0.9443	0.9302	0.9203
DTAP	0.8867	0.8874	0.8851	0.7506	0.7320	0.7216	0.9459	0.9375	0.9331
CBBA-PR	0.9497	0.9490	0.9503	0.6663	0.5976	0.4918	0.8916	0.8567	0.8292
	$CP(\tau)$			$CP(\tau \mid DIS)$			$RP(\tau \mid DIS)$		

Figure 7. Comparison of system performance of each algorithm at different dynamic strengths (different number of *task unexpected changes*).

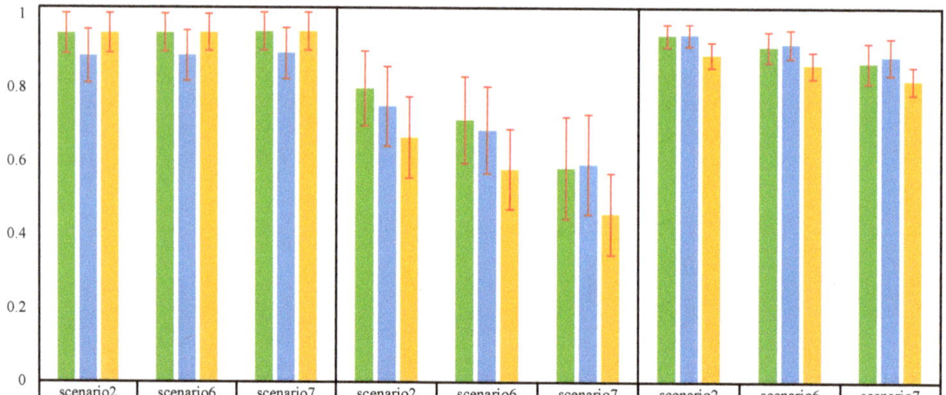

	scenario2	scenario6	scenario7	scenario2	scenario6	scenario7	scenario2	scenario6	scenario7
SAABoPA	0.9491	0.9508	0.9542	0.7992	0.7139	0.5833	0.9443	0.9132	0.8699
DTAP	0.8867	0.8887	0.8948	0.7506	0.6863	0.5934	0.9459	0.9210	0.8869
CBBA-PR	0.9497	0.9514	0.9542	0.6663	0.5798	0.4579	0.8916	0.8641	0.8227
	$CP(\tau)$			$CP(\tau \mid DIS)$			$RP(\tau \mid DIS)$		

Figure 8. Comparison of system performance of each algorithm at different dynamic strengths (different number of *UAV's number decreases*).

In summary, the capability performance of the SAABoPA proposed in this paper is similar to that of CBBA-PA under no interference and better than that of the DTAP; the capability performance of the SAABoPA under multiple interference is better than that of the DTAP and CBBA-PA; the resilience performance of the SAABoPA under multiple interference is similar to that of the DTAP and better than that of the CBBA-PA, and it is more adaptable to dynamic scenarios.

5. Conclusions

This paper presents a basic framework for applying UAVs as important components of EMDS to emergency material delivery scenarios, and proposes SAABoPA for capability performance and resilience performance optimization. Combined with the actual material delivery, the problem is modeled as MTTDDVRP-SD on the basis of the VRP problem, while several features are considered, including multi-trip per UAV, time-dependent emergency indicator, dynamics of the environment, split-delivery, and trip duration limit. Three types of dynamic interference scenarios are considered, including: *new task generation*, *task unexpected changes*, and *UAV's number decreases*. To solve this new problem, this paper proposes the SAABoPA algorithm, which adds a pre-authorization and sequential auction mechanism. Meanwhile, in order to describe the effect of dynamic disturbances on EMDS, we improve the integral resilience model under single interference and propose a resilience performance indicator adapted to multiple interference scenarios. Finally, through comparison experiments with DTAP and CBBA-PR in scenarios with different dynamic intensities, and using Friedman's test with 99% confidence interval, we verified the effectiveness of SAABoPA, which can improve the resilience performance of the system while maintaining a better capability performance, compensating for the shortcomings of CBBA-PR which only focuses on capability performance and DTAP algorithm which only focuses on resilience performance.

It should be noted that the scenario in this paper is material delivery under disaster area rescue, which mainly considers task survival measured by task emergency indicator as the optimization objective, and may need to trade-off more objectives if it is applied to other scenarios such as UAV logistics, combat equipment delivery, and cluster fire strike. In the future, we consider building a small hardware experiment bed to test the algorithm effectiveness and system performance, and try to solve more practical problems to extend to real applications.

Author Contributions: Conceptualization, J.Z. and Y.Z.; methodology, J.Z.; software, J.Z.; validation, J.Z., T.W. and W.W.; formal analysis, R.W.; investigation, X.L.; resources, X.L.; data curation, Y.Z.; writing—original draft preparation, J.Z.; writing—review and editing, T.W.; visualization, R.W. All authors have read and agreed to the published version of the manuscript.

Funding: This work is supported in part by the National Natural Science Foundation of China under Grant 72101263.

Institutional Review Board Statement: Not applicable.

Informed Consent Statement: Not applicable.

Data Availability Statement: Not applicable.

Conflicts of Interest: The authors declare no conflict of interest.

Notations

Some of the parameters involved in the model and their meanings are as follows.

Sets

U	Set of UAVs
V_B	Set of *MDC*, $V_B = \{V_0\}$
DIS^1	Set of dynamic interference types 1
DIS^2	Set of dynamic interference types 2
DIS^3	Set of dynamic interference types 3

Indices

i	Index of UAV serial numbers, $U_i \in U$
j	Index of task serial numbers, $T_j \in T$
k	Index of UAV trips, $k \in \{1, 2, ..., Ex_i\}$
n^1, n^2, n^3	Index of the serial numbers of dynamic interference types 1, 2 and 3, which are parameters of the stochastic process, $n^1 \in \{1, 2, ..., \lvert DIS^1 \rvert\}$, $n^2 \in \{1, 2, ..., \lvert DIS^2 \rvert\}$, $n^3 \in \{1, 2, ..., \lvert DIS^3 \rvert\}$

Operator	
$\lvert\bullet\rvert$	Number of elements in the set
$\tilde{\bullet}$	Random variable or random vector (bold font)
$\overline{\bullet}$	Upper limit of possible values of the random variable
$\underline{\bullet}$	Lower limit on the possible values of the random variable
$U(\bullet,\bullet)$	Continuous uniform distribution between two values
$DiscreteU(\bullet,\bullet)$	Discrete uniform distribution between two values
Parameters	
$T_i^{duration}$	Maximum duration of the UAV U_i
δ	Ratio coefficient of the speed of the UAV with the weight of the loading
a	Constant parameter
L_i^{max}	Upper limit of the loading capacity of the UAV U_i
V_i^{unload}	Speed of the UAV U_i at no-load
(x_j, y_j)	Two-dimensional coordinates of the task T_j
(x_0, y_0)	Two-dimensional coordinates of the *MDC* V_0
Variables	
t	Discrete time series
T_{end}	Moment of completion of emergency material delivery task
Ex_i	Number of UAV U_i trips
sT_i^k	Departure time of the k-th trip of the UAV U_i
aT_i^k	Arrival time of the k-th trip of the UAV U_i
$v_i(t)$	Speed of the UAV U_i at t moments
$E_j(t)$	Emergency indicator of the task T_j at t moments
$R_j(t)$	Quantity of material Requirement of the task T_j at t moments
$L_i^k(t)$	Loading of the k-th trip of the UAV U_i at t moments
$MD_{ij}(t)$	Quantity of material delivered by the UAV U_i to the task T_j at t moments
$(x_i(t), y_i(t))$	Two-dimensional coordinates of the UAV U_i at t moments
ΔR	Quantity of change in the material requirements of the task
ΔE	Value of change in the material emergency indicators of the task
MD_{ij}^k	Decision variable, quantity of material delivered by the UAV U_i to the task T_j in k-th trip
x_{ij}^k	Binary decision variable, if the UAV U_i execute task T_j in k-th trip, $x_{ij}^k = 1$; otherwise $x_{ij}^k = 0$

Appendix A

The results of pair-wise comparisons of 1000 random instances for 7 scenarios are shown in Figure A1, which provide the confidence intervals (adjusted for a familywise error rate of $\alpha = 0.01$) for all comparisons between the SAABoPA algorithm and the comparison algorithm. Note that in each subplot of Figure A1, blue and red indicate that the results of the two algorithms for this scenario have significant differences at the 99% confidence intervals, while blue and black indicate that the results of the two algorithms for this scenario have no significant differences at the 99% confidence intervals.

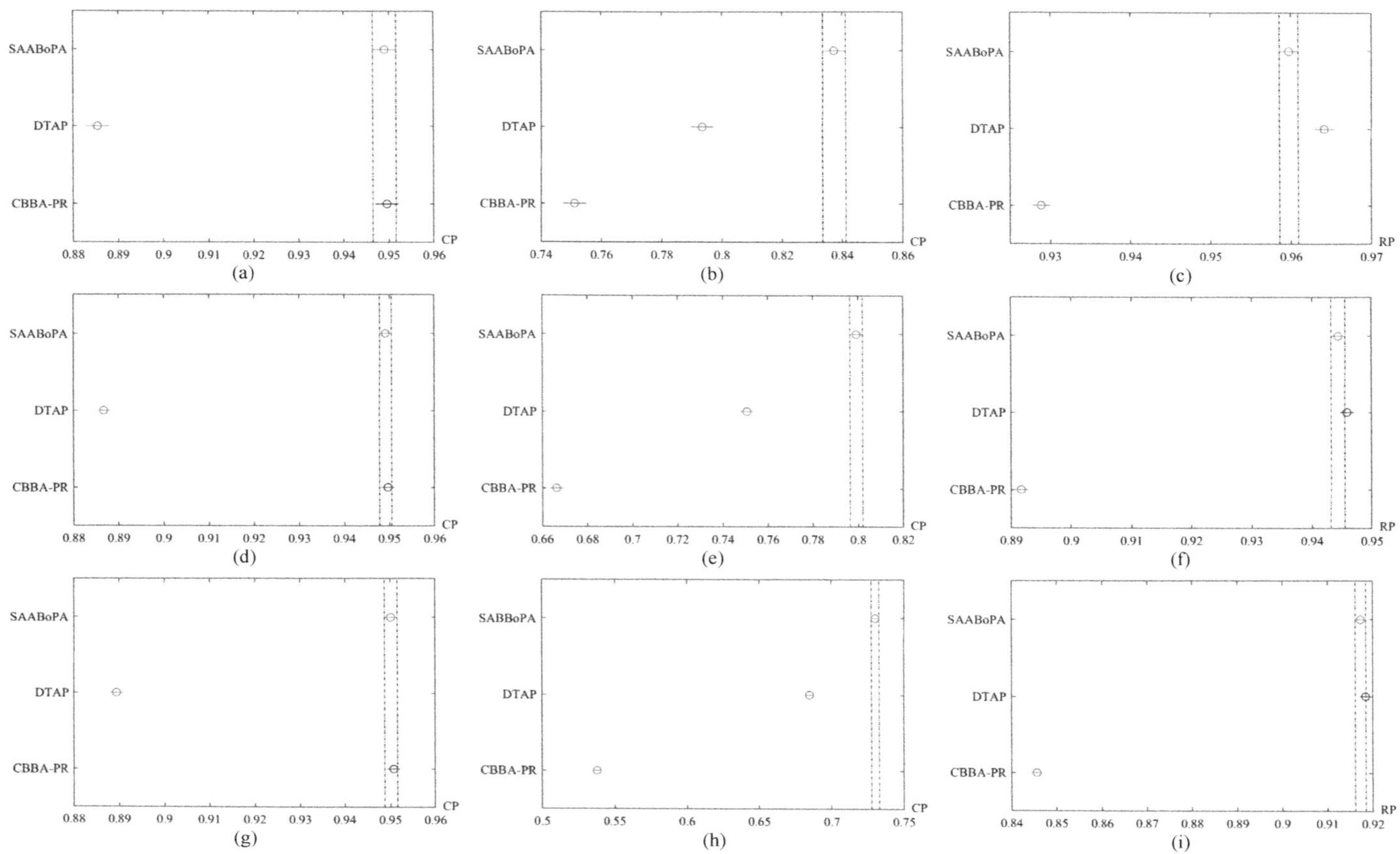

Figure A1. *Cont.*

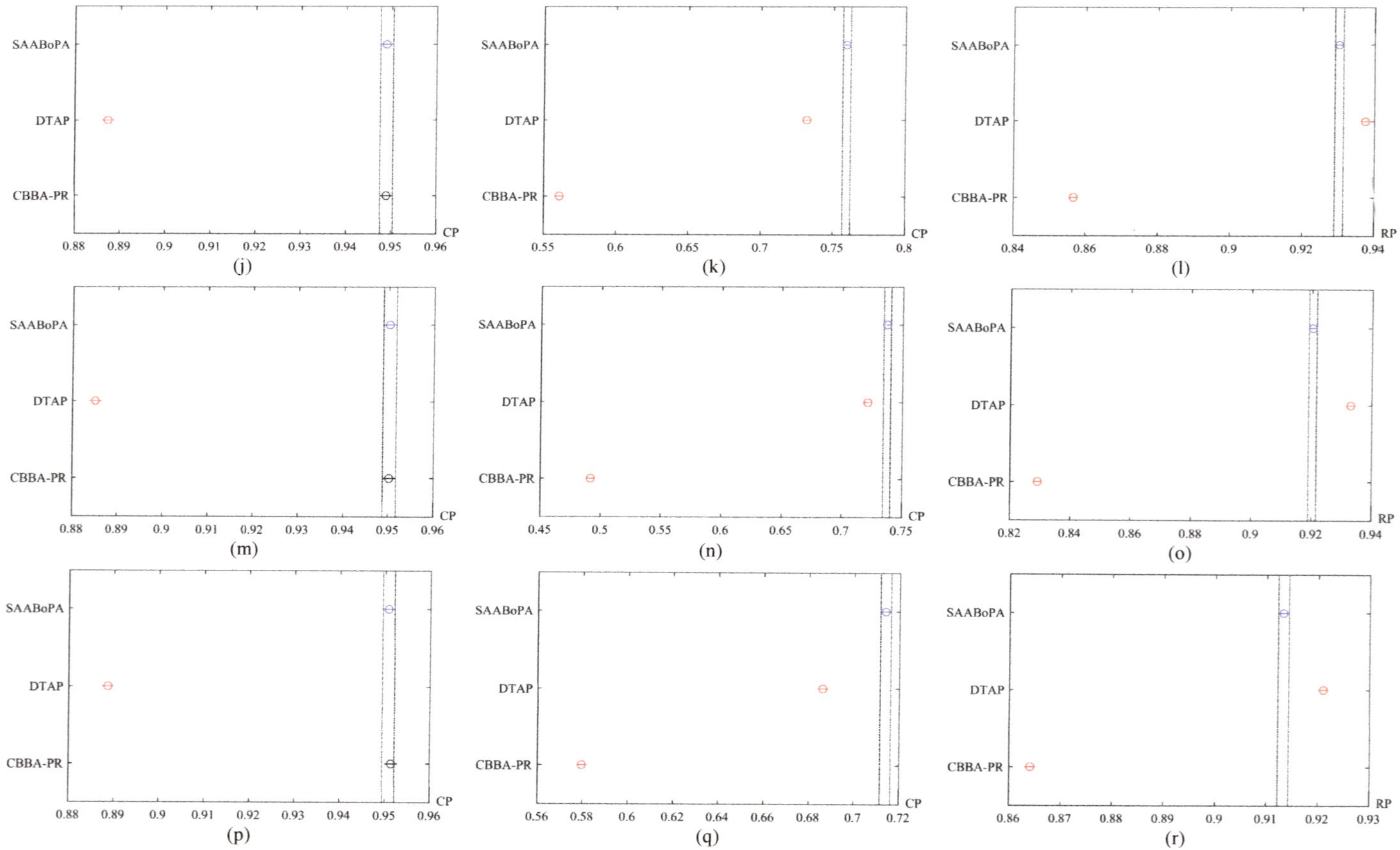

Figure A1. *Cont.*

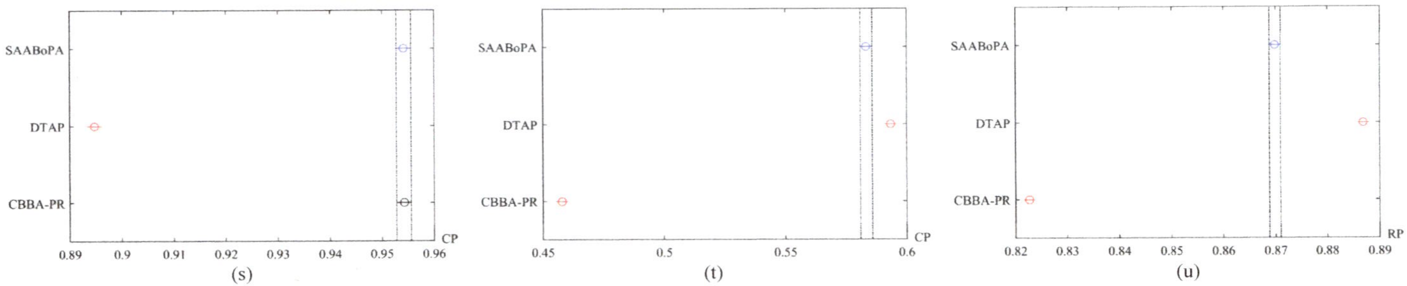

Figure A1. Pair-wise comparison of system performance under different algorithms in 7 scenarios: (**a,d,g,j,m,p,s**) Capability performance without dynamic interference of scenarios 1 to 7, respectively; (**b,e,h,k,n,q,t**) Capability performance with dynamic interference of scenarios 1 to 7, respectively; (**c,f,i,l,o,r,u**) Resilient performance of scenarios 1 to 7, respectively.

References

1. Pérez-Rodríguez, N.; Holguín-Veras, J. Inventory-allocation distribution models for postdisaster humanitarian logistics with explicit consideration of deprivation costs. *Transp. Sci.* **2016**, *50*, 1261–1285. [CrossRef]
2. Saini, K.; Sood, S.K. Exploring the emerging ict trends in seismic hazard by scientometric analysis during 2010–2019. *Environ. Earth Sci.* **2021**, *80*, 1–25. [CrossRef]
3. Ng, J.S.; Lim, W.Y.B.; Dai, H.-N.; Xiong, Z.; Huang, J.; Niyato, D.; Hua, X.-S.; Leung, C.; Miao, C. Joint auction-coalition formation framework for communication-efficient federated learning in uav-enabled internet of vehicles. *IEEE Trans. Intell. Transp. Syst.* **2020**, *22*, 2326–2344. [CrossRef]
4. Hou, H.; Yang, J.; Chen, Y.; Yu, M. A material delivery system built on internet of things and the role of libraries. *Libr. Tech.* **2019**, *38*, 195–209. [CrossRef]
5. Song, X.; Zheng, Y.; Chang, C. An emergency dispatch model based on variable precision rough sets. *Inf. Control.* **2011**, *40*, 858–864.
6. Guan, G.; Lin, Z.; Gong, Y.; Jiang, Z. Modeling and simulation of collaborative dispatching of disaster relief materials based on urgency. *Math. Probl. Eng.* **2020**, *2020*, 4274106. [CrossRef]
7. Taillard, É.D.; Laporte, G.; Gendreau, M. Vehicle routeing with multiple use of vehicles. *J. Oper. Res. Soc.* **1996**, *47*, 1065–1070. [CrossRef]
8. Liu, Y.; Liu, Z.; Shi, J.; Wu, G.; Pedrycz, W. Two-echelon routing problem for parcel delivery by cooperated truck and drone. *IEEE Trans. Syst. Man Cybern. Syst.* **2020**, *51*, 7450–7465. [CrossRef]
9. Sadrani, M.; Tirachini, A.; Antoniou, C. Vehicle dispatching plan for minimizing passenger waiting time in a corridor with buses of different sizes: Model formulation and solution approaches. *Eur. J. Oper. Res.* **2022**, *299*, 263–282. [CrossRef]
10. Cattaruzza, D.; Absi, N.; Feillet, D. Vehicle routing problems with multiple trips. *Ann. Oper. Res.* **2018**, *271*, 127–159.
11. Dorling, K.; Heinrichs, J.; Messier, G.G.; Magierowski, S. Vehicle routing problems for drone delivery. *IEEE Trans. Syst. Man, Cybern. Syst.* **2016**, *47*, 70–85. [CrossRef]
12. Sun, Y.; Wang, D.; Lang, M.; Zhou, X. Solving the time-dependent multi-trip vehicle routing problem with time windows and an improved travel speed model by a hybrid solution algorithm. *Clust. Comput.* **2019**, *22*, 15459–15470. [CrossRef]
13. Rios, B.H.O.; Xavier, E.C.; Miyazawa, F.K.; Amorim, P.; Curcio, E.; Santos, M.J. Recent dynamic vehicle routing problems: A survey. *Comput. Ind. Eng.* **2021**, *160*, 107604. [CrossRef]
14. Li, J.; Xiong, Y.; Jiang, B. Distribution fairness in emergency material vehicle scheduling based on uncertain time and demand. *J. Uncertain Syst.* **2021**, *14*, 2150014. [CrossRef]
15. Nan, L.; Chen, Y.; Zhang, Z. An improved adaptive large-scale neighborhood search algorithm solves hybrid vehicle path problems with dynamic demand. *Comput. Appl. Res.* **2021**, *38*, 9.
16. Sabar, N.R.; Bhaskar, A.; Chung, E.; Turky, A.; Song, A. A self-adaptive evolutionary algorithm for dynamic vehicle routing problems with traffic congestion. *Swarm Evol. Comput.* **2019**, *44*, 1018–1027. [CrossRef]
17. Ouaddi, K.; Mhada, F.; Benadada, Y. Memetic algorithm for multi-tours dynamic vehicle routing problem with overtime (mdvrpot). *Int. J. Ind. Eng. Comput.* **2020**, *11*, 643–662. [CrossRef]
18. Casazza, M.; Ceselli, A.; Calvo, R.W. A route decomposition approach for the single commodity split pickup and split delivery vehicle routing problem. *Eur. J. Oper. Res.* **2021**, *289*, 897–911. [CrossRef]
19. Hartomo, K.D.; Purnomo, H.D.; Anwar, M.T. Routing model for medium disaster relief operations. In Proceedings of the 2017 International Conference on Innovative and Creative Information Technology (ICITech), Salatiga, Indonesia, 2–4 November 2017; pp. 1–6.
20. Zhang, P.; Xiao, K.; Fu, C.; Yang, K. A fast dynamic programming algorithm for solving large-scale vcvrp problems. *Syst. Eng. Theory Pract.* **2016**, *36*, 12.
21. Mingozzi, A.; Roberti, R.; Toth, P. An exact algorithm for the multitrip vehicle routing problem. *INFORMS J. Comput.* **2013**, *25*, 193–207. [CrossRef]
22. Kilby, P.; Prosser, P.; Shaw, P. Dynamic vrps: A study of scenarios. *Univ. Strathclyde Tech. Rep.* **1998**, *1*, 11.
23. Montemanni, R.; Gambardella, L.M.; Rizzoli, A.E.; Donati, A.V. Ant colony system for a dynamic vehicle routing problem. *J. Comb. Optim.* **2005**, *10*, 327–343. [CrossRef]
24. Guo, X.; Ji, M.; Wen, D.; Zhang, X.; Tian, S. Distributed multi-uav tasking and path planning for 'last-mile' delivery. *Syst. Eng. Theory Pract.* **2021**. [CrossRef]
25. Choi, H.-L.; Brunet, L.; How, J.P. Consensus-based decentralized auctions for robust task allocation. *IEEE Trans. Robot.* **2009**, *25*, 912–926. [CrossRef]
26. Buckman, N.; Choi, H.-L.; How, J.P. Partial replanning for decentralized dynamic task allocation. In *AIAA Scitech 2019 Forum*; American Institute of Aeronautics and Astronautics, Inc.: San Diego, CA, USA, 2019; p. 0915.
27. Chen, C.; Bao, W.; Men, T.; Zhu, X.; Wang, J.; Wang, R. Nectar-an agent-based dynamic task allocation algorithm in the uav swarm. *Complexity* **2020**, *2020*, 6747985. [CrossRef]
28. Farinelli, A.; Iocchi, L.; Nardi, D. Distributed on-line dynamic task assignment for multi-robot patrolling. *Auton. Robot.* **2017**, *41*, 1321–1345. [CrossRef]
29. Luo, L.; Chakraborty, N.; Sycara, K. Distributed algorithms for multirobot task assignment with task deadline constraints. *IEEE Trans. Autom. Sci. Eng.* **2015**, *12*, 876–888. [CrossRef]

30. Chung, K.; Park, R.C. P2p cloud network services for iot based disaster situations information. *Peer-to-Peer Netw. Appl.* **2016**, *9*, 566–577. [CrossRef]
31. Vogel, R.M.; Fennessey, N.M.; Bolognese, R.A. Storage-reliability-resilience-yield relations for northeastern united states. *J. Water Resour. Plan. Manag.* **1995**, *121*, 365–374. [CrossRef]
32. Woods, D. Escaping failures of foresight. *Saf. Sci.* **2009**, *4*, 498–501. [CrossRef]
33. Yodo, N.; Wang, P.; Zhou, Z. Predictive resilience analysis of complex systems using dynamic bayesian networks. *IEEE Trans. Reliab.* **2017**, *66*, 761–770. [CrossRef]
34. Pumpuni-Lenss, G.; Blackburn, T.; Garstenauer, A. Resilience in complex systems: An agent-based approach. *Syst. Eng.* **2017**, *20*, 158–172. [CrossRef]
35. Liaghati, H.R.; Mazzuchi, T.A.; Sarkani, S. Utilizing a maximin optimization approach to maximize system resiliency. *Syst. Eng.* **2021**, *24*, 144–157. [CrossRef]
36. Ouyang, M.; Duenas-Osorio, L. Time-dependent resilience assessment and improvement of urban infrastructure systems. *Chaos Interdiscip. J. Nonlinear Sci.* **2012**, *22*, 033122. [CrossRef] [PubMed]
37. Dessavre, D.G.; Ramirez-Marquez, J.E.; Barker, K. Multidimensional approach to complex system resilience analysis. *Reliab. Eng. Syst. Saf.* **2016**, *149*, 34–43. [CrossRef]
38. Jing, T.; Wang, T.; Wang, W.; Li, X.; Zhou, X. An adaptive regulation method for cluster size of continuous reconnaissance uavs. *J. Comput. Res. Dev.* **2018**, *55*, 9.
39. Arya, S.R.; Ashokkumar, C.R.; Arya, H. Gamma and velocity tracking for uav obstacle avoidance in pitch plane. In Proceedings of the 2016 Indian Control Conference (ICC), Hyderabad, India, 4–6 January 2016; pp. 362–368.
40. Song, J.M.; Chen, W.; Lei, L. Supply chain flexibility and operations optimisation under demand uncertainty: A case in disaster relief. *Int. J. Prod. Res.* **2018**, *56*, 3699–3713. [CrossRef]
41. Zhou, Y.; Chen, N.; Li, Z.; Gong, Y. Optimal design of emergency logistics network at the initial stage of post-earthquake relief considering facility disruption scenarios. *Oper. Res. Manag.* **2020**, *29*, 6.
42. Lv, G.; Peng, Z.; Wang, D.; Dou, W. Target task assignment for unmanned ship cluster formation reconfiguration. *Chinese Nav. Res.* **2018**, *13*, 6.
43. Vincent, F.Y.; Widjaja, A.T.; Gunawan, A.; Vansteenwegen, P. The multi-vehicle cyclic inventory routing problem: Formulation and a metaheuristic approach. *Comput. Ind. Eng.* **2021**, *157*, 107320.
44. Peng, Y.; Li, Y. Collaborative truck-drone delivery path optimization considering the impact of epidemic. *Chinese J. Highw.* **2020**, *33*, 73.
45. Zhao, M. Research and Simulation of Distributed Multi-Type UAV Cooperative Mission Assignment. Ph.D. Thesis, Nanjing University of Science and Technology, Nanjing, China, 2009.
46. Song, X.; Wang, J.; Chang, C. Nonlinear continuous consumption emergency scheduling model and algorithm based on demand urgency. *Inf. Control* **2014**, *43*, 9.
47. Wang, Y.; Sun, B. Multiperiod optimal emergency material allocation considering road network damage and risk under uncertain conditions. *Oper. Res.* **2021**, *22*, 2173–2208. [CrossRef]
48. Patterson, M.D.; Wears, R.L. Resilience and precarious success. *Reliab. Eng. Syst. Saf.* **2015**, *141*, 45–53. [CrossRef]
49. Francis, R.; Bekera, B. A metric and frameworks for resilience analysis of engineered and infrastructure systems. *Reliab. Eng. Syst. Saf.* **2014**, *121*, 90–103. [CrossRef]
50. Campelo, F.; Wanner, E.F. Sample size calculations for the experimental comparison of multiple algorithms on multiple problem instances. *J. Heuristics* **2020**, *26*, 851–883. [CrossRef]

mathematics

MDPI

Article

MSGWO-MKL-SVM: A Missing Link Prediction Method for UAV Swarm Network Based on Time Series

Mingyu Nan, Yifan Zhu, Jie Zhang, Tao Wang and Xin Zhou *

College of System Engineering, National University of Defense Technology, Changsha 410000, China; nanmingyu@nudt.edu.cn (M.N.); yfzhu@nudt.edu.cn (Y.Z.); zhangjie@nudt.edu.cn (J.Z.); wangtao1976@nudt.edu.cn (T.W.)
* Correspondence: zhouxin09@nudt.edu.cn

Abstract: Missing link prediction technology (MLP) is always a hot research area in the field of complex networks, and it has been extensively utilized in UAV swarm network reconstruction recently. UAV swarm is an artificial network with strong randomness, in the face of which prediction methods based on network similarity often perform poorly. To solve those problems, this paper proposes a Multi Kernel Learning algorithm with a multi-strategy grey wolf optimizer based on time series (MSGWO-MKL-SVM). The Multiple Kernel Learning (MKL) method is adopted in this algorithm to extract the advanced features of time series, and the Support Vector Machine (SVM) algorithm is used to determine the hyperplane of threshold value in nonlinear high dimensional space. Besides that, we propose a new measurable indicator of Multiple Kernel Learning based on cluster, transforming a Multiple Kernel Learning problem into a multi-objective optimization problem. Some adaptive neighborhood strategies are used to enhance the global searching ability of grey wolf optimizer algorithm (GWO). Comparison experiments were conducted on the standard UCI datasets and the professional UAV swarm datasets. The classification accuracy of MSGWO-MKL-SVM on UCI datasets is improved by 6.2% on average, and the link prediction accuracy of MSGWO-MKL-SVM on professional UAV swarm datasets is improved by 25.9% on average.

Keywords: UAV swarm; missing links prediction; time series data; multiple kernel learning; multi-objective optimization; grey wolf optimizer; support vector machine; complex network

MSC: 68T20

1. Introduction

In modern intelligent warfare, the saturation assault of a UAV swarm is one of the most severe threats to the defender in many typical defense scenarios. It has been very urgent to develop an effective countermeasure to defend the saturation assaults of UAV swarm [1]. One purpose of link prediction in an UAV swarm network is to reconstruct its communication topology structure, so that a UAV swarm network disintegration strategy can be generated later. Recent studies have borne out that the fire control scheme based on the network disintegration strategy will improve the defensive effectiveness of UAV swarm interception significantly. The UAV swarm network disintegration strategy is shown in Figure 1.

A UAV swarm consists of a group of isomorphic or heterogeneous UAVs. The current UAV swarm command and control system still adopts the man-in-the-loop mode. The UAV swarm system receives the task instructions from the commander in the OODA (Observe, Orient, Decide, and Act) loop and completes the task semi-autonomously. The UAV swarm system is unable to be out of the commander's control completely.

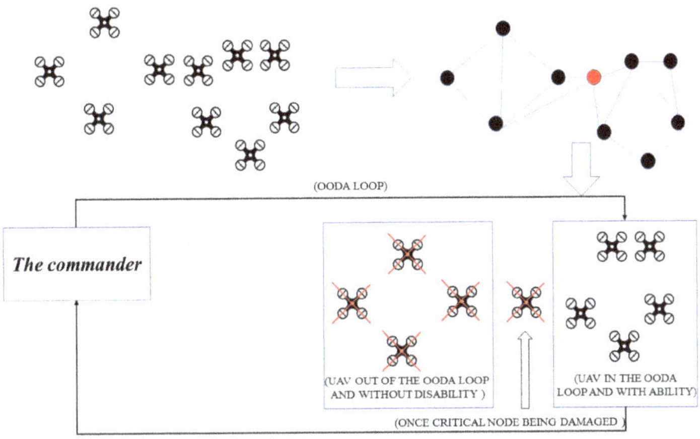

Figure 1. The flow of UAV swarm network disintegration strategy.

For the commander, the connectivity of the UAV swarm network is a prerequisite to realizing its characteristics of swarm intelligence and task coordination, and the two-connectivity character is a basic requirement for UAV swarm networks in a battlefield environment. In a UAV swarm, some nodes play an important role in the network's two-connectivity characteristics, which are called Critical Nodes, and the cut-vertex is one of those Critical Nodes.

The red node in Figure 1 is a cut-vertex of the given UAV swarm. Once the red node is damaged, the UAV swarm will be quickly split into multiple subblocks, and a large number of UAVs will break away from the network, not able to continue receiving the task instructions of a commander. At that time, the combat effectiveness of the UAV swarm will be greatly reduced.

UAV swarm network communication topology reconstruction is one of the technical routes to realize the identification of Critical Nodes of the UAV swarm network. The main contribution of this paper concentrates on reconstructing the UAV swarm network topology structure by the method of predicting missing links in complex networks. Missing link prediction (MLP) is a microscopic prediction in a complex network. Instead of predicting the global properties such as modularity, degree, and clustering coefficient, its goal is to assess the existence probability of each non-observed link, according to the known information from network structure and individuals' attributes [2,3].

So far, scholars have proposed many effective missing link prediction methods [4,5], in which the similarity-based methods are utilized widely, such as the Common Neighbors algorithm [6–8], the Adamic-Adar index algorithm [9–11], and the Local Random Walk algorithm [12]. Newman M. E. J. [6] studies empirically the time evolution of scientific collaboration networks in physics and biology. It shows that the probability of a pair of scientists collaborating increases with the number of other collaborators they have in common. Lada A. Adamic [9] attempts to predict the links among the activities of the internet network and reflect those activities of the internet network into the real world. He proposes some effective indicators of social connections and finds that these indicators vary drastically in different user populations. Those indicators generate far-reaching influence and have great significance in the field of MLP technology. However, as complex networks increase in size and node numbers, the computing burden of MLP technology has got heavier and heavier. To overcome the difficulties of the sparsity and huge size of the target networks, Liu [12] proposes a local random walk strategy, which can give better prediction while having a much lower computational complexity. Similarity-based MLP technology has also been utilized in many other networks, such as counter-terrorism [13], e-commerce [14], biological [15,16], and social [17–19].

However, similarity-based methods are mainly applicable to complex networks with some regularities, such as scale-free networks [20], regular networks, and small-world networks [21]. As for the UAV swarm system, it is an artificial network with strong randomness and high uncertainty, and the similarity-based method is hard to predict the missing link accurately for this scenario.

Current studies on complex network link prediction mainly focus on static and deterministic networks. In fact, many networks in the real world are dynamic and time-varying. For example, the UAV swarm network proposed in this work will evolve with the relative position of the UAV. The disintegration strategy and link prediction of time-varying complex networks is a challenge in the future [22]. Ren assumed that the UAV swarm would take some time to form a flying formation before performing reconnaissance, attack, and other tasks. During this period, the data link of the UAV swarm network can be predicted. However, Ren did not give a specific link prediction method and directly gave the disintegration strategy of the UAV swarm network under the premise of the known network links and topology reconstruction [23]. Shu and Qi conducted in-depth research on the problems of UAV swarm network link prediction independently. Aiming at the characteristics of the UAV swarm network, Shu proposed a temporal graph embedding model to reconstruct the UAV swarm network. The network structure features were mapped to the relationships between nodes, and the contextual semantic features of nodes were extracted by adversarial training. With the help of long and short-term memory networks, the temporal characteristics of the UAV swarm network are extracted to predict the link [24]. However, the method employed by Shu, is a black-box model that lacks interpretability and does not take full advantage of the velocity information of the UAV swarm network. Qi proposed a Markov chain-based link prediction algorithm for the UAV swarm network topology, which could predict the link between a pair of nodes. For the convenience of analysis, Qi employed a SYN-boid model to describe the swarming motions of nodes in the UAV swarm network [25]. The most important transition probability matrix is hard to obtain in the method of Qi. In order to make up for the defects of the method proposed by Shu and Qi, an equivalent transformation model from time series to complex network was adopted in this paper.

For a complex system, there are two paradigms to describe its intrinsic dynamic behavior, namely time series and complex networks. Hence, this paper attempts to develop a new missing link prediction technology, applicable to UAV swarm networks, based on the time series. In fact, the method of transformation from time series to complex networks has been developed for decades and could be summarized in the following three main categories: Neighbor-Joining [26,27], Visibility Graph [28–30], and Transfer [31,32].

Zhang and Small [26] first proposed converting time series into complex networks for analysis in 2006. They construct complex networks from pseudo-periodic time series, with each cycle represented by a single node in the network. Two nodes are deemed to be connected if the phase space distance between the corresponding cycles is less than a predetermined value D. On the basis of Zhang and Small, Yang [28] proposes a method of fixed length segmentation of time series and examines the correlation coefficient of individual time series segments. In 2014, Zhao [33] proposes a magnitude difference mapping method from one-dimensional time series to complex networks. The magnitude difference mapping method directly examines the magnitude difference between time series with respect to a given threshold value, so it provides the possibility of proving the equivalence relation between time series and complex networks, analytically. Peng [34], in 2020, studied the transformation between time series and complex networks both in theory and applications. He analyzes the equivalence of the amplitude difference mapping method from time series to complex networks. Two quasi-isometric isomorphism theories of metric space are summarized and their relations are found in the literature [35]. However, the analytical proof work is only based on a series of ideal non-linear differential equations, with the equation parameters and variables not having definite physical meanings. The overidealized mathematical model is a little far away from the real situation in the real world.

The preceding works have made significant contributions to the MLP problems of UAV swarm networks based on time series, but they also have the following issues:

1. The operations of the above algorithms of transformation between time series and complex networks are all processed in ordinary Euclidean space. However, many advanced relational features of the UAV swarm network's dynamic behaviors may not be obvious in ordinary Euclidean space;
2. The dimension of extracted features about time series is relatively low in the above algorithms of transformation between time series and complex networks, which may not be able to characterize the UAV swarm network sufficiently;
3. The determination of thresholds relies heavily on the experience of researchers and is absent with efficient methods, as used in the above algorithms of transformation between time series and complex networks.

To effectively solve the aforementioned problems, a multi-kernel learning algorithm based on a multi-strategy grey wolf optimizer (MSGWO-MKL-SVM) was proposed, and the framework of MSGWO-MKL-SVM is shown in Figure 2.

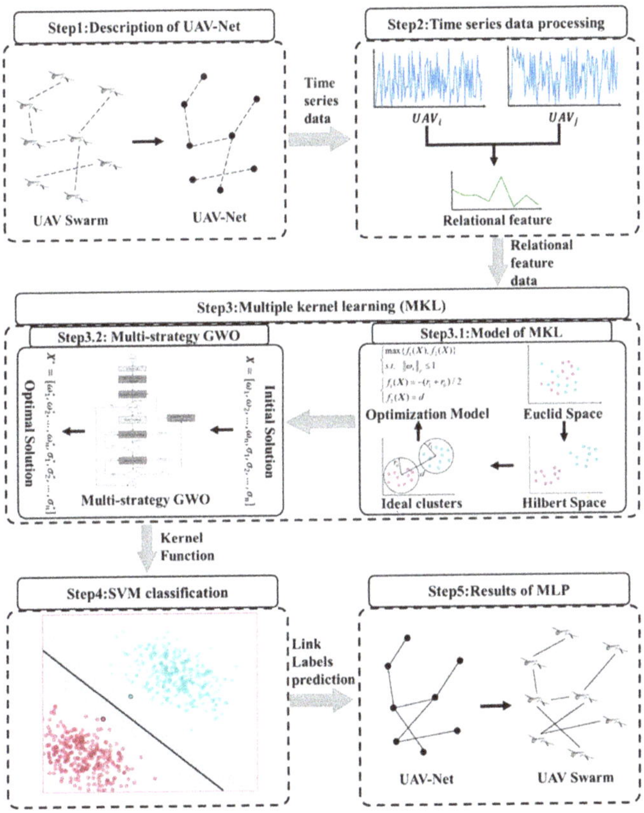

Figure 2. Framework of the MSGWO-MKL algorithm.

The MSGWO-MKL-SVM algorithm for predicting links of UAV swarm networks based on time series contains five steps. In step 1, the relationship between UAV swarms and complex networks was described. Nodes of networks represent UAVs, and edges of networks represent the communication links among a UAV swarm.

In step 2, the time series data of a UAV swarm were processed. The advanced relational features of UAV-*i* and UAV-*j* from the training set were extracted by correlation analysis.

In step 3, new indicators of multi-kernel learning were established based on the idea of clusters, transforming a multi-kernel learning problem into a multi-objective optimization problem. Besides that, a multi-strategy grey wolf optimizer algorithm was proposed to solve this problem, whose global searching ability was greatly enhanced compared with some state-of-the-art algorithms. In step 4, the trained kernel functions were put into the Support Vector Machine (SVM) algorithm, extracting the advanced features of time series in high dimensional space, and then determining the threshold hyperplane. In step 5, the time series data of two UAV-*i* and UAV-*j* from the test set were fed into the MSGWO-MKL-SVM algorithm, which determined whether UAV-*i* and UAV-*j* had a communication link.

The main contributions of this paper can be summarized as follows:

1. The multiple kernel learning (MKL) method was adopted to transform the features of time series from a linear Euclidean space to a non-linear Hilbert space, making the features of time series of a UAV swarm network more remarkable in the kernel space;
2. New indicators of multi-kernel learning (MKL) were established based on the idea of clusters, transforming a multi-kernel learning problem into a multi-objective optimization problem and reducing the computational complexity greatly;
3. Variable neighborhood search strategies and parameters adaptive operators were designed to enhance the global searching ability of grey wolf optimizer algorithm (GWO). Besides that, we adopted the opposition-based learning strategy to increase the diversity of the initial population. Eventually, a multi-strategy grey wolf optimization algorithm (MSGWO) was proposed in this paper. The MSGWO algorithm can enhance the balance between local and global search and maintain diversity. In the standard UCI dataset, the MSGWO algorithm performed better than some state-of-the-art algorithms;
4. Multiple kernel learning and Support Vector Machine (MKL-SVM) algorithms were adopted to calculate the threshold hyperplane of correlation features of the UAV swarm network in the kernel space directly, avoiding empirical estimation of the threshold;
5. The multifractal detrended cross-correlation analysis (MF-DCCA) method was used to analyze the correlation of time series between UAV-*i* and UAV-*j*. *K*-order cross-correlativity coefficient was defined to extract high-dimensional features of cross correlativity between UAV-*i* and UAV-*j*.

The rest of this paper is organized as follows. In Section 2, basic descriptions of the UAV swarm network and the missing link prediction (MLP) model are established. In Section 3, the time series data process and cross-correlation analysis are described. In Section 4, new indicators of multi-kernel learning (MKL) were established based on the idea of clusters, and a multi-strategy grey wolf optimization algorithm (MSGWO) is proposed. Sections 6 and 7, calculating samples are provided and discussed. In Section 8, several conclusions are given, in addition to a discussion on future research.

2. Description of UAV Swarm Networks

There is a UAV network containing n UAVs and the control equation of the UAV-i is represented in Equation (1) [36]:

$$\dot{\xi}_i = \varsigma_i, i = 1, \dots n \tag{1}$$

where ξ_i represents the displacement statement of the UAV-i; ς_i represents the velocity statement of the UAV-i.

A graph $G = (V, E)$ describes a directed communication network structure of the UAV swarms. The graph G consists of a node set $V(G)$ and an edge set $E(G)$, where an edge is an ordered pair of distinct nodes in the graph G. One node of the network represents one UAV in the swarm, and one edge between two distinct nodes represents that there exists a message delivery between the two UAVs.

It is assumed that the matrix $A(G) = [a_{ij}]$ is a $n \times n$ matrix, which is termed the adjacency matrix of the UAV network, and follows Equation (2) [37].

$$a_{ij} = \begin{cases} 1, \; if \; e_{ij} \in E(G) \\ 0, \; otherwise \end{cases} \tag{2}$$

where a_{ij} represents the message delivering conditions from the UAV-*i* to the UAV-*j*; e_{ij} is an edge between node-*i* and node-*j*.

In order to simulate the behavior of bird swarms, Reynolds proposed the Boid model in 1986 [38], in which swarms meet the following three principles:

1. Separation: One node is too close to another node in its repulsion zone, and the two nodes will repulse and move in opposite directions;
2. Aggregation: Each node will move closer to the central node of the swarm;
3. Coherence: Each node will adjust its speed and direction of movement, based on its neighbor nodes, to ensure the velocity consistency of the whole swarm.

Based on the above three principles, the formation and topology control illustration of UAV swarms are as in Figure 3.

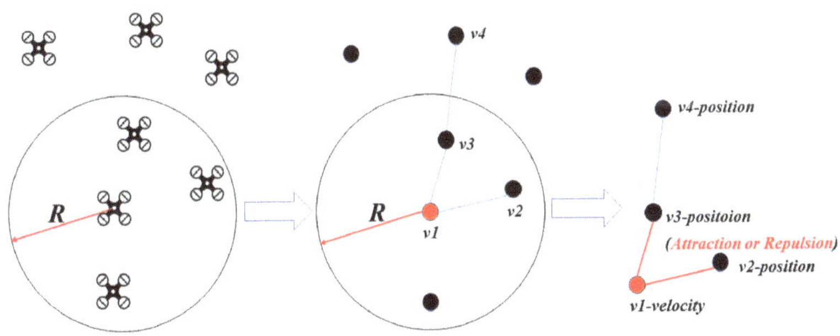

Figure 3. Formation and topology control illustration of UAV swarms.

The UAV node could establish data links with other nodes in its communication radius, R. However, limited by the number of channels and communication quality, each UAV node can only establish data links with part of the nodes. In Figure 3, The UAV node $v1$ only establishes connections with $v2$ and $v3$. Based on Boid's three principles, the relative distance and direction between nodes $v3$ and $v1$ will affect the velocity vector of node $v1$. Although node v4 can also exert indirect influence on node $v1$ through node $v3$, the influence degree is weaker than the direct influence of node $v3$. For node $v1$, the indirect influence degree of K-hop node v4 and the direct influence degree of 1-hop node $v3$ is different. The following work in this paper mainly focuses on the quantification of the influence degree between nodes and the determination of the threshold of direct influence of 1-hop nodes and indirect influence of K-hop nodes.

Therefore, $\{\xi_i(t), \xi_j(t)\}_{i=1}^{n}$ is defined as a set of time series of the UAV swarm network, $\xi_i(v_i, t)$ is the velocity time series of the UAV-*i*, $\xi_j(x_{ij}, t)$ is the relative displacement time series of the UAV-*i* and UAV-*j*, and ε is a threshold. We use the absolute metric of time series in high dimensional nonlinear Hilbert space as a transformation method, as in Equation (3).

$$a_{ij} = \begin{cases} 1, \; if \; \| \phi[\xi_i(t), \xi_j(t)] \| \geq \varepsilon \\ 0, \; otherwise \end{cases} \tag{3}$$

where t is the time, $\| \cdot \|$ is an absolute metric function, and $\phi(\cdot)$ is a mapping function.

3. Time Series Data Processing and Cross-Correlation Analysis

A Detrended Cross-Correlation Analysis (DCCA) algorithm [39] is proposed by Podobnik. The DCCA algorithm is designed to measure the cross correlativity about two nonstationary time series. The Multifractal Detrended Cross-Correlation Analysis (MF-DCCA) method [40,41] integrates multifractal theory on the basis of DCCA, measuring the multi-fractal properties about two nonstationary time series in different timescales. In this section, a new high-order cross correlativity coefficient based on MF-DCCA was proposed, which aims to extract the high dimensional cross correlativity features of the two nonstationary time series of UAV-*i* and UAV-*j*.

A construction equation for two new time series, $\{\check{\xi}_i(t)\}_{t=1}^{T}$ and $\{\check{\xi}_j(t)\}_{t=1}^{T}$, based on the UAV swarm network's dynamic behaviors, $\{\xi_i(v_i,t)\}_{t=1}^{T}$ and $\{\xi_j(x_{ij},t)\}_{t=1}^{T}$, about UAV-*i* and UAV-*j*, was devised. The parameter T is the length of the time series. The construction equation is represented in Equation (4).

$$\begin{cases} \check{\xi}_i(t) = \sum_{k=1}^{t}(\ \xi_i(k) - \overline{\xi_i}) \\ \check{\xi}_j(t) = \sum_{k=1}^{t}\ (\xi_j(k) - \overline{\xi_j}) \end{cases} \tag{4}$$

where, $\overline{\xi_i}$ and $\overline{\xi_j}$, are the mean value of $\{\xi_i(t)\}_{t=1}^{T}$ and $\{\xi_j(t)\}_{t=1}^{T}$.

The two new time series, $\{\check{\xi}_i(t)\}_{t=1}^{T}$ and $\{\check{\xi}_j(t)\}_{t=1}^{T}$, were equally divided into T_s inter-cells, as in Equation (5).

$$T_s = T/s \tag{5}$$

where, s, is the separation scale and T_s is the separation number.

We defined inter-cell time series $\check{\xi}_i[t,m]$ and $\check{\xi}_i[t,m]$, in Equation (6).

$$\begin{cases} \check{\xi}_i[t,m] = \left[\check{\xi}_i(t), t = 1,\ldots,T_s\right]_m \\ \check{\xi}_j[t,m] = \left[\check{\xi}_j(t), t = 1,\ldots,T_s\right]_m \end{cases} \tag{6}$$

where parameter, t, is from 1 to T_s and parameter m is from 1 to s.

We defined the detrended inter-cell time series $\hat{\xi}_i[t,m]$ and $\hat{\xi}_j[t,m]$, in Equation (7).

$$\begin{cases} \hat{\xi}_i[t,m] = \check{\xi}_i[t,m] - \xi_i^v[t,m] \\ \hat{\xi}_j[t,m] = \check{\xi}_j[t,m] - \xi_j^v[t,m] \end{cases} \tag{7}$$

where, $\xi_i^v[t,m]$, is the trend function of the time series $\check{\xi}_i[t,m]$ and $\xi_j^v[t,m]$ is the trend function of the time series $\check{\xi}_j[t,m]$.

The k-order co-variance detrend fluctuant function and k-order variance detrend fluctuant functions about the two time series, UAV-*i* and UAV-*j*, follow Equation (8).

$$\begin{cases} F_{k-YY}(s) = \left\{\frac{1}{s}\sum_{m=1}^{s}\left[\frac{1}{T_s}\sum_{t=1}^{T_s}\left[\xi_j[t,m] \times \xi_j[t,m]\right]\right]^k\right\}^{\frac{1}{k}} \\ F_{k-XX}(s) = \left\{\frac{1}{s}\sum_{m=1}^{s}\left[\frac{1}{T_s}\sum_{t=1}^{T_s}\left[\xi_i[t,m] \times \xi_i[t,m]\right]\right]^k\right\}^{\frac{1}{k}} \\ F_{k-XY}(s) = \left\{\frac{1}{s}\sum_{m=1}^{s}\left[\frac{1}{T_s}\sum_{t=1}^{T_s}\left[\xi_i[t,m] \times \xi_j[t,m]\right]\right]^k\right\}^{\frac{1}{k}} \end{cases} \tag{8}$$

where, $F_{k-YY}(s)$, is the k-order of the covariance detrend fluctuant function, and $F_{k-YY}(s)$ and $F_{k-XX}(s)$ are the k-order of the variance detrend fluctuant functions.

The k-order cross correlativity coefficient was defined in Equation (9).

$$\rho_k = F_{k-XY}(s)^2/F_{k-XX}(s) \times F_{k-YY}(s) \tag{9}$$

where ρ_k is the k-order cross correlativity coefficient.

Eventually, the two time series about UAV-i and UAV-j were transformed into a $1 \times k$ dimension matrix $[\rho_{ij}]_{1\times k}$, in Equation (10).

$$\left[\{\xi_i(t)\}_{t=1}^{T}; \{\xi_j(t)\}_{t=1}^{T}\right] \to [\rho_{ij}]_{1\times k} = \left[\rho_{ij}^1, \rho_{ij}^2, \ldots, \rho_{ij}^k\right] \tag{10}$$

4. MSGWO-MKL Algorithm

4.1. Model of MKL

For one pair of time series, $\{\xi_i(v_i, t)\}_{t=1}^{T}$ and $\{\xi_j(x_{ij}, t)\}_{t=1}^{T}$, about UAV-$i$ and UAV-j, the method of time series processing is able to transform them into a $1 \times k$ dimensional matrix ρ_{ij}.

Assuming that there exist such two clusters, S_0 and S_1, the two clusters were defined in Equation (11).

$$\begin{cases} S_1 = \left\{ \left[\rho_{ij}^1, \rho_{ij}^2, \ldots, \rho_{ij}^k, \overline{d}\right] \middle| a_{ij} = 1 \right\} \\ S_0 = \left\{ \left[\rho_{ij}^1, \rho_{ij}^2, \ldots, \rho_{ij}^k, \overline{d}\right] \middle| a_{ij} = 0 \right\} \end{cases} \tag{11}$$

where ρ_{ij}^k is the k-order cross correlativity coefficient of one pair of time series, $\{\xi_i(v_i, t)\}_{t=1}^{T}$ and $\{\xi_j(x_{ij}, t)\}_{t=1}^{T}$, about UAV-$i$ and UAV-j. The average distance of UAV-i and UAV-j in the time window is $\overline{d}$. The two clusters, S_0 and S_1, in an ideal kernel space are represented in Figure 4.

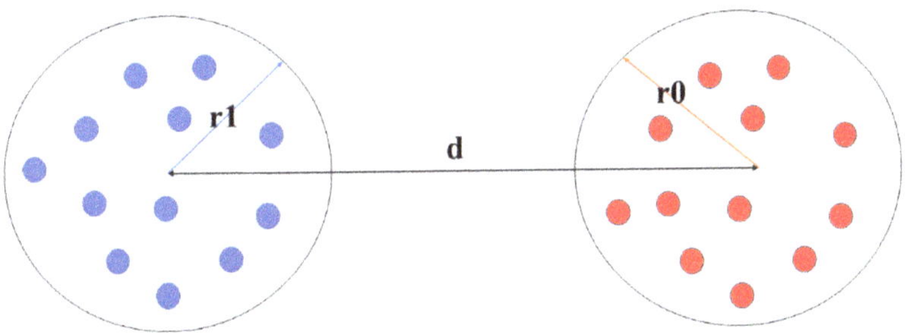

Figure 4. Clusters in an ideal kernel space.

The, r_1, is the character radius of the cluster S_1 in the ideal kernel space, r_0 is the character radius of the cluster, S_0, in the ideal kernel space, and d is the character distance between the cluster, S_0, and the cluster, S_1, in the ideal kernel space.

Equation (12) was established in the ideal kernel space, predicting the missing links of UAV swarm networks.

$$a_{ij} = \begin{cases} 1, \ if \ \| \phi(\rho_{ij}) - \phi\left(\rho_{center-(1)}\right) \| \le r_1 \\ 0, \ if \ \| \phi(\rho_{ij}) - \phi\left(\rho_{center-(0)}\right) \| \le r_0 \end{cases} \tag{12}$$

where, $\rho_{center-(1)}$ and $\rho_{center-(0)}$, are the center points of the two clusters, S_0 and S_1, in the ideal kernel space. $\phi(\ )$ is the mapping function of the ideal kernel functions.

Traditional indicators of Kernel function are easy to fall into a local optimum with a slow convergence speed in the process of kernel learning, such as CSK [42,43] and KTA [44], passing through all the elements of the training set and operation's computational complexity to achieve n^2. To solve these problems, new indicators based on the idea of clusters were proposed.

The larger the character distance of clusters d, and the narrower the character radius, r_1 and r_0, are, the stronger the kernel function's classification capacity is. The computational complexity of evaluating kernel functions was reduced from n^2 to $(2n + 1)$, which improved computation efficiency significantly.

The character radius, r_1 and r_0, were calculated in Equation (13).

$$\begin{cases} r_1 = \frac{1}{n_1}\sum_{i=1}^{n_1} d_K\left(\vec{S_1}[i], \vec{S}_{1-center}\right) \\ r_0 = \frac{1}{n_0}\sum_{i=1}^{n_0} d_K\left(\vec{S_0}[i], \vec{S}_{0-center}\right) \end{cases} \quad (13)$$

where, n_1 and n_0, are the number of elements in the cluster S_1 and S_0, $\vec{S_1}[i]$ is the i-th element of the cluster S_1, $\vec{S_2}[i]$ is the i-th element of the cluster S_2, $\vec{S}_{1-center}$ is the center of the cluster S_1, $\vec{S}_{2-center}$ is the center of the cluster S_2, and d_K is the distance in the kernel space.

The centers of the cluster, S_1 and S_0, were calculated in Equation (14).

$$\begin{cases} \vec{S}_{1-center} = \frac{1}{n1}\sum_{i=1}^{n1} \vec{S_1}[i] \\ \vec{S}_{0-center} = \frac{1}{n0}\sum_{i=1}^{n0} \vec{S_0}[i] \end{cases} \quad (14)$$

The distance in the kernel space, d_K, was calculated, in Equation (15).

$$d_K(X,Y) = Kernel(X,X) + Kernel(Y,Y) - 2\,Kernel(X,Y) \quad (15)$$

where $Kernel()$ is the kernel function, and X and Y are vectors in the Euclidean space.

The character distance d of the cluster, S_1, and cluster, S_0, was calculated in Equation (16).

$$d = d_H\left(\vec{S}_{1-center}, \vec{S}_{0-center}\right) \quad (16)$$

Eventually, the process of multi-kernel learning was transformed into a multi-objective optimization problem in Equation (17).

$$\begin{cases} max\{f1[Kernel(\omega,\sigma)], f2[Kernel(\omega,\sigma)]\}\ .st.\ \parallel \omega_i \parallel_p \leq 1 \\ f1 = -(r_1 + r_0)/2, f2 = d \end{cases} \quad (17)$$

where $f1(\ )$ and $f2(\ )$ are the objective functions and $Kernel(\ )$ is the kernel function to be optimized.

The kernel function $Kernel(\ )$ was defined in Equation (18).

$$Kernel(\ ) = \sum_{i=1}^{m} \omega_i \times \overline{Kernel_i}(\sigma_i) \quad (18)$$

where $\overline{Kernel_i}(\ )$ is the basis kernel function; ω_i is the weight of the basis kernel function $\overline{Kernel_i}(\ )$; σ_i is the parameter of the basis kernel function $\overline{Kernel_i}(\ )$, and m is the number of the basis kernel function $\overline{Kernel_i}(\ )$.

The optimization solution of $Kernel(\ )$ could be expressed as a one-dimensional matrix X, as in Equation (19).

$$X = [\omega_1, \omega_2, \ldots, \omega_m; \sigma_1, \sigma_2, \ldots, \sigma_m]_{1\times 2m} \quad (19)$$

4.2. MSGWO Algorithm

4.2.1. Grey Wolf Optimizer Algorithm (GWO)

The GWO is a swarm intelligence optimization algorithm based on the social structures and predation behaviors of the wolves [45]. The results of GWO are obviously superior to Particle Swarm Optimization (PSO) and Differential Evolution (DE) in 29 standard test functions.

The grey wolf swarms have a strict social hierarchy. The three wolves with the best performance are defined as leader wolves α, β, and δ, and the other wolves are defined as follower wolves ω. The follower wolves update their positions according to the condition of the leader wolves. The original optimization process of GWO is shown in Algorithm 1. The updating process of the wolf population is as shown in Figure 5.

Algorithm 1: Grey Wolf Optimizer

```
for iter in range (iter_max):
    for i in range (n):
        C_k = 2 × random(0,1), k = 1,2,3
        D_α = C_1 A_α − A_i(iter), D_β = C_2 A_β − A_i(iter), D_δ = C_3 A_δ − A_i(iter)
        K_i = (2 − iter/iter_max) × [2 × random(0,1) − 1], k = 1,2,3
        A_1 = A_α − K_1 D_α, A_2 = A_β − K_2 D_β, A_3 = A_δ − K_3 D_δ
        A_i(iter + 1) = (A_1 + A_2 + A_3)/3
    end for
end for
```

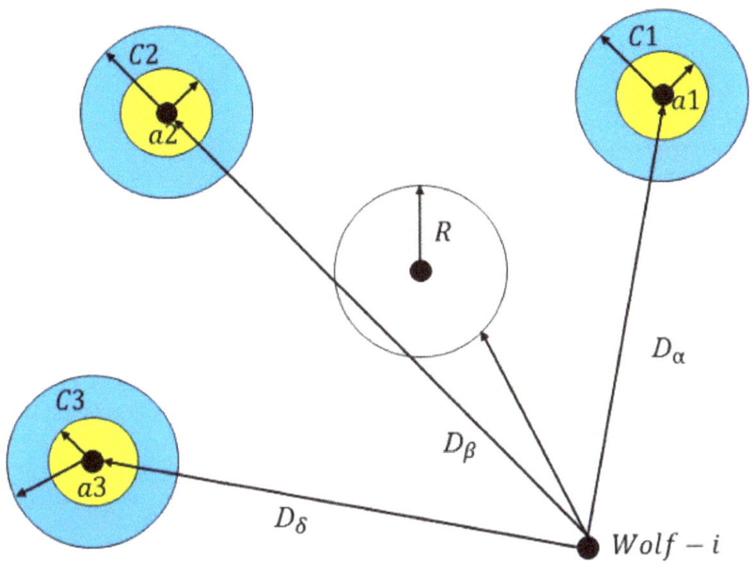

Figure 5. Updating process of wolves.

In Algorithm 1, A_α, A_β, and A_δ represent the positions of the leader wolves α, β, and δ; $A_i(iter)$ represents the position of the wolf- i in the generation- $iter$; D_α, D_β, and D_δ represents the search neighborhood generated by, α, β, and δ; $random(0,1)$ is a random number between (0,1), of which the randomness determines the uncertainty of the search neighborhood; $iter$ represents the generation of the wolf packs; $iter_{max}$ represents the maximum generation; the parameter K influences the wolf's neighborhood. If the absolute value of K is more than one, the wolf swarms will face the neighborhood searching. If the absolute value of K is less than one, the wolf swarms will leave the neighborhood to search. As shown in Figure 6, the uncertainty of the search neighborhood increases the global searching ability of the GWO.

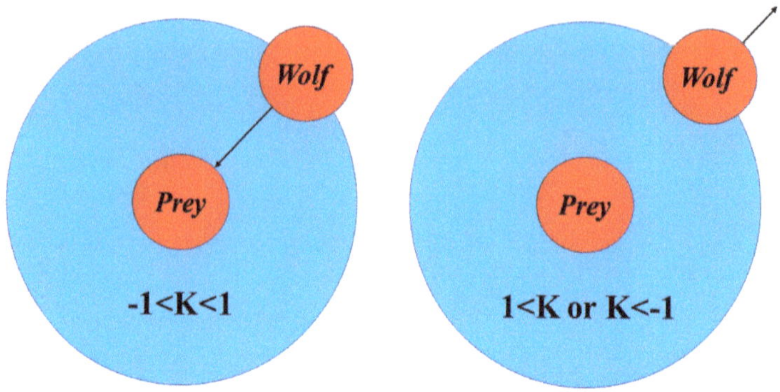

Figure 6. Search neighborhood.

4.2.2. Multi-Objective Design

This section modified the GWO algorithm into a multi-objective optimization algorithm. For multi-objective algorithms, the selection of leader wolves in each iteration is the most crucial step, which determines the superiority of the solutions directly.

Pareto Domination [46,47]: For multi-objective optimization algorithms, there are n objective functions $f_i(x), i = 1,2$. Given two decision variables, X_a and X_b, if the two decision variables satisfy following Equation (20), then the decision variable X_a is dominated by the decision variable X_b.

$$\begin{cases} f_i(X_a) \leq f_i(X_b), \forall\, i \in 1,2. \\ f_i(X_a) < f_i(X_b), \exists\, i \in 1,2. \end{cases} \tag{20}$$

where objective functions, $f_i(x), i = 1,2$ aim to maximize.

If there exists a decision variable X_{ND},which is not able to be dominated by other decision variables, then X_{ND} is termed a non-dominated solution.

Pareto Rank: In a set of solutions, the non-dominated solutions X_{ND} are termed rank one. Then the non-dominated solutions are removed from the original solution set. The non-dominated solutions, X_{ND}, in the new set of solutions are termed rank two. By analogy, the rank of all solutions in a solution set can be obtained, see Figure 7.

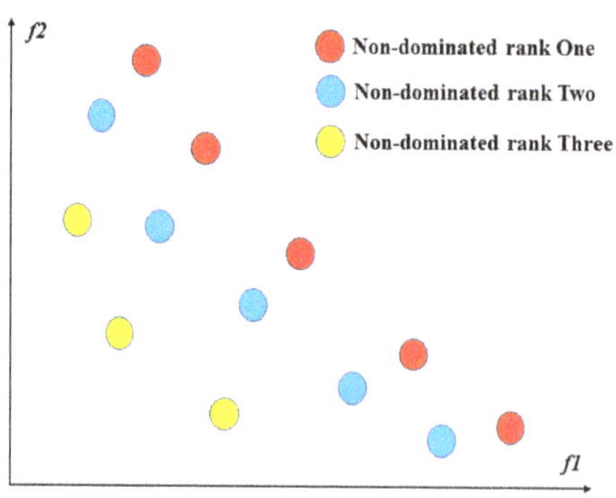

Figure 7. Non-dominated rank.

We selected leader wolves in the solution set of high non-dominated rank, according to the following Equation (21).

$$max\{RD = f_2(X_i)/(-f_1(X_i))\}, for\ X_i \epsilon\ Pareto \tag{21}$$

where *Pareto* is the solution set of high non-dominated rank, and *RD* is the relative distance between the character distance and character radius of two clusters.

The leader wolf selection process of MSGWO is shown in Algorithm 2.

Algorithm 2: Leader Wolves Selection
1: Define the scale of wolf population and position
2: for i in range(n):
3: for j in range(n):
4: if $f_i(X_a) \leq f_i(X_b), \forall\, i \in 1,2$ and $f_i(X_a) < f_i(X_b), \exists\, i \in 1,2.$:
5: Then X_a is dominated by X_b
6: Determine *Pareto* set
7: $max\{RD = f_2(X_i)/(-f_1(X_i))\}, for\ X_i \epsilon\ Pareto$
8: Determine the leader wolfs α,β and δ
9: end

4.2.3. Adaptive Parameters Strategy

In the process of kernel learning, we found that the two objective functions, character radius, f_1, and character distance, f_2, were highly correlated and contradictory. Once the character distance reaches a high level, the character radius will also increase rapidly. Eventually, they all would be at a relatively high level whose performance was bad in standard data sets. Rigorous non-dominated rank hierarchy causes the local convergence of solutions in the process of kernel learning. The Weak Pareto Domination was proposed in Equation (22) to increase the diversity of leader wolves while preserving superior solutions in the next iteration.

Weak Pareto Domination: For multi-objective optimization algorithms, there are n objective functions, $f_i(x), i = 1,2$. Given two decision variables, X_a and X_b, if the two decision variables satisfy the following Equation (22), then the decision variable, X_a, is weak-dominated by the decision variable, X_b.

$$\begin{cases} f_1(X_a) < f_1(X_b)\ and\ (1-\alpha) \times f_2(X_a) < f_2(X_b)\ (a) \\ (1+\alpha)f_1(X_a) < f_1(X_b)\ and\ f_2(X_a) < f_2(X_b)\ (b) \end{cases} \tag{22}$$

where objective functions, $f_i(x), i = 1,2$, aim to maximize; α is the adaptive parameter from 0 to 0.3, (a) and (b) correspond to the different two modules.

The Weak Pareto Domination was designed to encourage the wolf to explore while avoiding the local convergence at a relatively high level. The determination of adaptive parameters is in Equation (23)

$$\begin{cases} If\ |f_1(X_\alpha)| > k_1, then\ select\ (22.a)\ and\ let\ \alpha = 2 - |f_1(X_\alpha)| \\ If\ |f_2(X_\alpha)| < k_2, then\ select\ (22.b)\ and\ let\ \alpha = 2 \times |f_2(X_\alpha)| \end{cases} \tag{23}$$

where, *select* $(22.a)$, means that selecting the (a) module of the Equation (22); k_1 and k_2, are experience factors, recommending, k_1 = 1.7, and k_2 = 0.15.

The Adaptive Parameters Strategy is shown in Algorithm 3.

Algorithm 3: Adaptive Parameters Strategy
1: Define the leader wolf α
2: $if\ |f_1(X_\alpha)| > k_1$:
3: Weak Pareto Domination-(a):
4: $f_1(X_a) < f_1(X_b)\ \ and\ \ (1-\alpha) \times f_2(X_a) < f_2(X_b)$
5: $\alpha = 2 - |f1(X_\alpha)|$
6: $if\ |f_2(X_\alpha)| < k_2$:
7: Weak Pareto Domination-(b):
8: $(1+\alpha) \times f_1(X_a) < f_1(X_b)\ \ and\ \ f_2(X_a) < f_2(X_b)$
9: $\alpha = 2 \times |f_2(X_\alpha)|$
10: end

4.2.4. Opposition-Based Learning Strategy

The Opposition-Based Learning (OBL) strategy was proposed by H.Tizhoosh in 2005 [48,49], using opposite solutions, approximate opposite solutions, or inverse approximate opposite solutions to optimize the performance of an algorithm. It selects a total opposite solution based on the known best solution to increase the global searching ability. The method is widely used for algorithmic optimization in many algorithms.

In this section, the opposition-based learning strategy was adopted in the process of initializing the wolf population. We deleted three dominated wolves in the original wolf population and transformed the leader wolves into the opposite leader wolves, putting the opposite leader wolves into the new wolf population, which would increase the quality of leader wolves significantly and the diversity of the original population. The Opposition-based Learning (OBL) strategy is as Equation (24).

$$X_{OBL} = LB + UB - X_\alpha + r \cdot (X_\alpha - X) \tag{24}$$

where, X_{OBL}, is the solution generated by the Opposition-based Learning (OBL) strategy, LB is the lowest limit solution, LB is the uppermost limit solution, X_α is the solution of leader wolf α, X is the original solution, and r is a random number from 0 to 1.

The Opposition-Based Learning strategy is shown in Algorithm 4.

Algorithm 4: Opposition-Based Learning Strategy

```
Define the wolf i
For i in range (n):
    For j in range (20):
        X_OBL(i) = LB + UB − X_α + r · (X_α − X(i))
        IF (X(i) is dominated by X_OBL(i)):
            X(i) = X_OBL(i)
            Break
end
```

4.2.5. Neighbor Learning Strategy

In addition to group hunting, individual hunting is another interesting social behavior of grey wolves, which is our motivation to improve the GWO [50]. The Neighbor Learning Strategy (NLS) was proposed in this section. In NLS, each individual wolf was motivated by its neighbors to find another strategy for a better position. The following steps describe how NLS search strategies generate better positions.

Radius $R_i(t)$ was calculated using Euclidean distance between the current position of $X_i(t)$ and the position $X_{i-GWO}(t+1)$ generated by GWO, in Equation (25).

$$R_i(t) = \| X_i(t) - X_{i-GWO}(t+1) \| (1.5)^n \tag{25}$$

where , $n = 1, 2, \ldots$, to adjust the neighborhood scope of $X_i(t)$.

Then, the neighborhood scope of $X_i(t)$ was constructed by Equation (26).

$$N_i(t) = \{ X_j(t) | D_i(X_i(t), X_j(t)) < R_i(t) \} \tag{26}$$

where $N_i(t)$ is the neighborhood scope of the wolf $X_i(t)$; $D_i(X_i(t), X_j(t))$ is the Euclidean distance between $X_i(t)$ and $X_j(t)$.

$M_i(t)$ is the absolute complement of set $N_i(t)$, in Equation (27).

$$M_i(t) = \{ X_j(t) | X_j(t) \notin N_i(t), X_j(t) \in \Omega \} \tag{27}$$

where Ω is a set containing all the wolves' positions.

Once the neighborhood scope, $N_i(t)$ and $M_i(t)$, are constructed, Neighbor Learning Strategy is performed by Equation (28).

$$X_{NLS}(i) = X_i + random \cdot (X_N(i) - X_M(i)) \tag{28}$$

where, $X_N(i)$, is a random element selected from $N_i(t)$, $X_M(i)$ is a random element selected from $M_i(t)$, *random* is a random number from 0 to 1, and X_{NLS} is a solution generated by the Neighbor Learning Strategy.

The Neighbor Learning Strategy is shown in Algorithm 5.

Algorithm 5: Neighbor Learning Strategy

```
Define the wolf population
For i in range (n):
  For j in range (20):
    For n in range (100):
   R_i(t) =|| X_i(t) − X_{i−GWO}(t+1) || (1.5)^n
      N_i(t) = { X_j(t) | D_i(X_i(t), X_j(t)) < R_i(t) }
      IF N_i(t) ≠ ∅:
        Break
      M_i(t) = { X_j(t) | X_j(t) ∉ N_i(t), X_j(t) ∈ Ω }
       X_NLS(i) = X_i + random·(X_N(i) − X_M(i))
     IF (X(i) is dominated by X_NLS(i):
       X(i)= X_NLS(i)
       Break
end
```

4.2.6. Shuffle Learning Strategy

The Shuffle Learning strategy creates a new neighborhood by the shuffle method. The illumination of the Shuffle Learning strategy is shown in Figure 8.

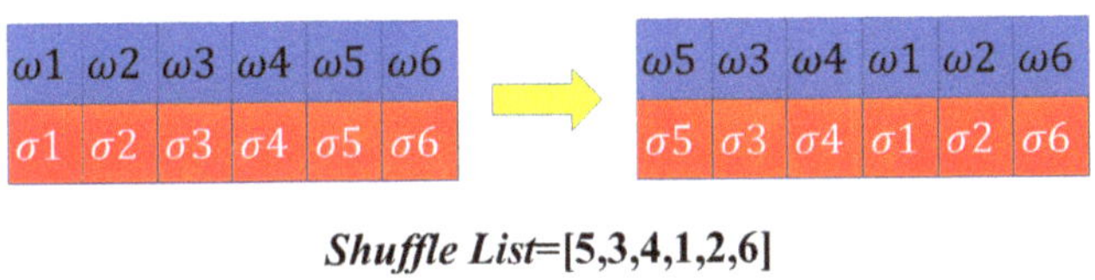

Figure 8. Shuffle Learning Strategy.

When the Opposition-Based Learning strategy and Neighbor Learning strategy are not able to generate superior solutions, it is time that shuffle learning is adopted. The shuffling operation will generate a random sequence, forming a set of new positions. Although the shuffling operation will explore considerable feasible solutions and improve the global searching ability, it will also destroy the original structure of the neighborhood and miss the superiority of leader wolves.

The Shuffle Learning strategy is shown in Algorithm 6.

Algorithm 6: Shuffle Learning Strategy

```
Define the wolf population
For i in range (n):
  For j in range (20):
    X_SLS(i) = np.random.shuffle(X[i])
    IF (X(i) is dominated by X_SLS(i)):
       X(i)= X_NLS(i)
       Break
end
```

4.2.7. Flow of the MSGWO

The flow of the MSGWO algorithm is shown in Figure 9. The red part means the components of the original GWO, the blue part means the judgement module, and the yellow component are improved in this paper.

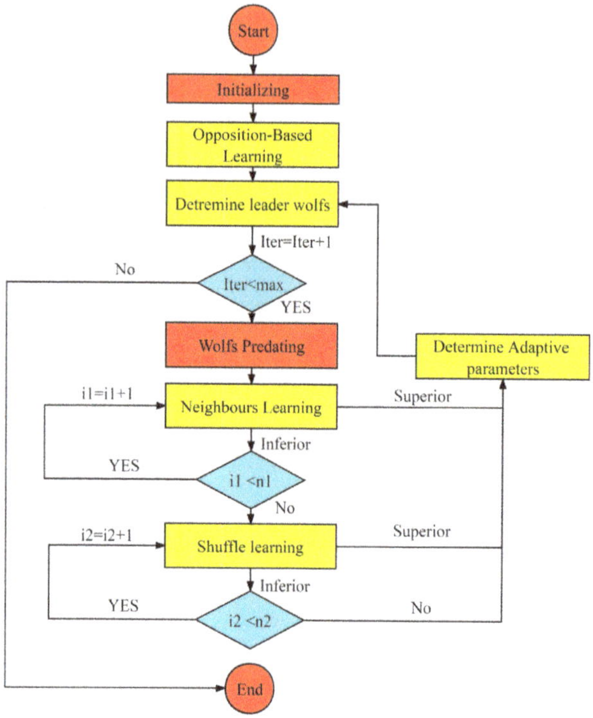

Figure 9. Flow of MSGWO.

When the MSGWO algorithm is launched, the initializer will generate the initial population of the grey wolves randomly. The weak Pareto rank norm will select leader wolves. Then we delete three dominated wolves from the original wolf population and transform the leader wolves into the opposite leader wolves, putting the opposite leader wolves into the new wolf population, which will increase the quality of leader wolves significantly and the diversity of the original population.

After that, the original GWO algorithm will generate a set of solutions to the multi-objective optimization problem. However, the GWO algorithms are easily trapped in local optimization, and the quality of solutions generated by the GWO algorithm should be enhanced further. To solve those problems, the neighbors' learning strategy and shuffle learning strategy are adopted. New neighborhoods generated by the neighbors' learning strategy and shuffle are able to increase the global searching ability of the GWO evidently. Once the solution generated by the neighbors learning strategy dominates the original solution, the shuffle learning strategy will be skipped directly. Eventually, the adaptive parameters will be adjusted according to the conditions of the leader wolves.

5. MSGWO-MKL-SVM Algorithm

As a general method for classification proposed by Vapnik [51,52], the support vector machine essentially uses a kernel function that maps the original input data space into a high-dimensional feature space so that the instances from two classes are as far apart as possible, preferably separable with a linear boundary in a Hilbert space.

Given a sample, $\{x_i, y_i; i = 1, \ldots, n\}$, where x_i is a vector of predictors in the input space and y_i represents the class index, which takes a value from $\{+1, -1\}$, a nonlinear support vector machine maps the input data $\{x_1, x_2, \ldots, x_n\}$ into a high-dimensional feature space, using a nonlinear mapping function ϕ, and finds a linear boundary in the feature space by maximizing the smallest distance of instances to this boundary. Mathematically, the idea is equivalent to solving the Equation (29).

$$\begin{cases} max \sum_{i=1}^{n} \alpha_i - \frac{1}{2} \sum_{i=1}^{n} \sum_{j=1}^{n} \alpha_i \alpha_j y_i y_j K(x_i, x_j) \\ subject\ to\ \sum_{i=1}^{n} \alpha_i y_i = 0, 0 \le \alpha_i \le C, i = 1, 2, \ldots n \end{cases} \tag{29}$$

where α_i is the dual variable and the scalar function $K(x_i, x_j)$ and is called a kernel function, adopting the multiple kernel functions learned in the last section.

The kernel form of the SVM boundary can be written as Equation (30).

$$\sum_{i \in SV} \alpha_i y_i K(x_i, x) + b = 0 \tag{30}$$

where SV is the set of support vectors.

We put the kernel functions optimized by the MSGWO algorithm into the SVM algorithm, forming the complete MSGWO-MKL-SVM algorithm.

6. Numerical Experiment

To illustrate the effectiveness of the MSGWO-MKL-SVM algorithm proposed in this paper, we designed three experiments:

1. Testing the multi-objective optimization ability of the MSGWO algorithm;
2. Testing the classification ability of the MSGWO-MKL algorithm;
3. Testing the missing links predicting ability of the MSGWO-MKL-SVM algorithm.

All experiments were conducted with Python 3.6, running on an Intel Core i7-8565CPU @ 1.80 GHz, and Windows 7 Ultimate Edition.

6.1. *Multi-Objective Optimization Ability Test of MSGWO*

This section selected the Blood Transfusion dataset in UCI to examine the MO-IGWO's optimization in the process of multi-objective optimization. The objective functions were adopted as in Equation (17). The relative distance (RD) is the ratio of character distance (CD) and character radius (CR) of clusters in kernel space. The MO-PSO [53], MO-GWO [54], and NSGA-2 [46] algorithms were used for comparison, demonstrating the superiority of the MSGWO algorithm.

As shown in Table 1, in all experiments, the parameters of the comparative algorithms were the same as the recommended settings.

Table 1. Parameters of algorithms.

	MO-PSO	MO-GWO	NSGA-2	MSGWO
Population	20	20	100	20
Generation	150	150	200	50

The optimization process of MO-PSO is as shown in Figure 10, and the relative distance of MO-PSO is as shown in Figure 11. The optimization process of NSGA-2 is as shown in Figure 12 and the relative distance of NSGA-2 is as shown in Figure 13. The optimization process of MO-GWO is as shown in Figure 14 and the relative distance of MO-GWO is as shown in Figure 15. The optimization process of MSGWO is as shown in Figure 16 and the relative distance of MSGWO is as shown in Figure 17.

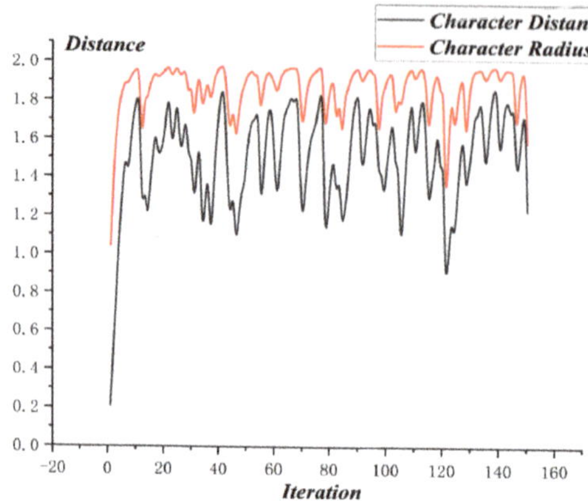

Figure 10. Optimization process of MO-PSO.

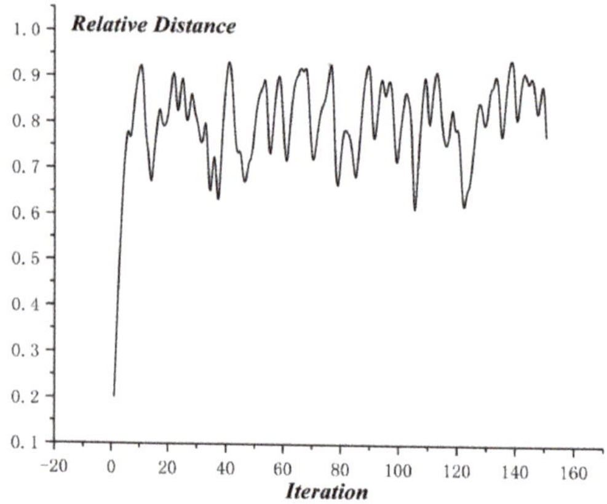

Figure 11. Relative distance of MO-PSO.

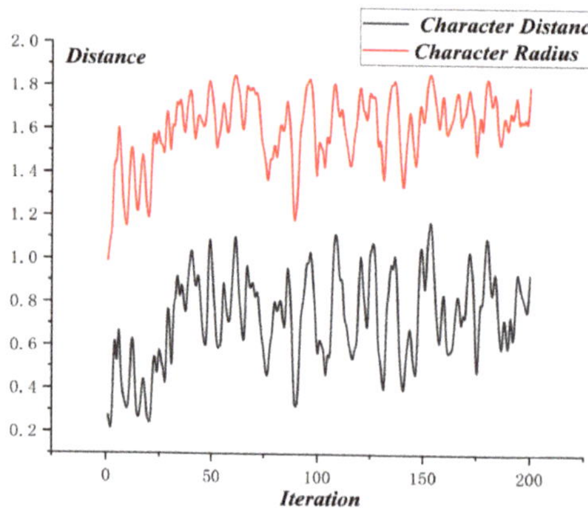

Figure 12. Optimization process of NSGA-2.

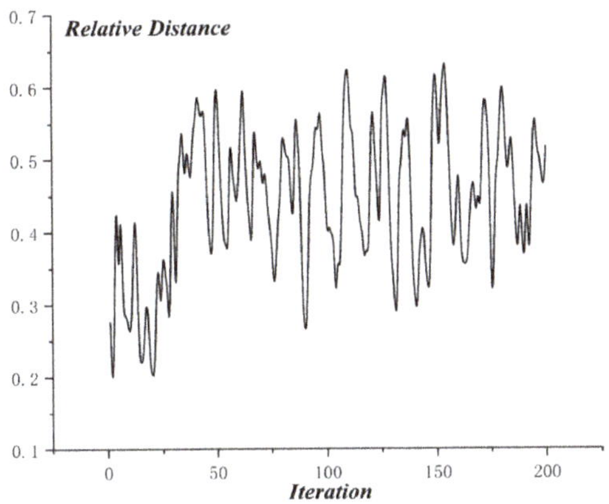

Figure 13. Relative distance of NSGA-2.

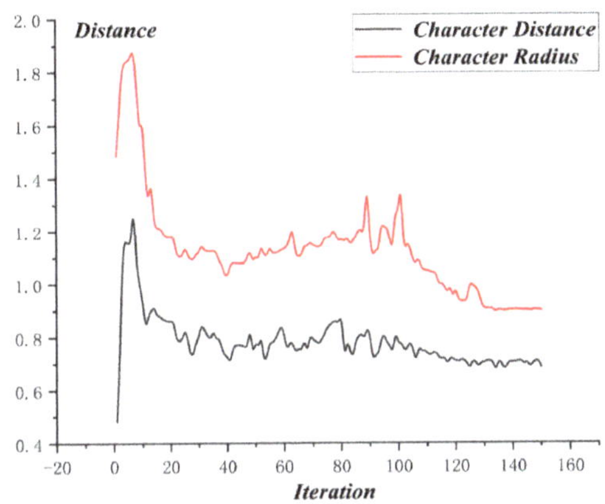

Figure 14. Optimization process of MO-GWO.

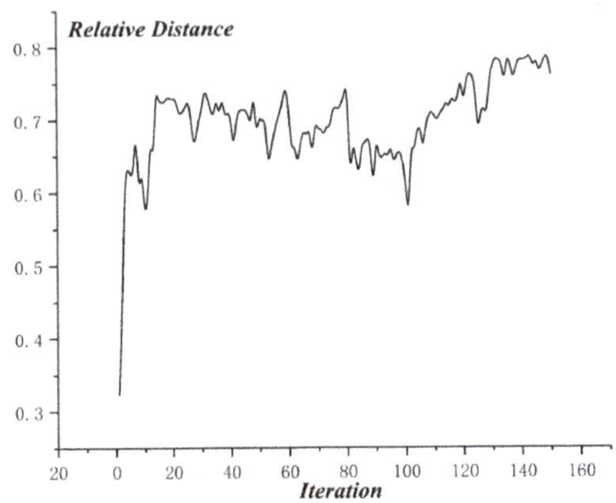

Figure 15. Relative distance of MO-GWO.

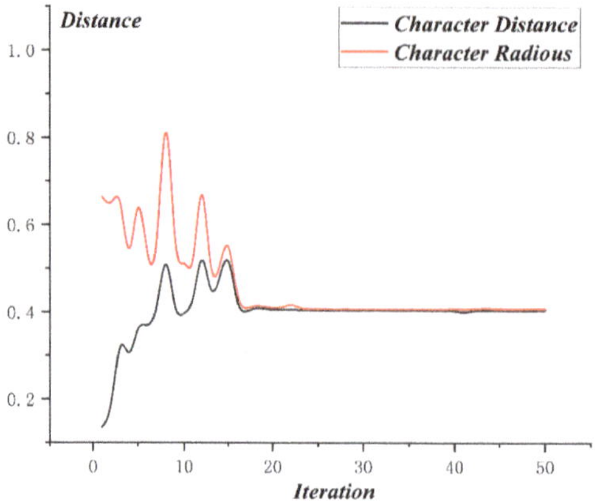

Figure 16. Optimization process of MSGWO.

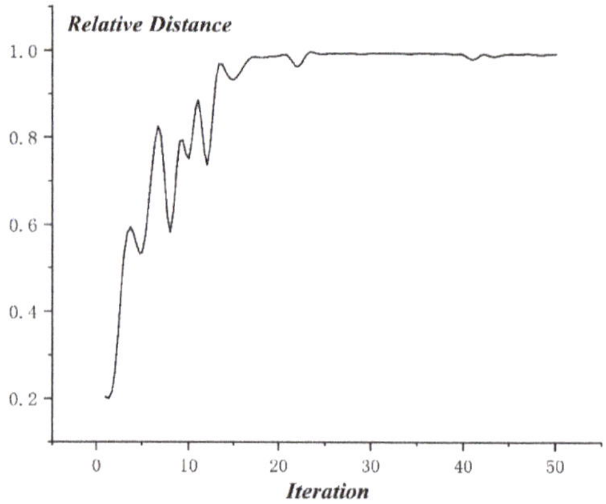

Figure 17. Relative distance of MSGWO.

In the optimization process of MO-PSO, the character distance and character radius both showed an increasing tendency, with considerable oscillation. In the finite 150 iterations, the algorithm MO-PSO didn't reach the state of convergence. However, the relative distance of MO-PSO was kept at a high level constantly, with slight oscillation.

In the optimization process of NSGA-2, the character distance showed an increasing tendency, and the character radius was kept at a low level. In the finite 200 iterations, the algorithm NSGA-2 didn't reach the state of convergence. The relative distance of NSGA-2 was kept at around 0.5, with violent oscillation.

In the optimization process of MO-GWO, the character distance and character radius vary almost simultaneously, and they both show a decreasing tendency. In the finite 150 iterations, the algorithm MO-GWO didn't reach a state of convergence. However, the relative distance of MO-GWO was kept at a high level constantly, with a tendency of convergence.

In the optimization process of MSGWO, the character distance shows an increasing tendency, and the character radius shows a decreasing tendency. In the finite 20 iterations, the algorithm MSGWO reached a state of convergence. The relative distance of MSGWO was kept at a high level constantly, without oscillation.

Then, the kernel functions optimized by the above algorithms were submitted into the SVM method, solving a classification problem in the Blood Transfusion data set. The results of Character Distance, Character Radius, Relative Distance and classification accuracy are shown in Table 2.

Table 2. Classification Results.

	MO-PSO	NSGA-2	MO-GWO	MSGWO
Character Distance	1.63	0.93	0.686	0.404
Character Radius	**1.870**	1.810	0.901	0.407
Relative Distance	0.869	0.513	0.761	0.993
Accuracy	62.4%	68.0%	67.1%	78.2%

For *Character Distance*, the MSGWO algorithm reached the minimum value of 0.404. For *Character Radius*, the MO-PSO algorithm reached the maximum value of 1.870. For *Relative Distance*, the MSGWO algorithm reached the maximum value of 0.993. It is not difficult to find that the MO-PSO and NSGA-2 algorithms are easy to increase *Character Distance* and *Character Radius* simultaneously, and the MO-GWO algorithm is easy to decrease *Character Distance* and *Character Radius* simultaneously. When the two objective functions, like *Character Distance* and *Character Radius* are conflicting and highly coupled, the MSGWO could balance the contradiction of different objective functions in the process of multi-objective optimization. From the number of iterations, the MSGWO algorithm used fewer iterations and obtained superior solutions, which is sufficient to demonstrate that the MSGWO algorithm has stronger global searching ability and faster convergence speed compared with the other state-of-the-art algorithms in this given multi-objective optimization problem. The classification accuracy in the Blood Transfusion data set also demonstrated the effectiveness of the MSGWO algorithm.

6.2. Classification Ability Test of MSGWO-MKL

The kernel function optimized by MSGWO was put into the SVM algorithm to verify the classification ability of the MSGWO-MKL algorithm. We repeated ten fold cross-validation 20 times in eight standard UCI data sets, comparing with other state-of-the-art SVM classification algorithms, such as SVM, TML-SVM [55], ISSML-SVM [56], LMN-SVM [57], and PCML-SVM [58]. The classification accuracy of eight UCI data sets is shown in Table 3.

Table 3. Classification Results.

Standard Dataset	SVM	TML-SVM	ISSML-SVM	LMNN-SVM	PCML-SVM	MSGWO-MKL
Blood Transfusion	65.3%	69.2%	68.3%	71.3%	70.9%	78.2%
Breast Cancer	75.3%	75.7%	76.5%	73.1%	74.9%	77.8%
German	74.8%	75.5%	75.7%	75.2%	76.4%	84.1%
Heart	85.8%	86.5%	86.0%	85.4%	85.1%	85.7%
Liver	74.0%	75.6%	74.5%	72.5%	73.3%	79.0%
Parkinson	85.8%	88.2%	89.5%	88.2%	88.5%	96.1%
Pima	77.0%	77.5%	78.7%	77.5%	78.2%	79.8%
Sonar	86.0%	86.5%	84.6%	83.7%	85.5%	92.6%

According to the results of Table 3, the classification accuracy of MSGWO-MKL was improved by 6.2% on average compared with the original SVM algorithm in eight standard UCI data sets. For the data set Blood Transfusion, German and Parkinson, the classification accuracy of MSGWO-MKL was increased by more than 10% compared with the best result. For the data set Breast Cancer, Liver, Pima, and Sonar, the classification accuracy of MSGWO-MKL was increased by less than 5% compared with the best result. For the data set Heart, the difference between the classification accuracy of all algorithms is within 1%.

The test results in eight standard UCI datasets proved that the kernel function optimized by the MSGWO algorithm could help the SVM algorithm increase the classification accuracy to some extent. The results also showed that the classification accuracy increments caused by the MSGWO-MKL algorithm were related to the given data set. The performance of the MSGWO-MKL algorithm differed widely in different data sets.

6.3. Missing Link Predicting Ability Test of MSGWO-MKL-SVM

When a UAV swarm was carrying out missions to check out or carry out a strike on adversarial airports, they would be confronted with a variety of highly intensive anti-air weapons and would be easily intercepted without any countermeasures. The formation control of a UAV swarm in enemy airspace is a common tactical movement. The time series data is observed from the process of formation control of a UAV swarm. Figure 18 depicts the completion of the simulation process in the Any-logic simulation platform. The topology structure of the UAV network was generated randomly, as in Equation (31).

$$A_{UAV} = \left[a_{ij}^{UAV}\right] = \begin{cases} 0, \ if\ x > P_0 \\ 1, \ if\ x \le P_0 \end{cases} \tag{31}$$

where A_{UAV} is the adjacency matrix of the UAV swarm, a_{ij}^{UAV} is the element of the matrix, A_{UAV}, x is a random number from 0 to 1, and P_0 is the probability parameter of two UAVs having communication links, recommending that $P_0 = 0.5$.

Figure 18. The simulation in Any-logic platform.

We repeated the simulation of UAV swarm formation control 500 times on the Any-logic platform, obtaining the time series of the UAV swarm network in a given topology network. Seven different scenarios were designed to verify the missing link predicting ability of the MSGWO-MKL-SVM algorithm. The conditions of different scenarios are shown in Table 4.

Table 4. Conditions of different scenarios.

Scenario	UAV Number	Observation Time Length/s
1	20	10
2	30	10
3	50	5
4	50	10
5	50	15
6	50	20
7	70	10

Then the ten fold cross-validation was repeated 120 times. The other state-of-the-art MLP algorithms, such as Common Neighbors (CN) [3] and Amplitude Difference Method (ADM) [18], were compared with the proposed MSGWO-MKL-SVM algorithm.

Link prediction results are shown in Figure 19A–G and Table 5. Figure 19A–G depicts a series of scatter diagrams corresponding to Scenarios 1–7.

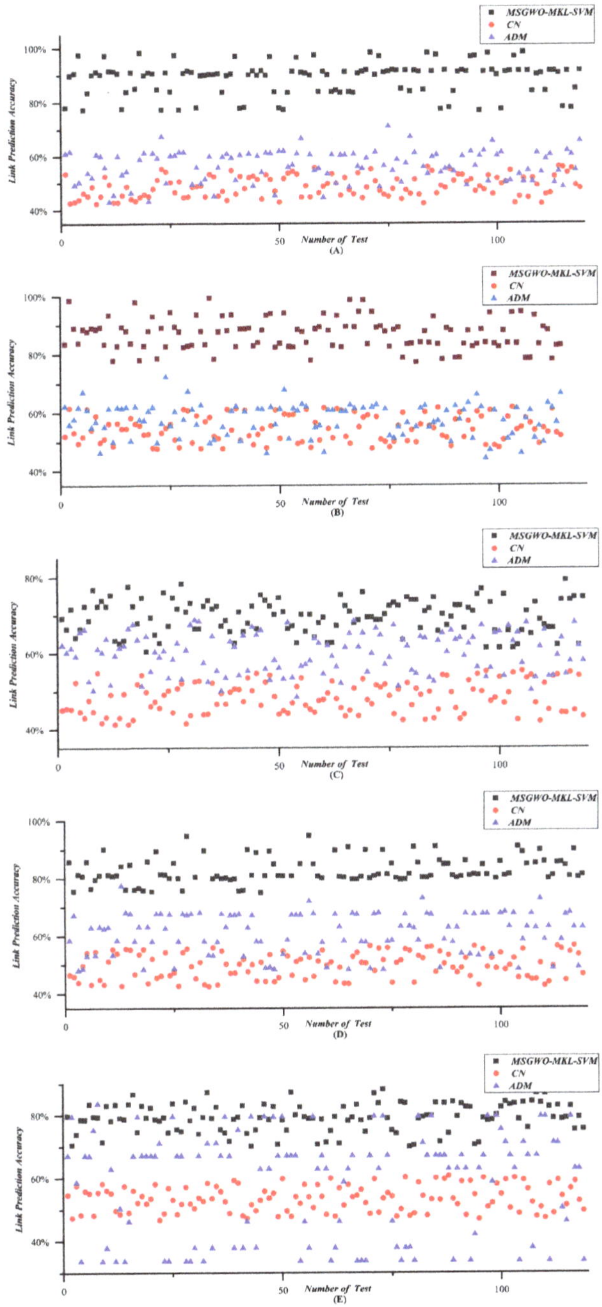

Figure 19. *Cont.*

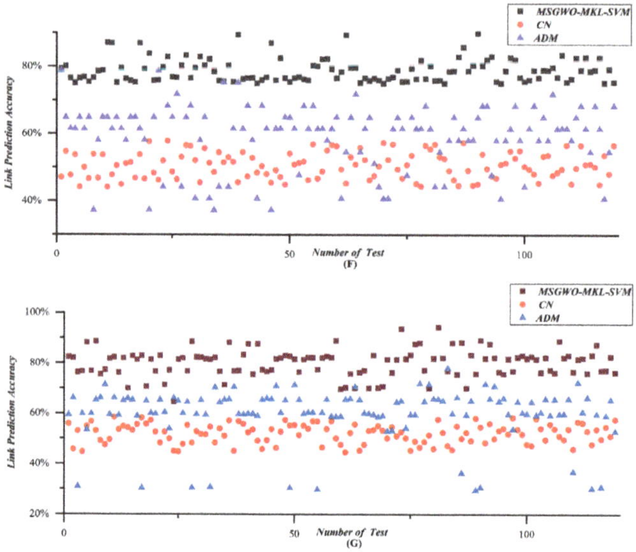

Figure 19. (**A**–**G**) Scatter diagrams of link prediction results.

Table 5. Results of link prediction.

Scenario	Accuracy	CN	ADM	MSGWO-MKL
Scen1	Average	48.62%	56.50%	89.03%
	Std.dev	3.84×10^{-2}	5.76×10^{-2}	5.77×10^{-2}
	Median	48.53%	57.31%	90.07%
	Maximum	55.95%	71.11%	98.33%
	Minimum	42.15%	43.03%	76.70%
Scen2	Average	54.52%	57.75%	86.78%
	Std.dev	4.42×10^{-2}	5.48×10^{-2}	5.33×10^{-2}
	Median	54.37%	57.76%	87.75%
	Maximum	61.68%	72.27%	99.42%
	Minimum	47.73%	44.22%	77.09%
Scen3	Average	48.26%	59.99%	69.40%
	Std.dev	3.98×10^{-2}	5.58×10^{-2}	4.30×10^{-2}
	Median	48.02%	59.72%	69.40%
	Maximum	55.24%	74.27%	78.35%
	Minimum	41.40%	46.22%	60.44%
Scen4	Average	49.68%	60.82%	82.67%
	Std.dev	4.33×10^{-2}	7.09×10^{-2}	4.44×10^{-2}
	Median	50.24%	62.72%	81.06%
	Maximum	56.42%	77.45%	94.73%
	Minimum	42.68%	48.13%	74.99%

Table 5. *Cont.*

Scenario	Accuracy	CN	ADM	MSGWO-MKL
Scen5	Average	53.51%	58.58%	79.25%
	Std.dev	4.06×10^{-2}	1.66×10^{-1}	4.47×10^{-2}
	Median	53.63%	67.01%	79.24%
	Maximum	60.59%	83.71%	88.11%
	Minimum	46.75%	33.68%	70.01%
Scen6	Average	50.05%	59.20%	78.85%
	Std.dev	3.86×10^{-2}	9.55×10^{-2}	3.49×10^{-2}
	Median	50.63%	61.47%	78.46%
	Maximum	57.79%	78.75%	89.86%
	Minimum	44.11%	37.28%	75.02%
Scen7	Average	51.94%	59.99%	80.09%
	Std.dev	3.82×10^{-2}	1.04×10^{-1}	5.45×10^{-2}
	Median	52.66%	60.31%	81.64%
	Maximum	58.47%	78.04%	84.29%
	Minimum	44.64%	60.31%	64.46%

According to the results of Figure 19A–G, and Table 5, the link prediction accuracy was improved by 25.9% by MSGWO-MKL-SVM, compared with the average results, which strongly demonstrated the validity of the MSGWO-MKL-SVM algorithm. The results also showed that when facing a UAV swarm network with strong randomness and high uncertainty, the similarity-based method CN performed badly. Although the ADM algorithm that coped with one-dimensional time series performed better than the similarity-based method CN, it was still at a low level. Besides that, the link prediction accuracy of the ADM algorithm is very unstable, especially for the scenarios of a large number of UAVs and long-time observation. The MSGWO-MKL-SVM algorithm has obvious advantages in both link prediction accuracy and stability.

The variation of prediction accuracy about UAV number is shown in Figure 20, and the variation of prediction accuracy about observation time length is shown in Figure 21.

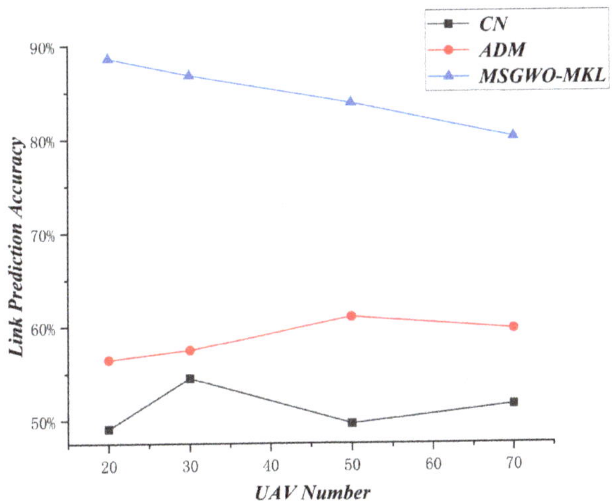

Figure 20. Variation of accuracy about UAV number.

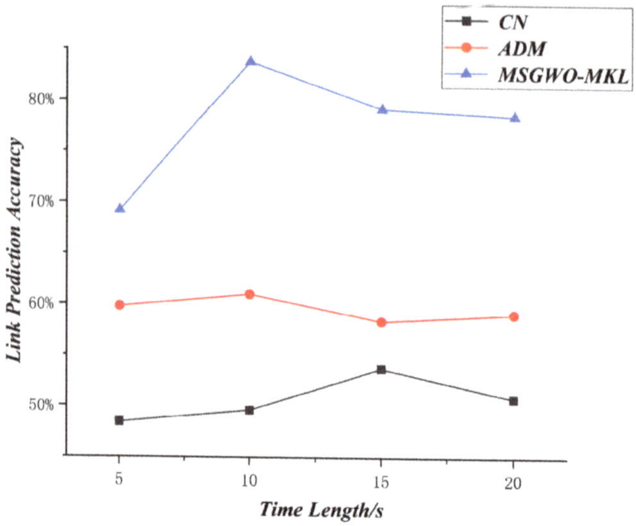

Figure 21. Variation of accuracy about time length.

According to the results of Figure 20, with the scale of the UAV swarm increasing, the missing link prediction accuracy of the MSGWO-MKL-SVM algorithm showed a downward trend. This is due to the fact that, with the scale of the UAV swarm increasing, the UAV swarm network will get more and more complicated, and the difficulty of link prediction will also increase at the same time.

According to the results of Figure 21, with the observation time length increasing, the missing link prediction accuracy of the MSGWO-MKL-SVM algorithm showed an upward trend and then a downward trend. This is due to the fact that, with the observation time length increasing, the information in the time series is increasing, and the difficulty of link prediction will also decrease at the same time. However, a UAV swarm is a dynamic, time-varying, complex network. If the observation time is too long, the UAV swarm network will undergo many changes, resulting in part of the time series data being invalid.

7. Discussion

This paper proposed a new algorithm, MSGWO-MKL-SVM, based on time series to solve the MLP problems of UAV swarm networks. In Section 6, the multi-objective optimization ability of the MSGWO algorithm, the classification ability of the MSGWO-MKL algorithm, and the missing links predicting ability of the MSGWO-MKL-SVM algorithm have been verified properly by a series of comparative experiments. Although the MSGWO-MKL-SVM algorithm exhibited excellent performance, the following several flaws remain when dealing with MLP problems of UAV swarm networks.

1. In the process of multi-kernel learning, the basement set of basic kernel functions is lack of completeness proof. However, in the absence of proper determination methods, the selection of basic kernel functions is heavily reliant on the experience of researchers. This means that the performance of the MSGWO-MKL algorithm may fluctuate in different scenarios. The investigation into the completeness of basic kernel functions should be brought to the forefront of the field of multi-kernel learning;
2. In the process of multi-kernel learning, heuristic algorithms were adopted to optimize the kernel functions. The calculating cost increases exponentially with the amount of data. The computational complexity of evaluating a kernel function's performance is $o(n^2)$, where, n, is the amount of data. The computational complexity of multi-objective optimization is $o(s!)$, where, s, is the scale of solution space, so the computational complexity of the MSGWO-MKL algorithm is $n^2 \times o(s!)$. The

new indicators of MKL transform the computational complexity of evaluating a kernel function's performance from $o(n^2)$ to $o(2n+1)$. The assumption is that the MSGWO algorithm transforms the computational complexity of the multi-objective optimization problem from $o(s!)$ to $o\left(s^k\right)$, k is a natural number, and that the computational complexity of the MSGWO-MKL algorithm is also $(2n+1) \times o\left(s^k\right)$. High computational complexity is a common problem in the process of multi-kernel learning, and there is no doubt that certain effective optimization algorithms with low computational complexity are urgently needed, such as some convex optimization algorithms;

3. In the real battlefield environment, the enemy UAV swarm do not tend to conduct formation control frequently and actively. This means that the effective information of the observing time series data is finite. The defenders should apply more electronic interference to the enemy UAV swarm, compelling enemy UAV swarms to enhance the frequency of formation control so that the observing time series data could contain more information that is effective.

8. Conclusions

Many developed countries are investigating and developing AUDT technologies to defend against advanced enemy UAV swarm attacks in the future battlefield environment. Accurate link prediction of UAV swarm networks can help the defender quickly generate an efficient dynamic weapon target assignment scheme to disintegrate the enemy UAV swarm at a very low cost.

This paper proposed a new algorithm, MSGWO-MKL-SVM, based on time series to solve the MLP problems of UAV swarm networks. In this paper, k-order cross-correlation features of time series data about UAV swarm networks were extracted. Then we introduced the multi-kernel learning (MKL) techniques into the process of link prediction of the UAV swarm network, and the multi-strategy grey wolf optimizer algorithm (MSGWO) was adopted to optimize the kernel function. The MSGWO algorithm can effectively avoid local convergence in the process of multi-objective optimization, while the proposed indicator of MKL based on cluster greatly reduces the computational complexity. In the end, the multi-objective optimization ability of the MSGWO algorithm, the classification ability of the MSGWO-MKL algorithm, and the missing links predicting ability of the MSGWO-MKL-SVM algorithm have been verified properly by a series of comparative experiments. Meanwhile, the proposed method can be used for some link prediction on some social networks as well. From the experimental results and discussions, the following conclusions can be drawn:

1. The k-order cross-correlativity coefficient used in this paper could quantify the influence degree between nodes effectively. Then, the MSGWO-MKL-SVM algorithm could calculate the threshold hyperplane of direct influence and indirect influence based on time series, distinguishing 1-hop nodes and k-hop nodes validly;
2. The observation length of time series should be moderate. Too long or too short, all will impair the link prediction accuracy of UAV swarm networks;
3. New indicators of multi-kernel learning (MKL) based on clusters, transformed a multi-kernel learning problem into a multi-objective optimization problem and greatly reduced the computational complexity in the process of optimization;
4. The design of multi-strategy can enhance the balance between local and global search of the GWO algorithm and maintain diversity. In the standard UCI dataset, the MSGWO algorithm performed better than some state-of-the-art algorithms.

Author Contributions: Writing—original draft, M.N.; Writing—review & editing, Y.Z., J.Z., T.W. and X.Z. All authors have read and agreed to the published version of the manuscript.

Funding: National Natural Science Foundation of China: No. 72101263.

Institutional Review Board Statement: Not applicable.

Informed Consent Statement: Not applicable.

Data Availability Statement: Not applicable.

Conflicts of Interest: The authors declare no conflict of interest.

References

1. Rui, Q.; Xu, G.; Cheng, Y.; Ye, Z.; Huang, J. Simulation and Analysis of Grid Formation Method for UAV Clusters Based on the 3×3 Magic Square and the Chain Rules of Visual Reference. *Appl. Sci.* **2021**, *11*, 11560. [CrossRef]
2. Lü, L.; Zhou, T. Link prediction in complex networks: A survey. *Phys. A Stat. Mech. Its Appl.* **2011**, *390*, 1150–1170. [CrossRef]
3. Lü, L.; Pan, L.; Zhou, T.; Zhang, Y.-C.; Stanley, H.E. Toward link predictability of complex networks. *Proc. Natl. Acad. Sci. USA* **2015**, *112*, 2325–2330. [CrossRef]
4. Ren, B.; Song, Y.; Zhang, Y.; Liu, H.; Chen, J.; Shen, L. Reconstruction of Complex Networks under Missing and Spurious Noise without Prior Knowledge. *IEEE Access* **2019**, 1. [CrossRef]
5. Guo, J.; Meng, Y. Link Prediction Algorithm using Relative Entropy to Measure Node Structure Similarity. *J. Lanzhou Jiaotong Univ.* **2022**, *41*, 9.
6. Newman, M.E.J. Clustering and preferential attachment in growing networks. *Phys. Rev. E* **2001**, *64*, 025102. [CrossRef] [PubMed]
7. Yasami, Y.; Safaei, F. A novel multilayer model for missing link prediction and future link forecasting in dynamic complex networks. *Phys. A Stat. Mech. Its Appl.* **2018**, *492*, 2166–2197. [CrossRef]
8. Kumar, M.; Mishra, S.; Biswas, B. PWAF: Path Weight Aggregation Feature for link prediction in dynamic networks. *Comput. Commun.* **2022**, *191*, 438–458. [CrossRef]
9. Adamic, L.; Adar, E. Friends and neighbors on the Web. *Soc. Networks* **2003**, *25*, 211–230. [CrossRef]
10. Martin, C.D.; Branzi, F.M.; Bar, M. Prediction is Production: The missing link between language production and comprehension. *Sci. Rep.* **2018**, *8*, 1079. [CrossRef]
11. Liben-Nowell, D.; Kleinberg, J. The link-prediction problem for social networks. *J. Am. Soc. Inf. Sci. Technol.* **2007**, *58*, 1019–1031. [CrossRef]
12. Liu, W.; Lu, L. Link prediction based on local random walk. *Europhys. Lett.* **2010**, *89*, 58007. [CrossRef]
13. Berlusconi, G.; Calderoni, F.; Parolini, N.; Verani, M.; Piccardi, C. Link prediction in criminal networks: A tool for criminal intelligence analysis. *PLoS ONE* **2016**, *11*, e0154244. [CrossRef] [PubMed]
14. Lü, L.; Medo, M.; Yeung, C.H.; Zhang, Y.-C.; Zhang, Z.-K.; Zhou, T. Recommender systems. *Phys. Rep.* **2012**, *519*, 1–49. [CrossRef]
15. Clauset, A.; Moore, C.; Newman, M.E. Hierarchical structure and the prediction of missing links in networks. *Nature* **2008**, *453*, 98–101. [CrossRef] [PubMed]
16. Redner, S. Networks: Teasing out the missing links. *Nature* **2008**, *453*, 48. [CrossRef] [PubMed]
17. Liu, H.; Kou, H.; Yan, C.; Qi, L. Link prediction in paper citation network to construct paper correlation graph. *EURASIP J. Wirel. Commun. Netw.* **2019**, *2019*, 233. [CrossRef]
18. Muniz, C.P.; Goldschmidt, R.; Choren, R. Combining contextual, temporal and topological information for unsupervised link prediction insocial networks. *Knowl.-Based Syst.* **2018**, *156*, 129–137. [CrossRef]
19. Songmuang, P.; Sirisup, C.; Suebsriwichai, A. Missing Link Prediction Using Non-Overlapped Features and Multiple Sources of Social Networks. *Information* **2021**, *12*, 214. [CrossRef]
20. Lv, C.; Yuan, Z.; Si, S.; Duan, D. Robustness of scale-free networks with dynamical behavior against multi-node perturbation. *Chaos Solitons Fractals* **2021**, *152*, 111420. [CrossRef]
21. Weeden, K.A.; Cornwell, B. The small-world network of college classes: Implications for epidemic spread on a university campus. *Sociol. Sci.* **2020**, *7*, 222–241. [CrossRef]
22. Wu, J.; Deng, Y.; Wang, Z.; Tan, S.; Li, Y. Status and Prospects on Disintegration of Complex Networks. Complex Systems and Complexity Science. Available online: https://kns.cnki.net/kcms/detail/37.1402.n.20220310.1849.004.html. (accessed on 12 March 2022).
23. Baoan, R. Research on Reconstruction and Disruption of Complex Network and Its Application. *Natl. Univ. Def. Technol.* **2019**, *520*, 196–207. [CrossRef]
24. Shu, J.; Wang, Q.; Liu, L. UAV ad hoc network link prediction based on deep graph embedding. *J. Commun.* **2021**, *42*, 137–149.
25. Qi, X.; Gu, X.; Zhang, Q.; Yang, Z. A Link-Prediction Based Multi-CDSs Scheduling Mechanism for FANET Topology Maintenance. In Proceedings of the 10th EAI International Conference on Wireless and Satellite Systems, WiSATS, Harbin, China, 12–13 January 2019; pp. 587–601.
26. Zhang, J.; Small, M. Complex Network from Pseudo periodic Time Series: Topology versus Dynamics. *Phys. Rev. Lett.* **2006**, *96*, 238701. [CrossRef]
27. Zou, Y.; Donner, R.V.; Marwan, N.; Donges, J.F.; Kurths, J. Complex network approaches to nonlinear time series analysis. *Phys. Rep.* **2019**, *787*, 1–97. [CrossRef]
28. Yang, Y.; Yang, H. Complex Network-Based Time Series Analysis. *Phys. A Stat. Mech. Its Appl.* **2008**, *387*, 1381–1386. [CrossRef]

29. Papadopoulos, L.; Porter, M.A.; Daniels, K.E.; Bassett, D.S. Network analysis of particles and grains. *J. Complex Netw.* **2018**, *6*, 485–565. [CrossRef]
30. Nie, C.X.; Song, F.T. Constructing financial network based on PMFG and threshold method. *Phys. A Stat. Mech. Its Appl.* **2018**, *495*, 104–113. [CrossRef]
31. Marwan, N.; Donges, J.F.; Zou, Y.; Donner, R.V.; Kurths, J. Complex Network Approach for Recurrence Analysis of Time Series. *Phys. Lett. A* **2009**, *373*, 4246–4254. [CrossRef]
32. Li, C.; Feng, B.; Li, S.; Kurths, J.; Chen, G. Dynamic analysis of digital chaotic maps via state-mapping networks. *IEEE Trans. Circuits Syst. I Regul. Pap.* **2019**, *66*, 2322–2335. [CrossRef]
33. Zhao, Y.; Weng, T.; Ye, S. Geometrical Invariability of Transformation Between a Time Series and a Complex Network. *Phys. Rev. E* **2014**, *90*, 012804. [CrossRef] [PubMed]
34. Peng, X.; Small, M.; Zhao, Y.; Moore, J.M. Detecting and predicting tipping points. *Int. J. Bifurc. Chaos* **2019**, *29*, 1930022. [CrossRef]
35. Zhao, Y.; Peng, X.; Small, M. Reciprocal characterization from multi variate time series to multilayer complex networks. *Chaos* **2020**, *30*, 013137. [CrossRef] [PubMed]
36. Jiang, Z.; Ge, J.; Xu, Q.; Yang, T. Terminal Distributed Cooperative Guidance Law for Multiple UAVs Based on Consistency Theory. *Appl. Sci.* **2021**, *11*, 8326. [CrossRef]
37. Hao, L.; Kim, J.; Kwon, S.; Ha, D., II. Deep learning-based survival analysis for high-dimensional survival data. *Mathematics* **2021**, *9*, 1244. [CrossRef]
38. Reynolds, C.W. Flocks, Herds and Schools: A Distributed Behavior Model. In Proceedings of the 14th Annual Conference on Computer Graphics and Interactive Techniques, Anaheim, CA, USA, 27–31 July 1987.
39. Podobnik, B.; Grosse, I.; Horvatić, D.; Ilic, S.; Ivanov, P.C.; Stanley, H.E. Quantifying cross-correlations using local and global detrending approaches. *Eur. Phys. J. B* **2009**, *71*, 243. [CrossRef]
40. Zhang, W.; Wang, P.; Li, X.; Shen, D. The inefficiency of cryptocurrency and its cross-correlation with Dow Jones Industrial Average. *Phys. A Stat. Mech. Its Appl.* **2018**, *510*, 658–670. [CrossRef]
41. Zhou, W.X. Multifractal detrended cross-correlation analysis for two nonstationary signals. *Phys. Rev. E* **2008**, *77*, 066211. [CrossRef]
42. Chen, Z.; Guo, Y.; Zhang, S.; Feng, T. Pattern classification differentiates decision of intertemporal choices using multi-voxel pattern analysis. *Cortex* **2019**, *111*, 183–195. [CrossRef]
43. Rocha, W.F.C.; Prado, C.B.; Blonder, N. Comparison of chemometric problems in food analysis using non-linear methods. *Molecules* **2020**, *25*, 3025. [CrossRef]
44. Ding, Y.; Tang, J.; Guo, F. Identification of drug-side effect association via multiple information integration with centered kernel alignment. *Neurocomputing* **2019**, *325*, 211–224. [CrossRef]
45. Mirjalili, S.; Mirjalili, S.M.; Lewis, A. Grey wolf optimizer. *Adv. Eng. Softw.* **2014**, *69*, 46–61. [CrossRef]
46. Deb, K.; Pratap, A.; Agarwal, S.; Meyarivan, T. A fast and elitist multi-objective genetic algorithm: NSGA-II. *IEEE Trans. Evol. Comput.* **2002**, *6*, 182–197. [CrossRef]
47. Xue, Y. Mobile Robot Path Planning with a Non-Dominated Sorting Genetic Algorithm. *Appl. Sci.* **2018**, *8*, 2253. [CrossRef]
48. Tizhoosh, H.R. Opposition-based learning: A new scheme for machine intelligence. In Proceedings of the International Conference on Computational Intelligence for Modelling Control and Automation and International Conference on Intelligent Agents, Web Technologies and Internet Commerce (CIMCA-IAWTIC'06), Vienna, Austria, 22 May 2006; IEEE: New York, NY, USA, 2005; Volume 1, pp. 695–701.
49. Gharehchopogh, F.S.; Gholizadeh, H. A comprehensive survey: Whale Optimization Algorithm and its applications. *Swarm Evol. Comput.* **2019**, *48*, 1–24. [CrossRef]
50. Nadimi-Shahraki, M.H.; Taghian, S.; Mirjalili, S. An improved grey wolf optimizer for solving engineering problems. *Expert Syst. Appl.* **2021**, *166*, 113917. [CrossRef]
51. Schuldt, C.; Laptev, I.; Caputo, B. Recognizing human actions: A local SVM approach. In Proceedings of the 17th International Conference on Pattern Recognition, ICPR 2004, Cambridge, UK, 26 August 2004; IEEE: New York, NY, USA, 2004; Volume 3, pp. 32–36.
52. Shao, J.; Liu, X.; He, W. Kernel based data-adaptive support vector machines for multi-class classification. *Mathematics* **2021**, *9*, 936. [CrossRef]
53. Coello, C.A.C.; Lechuga, M.S. MOPSO: A proposal for multiple objective particle swarm optimization. In Proceedings of the 2002 Congress on Evolutionary Computation. CEC'02 (Cat. No. 02TH8600), Honolulu, HI, USA, 12–17 May 2002; IEEE: New York, NY, USA, 2002; Volume 2, pp. 1051–1056.
54. Maadanpour Safari, F.; Etebari, F.; Pourghader Chobar, A. Modelling and optimization of a tri-objective Transportation-Location-Routing Problem considering route reliability: Using MOGWO, MOPSO, MOWCA and NSGA-II. *J. Optim. Ind. Eng.* **2021**, *14*, 99–114.
55. Shi, B.; Liu, J. Nonlinear metric learning for KNN and SVMs through geometric transformations. *Neurocomputing* **2018**, *318*, 18–29. [CrossRef]
56. Azar, A.T.; El-Said, S.A. Performance analysis of support vector machines classifiers in breast cancer mammography recognition. *Neural Comput. Appl.* **2014**, *24*, 1163–1177. [CrossRef]

both energy management and voyage scheduling in the field of all-electric shipboard microgrids to improve the overall energy efficiency [11,20–23]. Since energy management and voyage scheduling in the AESs are coupled due to the relationship between propulsion loads and ship speed, Shang et al. [20] formulated a multi-objective optimization model to achieve the joint generation and voyage scheduling for an AES with the integration of diesel generators and energy storage systems (ESSs). The results show that joint scheduling could reduce operational costs and GHG emissions simultaneously compared to fixed voyage scheduling. Huang et al. [21] regarded thermal storage and load as a virtual ESS, and proposed a multi-objective optimization model to optimize the voyage scheduling and power generation of the AES coordinately. The results also show the superiority of the joint optimization method over the fixed voyage scheduling methods.

ESS sizing based on the joint optimal generation–voyage scheduling has also been investigated in some studies [24–26]. Considering that a single ESS deployment ship may not meet the increasingly stringent regulation of GHG emissions in the future, Fang et al. [24] chose to install the carbon capture system (CCS) and ESS on board, and introduced a two-stage planning method to determine the optimal capacity. The capacity of CCS and ESS is determined in the first stage. Then, the joint scheduling is implemented in the second stage under the given capacity of components. Wen et al. [25] presented a biobjective bilevel optimization method to optimize voyage routing and ESS sizing coordinately based on solar power prediction. Zhao et al. [26] proposed a biobjective optimization model to optimize ESS size and voyage routine, considering the uncertainty of onshore electricity prices. However, the research objectives in these studies are the diesel/battery hybrid ship, which differs from the fuel cell/battery hybrid ship.

In the previous studies of fuel cell/battery hybrid AESs, some scholars focused on the energy management of the shipboard microgrid [17,27–30]. Banaei et al. [17] proposed an optimal energy management strategy considering different operation constraints of FCs and batteries. Then, the model predictive control (MPC) method was used to reduce the load forecast error. Some studies focus on the sizing of FC and battery on board [18,31]. Letafat et al. [18] investigated the energy management and component sizing method for the fuel cell/battery hybrid AES to minimize the total cost, including the operation cost and daily investment cost. The result shows that the sizes of FCs and batteries can be determined effectively while optimal energy management is achieved. Wang et al. [31] proposed a method to optimize the sizing of diesel engines, batteries, fuel cells, and energy management of a hybrid offshore support vessel. However, only energy management is considered in these sizing methods, and the voyage and load profiles are predetermined. Motivated by this problem, Pan et al. [32] proposed a hybrid energy configuration method based on the coordinated navigation routing and power generation scheduling model to optimize the capacity of the battery and FC. Nevertheless, the research objective of the passenger ferry in this paper usually has a fixed time window different from the cargo ship studied in [32].

The purpose of this paper is to propose an optimization method to determine the optimal component size for a fuel cell/battery hybrid ferry while optimizing the generation–voyage scheduling. This method can be used to offer guidance to the designer during the early stages of the ship design and building process, as well as to provide information to ship owners before the voyage. Our main contributions are twofold: (1) an optimal sizing and operation framework is proposed based on the bilevel optimization model; (2) a bilevel optimal sizing and operation method for the fuel cell/battery hybrid AES is proposed. At the upper level, the sizes of the components are optimized to minimize the total cost, while the energy management and voyage scheduling are optimized jointly at the lower level to minimize the operation cost, considering the constraints related to the practical operation of AESs, i.e., the output constraint, the ramp rate constraint, and the spinning reserve constraint.

The rest of this article is organized as follows. In Section 2, the problem is stated, and the framework of the proposed method is described. In Section 3, the mathematical model of AES and hydrogen fuel cell is established. In Section 4, the problem is formulated, and the solution algorithm is described. In Section 5, the solution algorithm is detailed. In Section 6, the numerical experiments are investigated, and their results are analyzed. Finally, conclusions are presented in Section 7.

2. Problem Statement

2.1. Topology of the AES

The topology of the shipboard microgrid of the AES is illustrated in Figure 1. The power of the fuel cell and the battery is distributed by the power network to satisfy the demand of propulsion and service loads on board. The fuel cell supplied by the hydrogen tank is selected as the primary energy source. The battery is used to balance the power source and loads, which ensures that the FCs can be operated at their optimal operating point and improves the flexibility of the ship's operation. Specifically, when the output power of the FCs exceeds the load demand, the battery will be charged. Conversely, when the load demand exceeds the output power of the FCs, the battery will be discharged. In addition, when the ship anchors at the port, the cold ironing can be connected to the shipboard microgrid to supply electricity to service loads and charge the battery. The loads on board involve the propulsion loads of two waterjet engines and service loads of lighting, radar, and air conditioning.

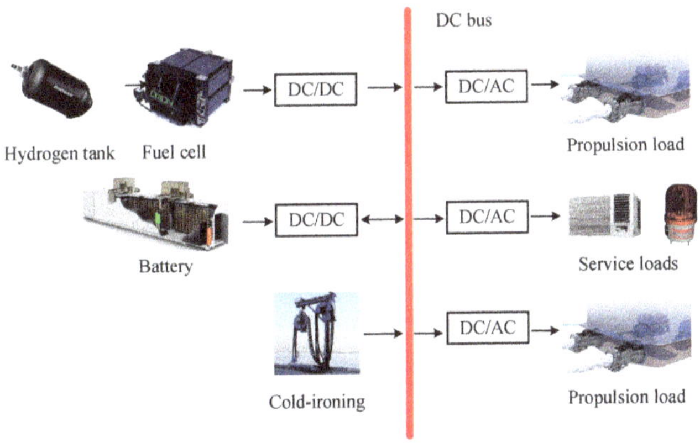

Figure 1. Topology of fuel cell/battery AES.

2.2. Framework of Proposed Method

The framework of the proposed method is given in Figure 2. The optimization of the design and operation for a fuel cell/battery hybrid ferry are closely connected. However, combining these problems into a single optimization challenge can result in an overwhelming number of variables and constraints that are difficult to solve computationally [33]. The bilevel optimization model has been proposed by researchers to solve similar problems, and is reported to exhibit good performance [24,25,32]. It is adopted in this paper to solve the problem of excessive variables and constraints. Bilevel optimization models are characterized by two optimization problems that are hierarchically related [34]. In such problems, an optimal solution in the lower-level problem must be associated with each feasible upper-level solution. In this paper, the upper level is used to determine the optimal sizing of the FC and battery while minimizing the total cost, which includes the investment cost of the FC and battery and operation cost at the lower level. The optimal operation of the AES is investigated at the lower level. With the given capacity of components from the upper level, the lower level is used to minimize the operation cost by determining the optimal ship speed and hourly output power of the FC and battery. Then, the joint optimization of energy management and voyage scheduling is achieved for the AES. Finally, the optimal results are sent to the upper level to determine the optimal sizes of the components. In addition, the optimization problems of the upper and lower level are solved by the particle swarm optimization (PSO) algorithm and mixed-integer linear programming (MILP) solver.

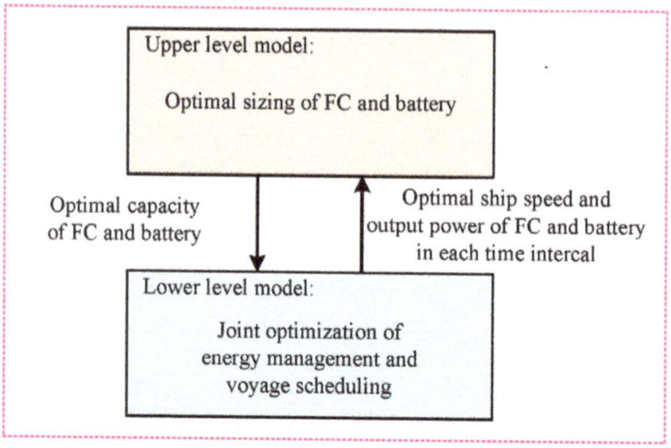

Figure 2. Framework of proposed optimal sizing method based on bilevel optimization model.

3. Mathematical Modeling

3.1. AES Voyage Model

In order to investigate the optimal voyage scheduling, the AES voyage model is established, which follows a specific voyage pattern, as illustrated in Figure 3. The ship departs from port 1 to visit intermediate ports 2 and 3 and returns to port 1. The voyage for the AES lasts for T time intervals, and the duration of each interval is Δt. The state of the ship during the voyage can be divided into three types based on the ship speed: the ship cruises at full speed in the period T_c; the ship cruises with a lower speed in the period T_p; the ship berths at the port in the period T_b. The periods T_c, T_p, and T_b are denoted as full-speed cruising, partial-speed cruising, and berthing periods, respectively. It is noted that there are three different ship speed constraints according to the three different periods. The voyage distance at the t-th time interval can be updated using Equation (1). The propulsion load is calculated according to the exponential relationship between propulsion load and cruising speed, as shown in Equation (2) [20,35].

$$Dist_t = \begin{cases} Dist_{t-1} + v_t \Delta t & t \in T \backslash \{1\} \\ v_t \Delta t & t = 1 \end{cases} \tag{1}$$

$$P_t^{pl} = c_1 \cdot (v_t)^{c_2} \tag{2}$$

where $Dist_t$ is the voyage distance at the t-th time interval; v_t is the ship cruising speed in the t-th time interval; Δt is the voyage time at the t-th time interval; P_t^{pl} is the power demand of propulsion load; c_1 and c_2 are the proportional and exponential coefficients of the propulsion–speed relationship, respectively; t is the t-th time interval; T is the number of time intervals.

3.2. Hydrogen Fuel Cell Operation Model

In this section, the relationship between the output power of the FC and the consumed mass of hydrogen is analyzed. During the voyage, the hydrogen stored in the tank will be consumed by the FC to output electric power. In this paper, a coefficient is used to convert the mass of hydrogen into the FC's generated power. Moreover, the FC's generated power is not equal to the FC's output power, as there is conversion efficiency between them. The efficiency curve is illustrated in Figure 4, where the efficiency of the FC changes with the variation in its output power. As a result, a nonlinear relationship exists between the FC's generated and output power.

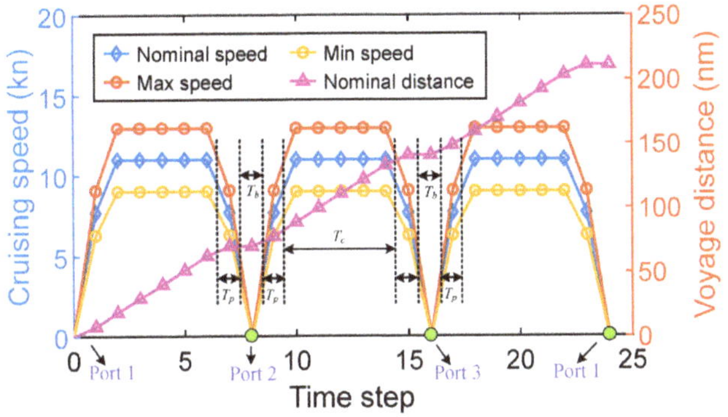

Figure 3. Voyage pattern of an all-electric ship (AES).

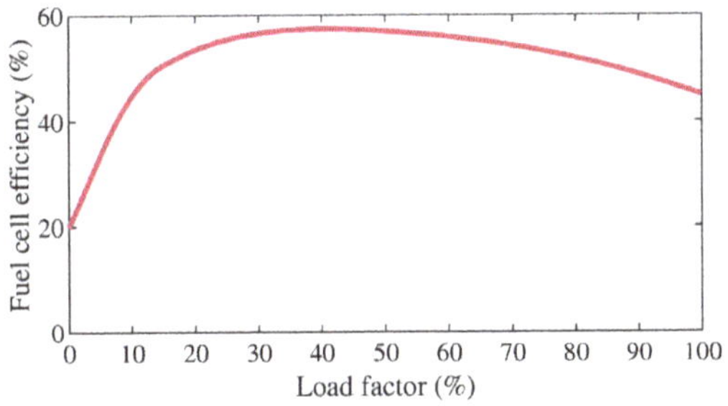

Figure 4. Efficiency curve of FC.

In this paper, a linear fitting function is employed to describe this relationship, as shown in Equation (3) [27]. Ultimately, with the given output power of the FC, the consumed mass of hydrogen can be calculated.

$$M_t^{H_2} = K^{E-m} P_t^{FC,gen} = K^{E-m}\left(\alpha^{FC} P_t^{FC} + o_t^{FC} \beta^{FC}\right), \forall t \in T \tag{3}$$

where $M_t^{H_2}$ is the consumed mass of hydrogen at the t-th time interval; $P_t^{FC,gen}$ and P_t^{FC} are the generated power and output power of fuel cell, respectively; K^{E-m} is the coefficient used to convert the generated power of the fuel cell into the mass of hydrogen; α^{FC} and β^{FC} are the fitting coefficients of the relationship between $P_t^{FC,gen}$ and P_t^{FC}; o_t^{FC} is the on/off state at the t-th time interval, $o_t^{FC} \in \{0,1\}, \forall t \in T$.

4. Problem Formulation

4.1. Upper Level

In this section, the bilevel optimal sizing and operation model is established for the fuel cell/battery hybrid AES.

4.1.1. Objective Function

The objective of the upper level is to minimize the total cost of the fuel cell/battery hybrid AES by determining the optimal sizing of the FC and battery, which is given as follows:

$$\min C = C_{INV} + C_{OP} \tag{4}$$

where C is the total cost of a single voyage, which includes the investment cost C_{INV} and operation cost C_{OP}. In this paper, the investments of the FC and battery are unified into a single voyage, which can be calculated by Equations (5) and (11), respectively.

$$C_{INV} = C_{INV}^{FC} + C_{INV}^{bat} = \frac{P_{\max}^{FC}\lambda_{INV}^{FC}T_{op}^{FC}}{T_{op,lifetime}^{FC}} + \frac{\left(\lambda_{INV}^{bat,E}E_{\max}^{bat} + \lambda_{INV}^{bat,P}P_{\max}^{bat}\right)N^{bat,cycle}}{N_{lifetime}^{bat,cycle}} \tag{5}$$

where C_{INV}^{FC} and C_{INV}^{bat} are the total investment cost of the fuel cell and battery, respectively; λ_{INV}^{FC}, $\lambda_{INV}^{bat,E}$, and $\lambda_{INV}^{bat,P}$ are the price of the fuel cell power (\$/kW), battery capacity (\$/kWh), and battery power (\$/kW), respectively; T_{op}^{FC} and $T_{op,lifetime}^{FC}$ are the operation times of the fuel cell for a single voyage and its lifetime, respectively; $N^{bat,cycle}$ and $N_{lifetime}^{bat,cycle}$ are the battery charging/discharging cycle numbers for a single voyage and its lifetime, respectively. T_{op}^{FC} and $N^{bat,cycle}$ can be calculated using Equations (6) and (7).

$$T_{op}^{FC} = \sum_{t\in T} o_t^{FC} \tag{6}$$

$$N^{bat,cycle} = \min\left(\sum_{t\in T}\left(X_t^{ch}\right), \sum_{t\in T}\left(1 - X_t^{ch}\right)\right) \tag{7}$$

where X_t^{ch} is battery charging/discharging state at the t-th time interval, $X_t^{ch} \in \{0,1\}, \forall t \in T$.

4.1.2. Constraints

The constraints in the upper level are mainly related to the capacity, which is determined by the limited onboard space, as shown in Equations (8)–(10).

$$0 \le P_{\max}^{bat} \le P_{sizing}^{bat} \tag{8}$$

$$0 \le E_{\max}^{bat} \le E_{sizing}^{bat} \tag{9}$$

$$0 \le P_{\max}^{FC} \le P_{sizing}^{FC} \tag{10}$$

where $P_{\max}^{bat}$ and $E_{\max}^{bat}$ are the maximum power and capacity of the battery, respectively; $P_{\max}^{FC}$ is the maximum power of the fuel cell; P_{sizing}^{bat} and E_{sizing}^{bat} are the maximum sizing power and capacity of the battery, respectively; P_{sizing}^{FC} is the maximum sizing power of the fuel cell.

4.2. Lower Level

4.2.1. Objective Function

The objective function of the lower level is to minimize the operation cost, C_{OP}:

$$\min C_{OP} = C_{H_2} + C_{CI} = \sum_{t\in T}\left(\lambda^{H_2}M_t^{H_2} + \lambda_t^{CI}P_t^{CI}\right) \tag{11}$$

where C_{H_2} and C_{CI} are the operation costs of hydrogen and cold ironing, respectively; λ^{H_2} is the hydrogen price (\$/kg); λ_t^{CI} is the cold ironing price at the t-th time interval (\$/kWh); $M_t^{H_2}$ is consumed mass of hydrogen at the t-th time interval (kg); P_t^{CI} is the output power of cold ironing at the t-th time interval.

4.2.2. Constraints

1. Power Balance Constraint

In the AES, the output powers of the FC, battery, and cold ironing need to meet the demand of the propulsion and service loads at any time interval, as shown in Equation (12)

$$\eta_T\left(P_t^{FC}+P_t^{bat,dc}+P_t^{CI}\right)=P_t^{ser}+P_t^{pl}+P_t^{bat,ch},\forall t\in T \tag{12}$$

where η_T is the transmission efficiency of shipboard microgrid; P_t^{FC} is the fuel cell output power at the t-th time interval; $P^{bat,ch}$ and $P_t^{bat,dc}$ are the battery charging power and discharging power, respectively, at the t-th time interval; P_t^{pl} and P_t^{ser} are the power demands of propulsion load and service load at the t-th time interval, respectively.

2. Fuel Cell Output Power Constraint

The output power of the FC is determined by the on/off states and the loading factor

$$P_t^{FC}=o_t^{FC}l_t^{FC}P_{\max}^{FC},\forall t\in T \tag{13}$$

where l_t^{FC} is the loading factor of the FC at the t-th time interval. In order to avoid the overloading of the FC and to prolong its life, the loading factor is limited using Equation (14).

$$l_{\min}^{FC}\le l_t^{FC}\le l_{\max}^{FC},\forall t\in T \tag{14}$$

where $l_{\min}^{FC}$ and $l_{\max}^{FC}$ are the minimum and maximum loading factors of the FC, respectively.

3. Fuel Cell Ramp Rate Constraint

Considering the characteristics of the low dynamic reaction of the FC, the variation in the FCs' output power is limited, as illustrated by Equation (15).

$$r_{\min}^{FC}P_{\max}^{FC}\le P_t^{FC}-P_{t-1}^{FC}\le r_{\max}^{FC}P_{\max}^{FC},\forall t\in T \tag{15}$$

where $r_{\min}^{FC}$ and $r_{\max}^{FC}$ are the minimum and maximum ramp rates of the FC, respectively.

4. H_2 Tank Capacity Constraint

The hydrogen tank will be fully charged in the departure port and will not be charged during the voyage. The total mass of the hydrogen consumed during the voyage cannot surpass the maximum allowable mass of the hydrogen tank, as shown in Equation (16).

$$0\le\sum_{t\in T}M_t^{H_2}\le(1-\eta_{tank})M_{\max}^{H_2} \tag{16}$$

where $M_{\max}^{H_2}$ is the maximum hydrogen tank capacity; η_{tank} is the hydrogen tank mass reserve coefficient.

5. Battery Charging and Discharging Power Constraint

The charging and discharging powers of the battery are limited to its corresponding lower and upper bound

$$0\le P_t^{bat,ch}\le X_t^{ch}P_{t,\max}^{bat},\forall t\in T \tag{17}$$

$$0\le P_t^{bat,dc}\le\left(1-X_t^{ch}\right)P_{t,\max}^{bat},\forall t\in T \tag{18}$$

6. Battery Capacity Constraint

The battery capacity at any time intervals is obtained by calculating Equations (19) and (20)

$$E_t^{bat}=E_{t-1}^{bat}+\eta_{ch}P_t^{bat,ch}-\frac{P_t^{bat,dc}}{\eta_{dc}},\forall t\backslash\{1\} \tag{19}$$

$$E_t^{bat} = E^{bat} \cdot SOC_0 + \eta_{ch} P_t^{bat,ch} - \frac{P_t^{bat,dc}}{\eta_{dc}}, t = 1 \quad (20)$$

where E_t^{bat} is the stored energy of the battery at the t-th time interval; η_{ch} and η_{dc} are the battery charging and discharging efficiencies of the battery at the t-th time interval, respectively; SOC_0 is the initial state of charge (SOC) of the battery before the voyage, $SOC_0 = 0.5$.

7. SOC Constraint

Equation (21) is used to limit the SOC of the battery within a reasonable range.

$$(SOC_{\max} - DoD_{\max}) \leq SOC_t = \frac{E_t^{bat}}{E_{\max}^{bat}} \leq SOC_{\max}, \forall t \in T \quad (21)$$

where $SOC_{\max}$ is the maximum allowable SOC; $DoD_{\max}$ is the maximum allowable depth of discharge (DoD).

At the end of the voyage, the capacity of the battery should be no less than its initial capacity:

$$SOC_0 \leq SOC_t \leq \left(1 + \delta^{SOC}\right) SOC_0, t = T \quad (22)$$

where δ^{SOC} is the maximum allowable SOC mismatch.

8. System Reserve Constraint

In order to cope with the sudden changes in the load or outage of the FC, the reserve constraint is considered in this paper, as described in Equations (23)–(25).

$$R_t^{FC} = P_{\max}^{FC} - P_t^{FC}, \forall t \in T \quad (23)$$

$$R_t^{bat} = X_t^{ch} P_{\max}^{bat} + \left(1 - X_t^{ch}\right)\left(P_{\max}^{bat} - P_t^{bat}\right), \forall t \in T \quad (24)$$

$$R_t^{FC} + R_t^{bat} \geq \eta_R P_t^{FC}, \forall t \in T \quad (25)$$

where R_t^{FC} and R_t^{bat} are the power reserves of the FC and battery at the t-th time interval, respectively; η_R is the power reserve coefficient.

9. Cold Ironing Power Constraint

The cold ironing can be used to meet the power demand of the loads on board and to charge the battery when the ship arrives at the port, as shown in Equation (26).

$$\begin{cases} 0 \leq P_t^{CI} \leq P_{\max}^{CI}, & t \in T_b \\ P_t^{CI} = 0, & otherwise \end{cases} \quad (26)$$

where $P_{\max}^{CI}$ is the maximum power of cold ironing.

10. AES sailing Speed Constraint

The AES sailing speed constraints during the full-speed period T_c, the partial-speed period T_p, and the berthing period T_b are given in Equation (27).

$$\begin{cases} (1 - \delta_{\max}^{v}) \cdot v^n \leq v_t \leq (1 + \delta_{\max}^{v}) \cdot v^n, & \forall t \in T_c \\ \eta_p (1 - \delta_{\max}^{v}) \cdot v^n \leq v_t \leq \eta_p (1 + \delta_{\max}^{v}) \cdot v^n, & \forall t \in T_p \\ v_t = 0, & \forall t \in T_b \end{cases} \quad (27)$$

where v^n is the nominal sailing speed; η_p is the partial ratio; $\delta_{\max}^{v}$ is the maximum allowable sailing speed mismatch.

11. Voyage Constraint

The ferry investigated in this paper should arrive at each port punctually. Of course, a small quantity of mismatch with time is allowed. Thus, when the ship arrives at the intermediate and terminal port, the voyage constraints in Equations (28) and (29) should be satisfied:

$$\left(1-\delta_{\max}^{D}\right)Dist_{t}^{n}\leq Dist_{t}\leq\left(1+\delta_{\max}^{D}\right)Dist_{t}^{n},\forall t\in T_{b}\backslash\{T\} \tag{28}$$

$$Dist_{T}^{n}\leq Dist_{T}\leq\left(1+\delta_{\max}^{D}\right)Dist_{T}^{n} \tag{29}$$

where $\delta_{\max}^{D}$ is the maximum allowable voyage distance inaccuracy; $Dist_{t}^{n}$ is the nominal voyage distance at the t-th time interval.

5. Solution Algorithm

The flow chart of the proposed method is shown in Figure 5. As illustrated in Figure 5, the PSO algorithm is used in the upper level to determine the fuel cell and battery size, and the MILP is used in the lower level to determine the optimal ship speed and hourly output of the FC and battery. PSO, developed by Kennedy and Eberhart in 1995 [36,37], is a heuristic optimization technique that is easy to implement compared with other optimization algorithms, and has been widely used in many areas [38–40]. The optimization model in the lower level is a mixed-integer nonlinear programming (MINLP) model due to the nonlinear function of Equation (2). In this paper, the piecewise linear model used in [17] is adopted to turn the nonlinear function into a linear function. Correspondingly, the MINLP model is transformed into a MILP model. MILP has many advantages over other optimization techniques, such as its ability to achieve globally optimal solutions based on the convexity of linear problems. Additionally, MILP can be solved very quickly and effectively by commercial solvers [33], especially when dealing with small-scale optimization problems. The solution algorithm is detailed as follows.

Step 1: Initialization. The initialization of PSO is implemented by randomly generating M particles with the position with N dimensions and velocity.

Step 2: Update the position and velocity of each particle. The position and velocity of each particle are updated using Equation (30).

$$\begin{cases} V_{i}^{k+1}=wV_{i}^{k}+c_{1}r_{1}\left(p_{best,i}^{k}-X_{i}^{k}\right)+c_{2}r_{2}\left(g_{best}^{k}-X_{i}^{k}\right) \\ X_{i}^{k+1}=X_{i}^{k}+V_{i}^{k+1} \end{cases} \tag{30}$$

where X_{i}^{k} and V_{i}^{k} are the position and velocity of the i-th particle in the k-th iteration, $X_{i}^{k}=\left[x_{i1}^{k},x_{i2}^{k},\ldots,x_{iN}^{k}\right]$; i is the i-th particle; k is the number of current iteration; w is the inertia weight; c_1 and c_2 are two positive constants; r_1 and r_2 are two random numbers within range [0,1]; $p_{best,i}^{k}$ is the previous best particle position of the i-th particle in the k-th iteration, $p_{best,i}^{k}=\left[x_{i1}^{p_{best}},x_{i2}^{p_{best}},\ldots,x_{iN}^{p_{best}}\right]$; g_{best}^{k} is the global best particle position in the k-th iteration, $g_{best}^{k}=\left[x_{1}^{g_{best}},x_{2}^{g_{best}},\ldots,x_{N}^{g_{best}}\right]$.

In order to enhance the performance of the algorithm, a dynamic update method of inertia weight is adopted, as shown in Equation (31). This approach ensures the strong global search ability of the algorithm at the beginning of the iteration with a larger inertia weight, and the accurate local search ability in later iterations with a smaller inertia weight.

$$w=w_{\max}-\frac{(w_{\max}-w_{\min})}{k_{\max}}\cdot k \tag{31}$$

where $w_{\max}$ and $w_{\min}$ are the maximum and minimum inertia weights, respectively; $k_{\max}$ is the maximum iteration number.

Step 3: Fitness calculation. Based on the given capacity of the FC and battery delivered from the upper level, the model in the lower level is optimized to minimize the operation cost of the AES. Once this optimization of the lower level is complete, the fitness of the upper level can be calculated using Equation (5) based on its corresponding fitness of the lower level.

Step 4: Update the global best particle g_{best}^{k} and current best particle $p_{best,i}^{k}$. After the fitness of all particles is calculated, the global and present best particle position is updated.

Step 5: Repeat Steps 2–5 until the stopping criterion of the algorithm is satisfied.

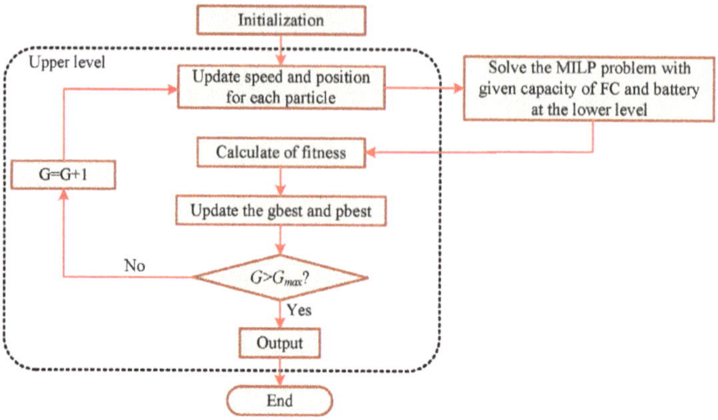

Figure 5. Flow chart of the proposed method.

6. Case Study

6.1. System Configuration

In this paper, a fuel cell/battery passenger ferry is applied in the case study. The navigation route is shown in Figure 6. The system parameters for the case study are detailed in Table 1. The service loads during the voyage are demonstrated in Figure 7. These parameters were obtained from refs. [17,18].

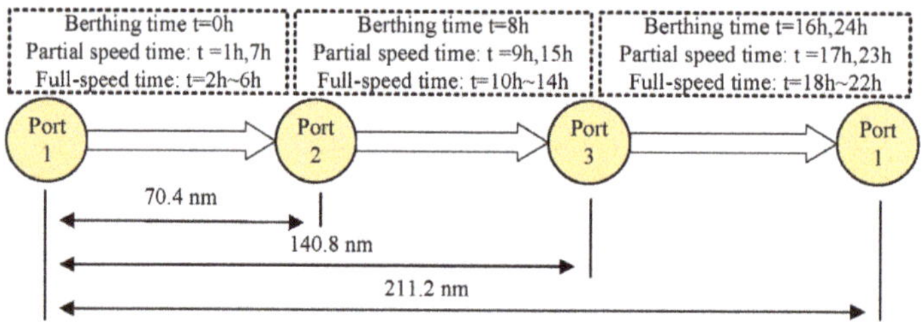

Figure 6. Navigation route for case study.

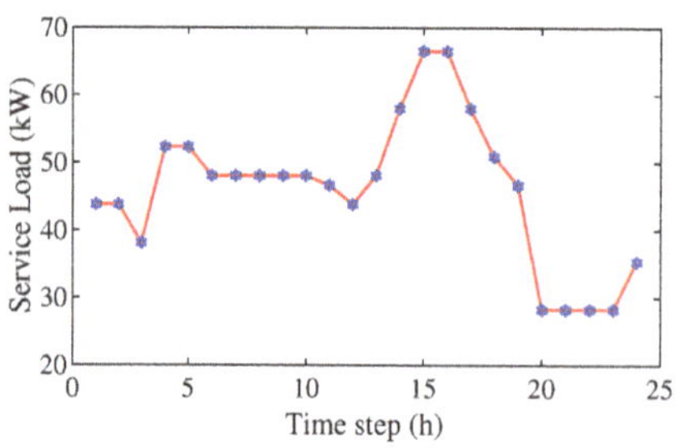

Figure 7. Service load profile.

Table 1. System parameters for case study.

Item	Parameter of Upper level
	λ_{INV}^{FC} = 40 \$/kW, $\lambda_{INV}^{bat,E}$ = 17.8 \$/kWh, $\lambda_{INV}^{bat,P}$ = 17.8 \$/kW $T_{op,lifetime}^{FC}$ = 40,000 h, $N_{lifetime}^{bat,cycle}$ = 1460 times P_{sizing}^{bat} = 300 kW, E_{sizing}^{bat} = 800 kWh, P_{sizing}^{FC} = 800 kW
Voyage	ΔT =1 h, T = 24 h v_n = 11 knots, c_1 = 0.346, c_2 = 3, η_P = 0.7, $\delta_{\max}^{v}$ = 18%, $\delta_{\max}^{D}$ = 1% T_c = {2, ..., 6, 10, ..., 14, 18, ..., 22}, T_p = {1, 7, 9, 15, 17, 23}, T_b = {8, 16, 24}
Fuel cell and Hydrogen tank	$\alpha^{FC} = 1.776$, $\beta^{FC} = -41.44$, $M_{\max}^{H_2}$ = 450 kg, K^{E-m} = 0.03 kg/kWh, λ^{H_2} = 5 \$/kg $l_{\max}^{FC}$ = 0.9, $l_{\min}^{FC}$ = 0.1, $r_{\max}^{FC}$ = 50%, $r_{\min}^{FC}$ = −50%, η_R = 15%, η_{tank} = 10%
Battery	$SOC_{\max}$ = 0.9, $DoD_{\max}$ = 0.8, η_{ch} = 85%, η_{dc} = 100%, δ^{SOC} = 1%, SOC_0 = 0.5
Cold ironing	$P_{\max}^{CI}$ = 150 kW, $\lambda_t^{CI} = \begin{cases} 0.32\$/kWh & t \in \{2,\ 3,\ 4,\ 13,\ 14\} \\ 0.16\$/kWh & t \in \{1,\ 5,\ \ldots,\ 12,\ 15,\ 16\} \\ 0.07\$/kWh & t \in \{17,\ \ldots,\ 24\} \end{cases}$

6.2. Optimization Results

In this section, three cases are designed to verify the effectiveness of the proposed method, and their results are compared with each other.

Case 1: Optimal result analysis under optimal energy management but without voyage scheduling.

Case 2: Optimal result analysis by proposed method considering FC only.

Case 3: Optimal result analysis by proposed method considering FC and battery.

The results of the optimal sizing scheme, investment cost, and operation cost for each case are listed in Table 2. The ship speed at each time interval for different cases is shown in Figure 8. The results of generation scheduling and the ship electric load for Cases 1–3 are shown in Figures 9–11, respectively.

Table 2. Optimization results summary.

Item	Case 1	Case 2	Case 3
Maximum power of FC $P_{\max}^{FC}$ (kW)	591	683	501
Maximum capacity of battery $E_{\max}^{bat}$ (kWh)	243	-	243
Maximum power of battery $P_{\max}^{bat}$ (kW)	161	-	152
Investment cost of FC($)	23,640	27,320	20,040
Investment cost of battery ($)	7191.2	-	7031
Total investment cost ($)	30,831.2	27,320	27,071
Daily investment cost of FC ($)	13.59	14.34	11.52
Daily investment cost of battery ($)	14.78	-	14.45
Total daily investment cost ($)	28.37	14.34	25.97
Daily consumed mass of H_2 (L)	455.01	446.11	430.90
Daily operation cost of H_2 ($)	2275.04	2230.57	2154.50
Daily operation cost of cold ironing ($)	58.50	20.97	58.47
Total daily operation cost ($)	2333.54	2251.54	2212.98
Total daily cost ($)	2361.91	2265.88	2238.95

Case 1: In this case, energy management is introduced to achieve optimal energy dispatch, and voyage scheduling is not considered, which means that the ship is assumed to sail at the nominal speed at each time interval. By observing Table 2, the planning FC capacity is 591 kW, and the planning battery capacity and power are 243 kWh and 161 kW. The investment costs for the FC and battery are $23,640 and $7191.2. Among the three cases, Case 1 has the highest total investment cost of $30,831.2 and total daily cost of $2361.91, primarily due to its high ship speed in the full-speed cruising period, as shown in Figure 8, which will require the huge installed capacity of the components and high

fuel consumption. In Figure 9, the power of the FC and the battery is utilized to meet the demands of shiploads in the full- and partial-speed cruising periods. During the berthing period, the power of the FC and cold ironing is used to meet the demands of shiploads and charge the battery.

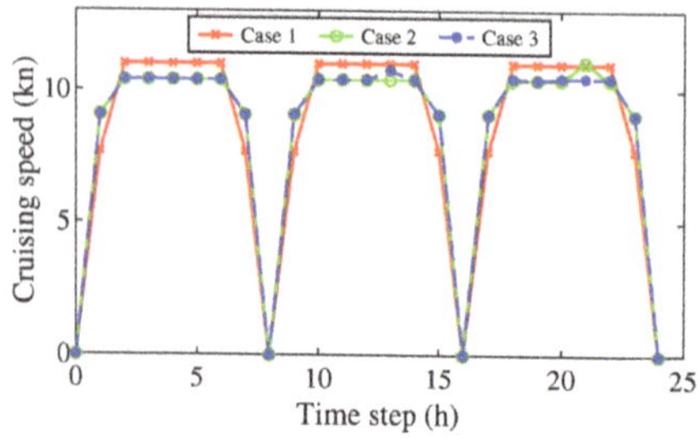

Figure 8. Ship speed at each time interval for different cases.

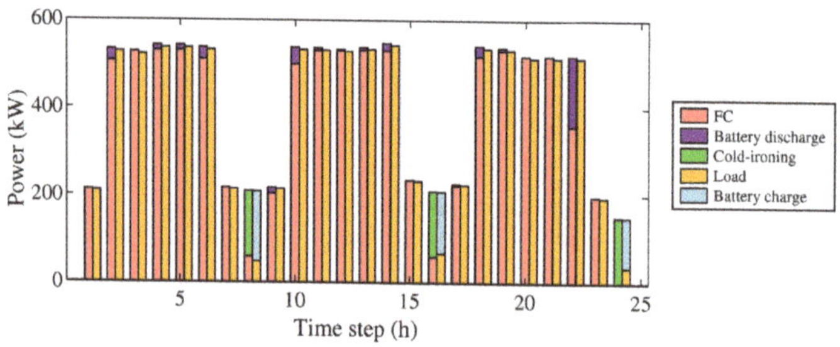

Figure 9. Generation scheduling and the ship electric load in Case 1.

Case 2: The FC is adopted as the sole energy source in this case. In Table 2, despite having the largest FC capacity of 683 kW among the three cases, Case 2 has the lowest daily investment cost of $14.34. The reason for this is that the battery's daily investment cost is zero, which makes a considerable difference. In Figure 10, the demands of shiploads during the full-speed and partial-speed cruising periods are satisfied by the power of FC. This leads to the higher consumed mass of hydrogen and daily operational cost of hydrogen compared to Case 3. Therefore, ESS integration is essential and unignorable. Since the price of cold ironing is lower than that of hydrogen, the power of cold ironing is used to meet the demands of shiploads, and the FC is turned off during the berthing period.

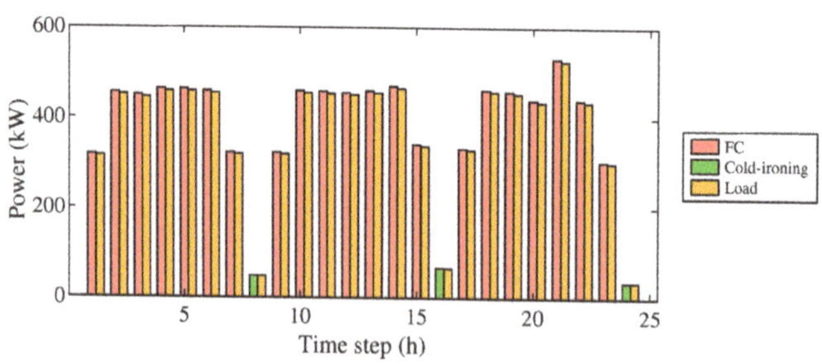

Figure 10. Generation scheduling and the ship electric load in Case 2.

Case 3: The proposed method is used in this case to investigate the impact of ESS integration and joint optimal energy management and voyage scheduling. In Table 2, Case 3 has the lowest planning FC power of 501 kW and the lowest planning battery capacity and power of 243 kWh and 152 kW. Correspondingly, the total investment cost of Case 3 also is the lowest, with the investment cost of $20,040 for the FC and $7031 for the battery. Under optimal voyage scheduling, the ship speed is reduced in the partial-speed cruising period and increased in the full-speed cruising period, as shown in Figure 8. This led to a decrease in shiploads of Case 1 in the full-speed cruising period and an increase in the partial-speed cruising period. On this basis, the power demand in Figure 11 is decreased in the full-speed cruising period and increased in the partial-speed cruising period, resulting in decreased total fuel consumption. In Table 2, the daily consumed mass of H_2 decreases from 455.01 L to 430.90 L, a reduction of 5.3%. Then, the daily operation cost of H_2 is reduced from $2333.54 in Case 1 to $2212.98 in Case 3, while the cost of cold ironing remains similar for both cases. So, the total daily cost is reduced from $2361.91 in Case 1 to $2238.95 in Case 3, a reduction of 5.2%. In addition, although the ship speed at each time interval of Case 2 and Case 3 are similar, the ESS integration in Case 3 allows for a portion of the fuel consumption to be shared by the battery, which is charged at a lower price in the port. Thus, the daily operation cost of Case 1 is lower than that of Case 2. Ultimately, Case 3 is demonstrated to be the most economical sizing scheme, with the lowest total investment cost and total daily cost among the three cases.

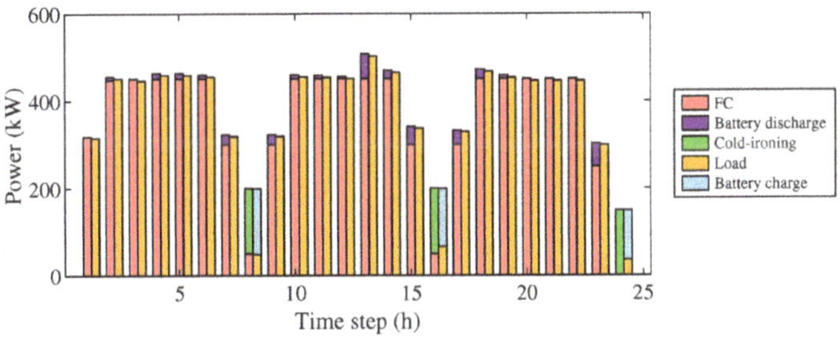

Figure 11. Generation scheduling and the ship electric load in Case 3.

The SOC profiles of the three cases are illustrated in Figure 12. In Figure 12, the battery in Cases 1 and 3 is mainly discharged in the cruising period and charged in the berthing period. However, the maximum depths of discharge (DoDs) during the voyage of Case 1 and Case 3 are 0.79 and 0.66, respectively. The smaller maximum DoD in Case 3 is more beneficial to the health of the battery. The reason behind this is that the heavier load in Case 1 requires a larger DoD to maintain a balance between the energy source and loads. Thus, the proposed optimal sizing method could help improve the performance of ESS and the overall system efficiency.

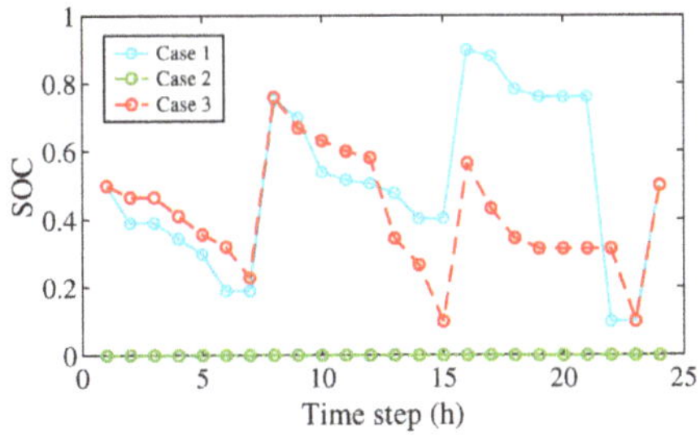

Figure 12. SOC profile for each case.

In order to illustrate the computation efficiency of the algorithm of the improved PSO used in this paper, its result is compared to that of the proposed method solved by other famous metaheuristic algorithms, such as the genetic algorithm (GA) [41], Archimedes optimization algorithm (AOA) [42], and the original PSO. These algorithms have been set with the same population size and iteration number and tested under Intel Core i7 and GPU 3.69 GHz. The iteration figures of these algorithms are described in Figure 13. As can be seen from the figure, the improved PSO algorithm converges at a higher descending speed and has a superior optimal fitness value compared to other algorithms. Therefore, the computation efficiency of adopting the improved PSO to solve the proposed method is confirmed.

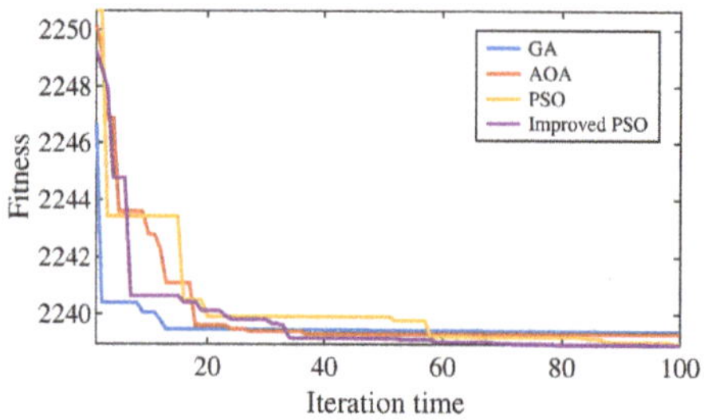

Figure 13. Iteration figure.

7. Conclusions

In this paper, the method to optimize the size of ferry components while considering joint optimal energy management and voyage scheduling is explored. First, the topology of the shipboard microgrid is analyzed, and a bilevel optimization framework is proposed to optimize the components' size and operation for the fuel cell/battery AES. Second, the mathematical model of AES voyage and hydrogen fuel cell operation is established. Third, considering the multiple operational and technical constraints, the bilevel optimal sizing and operation method is proposed. The upper level optimizes the FC and battery size by minimizing the total cost comprised of the investment and operation costs, while the lower level is used to optimize the generation and voyage scheduling of AES. Then, the PSO algorithm and MILP solver are applied to solve the upper- and lower-level optimization model, respectively. Finally, a case study is performed on a passenger ferry, demonstrating the proposed method's validity and superiority. The results show that the proposed method can reduce the total consumed mass of hydrogen by 5.3% and total daily cost by 5.2% compared with the AES using fixed voyage scheduling. The necessity of ESS integration on board is also proved in this paper.

In our future study, the MPC strategy will be introduced to improve the robustness of the model, and the environment parameters of the wave, wind, shallow water, and current will be considered in the ship voyage to improve the precision of the study. In addition, the famous simulation software entitled the Hybrid Optimization Model for Multiple Energy Resources (HOMER) will also be explored on the components sizing problem of the hybrid-powered ship.

Author Contributions: Conceptualization, H.J. and X.Y.; methodology, H.J. and X.Y.; software, H.J. and X.Y.; validation, H.J. and X.Y.; formal analysis, H.J. and X.Y.; resources, H.J.; writing—original draft preparation, H.J. and X.Y.; writing—review and editing, H.J. and X.Y.; visualization, H.J. All authors have read and agreed to the published version of the manuscript.

Funding: This research received no external funding.

Data Availability Statement: Not applicable.

Conflicts of Interest: The authors declare no conflict of interest.

References

1. Faber, J.; Hanayama, S.; Zhang, S.; Pereda, P.; Comer, B.; Hauerhof, E.; Schim van der Loeff, W.; Smith, T.; Zhang, Y.; Kosaka, H.; et al. *Fourth IMO GHG Study 2020*; Technical report; International Maritime Organization (IMO): London, UK, 2020.
2. Balcombe, P.; Brierley, J.; Lewis, C.; Skatvedt, L.; Speirs, J.; Hawkes, A.; Staffell, I. How to Decarbonise International Shipping: Options for Fuels, Technologies and Policies. *Energy Convers. Manag.* **2019**, *182*, 72–88. [CrossRef]
3. Joung, T.H.; Kang, S.G.; Lee, J.K.; Ahn, J. The IMO initial strategy for reducing Greenhouse Gas(GHG) emissions, and its follow-up actions towards 2050. *J. Int. Marit. Safety Environ. Aff. Shipp.* **2020**, *4*, 1–7. [CrossRef]
4. Gray, N.; McDonagh, S.; O'Shea, R.; Smyth, B.; Murphy, J.D. Decarbonising Ships, Planes and Trucks: An Analysis of Suitable Low-Carbon Fuels for the Maritime, Aviation and Haulage Sectors. *Adv. Appl. Energy* **2021**, *1*, 100008. [CrossRef]
5. Al-Enazi, A.; Okonkwo, E.C.; Bicer, Y.; Al-Ansari, T. A Review of Cleaner Alternative Fuels for Maritime Transportation. *Energy Rep.* **2021**, *7*, 1962–1985. [CrossRef]
6. Wan, Z.; el Makhloufi, A.; Chen, Y.; Tang, J. Decarbonizing the International Shipping Industry: Solutions and Policy Recommendations. *Mar. Pollut. Bull.* **2018**, *126*, 428–435. [CrossRef]
7. Jin, Z.; Sulligoi, G.; Cuzner, R.; Meng, L.; Vasquez, J.C.; Guerrero, J.M. Next-Generation Shipboard DC Power System: Introduction Smart Grid and dc Microgrid Technologies into Maritime Electrical Netowrks. *IEEE Electrif. Mag.* **2016**, *4*, 45–57. [CrossRef]
8. Geertsma, R.; Negenborn, R.; Visser, K.; Hopman, J. Design and Control of Hybrid Power and Propulsion Systems for Smart Ships: A Review of Developments. *Appl. Energy* **2017**, *194*, 30–54. [CrossRef]
9. Nuchturee, C.; Li, T.; Xia, H. Energy Efficiency of Integrated Electric Propulsion for Ships—A Review. *Renew. Sustain. Energy Rev.* **2020**, *134*, 110145. [CrossRef]
10. Nguyen, H.P.; Hoang, A.T.; Nizetic, S.; Nguyen, X.P.; Le, A.T.; Luong, C.N.; Chu, V.D.; Pham, V.V. The electric propulsion system as a green solution for management strategy of CO_2 emission in ocean shipping: A comprehensive review. *Int. Trans. Electr. Energy Syst.* **2021**, *31*, e12580. [CrossRef]
11. Fang, S.; Xu, Y.; Li, Z.; Zhao, T.; Wang, H. Two-Step Multi-Objective Management of Hybrid Energy Storage System in All-Electric Ship Microgrids. *IEEE Trans. Veh. Technol.* **2019**, *68*, 3361–3373. [CrossRef]
12. Xing, H.; Stuart, C.; Spence, S.; Chen, H. Fuel Cell Power Systems for Maritime Applications: Progress and Perspectives. *Sustainability* **2021**, *13*, 1213. [CrossRef]
13. Lotrič, A.; Sekavčnik, M.; Pohar, A.; Likozar, B.; Hočevar, S. Conceptual Design of an Integrated Thermally Self-Sustained Methanol Steam Reformer—High-Temperature PEM Fuel Cell Stack Manportable Power Generator. *Int. J. Hydrogren Energy* **2017**, *42*, 16700–16713. [CrossRef]
14. Pohar, A.; Hočevar, S.; Likozar, B.; Levec, J. Synthesis and Characterization of Gallium-Promoted Copper—Ceria Catalyst and Its Application for Methanol Steam Reforming in a Packed Bed Reactor. *Catal. Today* **2015**, *256*, 358–364. [CrossRef]
15. Rubin, K.; Pohar, A.; Dasireddy, V.D.; Likozar, B. Synthesis, Characterization and Activity of CuZnGaOx Catalysts for the Water–Gas Shift (WGS) Reaction for H2 Production and CO Removal after Reforming. *Fuel Process. Technol.* **2018**, *169*, 217–225. [CrossRef]
16. Shakeri, N.; Zadeh, M.; Bremnes Nielsen, J. Hydrogen Fuel Cells for Ship Electric Propulsion: Moving toward Greener Ships. *IEEE Electrif. Mag.* **2020**, *8*, 27–43. [CrossRef]
17. Banaei, M.; Rafiei, M.; Boudjadar, J.; Khooban, M.H. A Comparative Analysis of Optimal Operation Scenarios in Hybrid Emission-Free Ferry Ships. *IEEE Trans. Transp. Electrif.* **2020**, *6*, 318–333. [CrossRef]
18. Letafat, A.; Rafiei, M.; Sheikh, M.; Afshari-Igder, M.; Banaei, M.; Boudjadar, J.; Khooban, M.H. Simultaneous Energy Management and Optimal Components Sizing of a Zero-Emission Ferry Boat. *J. Energy Storage* **2020**, *28*, 101215. [CrossRef]
19. Li, Y.; Zhang, H.; Liang, X.; Huang, B. Event-Triggered-Based Distributed Cooperative Energy Management for Multienergy Systems. *IEEE Trans. Ind. Inform.* **2019**, *15*, 2008–2022. [CrossRef]
20. Shang, C.; Srinivasan, D.; Reindl, T. Economic and Environmental Generation and Voyage Scheduling of All-Electric Ships. *IEEE Trans. Power Syst.* **2016**, *31*, 4087–4096. [CrossRef]
21. Huang, Y.; Lan, H.; Hong, Y.Y.; Wen, S.; Fang, S. Joint Voyage Scheduling and Economic Dispatch for All-Electric Ships with Virtual Energy Storage Systems. *Energy* **2020**, *190*, 116268. [CrossRef]
22. Fang, S.; Gou, B.; Wang, Y.; Xu, Y.; Shang, C.; Wang, H. Optimal Hierarchical Management of Shipboard Multibattery Energy Storage System Using a Data-Driven Degradation Model. *IEEE Trans. Transp. Electrif.* **2019**, *5*, 1306–1318. [CrossRef]
23. Wen, S.; Zhao, T.; Tang, Y.; Xu, Y.; Zhu, M.; Fang, S.; Ding, Z. Coordinated Optimal Energy Management and Voyage Scheduling for All-Electric Ships Based on Predicted Shore-Side Electricity Price. *IEEE Trans. Ind. Appl.* **2021**, *57*, 139–148. [CrossRef]
24. Fang, S.; Xu, Y.; Li, Z.; Ding, Z.; Liu, L.; Wang, H. Optimal Sizing of Shipboard Carbon Capture System for Maritime Greenhouse Emission Control. *IEEE Trans. Ind. Appl.* **2019**, *55*, 5543–5553. [CrossRef]
25. Wen, S.; Zhao, T.; Tang, Y.; Xu, Y.; Zhu, M.; Huang, Y. A Joint Photovoltaic-Dependent Navigation Routing and Energy Storage System Sizing Scheme for More Efficient All-Electric Ships. *IEEE Trans. Transp. Electrif.* **2020**, *6*, 1279–1289. [CrossRef]
26. Zhao, T.; Qiu, J.; Wen, S.; Zhu, M. Efficient Onboard Energy Storage System Sizing for All-Electric Ship Microgrids via Optimized Navigation Routing under Onshore Uncertainties. *IEEE Trans. Ind. Appl.* **2022**, *58*, 1664–1674. [CrossRef]
27. Banaei, M.; Ghanami, F.; Khooban, M.H.; Boudjadar, J. Cost-effective control of Roll-on/Roll-off Emission-Free Ships. In Proceedings of the 2021 25th International Conference on Methods and Models in Automation and Robotics (MMAR), Międzyzdroje, Poland, 23–26 August 2021; IEEE: Toulouse, France, 2021; pp. 315–320.

28. Banaei, M.; Boudjadar, J.; Dragičević, T.; Khooban, M.H. Cost Effective Operation of a Hybrid Zero-Emission Ferry Ship. In Proceedings of the 2020 IEEE 11th International Symposium on Power Electronics for Distributed Generation Systems (PEDG), Dubrovnik, Croatia, 28 September–1 October 2020; IEEE: Toulouse, France, 2020; pp. 23–28.
29. Letafat, A.; Rafiei, M.; Ardeshiri, M.; Sheikh, M.; Banaei, M.; Boudjadar, J.; Khooban, M.H. An Efficient and Cost-Effective Power Scheduling in Zero-Emission Ferry Ships. *Complexity* **2020**, *2020*, 6487873. [CrossRef]
30. Han, J.; Charpentier, J.F.; Tang, T. An Energy Management System of a Fuel Cell/Battery Hybrid Boat. *Energies* **2014**, *7*, 2799–2820. [CrossRef]
31. Wang, X.; Shipurkar, U.; Haseltalab, A.; Polinder, H.; Claeys, F.; Negenborn, R.R. Sizing and Control of a Hybrid Ship Propulsion System Using Multi-Objective Double-Layer Optimization. *IEEE Access* **2021**, *9*, 72587–72601. [CrossRef]
32. Pan, X.; Zhu, X.; Zhao, F. More Environmental Sustainability Routing and Energy Management for All Electric Ships. *Front. Energy Res.* **2022**, *9*, 821236 . [CrossRef]
33. Urbanucci, L. Limits and Potentials of Mixed Integer Linear Programming Methods for Optimization of Polygeneration Energy Systems. *Energy Procedia* **2018**, *148*, 1199–1205. [CrossRef]
34. Angelo, J.S.; Krempser, E.; Barbosa, H.J. Differential evolution for bilevel programming. In Proceedings of the 2013 IEEE Congress on Evolutionary Computation, Cancun, Mexico, 20–23 June 2013; IEEE: Toulouse, France, 2013; pp. 470–477.
35. Kanellos, F.D. Optimal Power Management With GHG Emissions Limitation in All-Electric Ship Power Systems Comprising Energy Storage Systems. *IEEE Trans. Power Syst.* **2014**, *29*, 330–339. [CrossRef]
36. Kennedy, J.; Eberhart, R. Particle swarm optimization. In Proceedings of the ICNN'95—International Conference on Neural Networks, Perth, WA, Australia, 27 November–1 December 1995; IEEE: Toulouse, France, 1995; Volume 4, pp. 1942–1948.
37. Shi, Y.; Eberhart, R. A modified particle swarm optimizer. In Proceedings of the 1998 IEEE International Conference on Evolutionary Computation Proceedings, Anchorage, AK, USA, 4–9 May 1998; IEEE: Toulouse, France, 1998; pp. 69–73.
38. Yan, X.; Wang, K.; Yuan, Y.; Jiang, X.; Negenborn, R.R. Energy-Efficient Shipping: An Application of Big Data Analysis for Optimizing Engine Speed of Inland Ships Considering Multiple Environmental Factors. *Ocean. Eng.* **2018**, *169*, 457–468. [CrossRef]
39. Ahmed, E.M.; Rathinam, R.; Dayalan, S.; Fernandez, G.S.; Ali, Z.M.; Abdel Aleem, S.H.E.; Omar, A.I. A Comprehensive Analysis of Demand Response Pricing Strategies in a Smart Grid Environment Using Particle Swarm Optimization and the Strawberry Optimization Algorithm. *Mathematics* **2021**, *9*, 2338. [CrossRef]
40. Yu, H.; Gao, Y.; Wang, L.; Meng, J. A Hybrid Particle Swarm Optimization Algorithm Enhanced with Nonlinear Inertial Weight and Gaussian Mutation for Job Shop Scheduling Problems. *Mathematics* **2020**, *8*, 1355. [CrossRef]
41. Holland, J.H. *Adaptation in Natural and Artificial Systems*; University of Michigan Press: Ann Arbor, MI, USA, 1975.
42. Hashim, F.A.; Hussain, K.; Houssein, E.H.; Mabrouk, M.S.; Al-Atabany, W. Archimedes Optimization Algorithm: A New Metaheuristic Algorithm for Solving Optimization Problems. *Appl. Intell.* **2021**, *51*, 1531–1551. [CrossRef]

mathematics

Article

Methods of Fuzzy Multi-Criteria Decision Making for Controlling the Operating Modes of the Stabilization Column of the Primary Oil-Refining Unit

Batyr Orazbayev [1], Yerbol Ospanov [2], Valentina Makhatova [3], Lazzat Salybek [4], Zhanat Abdugulova [1], Zhumazhan Kulmagambetova [5], Salamat Suleimenova [1] and Kulman Orazbayeva [6,*]

1 Department of System Analysis and Control, L.N. Gumilyov Eurasian National University, Astana 010000, Kazakhstan
2 Department of Automation and Information Technology, Shakarim University, Semey 070014, Kazakhstan; 78oea@mail.ru
3 Department of Software Engineering, Dosmukhamedov Atyrau University, Atyrau 010008, Kazakhstan
4 Department of Automation, Telecommunications, M. Auezov South Kazakhstan University, Shymkent 160000, Kazakhstan
5 Department of Informatics and Information Technologies, Aktobe Regional University Named after K. Zhubanov, Aktobe 030212, Kazakhstan
6 Faculty of Business and Management, Esil University, Astana 010005, Kazakhstan
* Correspondence: kulman_o@mail.ru; Tel.: +7-701-174-2473

Abstract: Many technological systems are characterized by fuzzy initial information, necessary for the development of their models, optimization and control of operating modes. Therefore, the purpose of this study is to formulate decision making problems for optimizing and controlling operating modes of such systems in a fuzzy environment and to develop methods for solving them. The developed heuristic methods of fuzzy multi-criteria decision making are based on the modification and combination of different principles of optimality. The proposed methods based on system models, knowledge and experience of the decision maker allow iterative improvement and effective decision making. On the basis of experimental–statistical methods, methods of expert evaluation, statistical and fuzzy models of the stabilization column have been developed. The conditions for judging the fuzzy model's effectiveness are determined and investigated. Using the proposed heuristic method based on the main criterion and maximin, the problem of two-criterion optimization of the stabilization column parameters in a fuzzy environment is solved. The results obtained confirm the advantages of the proposed method of fuzzy decision making in comparison with the results of known methods. The developed heuristic methods differ from known ones because they allow making adequate decisions in a fuzzy environment by maximizing the use of the collected fuzzy information.

Keywords: multicriteria optimization; fuzzy decision making; decision maker; principles of optimality; heuristic methods

MSC: 49N30; 76B75; 90B50

1. Introduction

Technological processes of oil refining, petrochemistry, metallurgy and other industries are carried out mainly through chemical–technological systems (CTS). The complexity of such CTSs lies in a large number of interconnected technological units, which are characterized by many parameters, the influence of which on their operating modes, as well as on the volume and quality of products, is often non-formalizable and characterized by fuzziness [1,2]. This situation complicates the processes of developing mathematical models and optimizing the operating modes of CTS to control them [3]. Since CTSs are the main factor in the development of the economy of any country, increasing their efficiency through the use of modern mathematical methods of optimization and management is an important and urgent task of science and practice.

Multicriteria optimization problems in the presence of conflicting criteria are decision-making problems that are solved with the knowledge of a person—a decision maker (DM), taking into account his preferences. In practice, many complex production facilities are characterized by a lack and fuzziness of initial information. Such objects, in the presence of experienced operators—DMs, experts who manage the operating modes—are effectively managed due to their experience, knowledge and intuition. At the same time, many control criteria and restrictions are not clearly described in the natural language of DM experts. Therefore, to solve the problems of controlling the operating modes of fuzzy complex objects, it is more appropriate to use fuzzy multi-criteria decision making with the participation of DMs. It can be noted that at present, with the development of fuzzy set theory and decision-making methods, this approach has become more promising for solving decision-making problems for control in a fuzzy environment. Since many CTSs are described as fuzzy, the importance of research and development of decision-making methods in a fuzzy environment is increasing.

Currently, there are many works in which optimization and decision-making methods [4–19] are investigated and proposed, which are used or can be applied to optimize various complex CTSs, including in a fuzzy environment [20–27]. Let us consider the main results of studying the current state of the research area—tasks and decision-making methods, including in a fuzzy environment. One of the approaches to solving problems of multicriteria optimization is the application of the Pareto principle [4,5]. In this approach, not just a single solution is taken, but a set of solutions—points of the multidimensional search space that are the best from the point of view of one of the criteria. The resulting set of optimal points is the Pareto-optimal set (POS).

In [6], Petrovet. al. used a genetic algorithm related to the evolutionary method, which is characterized by high computational costs in order to optimize synchronous motors. The main reasons for this are that evolutionary methods are iterative methods that require large computational costs in the learning process [7]; to determine the best result, these methods iterate over all elements of the population through several iterations [8]. Saibal Majumder et al. in [9] proposed an efficient genetic algorithm based on uncertainties with a variable population for a random fuzzy maximum-flow problem.

Recently, numerous studies have been carried out, for example [10–12], aimed at reducing the computational costs of evolutionary methods due to a priori information about the initial population. Tan Liguo and Novikova in [10] proposed a multicriteria evolutionary algorithm with a step-by-step learning model, which allows a drastic reduction in the number of calculations compared to the classical genetic multivariate method. The peculiarity of this method is that the evolutionary search is purposeful due to the approximation of the POS based on the modification of the evolutionary genetic algorithm of multicriteria optimization using the stages of learning and forgetting. The paper [11] proposes a method of evolutionary multi-objective optimization for the control of generative adversarial networks, which makes it possible to reduce computational costs. Liand Kwong proposed an evolutionary method for multi-objective optimization through multiple learning, providing a reduction in the number of calculations [12]. Various multicriteria evolutionary algorithms (MEA) have been developed that allow obtaining an arbitrarily close approximation to the real continuous surface of the POS [13,14].

In order to provide direction to the evolutionary search, some researchers have attempted to extract knowledge from the regularity property of the POS in the MEA, which is based on learning. The regularity property of the POS was proved by Zhang et al. in [15]. This makes it possible to represent the POS as a continuous multi-criteria problem with m goals. Based on this statement, some authors of the study used various methods of supervised or unsupervised machine learning, such as Bayesian networks [16], Gaussian process [17], a restricted Boltzmann machine [17] and self-organizing maps [18], to evaluate POS.

The authors of [19] proposed an online strategy for self-adaptive pairing constraints based on agglomerative clustering. In this strategy, learning occurs only when the similarity between the populations of two successive generations is greater than the threshold value. In [20], Cheng et al. proposed an MEA using Gaussian process inverse modeling to reduce the number of Gaussian models. Li and Kwong incorporated manifold learning into multi-criteria optimization, which allows dimensionality reduction to extract the geometric properties of the structure of low-dimensional manifolds embedded in a high-dimensional space [12]. However, it should be noted that despite these efforts, the problems of excessive computational costs due to numerous iterations or retraining, especially at the completion stage, when the set of solutions approaches the Pareto set, are still not solved.

Decision making consists of evaluating possible solutions (alternatives) and choosing the best one according to given criteria. An important area of decision making is related to production. The larger the volume of production, the more difficult it is to make decisions when managing it, i.e., the problems of formalization and solving decision-making problems become relevant. The authors of [21,22] proposed decision-making methods for incomplete data based on the intuitionistic fuzzy approach, which allow making more adequate decisions in a fuzzy environment. The problems of fuzzy optimization and fuzzy decision making are studied in [23,24], where methods for their solution are proposed based on the α-level set of fuzzy set theories. The problems of applying multi-parameter fuzzy optimization in practice are studied in [25,26], and approaches to optimization in a fuzzy environment by oil refining are proposed in [27,28]. Aspects of technological systems such as power grids and the multi-criteria decision-making structure between the designer of a renewable power plant and an independent system operator are explored in [29,30]. The study [29] proposes an approach to improve fault tolerance, allowing power system planners to effectively manage multi-criteria sustainability indicators in a two-objective optimization planning model at the same time. In [30], a combination of a multi-criteria decision-making approach and a multi-agent modeling method was developed to obtain the maximum possible profit from a renewable generation plan. An approach to power market modeling based on fuzzy Q-learning coupled with a similarity order preference method (TOPSIS) is proposed as a new decision support system for renewable energy promotion.

Concretizing the literature review, it can be noted that in the above works [9,11–15, 17–19,22–25,30], the authors conducted studies using similar methods of multicriteria optimization and decision making. Furthermore, the authors of works [23,27,28] used in their research methods multicriteria optimization in a fuzzy environment to control the operating modes of technological systems. However, in these studies, fuzzy optimization problems, in contrast to our approach, are solved by converting them to a set of crisp problems based on the α-level set, which leads to the loss of some of the original fuzzy information and a decrease in the adequacy of the solutions obtained.

In the analyzed studies [23,27,28] for solving decision-making problems in a fuzzy environment, at the stage of formulation, a fuzzy task based on a α-level set is transformed into a set of equivalent crisp tasks. Further, the obtained crisp problems at α-levels are solved by known methods; then, by combining the obtained solutions, the solution of the original fuzzy problem is determined. However, such an approach can often lead to the loss of an important part of the original fuzzy information, which will lead to a decrease in the adequacy of the solutions obtained in a fuzzy environment. This motivates the development of a new approach that ensures the high adequacy of decisions made in a fuzzy environment.

In this regard, the main goal of this study is the formalization and formulation of fuzzy decision-making problems and the development of heuristic methods for solving them, which make it possible to obtain highly adequate solutions in a fuzzy environment. To do this, a fuzzy production problem based on the modification of various principles of optimality is posed and solved in a fuzzy environment without converting it to a set of crisp problems. At the same time, due to the experience, knowledge and intuition of DMs, the best decision is made, taking into account the current situation in production, the market for the sale of products, and the preferences of DMs. Thus, the main contribution of our research to the development of decision-making methods in a fuzzy environment is to provide the possibility of setting and solving fuzzy problems without reducing them to clear problems. This makes it possible to increase the adequacy and efficiency of decisions made when solving real production problems in a fuzzy environment.

The structure of the study is as follows. A review of the literature is presented in detail in Section 1. Section 2 describes the materials and the object of study and proposes methods for solving problems of multi-criteria decision making in a fuzzy environment. Section 3 describes the results obtained: models of the C-8 stabilization column of the EDP-AVT primary oil-refining unit; formulated and proved theorems on the adequacy of fuzzy models; the problem of fuzzy multi-criteria decision making for controlling the operating modes of the C-8 stabilization column of the primary oil refining-unit of Atyrau refinery was solved. Section 4 discusses the results of the study. Section 5 presents the study's limitations. Section 6 formulates conclusions and further directions for research.

2. Materials and Methods

The research materials in this work are experimental and statistical data, theoretical information and expert information, presented mainly in the form of fuzzy information, describing the states and operating modes of technological systems of oil refining production. These systems are a set of interconnected technological units with various streams and functioning as a whole, in which the chemical and physical processes of oil refining proceed and are often characterized by the fuzziness of some part of the initial information. To effectively control the operating modes of technological systems in a fuzzy environment, it is necessary to develop heuristic decision-making methods [3,22,31], that, based on models of the control object, allow DMs to choose the best operating mode.

In this paper, as a specific CTS, we study the EDP-AVT (Electric desalination plant-atmospheric-vacuum tubular) primary oil-refining unit using a simplified scheme, which is shown in Figure 1. The decision-making problem is solved in a fuzzy environment to control the operating modes of the C-8 stabilization column, where the target product is produced—stable gasoline.

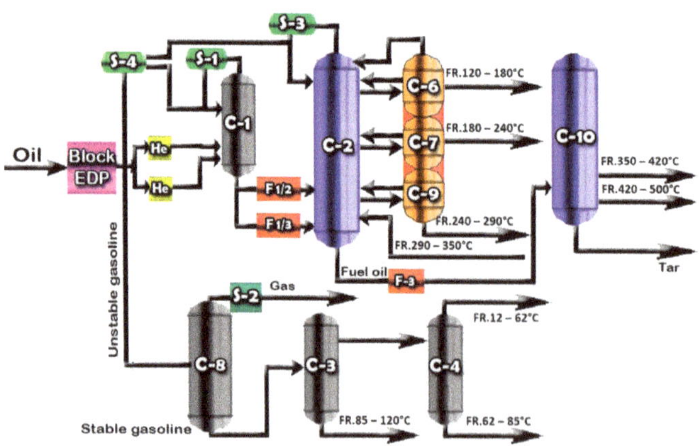

Figure 1. Simplified process flow diagram of the EDP-AVT unit.

The processed oil, having passed through the heat exchangers, enters the electric dehydrators of the EDP unit; then, after passing through the heat exchangers again, it enters C-1 oil topping column. Oil from C-1 outlet is heated in furnaces F-1/2, F-1/3 and transferred to C-2 atmospheric column. For the selection of narrow fractions of oil products

120–180, 180–240 and 240–290 °C, their overflows into the stripping columns C-6, C-7, C-9, respectively, are provided, from which, after cooling, these fractions are removed from the unit. The fuel oil from the C-2 column is heated in the F-3 furnace and enters the C-10 vacuum column. The gas is cooled in the C-8 column and enters the S-2 separator, from which the gas head is discharged. Stable gasoline from the bottom of the C-8 column enters the C-3 column, where gasoline fractions 85–120 °C are separated, then to C-4, where it is separated into gasoline fractions and 62–85 °C.

One of the main technological blocks of the EDP-AVT unit is the atmospheric unit, which includes columns C-1 and C-2. Fractions of light oil products are shipped from C-2 to the commodity park: 120–180; 180–240 and 240–290 °C, and unstable gasoline from columns C-1, C-2 is supplied as a raw material for the C-8 stabilization column and C-3 distillation column [26,28].

The described EDP-AVT primary oil-refining unit is characterized by the fuzziness of some of the initial information, which requires a fuzzy approach to make decisions on the management of its operating modes and the development and application of a fuzzy approach.

Fuzzy multi-criteria decision-making problems arise when it is required to choose the best solution at once according to several conflicting local criteria under conditions of fuzzy criteria and/or constraints. Since there is usually no solution that is best for all criteria at the same time, a reasonable compromise is necessary. Since only a person—a DM—can know which indicators are more important in the current situation, the solution of a multi-criteria fuzzy decision-making problem should be based on information about the preferences of the DM, his knowledge, experience and intuition.

For a unified description of the criteria, we will normalize them by reducing the range of their values to the segment [0, 1]. Such a description of the criteria is convenient for comparing their values with the values of the membership functions and for comparing the dimensionless values of various criteria. We present fuzzy decision-making statements and develop methods for solving them based on the heuristics and intelligence of a DM.

Let $\mu_c^1(\mathbf{x}), \ldots, \mu_c^m(\mathbf{x})$ be local criteria normalized in the interval [0, 1] that evaluate the efficiency of the modes of the control object, and $\varphi_q(\mathbf{x})\tilde{\geq}b_q, q=\overline{1,L}$ be fuzzy constraints in the form of fuzzy instructions. Let us assume $\boldsymbol{\mu}_q(\mathbf{x}),\ q=\overline{1,L}$ as the membership functions of fuzzy constraints. As you can see, the local criterion and constraints depend on the vector of input, mode parameters $\mathbf{x}=(x_1,\ldots,x_n)$. All or some local criteria can also be fuzzy, in which case the corresponding $\mu_c^i(\mathbf{x})$ are their membership functions [3,23,24]. Let us assume that a number of local criteria priorities $I_C=\{1,\ldots,m\}$ and the vector of weight coefficients $\boldsymbol{\beta}=(\beta_1,\ldots,\beta_L)$, reflecting the mutual importance of constraints, can be defined [3,10].

Then, modifying the ideas of the methods of the main criterion (MC) and maximin (MM) for working in a fuzzy environment, the decision-making problem for controlling the operating modes of an object can be written as the following formulation:

$$\max_{\mathbf{x}\in X}\mu_C^1(\mathbf{x}), \tag{1}$$

$$X=\left\{\mathbf{x}:x\in\Omega\wedge\arg\left(\mu_C^i(\mathbf{x})\geq\mu_R^i\right)\wedge\arg\left(\max_{\mathbf{x}\in X}\min_{q}(\beta_q\mu_q(\mathbf{x})),i=\overline{2,m},q=\overline{1,L}\right)\right\} \tag{2}$$

where $\wedge$—logical "and", requiring the truth of all statements connected through it, μ_R^i—boundary values of local criteria $\mu_C^i(\mathbf{x}),\ i=\overline{2,m}$, set by the DM.

By changing the boundary values of local criteria $\mu_R^i,\ i=\overline{2,m}$ and the vector of weight coefficients $\boldsymbol{\beta}=(\beta_1,\ldots,\beta_L)$ we can obtain a vector of solutions, i.e., input, mode parameters of the problem (1) and (2): $\mathbf{x}(\mu_R^i,\boldsymbol{\beta})$. The choice of the best solution is made in an iterative mode with the participation of the DM based on his preference, experience, knowledge and intuition [3,16,30].

Based on the principles of MC (for criteria) and MM (for constraints), the following heuristic method is proposed for solving the fuzzy decision-making problem (1) and (2), formulated to control the operating modes of an object [32]. The main points of the proposed heuristic method for solving the problem are set out as follows (1) and (2):

1. The number of steps for each q-th coordinate $p_q, q = \overline{1, L}$ and a number of local criteria priorities $I_C = \{1, \ldots, m\}$ are set, where L and m are thenumber of constraints and criteria [33]. The main criterion should be given the highest priority of 1;
2. The DM sets the value of the weight vector $\boldsymbol{\beta} = (\beta_1, \ldots, \beta_L)$, reflecting the relative importance of fuzzy constraints [33].
3. The DM assigns boundary values for local criteria $\mu_R^i, i = \overline{2, m}$, which are transferred to the composition of constraints and are taken into account as constraints.
4. To change the coordinates of the vector $\boldsymbol{\beta}$ according to the formula $h_q = \frac{1}{p_q}, q = \overline{1, L}$ the values of each step specified in paragraph 1 are calculated [3].
5. A set of weight vectors $\boldsymbol{\beta}^1, \boldsymbol{\beta}^2, \ldots, \boldsymbol{\beta}^N, N = (p_1 + 1) \cdot (p_2 + 1) \cdot, \ldots, \cdot (p_L + 1)$ are built by changing the coordinates in the interval [0, 1] with a step h_q [10].
6. The term set is defined, for which 'fuzzy' describes the parameters of the object and the process [24,27].
7. Membership functions $\mu_q(\mathrm{x}), q = \overline{1, L}$ of fuzzy constraints are constructed (fuzzification procedure) [3,27].
8. Based on the CTS mathematical models, a search is performed for the maximum of the main criterion (1) on the admissible set X, determined by the maximin principle (2), and the current solutions are determined: $\mathbf{x}(\mu_R^i, \boldsymbol{\beta}); \mu_C^1(\mathbf{x}(\mu_R^i, \boldsymbol{\beta})); \mu_C^2(\mathbf{x}(\mu_R^i, \boldsymbol{\beta})), \ldots, \mu_C^m(\mathbf{x}(\mu_R^i, \boldsymbol{\beta})), i = \overline{2, m}; \mu_1(\mathbf{x}(\mu_R^i, \boldsymbol{\beta})), \ldots, \mu_L(\mathbf{x}(\mu_R^i, \boldsymbol{\beta}))$ [7,10].
9. The results obtained are presented to the DM. If the current solutions do not satisfy the DM, then new values $\mu_R^i, i = \overline{2, m}$; are assigned to them and/or the values of the constraint weight vector $\boldsymbol{\beta}$ are adjusted and a return to step 3 follows. Otherwise, go to the next item [3].
10. The search for a solution stops; the results of the final choice of DM are displayed: the optimal values of the vector of parameters $\mathbf{x}^*(\mu_R^i, \boldsymbol{\beta})$; maximum value of the main criterion $\mu_C^1(\mathbf{x}^*(\mu_R^i, \boldsymbol{\beta}))$; required values of local criteria $\mu_C^2(\mathbf{x}^*(\mu_R^i, \boldsymbol{\beta})), \ldots, \mu_C^m(\mathbf{x}^*(\mu_R^i, \boldsymbol{\beta}))$ and maximum degrees of fulfillment of fuzzy constraints $\mu_1(\mathbf{x}^*(\mu_R^i, \boldsymbol{\beta})), \ldots, \mu_L(\mathbf{x}^*(\mu_R^i, \boldsymbol{\beta}))$, $i = \overline{2, m}$.

The preferences, weights, or priorities assigned to the decision maker's criteria significantly influence the decision-making process. The DM's preferences in the decision-making process in the described MC + MM heuristic method are taken into account by determining priorities and assigning weights to the criteria in paragraphs 1,2. At the same time, the DM determines priorities and weighting factors based on his experience and knowledge, taking into account the current situation in production and the market for the products produced.

Now suppose there are conditions for applying the principles of Pareto optimality and the ideal point. Then, modifying the principles of Pareto optimality and the ideal point, for fuzziness, we can write the following formulation of fuzzy decision making (3) and (4): [4,5]:

$$\max_{\mathbf{x} \in X} \boldsymbol{\mu}_C(\mathbf{x}), \ \boldsymbol{\mu}_C(\mathbf{x}) = \sum_{i=1}^{m} \gamma_i \mu_C^i(\mathbf{x}), \tag{3}$$

$$X = \left\{ \mathbf{x} : x \in \Omega \wedge \arg\left(\mu_q(\mathbf{x}) \geq \min \| \mu_q(\mathbf{x}) - \mu_q^p \|_D \right), \ q = \overline{1, L} \right\}, \tag{4}$$

where $\boldsymbol{\mu}_C(\mathbf{x})$ is theintegrated criterion obtained on the basis of the Pareto optimality principle, taking into account the weight of local criteria; $\gamma_i, \ i = 1, m$ are theweight coefficients of local criteria; Ω is the initial set of alternatives; μ_q^p are thecoordinates of an ideal point—the required degree of fulfillment of fuzzy constraints. In this formulation of the fuzzy decision-making problem, $\| \mu_q(\mathbf{x}) - \mu_q^p \|_D$ is a selectable metric D, which determines the distance between the current and ideal degrees of fulfillment of fuzzy constraints, wherein $\mu_q^p = (\max \mu_1(\mathbf{x}), \ldots, \max \mu_L(\mathbf{x}))$. If $\mu_q(\mathbf{x}), q = \overline{1, L}$ is normal, then $\mu_q^p = (1, \ldots, 1)$.

To solve the obtained decision-making problem in a fuzzy environment, the following heuristic method is proposed, developed on the basis of a modification of the Pareto optimality (PO) and ideal point (IP) principles [3–5]. The block diagram of the PO + IP heuristic method is shown in Figure 2.

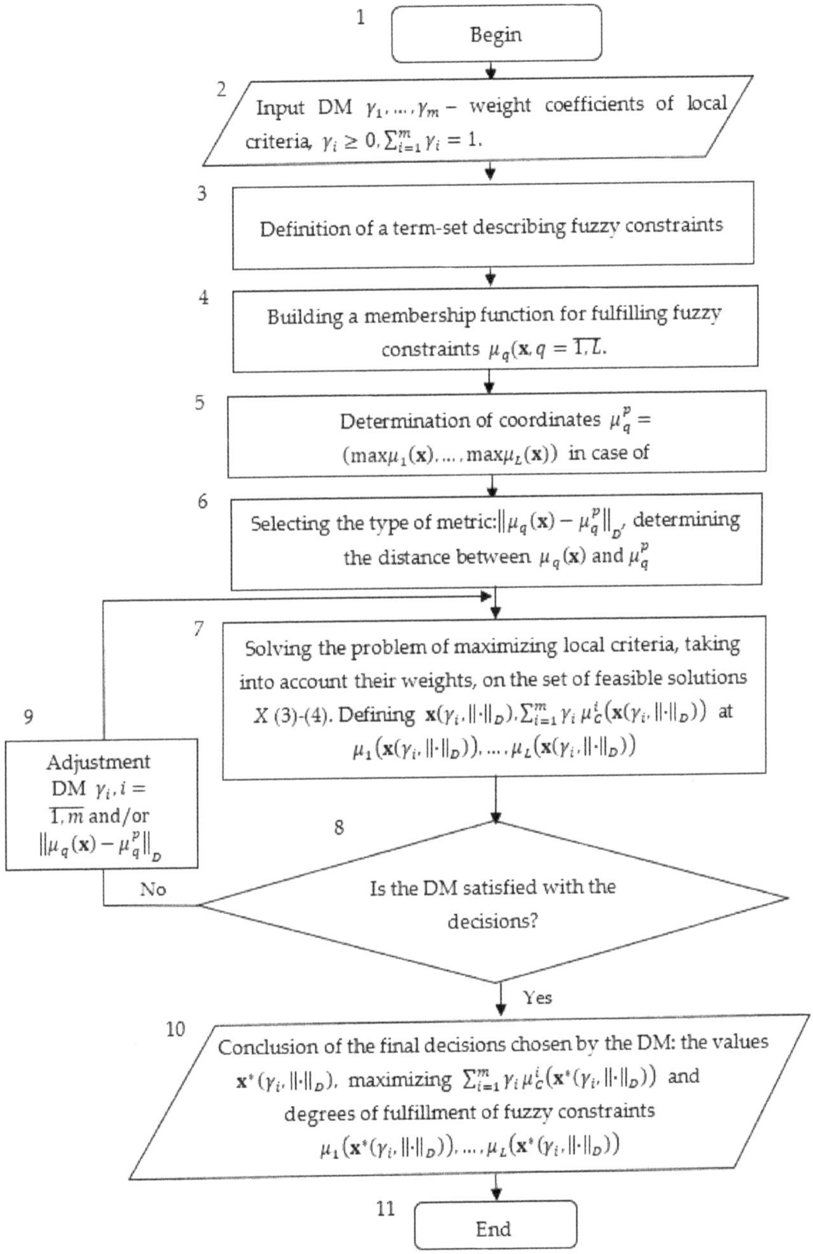

Figure 2. PO + IP heuristic block diagram.

In block 2, with the help of the DM and experts based on Pareto optimality [5], the weight coefficients of the criteria are set, which evaluate their importance.

In blocks 3 and 4, if expert evaluation is required, a term set describing fuzzy constraints is selected, and membership functions are built for them [3]. Membership functions can be built using the Fuzzy Logic Toolbox application of the MATLAB system [34].

In blocks 5 and 6, with the participation of DM, the coordinates of ideal points (solutions) are determined, i.e., the necessary degrees of fulfillment of fuzzy constraints, and the type of metric is selected. The chosen metric should determine the minimized distance between ideal points and the obtained degrees of fulfillment of fuzzy constraints [33].

In block 7, with the participation of the DM, the integrated criterion is maximized, taking into account the weight of local criteria (3) on the set of feasible solutions X (4) [33]. As a result, the values of the vector of input, mode parameters $\mathbf{x}(\gamma_i, \|\cdot\|_D)$, the corresponding values of the integrated criterion $\mu_C(\mathbf{x})$ and degrees of fulfillment of fuzzy constraints $\mu_1(\mathbf{x}(\gamma_i, \|\cdot\|_D)), \ldots, \mu_L(\mathbf{x}(\gamma_i, \|\cdot\|_D))$ are determined.

In block 8, the DM analyzes the resulting solutions to select the final, best solution. If the current results do not satisfy the DM, then in order to improve the solution, the values $\gamma_i, i = \overline{1,m}$ and/or type of the metric $\|\mu_q(\mathbf{x}) - \mu_q^p\|_D$ (block 9) are adjusted and the iteration of the search for the best solution is repeated starting from block 7. In the case of obtaining a solution that satisfies the DM, he chooses the best solution and to derive the final solution, the transition to block 10 is carried out.

Block 10 displays the selected final decision $\mathbf{x}^*(\gamma_i, \|\cdot\|_D)$, providing local criteria $\sum_{i=1}^{m} \gamma_i \mu_C^i(\mathbf{x})$ (3) as the maximum in the area of feasible solutions (4) and the maximum value of the degrees of fulfillment of fuzzy constraints $\mu_q(\mathbf{x}), q = \overline{1,L}$.

The work also uses methods of multicriteria optimization [10,13–17,35,36], and for the collection and processing of fuzzy information, methods of expert assessment [37,38] and fuzzy set theory [21–26,39–41] are used. To develop mathematical models of the optimization and control object, experimental and statistical methods [42–44] for developing fuzzy models [27,45] are used.

Let us note the advantage of the proposed approach to solving problems of decision-making in a fuzzy environment. This approach, based on the modification and combination of various principles of optimality, depending on the nature of the available information and the possibilities available to the DM, allows the choice of the most appropriate way to solve a specific decision-making problem in the current production situation.

3. Results

3.1. Mathematical Models of the C-8 Stabilization Column of the EDP-AVT Primary Oil Refining Unit

Based on the method of successive regressors [46] and experimental data and expert information, the following model structures have been identified that estimate the yield of gasoline and gas (y_1, y_2) and are characterized by the fuzzy quality of stable gasoline ($\tilde{y}_3, \tilde{y}_4$) from the output of the C-8 column:

$$y_j = a_0 + \sum_{i=1}^{5} a_i x_i + \sum_{i=1}^{5}\sum_{k=i}^{5} a_{ik} x_i x_k, \qquad j = 1,2, \tag{5}$$

$$\tilde{y}_j = \tilde{a}_0 + \sum_{i=1}^{5} \tilde{a}_i x_i + \sum_{i=1}^{5}\sum_{k=i}^{5} \tilde{a}_{ik} x_i x_j, \qquad j = 3,4, \tag{6}$$

where x_i, $i = 1,2$ arethe temperature of the top (x_1) and bottom (x_2) of the C-8 column; by changing these, an increase in the yield of stable gasoline is achieved, i.e., control variables; x_i, $i = \overline{3,5}$ are disturbing influences, namely the flow x_3, temperature x_4 and raw material density x_5.

After identifying the parameters of multiple regression models (5) based on the least-squares method [43], a model for estimating the yield of stable gasoline was obtained:

$$y_1 = 111.78 - 0.047x_1 + 0.13x_2 - 0.05x_3 - 0.01x_4 - 43.073x_5 - 0.003x_1^2 + 0.011x_2^2 - 0.001x_1x_2 + 0.022x_2x_4\,, \tag{7}$$

$$y_2 = 32.804 + 0.406x_1 - 0.302x_2 + 0.113x_3 - 0.084x_4 + 0.085x_5 - 0.001x_1^2 + 0.00007x_2^2 - 0.002x_2x_4\,, \tag{8}$$

To identify fuzzy parameters (regression coefficients) of models (6), fuzzy models are first presented as a set of crisp models based on the α-level set:

$$y_j^{\alpha_q} = a_0^{\alpha_q} + \sum_{i=1}^{5} a_i^{\alpha_q} x_i + \sum_{i=1}^{5}\sum_{k=1}^{5} a_{ik}^{\alpha_q} x_i x_k, \quad j = 3,4 \tag{9}$$

where α_q, $q = \overline{1,3}$ is the set of the α-level; we have chosen three levels, since the chosen function of the Gaussian type of the α-level has left and right levels, i.e., α = (0.5; 08; 1; 0.8: 0.5).

After identifying the regression coefficients at the α-levels of the model (9) based on the least-squares method, they are combined according to the formula [27,47]:

$$\tilde{a}_{ij} = \bigcup_{\alpha \in [0.5 \div 1]} a_{ij}^{\alpha_l} \text{ or } \mu_{\tilde{a}_{ij}}(a_{ij}) = \sup_{\alpha \in [0.5 \div 1]} \min\left\{\alpha_l, \mu_{a_{ij}}^{\alpha_l}(a_{ij})\right\}, \text{where } a_{ij}^{\alpha_l} = \left\{\tilde{a}_{ij} | \mu_{\tilde{a}_{ij}}(a_{ij})| \geq \alpha\right\}.$$

As a result, the following models for estimating the beginning of the boiling of gasoline y_2 and the end of its boiling y_2 are obtained, suitable for computer simulation, optimization and control of the operating modes of the C-8 column:

$$y_3 = 243.06 - 0.04x_1 - 0.057x_2 - 0.002x_3 + 0.001x_4 - 50.27x_5 - 0.001x_1^2 - 0.001x_2^2 - 0.0002x_1x_2 + 0.011x_2x_4, \tag{10}$$

$$y_4 = 15.87 + 0.05x_1 - 0.087x_2 + 0.0004x_3 + 0.032x_4 + 23.33x_5 + 0.0003x_1^2 - 0.002x_2^2 - 0.011x_1x_2 + 0.01x_1x_4\,, \tag{11}$$

In the obtained models (7), (8), (10) and (11), regressors with zero or near-zero coefficients are considered neglible.

3.2. Determination of the Adequacy of Fuzzy Models of Technological Systems

The efficiency of the process of optimization and control of the operating modes of technological systems operating in a fuzzy environment mainly depends on the adequacy of their fuzzy models. In this regard, the issue of assessing the adequacy of fuzzy models of technological systems is very important. To study the adequacy of fuzzy models, we consider that the system being modeled is described by a set of input $\{X_1, \ldots X_n\} \subset U$ and output $\{Y_1, \ldots Y_m\} \subset V$ fuzzy sets, where U and V are universes defining the input and output spaces of the system. Fuzzy sets $X_i, i = \overline{1,n}$ and $Y_j, j = \overline{1,m}$ are defined through their membership functions:

$$X_i = \{(x, \mu_{X_i}(x))\}; Y_j = \left\{\left(y, \mu_{Y_j}(y)\right)\right\}.$$

Then technological systems can be described by a fuzzy equation (model):

$$Y_j = X_i \circ R_{ij},\ i = \overline{1,n},\ j = \overline{1,m},$$

where ∘ is the sign of a composition operation, or membership function:

$$\mu_{Y_j}(y) = \underset{x}{maxmin}\left\{\mu_{X_i}(x),\ \mu_{R_{ij}}(x,y)\right\}, \tag{12}$$

where R_{ij} is a fuzzy binary relation between the input and output parameters of the system on $U \times V$. It can be represented as a set of control rules with the structure:

$$IF\ X_i\ \ THEN\ Y_j,\ i = \overline{1,n},\ j = \overline{1,m} \tag{13}$$

defined as follows: $R_{ij} = \underset{i=\overline{1,n},\ j=\overline{1,m}}{U} X_i \times Y_j$ or by the membership function: $\mu_{R_{ij}}(x.y) = maxmin\left\{\mu_{X_i}(x),\ \mu_{Y_j}(y)\right\}$,

In (12), the fuzzy relation R_{ij} is known. The use of such a fuzzy relation shows that the estimate $\hat{Y_j}$, which is determined by expression (12), does not coincide with the original fuzzy set of output parameters of the object Y_j [28]. This means the fuzzy relation R_{ij} does not adequately reflect the given statement (13).

The criterion for evaluating the adequacy of the fuzzy model (12) to the initial fuzzy output parameters of the object can be the following expression:

$$J = min\sum_{j=1}^{m}\left(\mu_{Y_j}(y) - \mu_{\hat{Y}_j}(y)\right)^2. \quad (14)$$

Criterion (14) minimizes the deviation of the membership functions of the output parameters of the control object $\mu_{Y_j}(y)$, which are used in the formation of the fuzzy mapping R_{ij}, from the membership functions of the fuzzy sets $\mu_{\hat{Y}_j}(y)$, calculated by (12).

The main reason for the inadequacy of the fuzzy model for the observed parameters of the technological system is the inaccurate implementation of the compositional inference rule in (12).

Let us consider the conditions for the exact fulfillment of the compositional inference rule, which minimizes the values of the fuzzy model adequacy criterion J (14).

Let us represent the condition for the adequacy of the fuzzy model. Let the fuzzy relation $\mathbf{R} = R_{ij} = \underset{i=\overline{1,n},\ j=\overline{1,m}}{U} X_i \times Y_j$ be given. Then, if for each $X_i,\ i = \overline{1,n}$:

$$Y_j = X_i \circ R_{ij},\ i = \overline{1,n},\ j = \overline{1,m}, \quad (15)$$

then the compositional inference rule is fulfilled exactly, i.e., the fuzzy model is adequate; otherwise, it is approximate, which indicates the inadequacy of the fuzzy model.

Now we give theorems on the adequacy of the fuzzy model, i.e., on the exact fulfillment of the compositional inference rule, which minimizes the criterion for the adequacy of the fuzzy model (14).

Theorem 1. $R_{ij} = \underset{i=\overline{1,n},\ j=\overline{1,m}}{U} X_i \times Y_j$ *is a regular relation matrix,* i.e., *n = m and* $det(R_{ij}) \neq 0$. *Then If* X_i *and* Y_j *are normal* ($max\mu_{X_i}(x) = 1,\ max\mu_{Y_j}(y) = 1$), *then condition (15) is exactly satisfied and the fuzzy model is adequate.*

Proof of Theorem 1. It is known that fuzzy sets X_i, Y_j and relation R_{ij} are described through their membership functions:

$$X_i = \{(x,\ \mu_{X_i}(x))\}; Y_j = \left\{\left(y,\ \mu_{Y_j}(y)\right)\right\}; R_{ij} = \left\{\left(\mu_{R_{ij}}(x,y), (x,y)\right)\right\}.$$

According to Tong's theorem [48], if the fuzzy sets X_i and Y_j are normal, and the relation matrix R_{ij} is regular, then R_{ij} has a column x^* and a line y^*, for which

$$\mu_{X_i}(x) = \mu_{R_{ij}}(x^*, y);\ \ \mu_{y_j}(y) = \mu_{R_{ij}}(x, y^*), \quad (16)$$

or

$$\mu_{X_i}(x) = \underset{y}{max}\mu_{R_{ij}}(x,y);\ \ \mu_{y_j}(y) = \underset{x}{max}\ \mu_{R_{ij}}(x,y), \quad (17)$$

Whence it follows that for the elements (x, y) of the relation R_{ij}, the following relations are met $\mu_{R_{ij}}(x^*, y) \geq \mu_{R_{ij}}(x, y)$ *and* $\mu_{R_{ij}}(x, y^*) \geq \mu_{R_{ij}}(x, y)$; consequently:

$$min\left\{\mu_{R_{ij}}(x^*, y), \mu_{R_{ij}}(x,y)\right\} = \mu_{R_{ij}}(x,y);\ \ min\left\{\mu_{R_{ij}}(x, y^*), \mu_{R_{ij}}(x,y)\right\} = \mu_{R_{ij}}(x,y). \quad (18)$$

Since

$$\mu_{Y_j}(y) = \underset{x}{max}min\left\{\mu_{X_i}(x),\ \mu_{R_{ij}}(x,y)\right\}, \quad (19)$$

then, substituting (16) into (19), taking into account (17) and (18), we obtain:

$$\mu_{Y_j}(y) = \underset{x}{maxmin}\left\{\mu_{X_i}(x),\ \mu_{R_{ij}}(x,y)\right\} = \underset{x}{maxmin}\left\{\mu_{R_{ij}}(x^*,y),\ \mu_{R_{ij}}(x,y)\right\} = \underset{x}{max}\mu_{R_{ij}}(x,y) = \mu_{Y_j}(y).$$

□

Let us give a crisp explanation of Equations (15) and (19) given above. Equation (15) is a compositional inference rule known from fuzzy set theories [24,27,38]. Equations (16) and (17) mean that if fuzzy sets X_i and Y_j are normal, i.e., the maximum value of their membership function reaches 1, then their membership functions are determined by the maximum values of the membership function of the relation matrix R_{ij}. In this case, the ratio matrix R_{ij} must be regular. In B (16), x^*, y^* column and row, these conditions are satisfied, and are proved by Tong's theorem [46]. Equation (18) follows from condition (17) and shows that the minimum values of the membership function of fuzzy relations $\mu_{R_{ij}}(x^*,y)$, $\mu_{R_{ij}}(x,y)$ and $\mu_{R_{ij}}(x,y^*)$, $\mu_{R_{ij}}(x,y)$, i.e., their intersections will be equal to $\mu_{R_{ij}}(x,y)$. Equation (19) represents the record of the compositional inference rule (15) through the membership functions of the fuzzy sets Y_j and X_i and the relation matrix R_{ij}.

Theorem 2. *Let* $\mathbf{R} = \underset{i=\overline{1,n},\ j=\overline{1,m}}{U} X_i \times Y_j$ *be an irregular ratio matrix,* i.e., $R = \underset{i=\overline{1,n}}{U} R_i$, *where* $R_i = X_i \times Y_i$ *is a regular relation matrix. If fuzzy sets* X_i, $Y_i, i = \overline{1,n}$ *are normal* ($max\ \mu_{X_i}(x) = 1$, $max\mu_{Y_i}(y) = 1$) *and* $\underset{i=\overline{1,n}}{\cap} X_i = \emptyset$, *and* $\underset{j=\overline{1,n}}{\cap} Y_i = \emptyset$, *then condition (15) is exactly satisfied and the fuzzy model is adequate.*

Proof of Theorem 2. We represent fuzzy sets X_i, Y_i in terms of their membership function $X_i = \left\{\left(\mu_{X_i}(x), x\right)\right\}; Y_i = \left\{\left(\mu_{Y_i}(y), y\right)\right\}$. Then, the fuzzy model is defined as

$$\mu_{Y_i}(y) = \underset{x}{maxmin}\{\mu_{X_i}(x),\ \mu_R(x,y)\}. \tag{20}$$

Matrix $\mathbf{R} = \underset{i=\overline{1,n}}{U} R_i$ is unregular, where

$$R_i = X_i \times Y_i. \tag{21}$$

By the conditions of the theorem

$$\underset{i=\overline{1,n}}{\cap} X_i = ,\ \underset{j=\overline{1,n}}{\cap} Y_i = . \tag{22}$$

Then from expression (21), taking into account condition (22), we can write:

$$\mu_{R_i} = \begin{cases} \mu_{R_i}, & if\ (x,y) \in \text{supp } X_i \times \text{Y}_\text{i}; \\ 0, & if\ (x,y) \notin \text{supp } X_i \times \text{Y}_\text{i}, \end{cases}$$

From the last entry

$$\mu_{\mathbf{R}} = \begin{cases} \mu_{R_1}, & if\ (x,y) \in \text{supp } X_1 \times Y_1; \\ \mu_{R_2}, & if\ (x,y) \in \text{supp } X_2 \times Y_2; \\ . & . \\ . & . \\ . & . \\ \mu_{R_n}, & if\ (x,y) \in \text{supp } X_n \times Y_n \end{cases}$$

therefore, for all $\mu_{\mathbf{R}} = \mu_{R_j}$, $j = \overline{1,n}$,$\min(\mu_{X_i}, \mu_{\mathbf{R}}) = 0$, except $\mu_{\mathbf{R}} = \mu_{R_i}$, $j = i$,

Taking this into account, in (20) we obtain:

$$\mu_{Y_i}(y) = \underset{x}{\text{maxmin}}\{\mu_{X_i}(x),\ \mu_{\mathbf{R}}(x,y)\} = \underset{x}{\text{maxmin}}\{\mu_{X_i}(x),\ \mu_{R_i}(x,y)\}.$$

Since according to the condition X_i, $i = \overline{1,n}$ are normal fuzzy sets, $R_i = X_i \times Y_i$—a regular relation matrix, according to Theorem 1, condition (15) is strictly satisfied; i.e., the fuzzy model is adequate. □

3.3. Solving the Problem of Fuzzy Multi-Criteria Decision-Making for Controlling the Operating Modes of the C-8 Stabilization Column of the Primary Oil Refining Unit of Atyrau Refinery

To support the proposed concept of solving problems of multi-criteria decision making in a fuzzy environment based on the developed heuristic method PO + IP of synthesized models of the C-8 stabilization column of Atyrau refinery, we will give the following example from real life.

In real practice, the task of fuzzy multi-criteria decision making of the process of controlling the operating modes of the stabilization column is to determine such values of the components of the vector $x = (x_1, x_2, x_3, x_4, x_5)$, providing that:

$$\max_{\mathbf{x}\in X} f_i(\mathbf{x}), i = 1,2, \tag{23}$$

$$X = \{\mathbf{x} : \mathbf{x} \in \Omega \wedge (\varphi_1(x) \tilde{\geq} b_1, \varphi_2(x) \tilde{\leq} b_2)\}, \tag{24}$$

where $f_i(\mathbf{x})$, $j = 1,2$ are local criteria for evaluating the yield of stable gasoline and gas from the C-8 column; $\mathbf{x} = (x_1, x_2, x_3, x_4, x_5)$ are the vector of input, mode parameters, and changes which optimize the operating modes of the object; and $\Omega = \lceil x_i^{min}, x_i^{max} \rceil$, $i = \overline{1,5}$ are the minimum and maximum values of the vectors specified by the object regulations. The C-8 operating procedure defines the following intervals for changing parameters x_i, $i = \overline{1,5} : x_1 = \lceil 140,\ 160 \rceil$, °C; $x_2 = \lceil 250,\ 260 \rceil$; °C; $x_3 = \lceil 210,\ 350 \rceil$, m^3/h;$x_4 = \lceil 70,\ 90 \rceil$, °C; $x_5 = \lceil 0.70,\ 1.00 \rceil$, kg/cm^2. The quality of gasoline is described by fuzzy constraints in the form of fuzzy instructions "beginning of boiling of gasoline $\tilde{y}_2$ should not be lower than 30 °C", "end of boiling of gasoline $\tilde{y}_3$ should not be higher than 180 °C". These fuzzy constraints in (23) and (24) are formalized as $\varphi_1(x) \tilde{\geq} b_1$ and $\varphi_2(x) \tilde{\leq} b_2$.

The current values of the input, parameters relating to operation and affecting the performance of operating modes, as well as the decision-making process are available and determined using appropriate measuring instruments. Their accuracy is guaranteed by the accuracy classes of these instruments, and the intervals of their values are determined by the technological regulations of the primary oil-refining unit [32]. Furthermore, information related to fuzzy constraints is evaluated as fuzzy by DM experts, and membership functions are built for them, allowing them to process such fuzzy information [3]. The quality of fuzzy information is determined by the experience, knowledge and intuition of DM experts and, if necessary, can be improved through additional surveys and examinations [37].

We note the importance when solving a more general decision-making problem of taking into account production management and additional restrictions, such as restrictions on different resources, performance indicators, or expert knowledge, so that decision-making methods provide more specific solutions.

We present the Pareto front in a graphical format for this decision-making problem with fuzzy restrictions in the presence of two criteria, $f_i(\mathbf{x})$, $j = 1,2$, estimating the yield of stable gasoline and gas from the stabilization column.

The set of Pareto optimal non-dominated solutions is called the Pareto front (boundary). Non-dominated solutions are a pair of solutions x and x', for which $\exists i \in \overline{1,K}$: $f_i(x) > f_i(x') \wedge \exists j \in \overline{1,K}$, $j \neq i$: $f_j(x') > f_i(x)$. Pareto front P(X) includes points x satisfying the conditions $P(X) = \{x \in X:\{ x' \in X: x' \leq x,\ x' \neq x\} = 0\}$. The most obvious is the Pareto front, i.e., the compromise curve is presented for the case of two mutually contradictory criteria, as is the case of our task; for example, in the form of a graph (Figure 3).

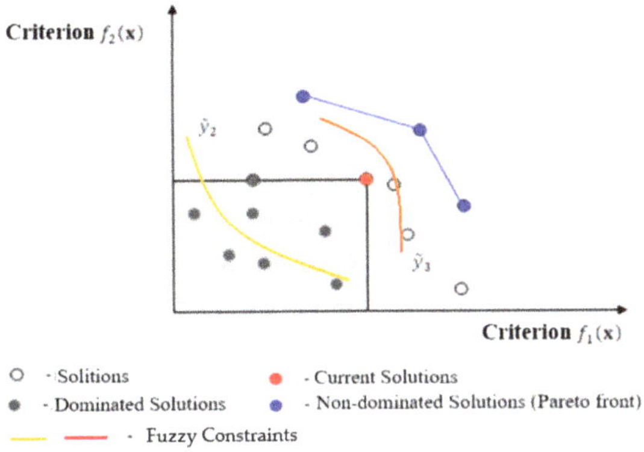

Figure 3. Pareto front for a two-criteria decision problem with two fuzzy constraints.

Having normalized local criteria and based on the formulation of the problem of fuzzy multi-criteria decision making (1) and (2), based on the principles of MC and MM, problems (23) and (24) can be written in the following form:

$$\max_{\mathbf{x}\in X} \mu_C^1(\mathbf{x}), \tag{25}$$

$$X = \left\{\mathbf{x} : \mathbf{x} \in \Omega \wedge \arg\left(\mu_C^2(\mathbf{x}) \geq \mu_R^2\right) \wedge \arg\left(\max_{\mathbf{x}\in X}\min_{q}(\beta_q \mu_q(\mathbf{x})), q = \overline{1,2}\right)\right\}, \tag{26}$$

where $\mu_C^1(x)$ is the main criterion, in our case, the yield of stable gasoline, and its value is determined by the model y_1 (7); $\mu_C^2(x)$ is the criterion estimating the gas yield, determined by the model y_2 (8), counted as a constraints; μ_R^2 is the boundary value set by the DM for the gas outlet, in our case $\mu_R^2 = 28$ m^3/h; β_q, $q = 1,2$ are weight coefficients of fuzzy constraints; and $\mu_q(x)$, $q = 1,2$ are membership functions that evaluate the degree of fulfillment of fuzzy constraints.

The problem of fuzzy multicriteria decision making (25) and (26) for controlling the operating modes of the C-8 gasoline stabilization column based on the models obtained in Section 3 can be rewritten as a problem of fuzzy mathematical programming:

$$y_1 = 111.78 - 0.047x_1 + 0.13x_2 - 0.05x_3 - 0.01x_4 - 43.073x_5 - 0.003x_1^2 + 0.011x_2^2 - 0.001x_1x_2 + 0.022x_2x_4 \rightarrow \max$$

under constraints:

$$y_2 = 32.804 + 0.406x_1 - 0.302x_2 + 0.113x_3 - 0.084x_4 + 0.085x_5 - 0.001x_1^2 + 0.00007x_2^2 - 0.002x_2x_4 \geq 28;$$

$$y_3 = 243.06 - 0.04x_1 - 0.057x_2 - 0.002x_3 + 0.001x_4 - 50.27x_5 - 0.001x_1^2 - 0.001x_2^2 - 0.0002x_1x_2 + 0.011x_2x_4 \gtrsim 30;$$

$$y_4 = 15.87 + 0.05x_1 - 0.087x_2 + 0.0004x_3 + 0.032x_4 + 23.33x_5 + 0.0003x_1^2 - 0.002x_2^2 - 0.011x_1x_2 + 0.01x_1x_4 \lesssim 180;$$

$$140 \leq x_1 \leq 160; 250 \leq x_2 \leq 260; 210 \leq x_3 \leq 330; 70 \leq x_4 \leq 90; 0.70 \leq x_5 \leq 1.00.$$

Let us present the results of solving the decision-making problem in a fuzzy environment (25) and (26) based on the MC+MM heuristic method proposed in Section 2.

1. The main criterion and the number of steps along each q-th coordinate are $p_q, q = \overline{1,2} : p_1 = 5$; and $p_2 = 4$; an order of priority of local criteria $I_C = \{1,2\}$ is determined, where 1 is the priority of the main criterion $\mu_C^1(\mathbf{x})$, estimating the yield of stable gasoline, 2—the priority of the criterion estimating the yield of gas from C-8 column;

2. DM introduced the value of the weight vector $\boldsymbol{\beta} = (0.55, 0.35)$, reflecting the mutual importance of fuzzy constraints on the beginning of the boil and the end of the boil of the produced stable gasoline.
3. DM has assigned a boundary value for the local criterion μ_R^2, which is taken into account as constraints: $\mu_R^2 = 8\ \mathrm{m}^3/\mathrm{h}$;.
4. To change the coordinates of the vector $\boldsymbol{\beta}$ the steps $h_1 = \frac{1}{p_1} = \frac{1}{5} = 0.20, h_2 = \frac{1}{4} = 0.25$ are calculated.
5. A set of weight vectors $\boldsymbol{\beta}^1, \boldsymbol{\beta}^2, \ldots, \boldsymbol{\beta}^N, N = (5+1)\cdot(4+1) = 30$ is constructed by changing the coordinates in the interval [0, 1] with steps $h_1 = 0.20$ and $h_2 = 0.25$.
6. The term set is defined, which is fuzzy and described by the instructions for the constraints: "not lower than 30 °C", "not higher than 180 °C".
7. Membership functions of fuzzy constraints $\mu_q(\mathbf{x}), q = \overline{1,2}$ are constructed, which are presented in the form of exponential functions $\mu_q^t(\tilde{y}_j) = \exp\left(Q_{\tilde{B}_j}^t \left| \left(y_j - y_j^{md}\right)^{N_{\tilde{B}_j}^t} \right|\right)$, where t is the quantum number; $Q_{\tilde{B}_j}^t$—is a parameter characterizing the degree of fuzziness, whose value is identified when constructing the membership function; $N_{\tilde{B}_j}^t$ is a coefficient that allows more accurate approximation of the graph of the membership function; y_j^{md} is a fuzzy variable that more closely matches the selected term and is defined by the expression $\mu_{\tilde{B}_j}^t(\tilde{y}_j) = \max_j \mu_{\tilde{B}_j}^t(y_j)$.

$$\mu_1^1(\tilde{y}_3) = \exp\left(0.5\left|(y_3 - 25)^{0.6}\right|\right); \mu_2^1(\tilde{y}_3) = \exp\left(0.5\left|(y_3 - 170)^{0.6}\right|\right);$$

$$\mu_1^1(\tilde{y}_3) = \exp\left(0.7\left|(y_3 - 30)^{0.8}\right|\right); \mu_2^2(\tilde{y}_3) = \exp\left(0.6\left|(y_3 - 180)^{0.7}\right|\right);$$

$$\mu_1^1(\tilde{y}_3) = \exp\left(0.8\left|(y_3 - 35)^{0.9}\right|\right); \mu_2^3(\tilde{y}_3) = \exp\left(0.7\left|(y_3 - 190)^{0.8}\right|\right);$$

8. On the basis of mathematical models of the C-8 stabilization column and using the Manager software package, a search was made for the maximum of the main criterion, taking into account the imposed constraints. In each iteration, the current solutions are determined: the vector of control and disturbing actions $\mathbf{x}(\mu_R^i, \boldsymbol{\beta})$, maximizing the main criterion $\mu_C^1(\mathbf{x}(\mu_R^i, \boldsymbol{\beta}))$, providing the required value of the criterion $\mu_C^2(\mathbf{x}(\mu_R^i, \boldsymbol{\beta}))$ and degrees of fulfillment of fuzzy constraints $\mu_1(\mathbf{x}(\mu_R^i, \boldsymbol{\beta})), \mu_2(\mathbf{x}(\mu_R^i, \boldsymbol{\beta}))$.
9. The DM analyzes the received solutions. Since, in the first four iterations, the DM is not satisfied with the current solutions, in order to improve the solution, he corrects μ_R^2 and/or β_1, β_2 and the transition returns to step 8. On the 5th cycle, results are obtained that satisfy the DM and the transition to the next step 10 was carried out.
10. The best solutions selected by DM are derived: the optimal value $\mathbf{x}^*(\mu_R^2, \boldsymbol{\beta})$, which maximizes the main criterion $\mu_0^1(\mathbf{x}^*(\mu_R^2, \boldsymbol{\beta}))$, providing the required criterion value $\mu_0^2(x^*(\mu_R^2, \boldsymbol{\beta}))$ and maximum degrees of fulfillment of fuzzy constraints $\mu_1(x^*(\mu_R^2, \boldsymbol{\beta}))$, $\mu_2(x^*(\mu_R^2, \boldsymbol{\beta}))$. These results are listed in Table 1.

Table 1. Comparison of the results of optimizing the operating modes of the stabilization column according to the proposed MC + MM heuristic method, according to the known method and real data on the object optimization.

Criteria and Constraint Values	Known Results [49]	Proposed MC + IP Heuristic Method	Real Data
The yield of stable gasoline—the main criterion $y_1 = f_1(\mathbf{x}^*)$, m^3/h	125.3	128.7	126
Gas yield $y_2 = f_2(\mathbf{x}^*)$, m^3/h	-	28.5	28.3
Fuzzy constraint on the onset of boiling of stable gasoline, $\mu_1(\mathbf{x}) = y_3$, °C	-	$\mu_1(\mathbf{x}) = 1$, $y_3 = 35$	$(33)^L$
Fuzzy constraint at the end of boiling of stable gasoline, $\mu_2(\mathbf{x}) = y_4$, °C	-	$\mu_2(\mathbf{x}) = 1$, $y_4 = 178$	$(180)^L$
Optimal values of input and operating parameters $\mathbf{x}^* = (x_1^*, x_2^*, x_3^*, x_4^*, x_5^*)$: x_1^*—temperature of the top of the C-8 stabilization column, °C;	160	157	158
x_2^*—temperature of the bottom of the C-8 stabilization column, °C;	258	250	253
x_3^*—raw material consumption, m^3/h;	158	158	158
x_4^*—raw material temperature, °C;	90	87	88
x_5^*—raw material density, kg/cm^2.	0.95	0.95	0.95

Notes: $(\cdot)^L$ means that these quality indicators are determined by the laboratory and require human participation; (-) means that these indicators cannot be determined by known methods. The solution search time in the compared methods is the same: about one minute.

Consider the results of the sensitivity analysis to the problem from the point of view of the variation of the membership function of fuzzy constraints in paragraph 7. The variation in the value of the membership function built according to the exponential formula proposed in this paragraph and the shape of its graph depends on the tuning coefficients $Q^t_{\tilde{B}_j}$ и $N^t_{\tilde{B}_j}$. The variation in the values of these coefficients allows quickly (roughly) and slowly (exactly) selecting the values that are more consistent with the graph of the constructed membership function. Thus, the values of the membership function are sensitive to changes in the values of these coefficients, allowing the building of membership functions that are more adequate for fuzzy descriptions.

Let us give an illustration of the contradictory nature of the set of goals (criteria). The goals of the solved problem are to maximize the value $f_i(\mathbf{x})$, $j = 1,2$, i.e., criteria that estimate the volume of stable gasoline and gas from the outlet of the stabilization column using the developed models (7), (8). At the same time, it is necessary to maximize $f_i(\mathbf{x})$, $j = 1,2$ taking into account the imposed fuzzy restrictions on the quality of gasoline, estimated according to the models (10) and (11) developed in Section 3.1.

It follows from the general material balance of products that an increase in the volume of stable gasoline leads to a decrease in the volume of gas, i.e., these criteria are mutually contradictory. In addition, maximizing the volume of gasoline on a Pareto optimal set leads to a deterioration in its quality indicators. An illustration of the contradictory nature of the criteria for problem (23) and (24) is shown in Figure 4.

When determining the main criterion, the value of the weight vectors and the boundary value of the local criterion transferred to the composition of the restriction, eight specialists in the object of study and the subject area participated. The participants included three senior operators of the primary oil refinery (DM) and five subject area experts (head, technologist and plant engineer, as well as two specialists of the plant laboratory for determining the quality of gasoline). All participants are employees of the Atyrau Oil Refinery, where primary oil-refining units operate; their age ranged from 35 to 50 years; in terms of gender, two participants from the laboratory are female and the rest are male.

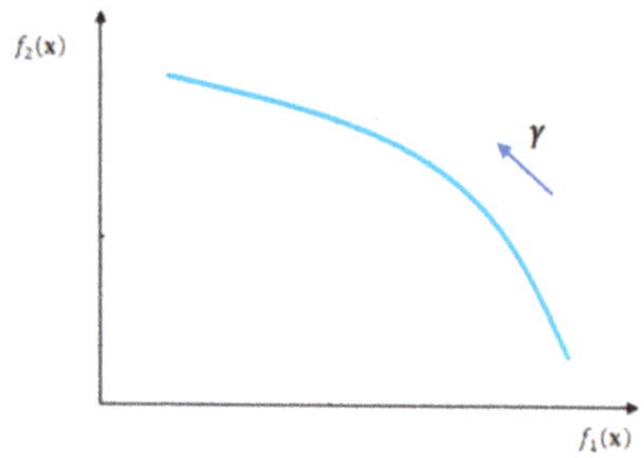

Figure 4. Contradictory character of criteria $f_1(\mathbf{x})$ and $f_2(\mathbf{x})$, γ—parameter that takes into account the ratio of the importance of criteria (weight coefficients).

In Table 1, for comparison, in addition to the well-known results of optimizing the operating modes of the stabilization column under deterministic conditions [49] and the results of fuzzy optimization, real optimization data from the object of study are also listed. Real data were obtained experimentally on the C-8 column of the EDP-AVT Atyrau refinery.

Theoretical contributions of this research are formulated and theorems on the adequacy of fuzzy models are proved, as well as by modifying, combining various principles of optimality, new formulations of problems of fuzzy multi-criteria decision making are formulated and heuristic methods for their solution are developed. The business contribution of the study lies in the ability of the DM to make more efficient decisions in a fuzzy environment based on their preferences, while also taking into account the current production situation and the product market. In addition, the proposed approach can be exported to control the operation modes of other fuzzy objects of various industries.

4. Discussion

The formulated problem statements for fuzzy multi-criteria decision making (1) and (2) and (3) and (4) are based on the modification and combination of various principles of optimization for fuzziness and for choosing the best compromise solution depending on the production situation. The proposed heuristic methods for solving the formulated problems of fuzzy multi-criteria decision making are iterative and based on the involvement of a DM in the decision process and in the choice of the final decision. At the same time, the DM selects the best solutions based on his preferences, experience, knowledge and intuition, as well as taking into account the current situation in production and the market.

The proposed heuristic method for the problem of fuzzy multi-criteria choice (1) and (2) is obtained by modifying the principles of optimization of the main criterion (for criteria) and maximin (for fuzzy constraints). This method is effectively used where there is a possibility of highlighting the main criterion, determining the boundary values for the rest of the local criteria and the need for guaranteed degrees of fulfillment of fuzzy constraints. Furthermore, the PO+IP heuristic method for solving problem (3) and (4) is based on the modification and combination of the Pareto optimality principles and the ideal point method. Accordingly, this method allows to effectively solve the problem of fuzzy multi-criteria decision making with the possibility of DM involvement to determine the weight coefficients of local criteria and the ideal points—the degrees of fulfillment of fuzzy constraints.

The structure of mathematical models of the C-8 stabilization column of the EDP-AVT primary oil-refining unit, used to make decisions on managing its operating modes, has been identified based on modified methods for the sequential inclusion of regressors. In addition, the identifications of crisp and fuzzy model parameters are identified using the REGRESS software package [50] which implements the least-squares method.

The formulated problem of fuzzy multi-criteria decision making for controlling the operating modes of the stabilization column based on its developed models is presented in the form of an FMP problem. Then, the obtained FMP problem was solved based on the proposed MC+MM heuristic method and the Manager software package with the participation of an experienced operator DM of the EDP-AVT Atyrau refinery primary oil-processing unit.

Analysis of the comparison results shows that the proposed fuzzy decision-making approach based on the heuristic MC+MM method allows obtaining better and more efficient solutions compared to the known deterministic method. In addition, the results of the fuzzy approach more closely match the real data obtained experimentally when optimizing the control object. As a result of the analysis and discussion of the data in Table 1, as an advantage of the proposed approach to solving problems of fuzzy decision making to control the operating modes of the object of study, we can note:

- the yield of the target product, stable gasoline (the main criterion), is increased by 3.4 m^3/h (2.7%), or allows the production of 81.6 m^3 more stable gasoline per day;
- The MC+MM heuristic method allows determining the yield of a by-product—gas from the top of the stabilization column—which makes it possible to determine the material balance of the column;
- the proposed fuzzy approach to solving decision-making problems allows estimation of the degree of fulfillment of fuzzy constraints ($\mu_1(\mathbf{x})$, $\mu_2(\mathbf{x})$), which are not determined by other methods;
- the proposed approach makes it possible to obtain better solutions with lower thermal energy (temperature), which ensures the effectiveness of the approach;

In addition, when solving the problem of fuzzy decision-making to control the operating modes of the object of study based on the proposed heuristic method, the adequacy of the decision is increased. This is achieved by taking into account additional fuzzy information (experience, knowledge, intelligence of the DM and experts) that more fully describes the real situation without idealization.

5. Study Limitations

The main limitations of the proposed heuristic approach to solving problems of multi-criteria decision making in a fuzzy environment include some difficulties in assessing the degree of belonging of fuzzy constraints to fuzzy sets, adequately describing them and possible difficulties for less experienced DMs in the process of choosing the best solution.

In the future, these limitations can be eliminated by developing a special system for assessing the degree of belonging of fuzzy indicators to fuzzy sets and preparing and training DMs for the decision-making process. For the development of this study, it is planned to automate and algorithmize the process of evaluating and choosing the best solution as much as possible.

6. Conclusions

The problems of setting and solving problems of fuzzy multi-criteria decision making for controlling the operating modes of technological systems on the basis of a heuristic approach are studied. Details of the main findings of the study and conclusions include:

(1) By modifying the principles of the main criterion and maximin, as well as Pareto optimality and the ideal point, mathematical formulations of fuzzy multi-criteria decision-making problems are obtained and heuristic methods for their solution are developed. The proposed heuristic method, in contrast to the well-known ones based on the transformation of the original fuzzy problem into a set of crisp problems, allows the fuzzy problem to be set and solved in a fuzzy environment without converting to crisp problems. Due to the preservation and maximum use of the collected fuzzy information, i.e., the knowledge, experience and intuition of expert DMs, the proposed methods allow obtaining more efficient and adequate solutions to a production problem in a fuzzy environment;

(2) Based on the adaptation of the methods of successive inclusion of regressors and least squares, effective mathematical models of the C-8 stabilization column of the EDP-AVT primary oil refining unit were developed, taking into account the available

fuzzy information. The main reason for choosing the method of sequential inclusion of regressors in our case is the availability of a priori information about the structure of the developed models, which facilitates the process of developing models;

(3) The questions of determining the adequacy of fuzzy models are investigated and the corresponding theorems and their proofs are given.

(4) Based on the developed models and the proposed heuristic method MC + MM, the problem of two-criteria decision making with fuzzy constrains for controlling the operating modes of the C-8 stabilization column is solved

The main contribution of this study to the development of decision-making methods in a fuzzy environment and the novelty of the proposed heuristic methods for solving such problems lies in the effective use of knowledge, experience and intuition of DMs and experts in solving fuzzy problems of multicriteria optimization. The proposed approach, due to the maximum use of available fuzzy information in the form of DM experience and intuition, allows obtaining more efficient and adequate solutions when making a decision on the management of real production facilities.

As a direction for further research, the authors plan to:

- develop methods for fuzzy multi-criteria decision making based on the modification for fuzziness of other principles of optimality; for example, the lexicographic principle of optimality, the principles of equality, quasi-equality, concessions, etc. Such methods can effectively solve decision-making problems when the proposed methods are difficult due to a lack or absence of the necessary information for their application. Thus, the DM will be able to choose the most efficient method for the fuzzy decision problem under various possible situations and depending on the availability of various types of initial information;
- create and apply neuro-fuzzy systems [51,52], which allow combining the learning ability of a neural network with the representation of fuzzy logic knowledge, which will help to further enhance the effect of solving decision-making problems under conditions of uncertainty;
- apply the following methods to solve similar problems of decision making: Analytic Hierarchy Process (AHP), Elimination and Choice Translating REality (ELECTRE), Preference Ranking Organization Method for Enrichment Evaluation (PROMETHEE), Fuzzy TOPSIS [53–55].

The future field of application of the obtained research results is solving decision-making problems for controlling the operating modes of other complex, fuzzy described objects of oil refining, petrochemistry, metallurgy and other industries.

Author Contributions: Conceptualization, B.O. and K.O.; methodology, K.O., Y.O. and Z.A.; validation, V.M. and B.O.; formal analysis, K.O. and S.S.; investigation, K.O. and L.S.; resources, V.M., L.S. and Y.O.; data curation, Z.A. and Z.K.; writing—original draft preparation, K.O.; writing—review and editing, B.O., K.O., Y.O. and Z.A.; visualization, S.S. and L.S.; supervision, B.O.; funding acquisition, Z.K. All authors have read and agreed to the published version of the manuscript.

Funding: The Science Committee of the Ministry of Education and Science of the Republic of Kazakhstan funded this research (Grant No. AP08855680—Intelligent decision support system for controlling the operating modes of the catalytic reforming unit).

Data Availability Statement: Not applicable.

Conflicts of Interest: The authors declare no conflict of interest.

References

1. Vakhrushev, A.V.; Omari, V.; Mukbaniani, O.V.; Susanto, H. *Chemical Technology and Informatics in Chemistry with Applications*; Apple Academic Press: Waretown, NJ, USA, 2021; pp. 1–376.
2. Fayaz, M.; Ahmad, S.; Ullah, I.; Kim, D. A Blended Risk Index Modeling and Visualization Based on Hierarchical Fuzzy Logic for Water Supply Pipelines Assessment and Management. *Processes* **2018**, *6*, 61. [CrossRef]
3. Orazbayev, B.B.; Ospanov, Y.A.; Orazbayeva, K.N.; Serimbetov, B.A. Multicriteria Optimization in Control of a Chemical-technological System for Production of Benzene with Fuzzy Information. *Bull. Tomsk Polytech. Univ. Geo Assets Eng.* **2019**, *330*, 182–194.
4. Mornati, F. Pareto Optimality in the work of Pareto. *Eur. J. Soc. Sci.* **2013**, *51*, 65–82. [CrossRef]
5. Ng, Y.-K. Pareto Optimality. In *Welfare Economics*; Springer: Berlin/Heidelberg, Germany, 2004; pp. 26–46.
6. Petrov, T.I.; Safin, A.R.; Nizamiev, M.F.; Basenko, V.R. Application of genetic algorithm in the development of software for selecting materials in the optimization of synchronous motors. *Kazan State Power Eng. Univ. Bull.* **2022**, *14*, 96–105.
7. Lebedeva, A.V.; Pakulina, A.N. *Practicum on Computational Methods*; Part 1; BHV: St. Petersburg, Russia, 2021; pp. 1–156.
8. Li, X.; Zhang, H.; Song, S. A self-adaptive mating restriction strategy based on survival length for evolutionary multiobjective optimization. *Swarm Evol. Comput.* **2018**, *43*, 31–49. [CrossRef]
9. Majumder, S.; Saha, B.; Anand, P.; Kar, S.; Pal, T. Uncertainty based genetic algorithm with varying population for random fuzzy maximum flow problem. *Expert Syst.* **2018**, *35*, e12264. [CrossRef]
10. Liguo, T.; Novikova, S.V. Application of the step learning method for the evolutionary algorithm in problems of multi-criteria optimization. *Kazan State Power Eng. Univ. Bull.* **2022**, *14*, 100–111.
11. He, C.; Huang, S.; Cheng, R.; Tan, K.C.; Jin, Y. Evolutionary Multi-Objective Optimization Driven by Generative Adversarial Networks (GANs). *IEEE Trans. Cybern.* **2020**, *51*, 3129–3142. [CrossRef]
12. Li, K.; Kwong, S. A general framework for evolutionary multi-objective optimization via manifold learning. *Neurocomputing* **2014**, *146*, 65–74. [CrossRef]
13. Zhang, H.; Zhou, A.; Song, S.; Zhang, Q.; Gao, X.Z.; Zhang, J. A Self- Organizing Multi-objective Evolutionary Algorithm. *IEEE Trans. Evol. Comput.* **2016**, *20*, 792–806. [CrossRef]
14. Gu, F.; Liu, H.L.; Tan, K.C. A multi-objective evolutionary algorithm using dynamic weight design method. *Int. J. Innov. Comput. Inf. Control* **2012**, *8*, 3677–3688.
15. Zhang, Q.; Zhou, A.; Jin, Y. RM-MEDA: A regularity model-based multi-objective estimation of distribution algorithm. *IEEE Trans. Evol. Comput.* **2008**, *12*, 41–63. [CrossRef]
16. Karshenas, H.; Santana, R.; Bielza, C.; Larranaga, P. Multi-objective estimation of distribution algorithm based on joint modeling of objectives and variables. *IEEE Trans. Evol. Comput.* **2014**, *18*, 519–542. [CrossRef]
17. Faruntsev, S.D. Decomposition method for real time optimization tasks in multilevel chemical-technological systems based on identification of compromise sets. *Dyn. Syst. Mech. Mach.* **2019**, *7*, 161–170. [CrossRef]
18. Shim, V.A.; Tan, K.C.; Cheong, C.Y.; Chia, J.Y. Enhancing the scalability of multi-objective optimization via restricted Boltzmann machine-based estimation of distribution algorithm. *Inf. Sci.* **2013**, *248*, 191–213. [CrossRef]
19. Li, X.; Zhang, H.; Song, S. MOEA/D with the online agglomerative clustering based self-adaptive mating restriction strategy. *Neurocomputing* **2019**, *339*, 77–93. [CrossRef]
20. Cheng, R.; Jin, Y.; Narukawa, K.; Sendhoff, B. A multi-objective evolutionary algorithm using Gaussian process-based inverse modeling. *IEEE Trans. Evol. Comput.* **2015**, *19*, 838–856. [CrossRef]
21. Abbas, S.H.; Hussain, Z.; Hussain, S.; Sharif, R.; Hussain, S. Intuitionistic fuzzy entropy and its applications to multicriteria decision-making with IF-TODIM. *J. Mech. Contin. Math. Sci.* **2021**, *16*, 99–119. [CrossRef]
22. Batool, N.; Hussain, S.; Kausar, N.; Munir, M.; Yi, M.R.; Li, M.; Khan, S. Decision-Making Under Incomplete Data: Intuitionistic Multi Fuzzy Ideals of Near-Ring Approach. *Decis. Mak. Appl. Manag. Eng.* **2023**, *6*, 1–19.
23. Zaychenko, Y.P. *Operation Research: Fuzzy Optimization*; Graduate School: Kyiv, Ukraine, 2015; pp. 1–195.
24. Kahraman, C. Multi-criteria decision-making methods and fuzzy sets. In *Fuzzy Multi-Criteria Decision-Making*; Springer: Berlin/Heidelberg, Germany, 2008; pp. 1–18.
25. Xia, M.; Zhang, F. Application of multi-parameter fuzzy optimization to enhance performance of a regulated two-stage turbocharged diesel engine operating at high altitude. *Energies* **2020**, *13*, 4278. [CrossRef]
26. Kumar, S.; Maity, S.R.; Patnaik, L. Optimization of wear parameters for duplex-tialn coated mdc-k tool steel using fuzzy mcdm techniques. *Oper. Res. Eng. Sci. Theory Appl.* **2022**, *5*, 40–67. [CrossRef]
27. Aliev, R.A.; Tserkovny, A.E.; Mamedova, G.A. *Production Management with Fuzzy Initial Information*; Energoatomizdat: Moscow, Russia, 1991; pp. 1–250.
28. Matveykin, V.G.; Dmitrievsky, B.S.; Kokuev, A.G.; Dzhambekov, A.M. Problem of Control of Catalytic Reforming and Method of its Solutions. *Bull. Tomsk Polytech. Univ. Geo Assets Eng.* **2019**, *330*, 59–67.
29. Salehizadeh, M.R.; Koohbijari, M.A.; Nouri, H.; Taşcıkaraoğlu, A.; Erdinç, O.; Catalão, J.P. Bi-Objective Optimization Model for Optimal Placement of Thyristor-Controlled Series Compensator Devices. *Energies* **2019**, *12*, 2601. [CrossRef]
30. Soltaniyan, S.; Salehizadeh, M.R.; Taşcıkaraoğlu, A.; Erdinç, O.; Catalão, J.P. An interactive multi-criteria decision-making framework between a renewable power plant planner and the independent system operator. *Sustain. Energy Grids Netw.* **2021**, *26*, 100447. [CrossRef]

31. Valiakhmetov, R.I. Application of heuristic algorithms in analyzing data to solve the problem of detection of electric centrifugal pumping units. *Bull. Tomsk Polytech. Univ. Geo Assets Eng.* **2018**, *329*, 159–167.
32. Suleimenov, E.B.; Tuleuov, Z.N. *Technological Regulations for the Installation of EDP-AVT 10/6-2*; Academic Press: Atyrau, Kazakhstan, 2019; pp. 1–117.
33. Rykov, A.S. *Search engine optimization. Methods of Deformable Configurations*; Sciences: Moscow, Russia, 1999; pp. 1–216.
34. Fuzzy Logic Toolbox. Available online: http://www.matlab.ru (accessed on 11 June 2023).
35. Ostrovsky, G.M.; Ziyatdinov, N.N.; Lapteva, T.V.; Silvestrova, A. Optimization of Chemical Process Design with Chance Constraints by an Iterative Partitioning Approach. *J. Ind. Eng. Chem.* **2015**, *54*, 3412–3437. [CrossRef]
36. Chen, Y.; He, L.; Li, J.; Zhang, F. Multi-criteria design of shale-gas-water supply chains and production systems towards optimal life cycle economics and greenhouse gas emissions under uncertainty. *Comput. Chem. Eng.* **2018**, *109*, 216–235. [CrossRef]
37. Lukianova, V.; Shutyak, Y.; Polozova, V. Expert assessment method in socio-economic research and Scales transformations. *Adv. Econ. Bus. Manag. Res.* **2019**, *99*, 355–360.
38. Boiko, Y. Methods of forming an expert assessment of the criteria of an information system for managing projects and programs. *Comput. Sci.* **2018**, *5*, 9–11. [CrossRef]
39. Zimmermann, H.-J. *Fuzzy Set Theory—And Its Applications, Fifth ed.*; Springer Science + Business Media, LLC: New York, NY, USA, 2018; pp. 1–525. [CrossRef]
40. Chen, F.; Qiu, X.; Alattas, K.A.; Mohammadzadeh, A.; Ghaderpour, E. A New Fuzzy Robust Control for Linear Parameter-Varying Systems. *Mathematic* **2022**, *10*, 3319. [CrossRef]
41. Chen, C.-T. Extensions of the TOPSIS for group decision-making under fuzzy environment. *Fuzzy Sets Syst.* **2020**, *114*, 1–9. [CrossRef]
42. Zhuang, W.; Li, Y.; Qiu, G. Statistical inference for a relaxation index of stochastic dominance under density ratio model. *J. Appl. Stat.* **2022**, *49*, 3804–3822. [CrossRef] [PubMed]
43. Zhao, Z.-W.; Wang, D.-H. Statistical inference for generalized random coefficient autoregressive model. *Math. Comput. Model.* **2012**, *56*, 152–166. [CrossRef]
44. Karmanov, F.I.; Ostreykovsky, V.A. *Statistical Methods for Processing Experimental Data Using the MathCad Package*; Infra-M: Moscow, Russia, 2017; pp. 1–287.
45. Orazbayev, B.; Zhumadillayeva, A.; Orazbayeva, K.; Iskakova, S.; Utenova, B.; Gazizov, F.; Ilyashenko, S.; Afanaseva, O. The System of Models and Optimization of Operating Modes of a Catalytic Reforming Unit Using Initial Fuzzy Information. *Energies* **2022**, *15*, 1573. [CrossRef]
46. Valeev, S.G. *Regression Modelling in the Processing of Observations*, 3rd ed.; Nauka: Moscow, Russia, 2017; pp. 1–272.
47. Yakovis, L.M.; Strongin, P.Y. Adaptive Identification of Control Objects in Systems with Standard Controllers. *J. Phys. Conf. Ser.* **2021**, *1864*, 012110. [CrossRef]
48. Tong, R.M. Analysis of fuzzy control algorithms using the relation matrix. *Int. J. Man-Mach. Stud.* **1976**, *8*, 679–686. [CrossRef]
49. Shumsky, V.M.; Zyryanova, L.A. *Engineering Tasks in Oil Refining and Petrochemistry*; MPC Publishing: Moscow, Russia, 2014; pp. 1–475.
50. Clark, A.; Kuznetsov, A.G. *REGRESS Software Package*; Oxford University: Oxford, UK, 2018; pp. 1–118.
51. Kar, S.; Das, S.; Ghosh, P.K. Applications of neuro fuzzy systems: A brief review and future outline. *Appl. Soft Comput.* **2014**, *15*, 243–259. [CrossRef]
52. Halgamuge, S.K.; Glesner, M. Neural networks in designing fuzzy systems for real world applications. *Fuzzy Sets Syst.* **1994**, *65*, 1–12. [CrossRef]
53. Wardana, R.W.; Garside, A.K.; Anggara, A.T. Integrated analytic hierarchy process and preference ranking organization method for enrichment evaluation II for supplier selection. *AIP Conf. Proc.* **2022**, *2453*, 020049. [CrossRef]
54. Bianchini, A. 3PL Provider Selection by AHP and TOPSIS methodology. *Benchmarking Int. J.* **2018**, *25*, 31–48. [CrossRef]
55. Radev, M. Using the TOPSIS Method to Evaluate Projects for Virtualization. *Izv. J. Union Sci.* **2017**, *2*, 234–241.

mathematics

MDPI

Article

An Effective Method of Equivalent Load-Based Time of Use Electricity Pricing to Promote Renewable Energy Consumption

Xiaoqing Zeng [1,*], Zilin He [2,*], Yali Wang [1], Yongfei Wu [1] and Ao Liu [1]

1 School of Economics and Management, Changsha University of Science and Technology, Changsha 410075, China; wyalijgxy@csust.edu.cn (Y.W.); wuyongfei@csust.edu.cn (Y.W.); la@stu.csust.edu.cn (A.L.)
2 College of Information Engineering, Inner Mongolia University of Technology, Hohhot 010051, China
* Correspondence: zengxq@csust.edu.cn (X.Z.); 202310204067@imut.edu.cn (Z.H.); Tel.: +86-013755000221 (X.Z.)

Abstract: The variability and intermittency inherent in renewable energy sources poses significant challenges to balancing power supply and demand, often leading to wind and solar energy curtailment. To address these challenges, this paper focuses on enhancing Time of Use (TOU) electricity pricing strategies. We propose a novel method based on equivalent load, which leverages typical power grid load and incorporates a responsibility weight for renewable energy consumption. The responsibility weight acts as an equivalent coefficient that accurately reflects renewable energy output, which facilitates the division of time periods and the development of a demand response model. Subsequently, we formulate an optimized TOU electricity pricing model to increase the utilization rate of renewable energy and reduce the peak–valley load difference of the power grid. To solve the TOU pricing optimization model, we employ the Social Network Search (SNS) algorithm, a metaheuristic algorithm simulating users' social network interactions to gain popularity. By incorporating the users' mood when expressing opinions, this algorithm efficiently identifies optimal pricing solutions. Our results demonstrate that the equivalent load-based method not only encourages renewable energy consumption but also reduces power generation costs, stabilizes the power grid load, and benefits power generators, suppliers, and consumers without increasing end users' electricity charges.

Keywords: renewable energy consumption; equivalent load; time of use pricing; demand response

MSC: 90B50

1. Introduction

In the last decade, there has been a remarkable surge in the deployment of renewable energy, a steady rise in its contribution to electricity generation, and a substantial decline in the cost of electricity production. According to data released by China's National Energy Administration, the installed capacity of renewable energy reached 1.213 billion kilowatts, accounting for 47.3% of the total installed capacity of national power generation by the end of 2022. The capacity of non-fossil fuel power generation has surpassed that of thermal power. In 2021, the guiding prices for newly built wind and photovoltaic power projects in many provinces of China were lower than the benchmark prices for thermal power generation, with the exception of Qinghai and Hainan province. Building a new type of power system dominated by renewable energy has become an inevitable choice.

The increasing integration of renewable energy, particularly wind and photovoltaic power, into the power system, has introduced significant operational challenges due to the unpredictable nature of their output and intermittency [1,2]. This has led to the emergence of wind and photovoltaic power curtailment, underscoring the imperative to enhance power utilization efficiency. Leveraging market incentive mechanisms to mobilize demand-side resources, boost renewable energy consumption, and alleviate operational pressures on the system is imperative [3]. Time of Use (TOU) pricing is a vital market mechanism for demand-side management, playing a crucial role in encouraging users to adjust their power loads, fostering user participation in maintaining power system balance, and increasing renewable energy consumption [4]. Previous studies have explored various aspects of demand response to promote renewable energy consumption [5]. The authors of [6] studied the operating mode of demand response from aspects such as trading and pricing mechanisms, financing, and technical services. The authors of [7] proposed an economic dispatch strategy considering the uncertainty of renewable energy and demand-side response. The authors of [8] established an optimization model for a virtual power plant, considering both reliable response loads and stochastic response loads, providing a means for user-side resources to participate in power dispatch. The authors of [9] used a Time of Use pricing strategy to guide users to participate in demand response, achieve linkage between photovoltaic power generation and thermal power generation, and improve the consumption capacity of photovoltaic power generation.

The context for applying TOU pricing is undergoing new changes: firstly, the proportion of renewable energy with uncertain output on the generation side is increasing, and the power consumption structure on the demand side is changing rapidly, with bidirectional fluctuations in power production and consumption; secondly, after a large amount of renewable energy is connected, the marginal supply costs decrease significantly with the changes in the output structure of the power. In addition, the diversification of power consumption structure and the large-scale application of new energy storage devices in power consumption have increased the demand response capability of users. Therefore, there is an urgent need to enhance the Time of Use (TOU) pricing mechanism [10], taking into full account the power structure on the generation side, accurately reflecting electricity costs, and avoiding price distortions. By forming effective market-oriented TOU pricing signals, this approach aims to motivate and encourage users to optimize their power usage, engage in peak shaving, improve the power supply–demand balance, and foster the development of green and low-carbon energy solutions.

From a demand response perspective, this paper designs a TOU pricing mechanism based on equivalent load, taking into account renewable energy consumption and generation costs, to facilitate the transition of the new power system from "source following load changes" to "source–load interaction". Firstly, a method for computing equivalent load is proposed based on the typical load of the power grid. By introducing the responsibility weight of renewable energy power consumption as the equivalent coefficient, an equivalent load curve reflecting the power source structure is generated. Secondly, a demand response model is constructed to eliminate the influence of natural trends, avoiding overestimating the degree of user response to electricity prices. Finally, with the lowest cost on the power source side as the optimization goal, and increasing the utilization rate of renewable energy and reducing the peak–valley difference of the power grid load as constraints, a Time of Use pricing optimization model is designed. The TOU pricing model is solved using a metaheuristic algorithm known as the Social Network Search (SNS) algorithm. By incorporating four innovative optimization operators (moods): Imitation, Conversation, Disputation, and Innovation, the SNS algorithm efficiently identifies optimal pricing solutions through expressed opinions. The method proposed in this paper not only encourages the uptake of renewable energy but also achieves a reduction in generation costs without increasing electricity expenses for users. Moreover, it contributes to the stabilization of power grid loads, leading to a mutually beneficial outcome for all stakeholders within the power system. Figure 1 serves as a comprehensive structural diagram that delineates the organization of this paper.

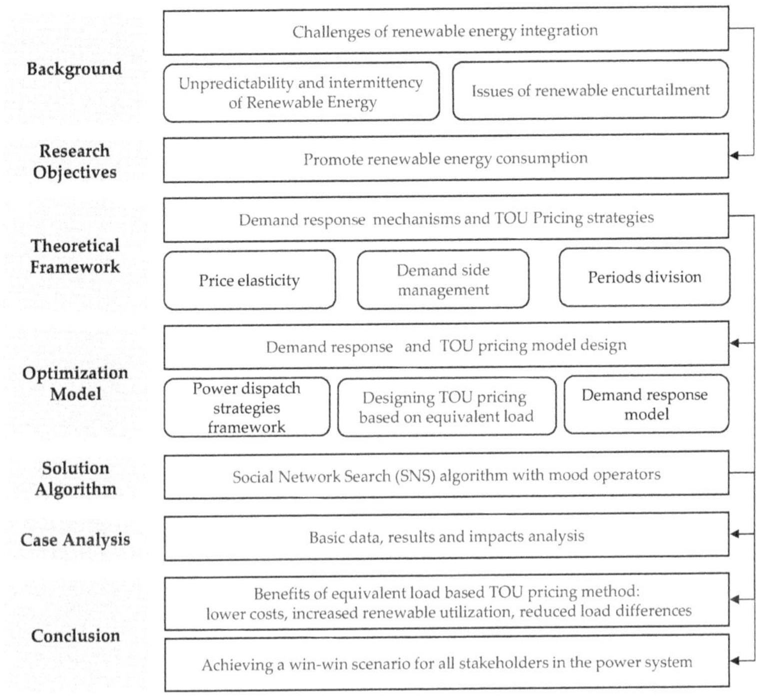

Figure 1. Structural diagram of Equivalent Load-based TOU Pricing optimization.

2. Time of Use Pricing Mechanism

Traditional Time of Use pricing is mainly designed based on the typical load curve of the power supply side. According to the typical load, the day is divided into peak, flat, and valley periods, with higher electricity prices during peak hours and lower electricity prices during off-peak and valley hours. Some provinces also set sharp prices, seasonal prices, or peak–load and off-peak–load prices. Through differentiated pricing, the pricing signals are fully utilized to instruct users to reduce electricity consumption as much as possible during peak hours and increase electricity usage during off-peak hours, achieving the goals of peak shaving, filling valleys, alleviating the imbalance between power supply and demand, and ensuring the security of the power system.

While electricity is homogeneous for users, there is a significant difference in the marginal generation cost of different energy types on the generation side. Compared to conventional thermal power, renewable energy has significantly reduced marginal generation costs due to the expansion of installed capacity and technological progress. Designing Time of Use pricing solely based on the typical load on the supply side poses challenges in effectively conveying the power source structure and cost information to the demand side. This could result in cost inversion, where users consume inexpensive electricity but pay higher prices. Figure 2 illustrates the multi-source output curve of a certain region's power generation side, showing higher total output from 10 a.m. to 12 p.m. During this period, if Time of Use pricing is designed based solely on the typical load, increasing electricity prices may not be conducive to the consumption of photovoltaic power, which peaks during these hours.

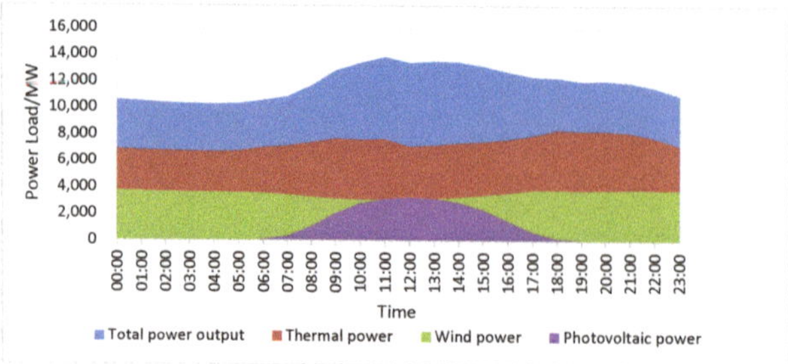

Figure 2. Energy output curve at power generation side.

Therefore, it is necessary to optimize the traditional Time of Use pricing design method based on the typical load of the power grid, taking into account factors such as the consumption of renewable energy and generation-side costs. In fact, since the issuance of the "Notice on Further Improving the Time of Use Pricing Mechanism" (Development and Reform Price [2021] No. 1093), various regions have continuously optimized Time of Use pricing policies based on specific circumstances and reasonably divided time periods. Nationwide, the period from 23:00 to 7:00 is mostly set as the valley period at night; however, in many provinces (regions), valley prices are implemented during midday when renewable energy output is relatively high. Shandong province has even divided 2–3 h of deep valley periods based on seasons. Time of Use pricing design should take into account the energy structure on the generation side.

2.1. Equivalent Load Considering Renewable Energy Consumption

Due to the volatility and intermittency of renewable energy output, its uncertainty over time, and its uneven distribution in space, significant challenges are posed to the balance of electrical power and the safe and reliable operation of a new power system. Optimizing the design of a Time of Use pricing mechanism to guide users to consume more electricity during peak periods of renewable energy output, and transforming the power balance mode from power generation tracking load to source-load interaction, are crucial for enhancing renewable energy consumption, promoting structural reforms on the power supply side, and driving the high-quality development of electric power.

Time of Use (TOU) pricing is primarily developed based on the power grid load curve and focuses on optimizing various types of loads such as typical load, baseline load, quasi-load, net load, and equivalent load. The typical load refers to the average or expected electricity load on the grid under normal conditions. The baseline load is the amount of electricity that would have been consumed without any interventions. Quasi-load is defined by the ideal load shape that the system aims to achieve. Net load represents the actual electricity load on the grid after subtracting the generation from renewable sources like solar and wind. The equivalent load proposed in this paper is a theoretical load, composed by considering the contribution and variability of renewable energy sources. In reference [11], a TOU pricing optimization model uses a BP neural network and grey prediction method to forecast the typical load curve, taking into account factors like load development and user behavior. Reference [12] discusses demand response by classifying it into two types: baseline and quasi-load. The baseline type assesses user contributions by assuming a baseline value for times when they do not participate in demand response, using methods such as averaging or regression of load data. Although adjustment factors are introduced to enhance prediction accuracy, establishing a reliable baseline remains a challenge, particularly in gaining user acceptance. The quasi-load type evaluates user contributions based on the ideal load shape provided by the system, as noted in references [13,14]. This load is determined by the demand response center based on overall network operation parameters, aiming to minimize operating costs and enhance renewable energy consumption. However, this model does not account for the impact of uncertainty factors and fails to capture the benefits of complementary user load. Despite proposals for dynamic self-organizing aggregation solutions, their practical application remains complex.

Many scholars base their Time of Use pricing designs on net load [15–17], which directly corresponds to the high-cost non-renewable energy output. In reference [15], an autoregressive moving average method is used for wind speed simulation, and a segmented function relationship between wind power output and wind speed is determined using historical data. The wind power output is then obtained, and the system's net load, with the goal of minimizing the peak–valley difference in the expected value of net load generated by conventional units after complete wind power consumption, is used as the target function for Time of Use pricing model optimization. However, this method assumes "complete wind power consumption" as a prerequisite in the optimization objective, which does not fully align with reality, and it does not indicate how the design of a Time of Use pricing mechanism can promote consumption. Reference [16] refers to the net load curve obtained by subtracting wind and photovoltaic power generation output from the grid load curve as the equivalent load curve. Equivalent load is used as the optimization target for Time of Use pricing, dividing the equivalent load curve into periods using fuzzy membership functions. It suggests that implementing new Time of Use pricing will encourage consumers to change their electricity usage habits and amounts, leading to a decrease in user comfort. The paper introduces two main concepts, "load transfer rate" and "user comfort", considering consumer psychology. It transforms the optimization objectives of minimizing peak–valley differences and maximizing user comfort into a single objective through linear weighting conversion, and uses a genetic algorithm for optimization, but it does not provide principles and methods for determining weighting factors, nor does it compare the improvement in renewable energy consumption before and after optimization. Reference [17] models peak–valley Time of Use pricing optimization based on the contributions of load and new energy output to the "duck curve" membership degree during different periods. This method aims to maximize renewable energy consumption under the constraint that the total electricity cost change before and after optimization is between 0–1%, but it does not consider the impact on the peak–valley load difference in the power grid and generation-side costs.

The limitation of the net load method is that the net load is only a part of the grid supply load, making it unsuitable for period division based on the net load. Moreover, the improvement in the peak–valley difference of the net load does not necessarily indicate a better effect on promoting renewable energy consumption. Considering the advantages and limitations of various load curves, this paper designs an equivalent load indicator, provides its computation method, and conducts Time of Use pricing optimization based on the equivalent load.

2.1.1. Definition and Computation of Equivalent Load

The term "equivalent" refers to a comprehensive indicator or value equivalent to a specific numerical value, such as the "pollution equivalent" measuring different pollutants' environmental impact, or the "equivalent electricity price" considering integrated capacity costs and electricity costs. Drawing on the basic idea of "equivalence", the load indicator considering renewable energy consumption and transformed through computation is defined as the "equivalent load". Unlike the power grid's typical load, the equivalent load is computed by considering various factors that influence the demand and supply dynamics of the power grid, particularly focusing on the contribution and variability of renewable energy sources. By introducing the responsibility weight of renewable energy consumption as the equivalent coefficient and basing it on the typical load, the equivalent load is adjusted according to the proportion of renewable energy in the total energy mix, effectively weighting the renewable energy output more heavily when it is available in abundance and less during scarcity. The total electricity corresponding to the equivalent load curve and the typical load curve is the same; hence, it is called "equivalent load". The equivalent load curve is significant because it provides a more accurate representation of the actual load on the grid that accounts for renewable energy fluctuations. By doing so, it allows for a TOU pricing strategy that not only responds to traditional demand patterns but also aligns closely with the availability of renewable energy, encouraging a more efficient and sustainable energy usage pattern.

The computation method of equivalent load is as follows:

Step One: Standardize the typical load on the supply side using the Min–Max normalization method, mapping the load data to a value between [0, 1], making it dimensionless and comparable across different scales or units:

$$L(t)' = \frac{L(t) - \min(L)}{\max(L) - \min(L)} \tag{1}$$

where $L(t)'$ is the standardized typical power grid load at time t; L is the typical power grid load, $L(t)$ is the power grid load at time t, and $\max(L)$ and $\min(L)$ are the maximum and minimum values of the typical power grid load.

Step Two: Standardize the renewable energy output on the generation side using the Max–Min method to [0, 1]:

$$L_r(t)' = \frac{\max(L_r) - L_r(t)}{\max(L_r) - \min(L_r)} \tag{2}$$

where $L_r(t)'$ is the standardized renewable energy consumption at time t; $L_r(t)$ is the renewable energy consumption at time t, and $\max(L_r)$ and $\min(L_r)$ are the maximum and minimum values of the renewable energy consumption.

The Max–Min method inversely scales the values, where higher original values are translated into lower normalized values, and vice versa. This inverse scaling is particularly advantageous in a demand-response context, as lower normalized values correspond to periods of high renewable energy production. This alignment encourages increased energy usage during these periods, promoting the consumption of renewable energy when it is most abundant.

Step Three: Combine the two standardized values from steps One and Two using the renewable energy consumption responsibility weight ω with an adjustable coefficient β to obtain the standardized equivalent load:

$$L_e(t)' = (1 - \beta\omega)L(t)' + \beta\omega L_r(t)' \tag{3}$$

where $L_e(t)'$ is the standardized equivalent load at time t, $L_e(t)' \in [0, 1]$; ω is the renewable energy equivalent coefficient; β is the adjustment coefficient.

Step Four: Restore the standardized equivalent load $L_e(t)'$ using Formula (4) to obtain the equivalent load $L_e(t)$ at time t:

$$L_e(t) = \frac{L_e(t)' \times (\sum_t^N \delta(t)L(t) - N\delta(t)\min(L))}{\sum_t^N \delta(t)L_e(t)'} + \min(L) \tag{4}$$

where $L_e(t)$ is the equivalent load at time t, $\delta(t)$ is the unit interval when sampling load data, typically 1 h, so N =24.

The typical load $L(t)$ can be provided by the local power company or computed based on the actual load of the power grid. Computation methods include the maximum daily load method, mean method, weighted average method, fuzzy C-means clustering algorithm, etc. [18]. Some scholars have proposed methods that consider grid load data and fit the typical load based on a normal distribution [19]. These methods are complex, and since determining the typical load is not the focus of this research, this paper simplifies the process by collecting the daily load data and calculating the typical load $L(t)$ using the mean method.

2.1.2. Influences of Parameters

As indicated by Equation (3), the value of the standardized equivalent load $L_e(t)'$ is affected by parameters ω and β. The renewable energy equivalent coefficient ω is directly taken as the renewable energy power consumption responsibility weight value published annually by the national energy regulatory authority. The computation of ω is shown in Equation (5):

$$\omega = \frac{\sum_i^m Q_{ri}}{\sum_j^n Q_j} \tag{5}$$

where $\sum_i^m Q_{ri}$ is the total annual consumption of m kinds of renewable energy, and $\sum_j^n Q_j$ is the total consumption of various power sources.

As renewable energy output is standardized using the Max–Min method, according to Equations (3) and (4), under the same $\beta\omega$, the larger $L_r(t)$ is, the smaller the equivalent load will be. Conversely, the effect is similar to the "duck curve" where more photovoltaic power leads to lower "net load". However, unlike the "duck curve", the equivalent load does not completely deduct renewable energy output. Instead, it uses a relative conversion method determined by $\beta\omega$. Changing the values of β and ω, a larger product of $\beta\omega$ leads to a deeper deviation of the equivalent load curve from the power grid's typical load curve. Conversely, it becomes closer to the original typical load curve.

The equivalent coefficient ω represents the renewable energy power consumption responsibility weight, which indicates the target proportion of renewable energy usage. A higher proportion of renewable energy generation corresponds to a larger ω. Essentially, by tailoring TOU pricing according to the renewable energy power consumption responsibility weight ω, we can directly influence the demand side of electricity consumption based on the energy structure. This adjustment in electricity demand encourages the use of renewable energy, thereby creating a synergy between renewable energy consumption on the generation side and load management on the demand side. This approach facilitates the transition of the power system from a "source following load" model to a "source–load interaction" paradigm, promoting a more dynamic and responsive energy system.

As ω is determined externally and published annually by the national energy regulatory authority, it is not a parameter that can be adjusted internally. When TOU pricing does not match ω, adjustments to the degree to which the equivalent load is affected can be made based on β.

The parameter β is a scaling factor that adjusts the influence of the renewable energy equivalent coefficient ω on the equivalent load calculation. It directly affects how much weight is given to the renewable energy output relative to the typical load in the final equivalent load computation.

By adjusting β, the model can be fine-tuned to optimize both economic and environmental outcomes in the power sector. If $\beta = 0$, Equation (3) simplifies to $L_e(t)' = L(t)'$, meaning the equivalent load is entirely based on the typical load, with no influence from renewable energy. If $\beta = 1$, Equation (3) becomes $L_e(t)' = (1-\omega)L(t)' + \omega L_r(t)'$, indicating a balanced influence based on the value of ω.

Typically, β is set to 1, but it can be modified based on the specific requirements and objectives of TOU pricing management to better match local conditions and optimize the effectiveness of the pricing strategy. This flexibility in adjusting β provides a mechanism to adapt the model for varying regional energy dynamics and policy goals.

Figure 3 illustrates the equivalent load curves under three specific scenarios: when $\beta = 1$ with ω values of 0.16 and 0.32, and when $\beta = 0.5$ with $\omega = 0.16$. The dashed line represents the equivalent load, the solid black line represents the grid's typical load curve, and the solid green line represents the actual output curve of renewable energy.

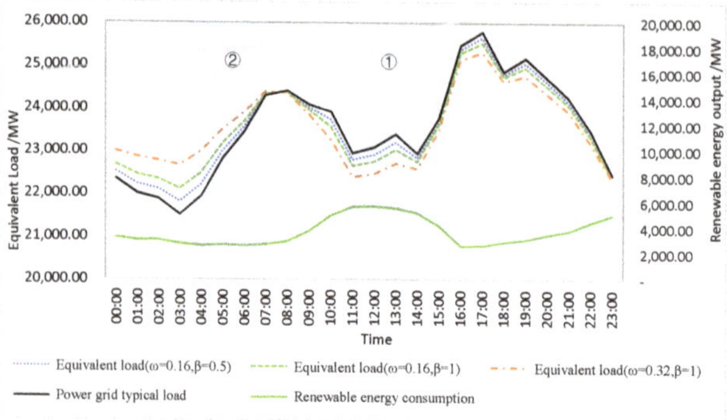

Figure 3. Equivalent load curve and renewable energy consumption curve.

According to Figure 3, during periods of high renewable energy output (such as zone ① from 11 a.m. to 2 p.m.), the equivalent load decreases. Because the equivalent load curve is below the typical load curve, according to demand response and compared to Time of Use pricing based on the typical load curve, the average electricity price in zone ① should be reduced when optimizing Time of Use pricing based on the equivalent load curve, thereby stimulating electricity consumption and increasing user electricity usage during that time period.

Figure 4 provides a detailed depiction of the impacts on both the load on the supply side and the output on the generation side before and after implementing Time of Use (TOU) pricing optimization based on typical and equivalent load methods.

In Figure 4a, the comparison between the pre-optimized grid's typical load and the post-optimization scenarios reveals that TOU pricing optimization, whether based on typical or equivalent load, effectively reduces the peak-to-valley difference in grid load. Notably, the equivalent load optimization method enhances grid stability more significantly. During the periods marked as zone ①, there is a noticeable increase in grid load, which strategically aligns with high renewable energy output periods, thereby promoting greater consumption of renewable energy.

Figure 4b illustrates the impact on non-renewable energy output, showing a flatter output curve post-optimization compared to the pre-optimization curve. This flattening indicates a more consistent and efficient operation of conventional power generation units, which contributes to the economic efficiency of these units by reducing the need for rapid ramping up and down in response to demand fluctuations.

Lastly, Figure 4c compares the effects on renewable energy consumption before and after optimization using both methods. It is evident that the equivalent load method is particularly effective in boosting renewable energy consumption. This method not only aligns demand with renewable energy availability more closely but also facilitates a higher integration of renewable energy into the grid. This is quantitatively reflected in the increased proportion of renewable energy in the total energy mix and a corresponding decrease in reliance on non-renewable sources.

Similarly, during periods of low renewable energy output (such as zone ② from 4 a.m. to 7 a.m.), the equivalent load curve is above the typical load curve. When designing Time of Use pricing based on the equivalent load curve, the average electricity price in zone ② increases compared to the typical load method, which is consistent with the characteristics of low renewable energy output in zone ②.

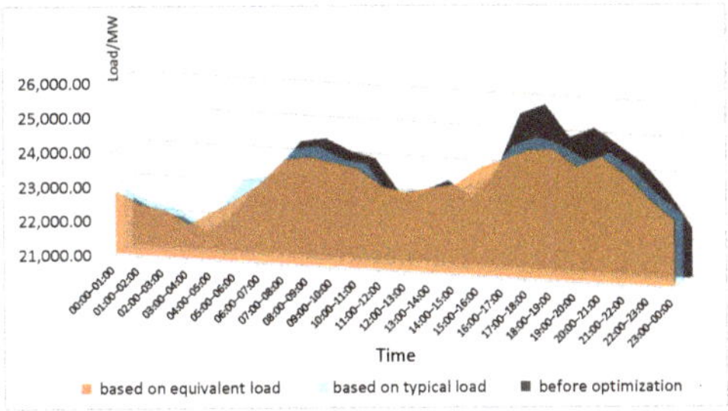

(a)

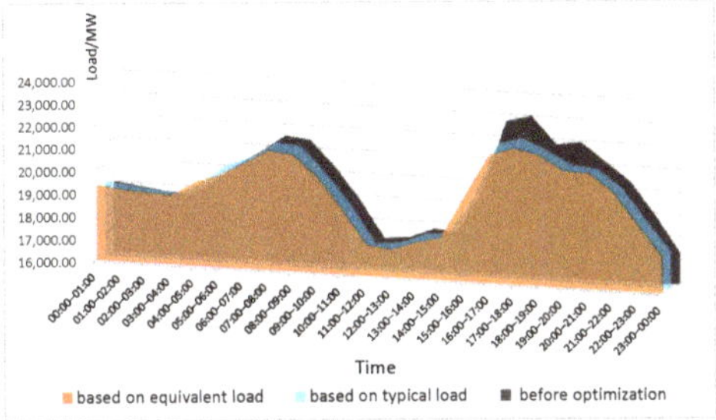

(b)

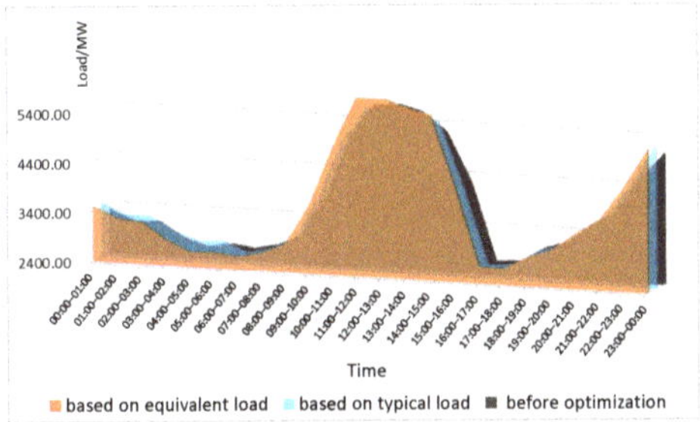

(c)

Figure 4. Loading comparison based on equivalent load and typical load. (**a**) power grid load; (**b**) non-renewable energy output; (**c**) renewable energy consumption.

Overall, the quantitative analysis in Figure 4 underscores the effectiveness of TOU pricing optimization, especially when using the equivalent load method, in promoting a more stable and economically efficient grid operation while enhancing the consumption of renewable energy.

2.2. Dispatch Strategies to Promote Renewable Energy Consumption

"Source–load interaction" to promote the consumption of renewable energy also requires corresponding implementation of dispatch strategies [17]. According to the requirements of the National Renewable Energy Law and the Comprehensive Supervision Work Plan for Clean Energy Consumption (National Energy Comprehensive Regulation [2021] No. 28) issued by the National Energy Administration, grid enterprises should prioritize the dispatch and full purchase of renewable energy generation. As weather forecasts become more accurate, wind farms and photovoltaic power stations gradually exhibit characteristics of observable and predictable conventional power sources [20,21].

At the same time, through the optimization of dispatch technology on the supply side, the space for renewable energy consumption can be further explored.

The dispatch strategies framework to promote renewable energy consumption is shown in Figure 5. This framework guides the decision-making process in adjusting energy outputs based on the changes in electricity load after demand response (ΔL) and the availability of renewable energy.

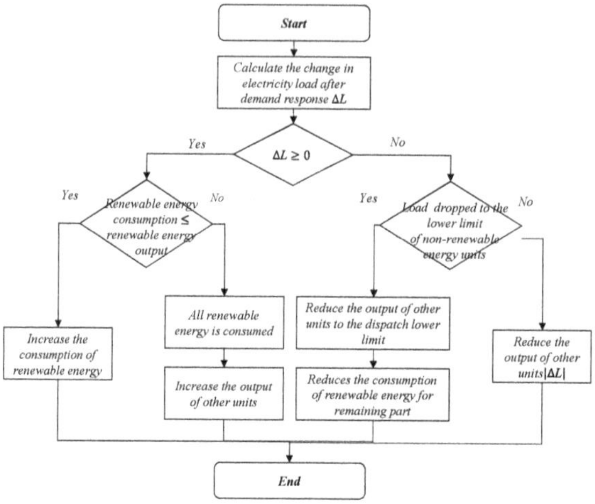

Figure 5. Dispatch strategies for promoting renewable energy consumption.

The framework begins by calculating the change in electricity load after demand response, denoted as ΔL. The decision-making process is as follows:

(1) If ΔL is non-negative, which implies an increase or no change in load:

Check if the renewable energy consumption is within the output limits. If yes, increase ΔL of the consumption of renewable energy. If no, ensure all available renewable energy output is fully utilized, and increase the output of other units to meet the total demand.

(2) If ΔL is negative, indicating a decrease in load:

Check if the load has dropped to the lower limit for non-renewable units. If so, reduce their output to the minimum dispatch limit, and adjust the renewable energy output to match the reduced load to maintain balance. If the load has not dropped to the lower limit, decrease ΔL of the output of other units accordingly.

The dispatch strategies framework provides a structured approach to adjusting power outputs based on changes in load, specifically aiming to maximize the use of renewable energy while maintaining system stability.

3. User Demand Response

Demand response is the market participation behavior of electricity users who respond to market price signals or incentive mechanisms and change their inherent electricity consumption patterns [22]. Demand response can be categorized into market price-based demand response and policy incentive-based demand response [23]. Price-based responses include peak–valley Time of Use pricing, real-time pricing, and others, while incentive-based responses involve interruptible loads, direct load control, emergency electricity demand response, etc. [24]. Time of Use pricing is an important mechanism designed based on the time value of electricity [25]. By setting different price levels for different time periods, Time of Use pricing is made to be closer to the supply cost of the power system. This maximizes the role of price signals, guiding electricity users to use less power during peak hours and more power during off-peak hours, to ensure the safe and stable operation of the power system, enhance overall system efficiency, and reduce the overall societal electricity costs. In this paper, based on user demand response and load curves, different time periods are defined, and different electricity prices are set.

3.1. Division of Periods

The division of peak–valley periods is the foundation for formulating and implementing Time of Use pricing. Peak–valley period division should reflect the actual peak–valley characteristics of the network supply load curve and also demonstrate the differences in electricity costs during different periods. Electricity users pay higher electricity fees for high-cost electricity during high-cost periods like sharp and peak periods and lower fees for low-cost electricity during valley period. This clarifies market signals to guide users to adjust their electricity consumption behavior. The "Notice on Further Improving the Time of Use Pricing Mechanism" proposes a scientific approach to period division, stating "Identify peak hours as periods of tight supply and high marginal supply cost, and off-peak hours as periods of relaxed supply and low marginal supply cost" [10]. Methods for period division typically include clustering based on load characteristics, cost-based methods based on supply cost, and factor analysis methods [26]. Among them, clustering methods evaluate the likelihood of each point on the load curve being in various periods based on the numerical characteristics of the load, using membership or similarity functions to determine sharp, peak, flat, and valley periods. Clustering methods include fuzzy clustering [27], C-means clustering, and SOM neural network clustering [28]. These clustering methods are based on load values and ignore time sequence, making the division of periods too separated and not conducive to users adjusting their electricity consumption behavior based on Time of Use pricing. The cost-based method involves period division based on the changing characteristics of actual supply costs over time [29]. This includes methods such as the day–load curve cost sudden change division method, cost time membership function method, and short-term marginal cost method, with a complex cost accounting process. Hierarchical clustering can merge loads into layers, providing a certain flexibility. This paper adopts the hierarchical clustering method to divide periods based on typical load curves and equivalent load curves.

3.2. Price Elasticity

The prerequisite for optimizing Time of Use pricing is to establish a response relationship model between user electricity consumption and electricity price. Typically, demand response uses price elasticity coefficients to describe this relationship, as they quantify the degree to which electricity consumption adjusts in response to price changes.

Price elasticity coefficients can be divided into self-elasticity coefficients and cross-elasticity coefficients [30,31]. The self-elasticity coefficient measures the immediate responsiveness of electricity consumption within the same time period to changes in its price, while the cross-elasticity coefficient captures the inter-period impact of price changes in one period to the consumption in another period. Specifically, price elasticity coefficients can be expressed as:

$$\varepsilon(t,t) = \frac{\Delta L_t / L_{0,t}}{\Delta P_t / P_{0,t}} \tag{6}$$

$$\varepsilon(t,h) = \frac{\Delta L_t / L_{0,t}}{\Delta P_h / P_{0,h}} \tag{7}$$

where $L_{0,t}$ is the electricity consumption in period t before responding; $P_{0,t}$ and $P_{0,h}$ are the electricity prices in period t and h before responding; ΔL_t is the relative change in electricity consumption in period t; ΔP_t and ΔP_h are the relative changes in electricity prices in periods t and h, respectively; $\varepsilon(t,t)$ is the self-elasticity coefficient. A higher self-elasticity value indicates that consumers are more sensitive to price changes, potentially leading to significant shifts in consumption patterns based on price variations. This sensitivity can be leveraged to flatten peak demand or fill valley hours by adjusting prices accordingly; $\varepsilon(t,h)$ is the cross-elasticity coefficient, which represents how price changes in one period

ensuring that the interests of all participants are not harmed, to truly fulfill its role as a price signal.

4.1. Objective Function and Decision Variables

TOU pricing optimization is a multi-objective planning problem [32,33]. Optimization goals include maximizing the utilization of renewable energy, minimizing environmental governance costs, reducing the purchasing cost of electricity on the generation side, and minimizing the peak–valley difference in grid load. Some objectives are mutually consistent, while others conflict. For example, a high utilization rate of renewable energy reduces carbon emissions and lowers environmental governance costs, but whether the total purchasing cost of electricity on the generation side decreases depends on the power structure and the actual generation cost of different sources. For multi-objective planning problems, some objectives can be placed in the constraint conditions, and solutions can then be carried out.

In this paper, the total generation-side cost C_T is minimized as the optimization goal, while the goals of increasing the utilization rate of renewable energy and reducing the peak–valley difference in grid load are considered as constraints, along with constraints related to electricity balance, user-side tariff stability, and maintaining a reasonable peak-to-valley price ratio.

The total cost on the power supply side, in addition to the purchase costs of renewable energy such as wind power and photovoltaic power generation, and non-renewable energy such as coal, oil, and gas, also includes the environmental management costs brought by thermal power generation [34]. The objective function is represented as follows:

$$\min C_T = P_r Q_r + (P_c + P_e) Q_c \tag{11}$$

where C_T is the total generation-side cost, Q_r and Q_c are the total electricity consumption of renewable energy and thermal power generation after implementing peak–valley TOU pricing, P_r is the guiding price for renewable energy, P_c is the benchmark price for thermal power, and P_e is the environmental governance cost per unit of thermal power generation. The purchasing cost of renewable energy is computed by multiplying the guiding price by the amount of renewable energy consumption, while the purchasing and environmental governance costs of non-renewable energy (typically thermal power) are computed by adding the benchmark price to the product of the environmental governance cost and the amount of thermal power generation.

$$Q_r = \sum_{s \in T_s} Q_{rs} + \sum_{p \in T_p} Q_{rp} + \sum_{f \in T_f} Q_{rf} + \sum_{v \in T_v} Q_{rv} \tag{12}$$

$$Q_c = \sum_{s \in T_s} Q_{cs} + \sum_{p \in T_p} Q_{cp} + \sum_{f \in T_f} Q_{cf} + \sum_{v \in T_v} Q_{cv} \tag{13}$$

Here, T_s, T_p, T_f, and T_v represent the different time periods for sharp, peak, flat, and valley loads, respectively.

The electricity consumption Q_i, during the i-th hour under the electricity price P_i, is expressed as follows:

$$Q_i = L_i \times T_i = e^{\beta_0 P_i + \beta_1} \times T_i \tag{14}$$

where the electricity price P_i is a function $f(.)$ of the sharp, peak, flat, and valley electricity prices P_s, P_p, P_f and P_v, respectively:

$$P_i = f(P_s, P_p, P_f, P_v, i) \tag{15}$$

The renewable energy and thermal power grid electricity consumption during the i-th hour, Q_{ri} and Q_{ci}, are determined by the dispatch strategy represented by the function $g(\cdot)$:

$$Q_{ri} = g(L_i, r) \times T_i \tag{16}$$

$$Q_{ci} = g(L_i, c) \times T_i \quad (17)$$

Here, i represents the i-th hour of a 24 h day, T_i is the duration of the i-th hour (with a value of 1), L_i is the grid load during the i-th hour, Q_i is the user-side electricity consumption during the i-th hour under the electricity price P_i, β_0 and β_1 are obtained through regression analysis based on historical electricity price and load data according to the demand response model in Equation (10), and the time period during the i-th hour is determined using the hierarchical clustering method described in Section 2.1. The electricity price P_i is determined by the function $f(\cdot)$, and the dispatch strategy is represented by the function $g(\cdot)$, which determines the output of renewable energy units and non-renewable energy units based on the grid load L_i. The values of Q_{ri} and Q_{ci} are then obtained using Equations (16) and (17). The decision variables of the TOU pricing optimization model are the sharp, peak, flat, and valley electricity prices, i.e., P_s, P_p, P_f and P_v.

4.2. Constraint Conditions

(1) Reduction in Peak–Valley Difference

To achieve peak–load shaving and stabilize the system load, the TOU pricing mechanism mandates a reduction in the peak–valley difference of the grid load before and after optimization. This is quantified in Equation (18):

$$(\max L_{TOU} - \min L_{TOU}) \leq (\max L_0 - \min L_0) \quad (18)$$

where L_{TOU} refers to the grid load during various time periods after TOU pricing optimization, and L_0 refers to the grid load during various time periods before TOU pricing optimization. The rationale behind this constraint is to ensure that the load distribution becomes more uniform, reducing the strain on grid resources and infrastructure during peak times.

(2) Increase in Renewable Energy Utilization

To promote the consumption of renewable energy, it is required that the utilization rate of renewable energy is increased after TOU pricing optimization, i.e.,:

$$\sum_{i \in R} \sum_{j \in T} Q_{ij}^{TOU} \geq \sum_{i \in R} \sum_{j \in T} Q_{ij}^{0} \quad (19)$$

where Q_{ij}^0 and Q_{ij}^{TOU} are the consumption amounts of the i-th type of renewable energy during the j-th time period before and after TOU pricing optimization, respectively. This condition is set to ensure that the TOU pricing model actively promotes the use of renewable energy sources, aligning with broader environmental goals and sustainability practices.

(3) Electricity Balance

Assuming TOU pricing optimization does not change the total daily electricity consumption, the following equation holds:

$$\sum_{i \in T} Q_i^0 = \sum_{j \in T} Q_j^{TOU} \quad (20)$$

where Q_i^0 is the electricity consumption of various user types during time period i before peak–valley TOU pricing optimization, and Q_j^{TOU} is the electricity consumption during time period i after optimization. The introduction of the equivalent load curve may result in slight variations in the divisions of time periods before and after optimization, but the overall daily consumption remains constant to ensure energy balance and prevent any unintended increase in total energy usage.

(4) No Increase in User-Side Electricity Costs

TOU pricing optimization is viable only if it does not lead to an increase in the total electricity cost for users. Assuming the total electricity consumption remains unchanged before and after optimization, the average electricity price on the user side should not rise, as expressed in Equation (21):

$$\sum_{i\in U}\sum_{j\in T} P_{ij}^{TOU} Q_{ij}^{TOU} \le \sum_{i\in U}\sum_{j\in T} P_{ij}^{0} Q_{ij}^{0} \tag{21}$$

where P_{ij}^{TOU} and Q_{ij}^{TOU} are the electricity price and consumption of the i-th user type during the j-th time period after TOU pricing optimization. This constraint ensures that the TOU pricing strategy is economically neutral for consumers, fostering acceptance and compliance without imposing additional financial burdens.

(5) Maintaining a Reasonable Peak-to-Valley Price Ratio

To ensure that the peak-to-valley price difference in electricity rates does not lead to excessive user reactions or insufficient response due to an unclear difference, it is crucial to maintain this ratio within a reasonable range. This is articulated in Equation (22):

$$\begin{cases} P_s > P_p > P_f > P_v > 0 \\ k_1 \le \frac{P_p}{P_v} \le k_2 \\ k_3 \le \frac{P_s}{P_p} \le k_4 \\ \frac{P_p - P_f}{P_f} \ge k_5 \\ \frac{P_f - P_v}{P_f} \ge k_6 \end{cases} \tag{22}$$

Here, parameters k_1 and k_2 restrict the peak-to-valley electricity price ratio, k_3 and k_4 restrict the ratio of sharp to peak electricity prices, and k_5 and k_6 restrict the fluctuation of peak and valley electricity prices based on flat-rate electricity prices. The notice "[2021]1093" from the National Development and Reform Commission (NDRC) provides specific requirements for the peak-to-valley electricity price difference and ratio: In regions where the predicted peak-to-valley ratio of the grid load exceeds 40% in the previous or current year, the price difference between peak and valley electricity rates should not be less than 4:1 in principle; in other regions, it should generally not be less than 3:1. The sharp electricity price should typically be increased by at least 20% above the peak-period electricity prices. According to the national implementation of Time of Use (TOU) pricing, the peak electricity prices are generally raised by 15% to 85% compared to flat-rate prices, sharp electricity prices are further increased by 20% to 25% above the peak rates, and valley electricity prices are reduced by 20% to 70% below flat-rate prices. Given the current landscape, and to allow for flexibility in adjustments, the parameters can be set as follows: $k_1 = 3$, $k_2 = 10$, $k_3 = 1.2$, $k_4 = 2$, $k_5 = 0.1$ and $k_6 = 0.2$.

This constraint ensures that TOU pricing remains effective and adaptable, promoting energy conservation and efficient use without causing undue stress or confusion among consumers.

4.3. The Social Network Search (SNS) Algorithm

The above Time of Use (TOU) pricing optimization model is calculated using a recent metaheuristic algorithm known as the Social Network Search (SNS) algorithm. As detailed in [35], the SNS algorithm was applied to solve various challenging optimization problems. The results demonstrate that SNS is highly capable of managing diverse optimization scenarios, consistently outperforming other algorithms. The SNS algorithm incorporates four innovative optimization operators: Imitation, Conversation, Disputation, and Innovation. These operators, referred to as "moods", are designed to mimic the real-world behaviors of social network users when they express their opinions, thereby enhancing the algorithm's effectiveness in solving complex problems.

4.3.1. Imitation

The Imitation mood is characterized by users' tendency to emulate others' expressions and viewpoints. This mood captures the essence of social learning, where individuals are influenced by the perspectives of their peers, often leading to a homogenization of thoughts and ideas within the network. This mental state can be represented quantitatively as follows:

$$X_{inew} = X_j + rand(-1,1) \times rand(0,1) \times (X_i - X_j) \tag{23}$$

where X_j represents the vector of the j-th user's view which is selected randomly and $i \neq j$, X_i is the vector of the i-th user's view. X_{inew} is the user's new location in the search space. Also, $rand(0,1)$ and $rand(-1,1)$ indicate two random vectors in intervals [0, 1] and [−1, 1], respectively.

4.3.2. Conversation

Conversely, the Conversation mood facilitates a more interactive exchange where users engage in dialogues, sharing and refining their thoughts through direct communication. This mood supports a collaborative environment where knowledge is co-created and shared among participants. This mental state can be represented as follows:

$$X_{inew} = X_k + rand(0,1) \times sign(f_i - f_j) \times (X_j - X_i) \tag{24}$$

where X_k demonstrates the vector of the issue which is randomly chosen to speak about it, X_j is the vector of a randomly selected user's view for a chat and X_i is the vector of view of the ith user, and it should be noted that $i \neq j \neq k$ in which j and k are selected randomly. In addition, $sign$ is the sign function and $sign(f_i - f_j)$ determines the moving direction of X_k.

4.3.3. Disputation

In the Disputation mood, users are inclined to engage in debates and discussions, often challenging and defending various viewpoints. This mood is crucial for the critical examination of ideas, fostering a platform where arguments can be tested and validated through collective scrutiny. The new impacted view can be expressed as follows:

$$X_{inew} = X_i + rand(0,1) \times \left(\frac{\sum_t^{N_r} X_t}{N_r} - (1 + round(rand)) \times X_i \right) \tag{25}$$

where the symbol ($round$) rounds the real input to the adjacent integer number, whereas the symbol (N_r) represents the group size or commenters.

4.3.4. Innovation

Lastly, the Innovation mood is observed when users initiate discussions based on novel ideas or personal experiences. As a result, a new concept will be generated, and the new impacted viewpoint may be expressed as follows:

$$\begin{gathered} x_{inew}^d = t \times x_j^d + (1-t) \times n_{new}^d \\ n_{new}^d = lb_d + rand_1 \times (ub_d - lb_d) \\ t = rand_2 \end{gathered} \tag{26}$$

where d is the d-th variable that is selected randomly in the interval [1, D], and D is the number of problem's variables. $rand_1$ and $rand_2$ are two random numbers in the interval [0, 1]. Also, ub_d and lb_d are the maximum and minimum values for the d-th variable. n_{new}^d represents the new idea about the d-th dimension of the problem. x_j^d is the current idea about the d-th variable presented by another user, (j-th represents the user selected randomly and $i \neq j$) and i-th shows the user wants to change it because of new idea

(n^d_{new}). Finally, the new view about the d-th dimension will be created as x^d_{inew}. x^d_{inew} is an interpolation of the current idea (x^d_j) and the new idea (n^d_{new}).

A change in one dimension (x^d_{inew}) causes a general change in the main concept, and can be considered as a new view to share. This process can be modeled as follows:

$$X_{inew} = \left[x_1, x_2, x_3, \ldots x^d_{inew} \cdots x_D\right] \tag{27}$$

where x^d_{inew} is a new insight into the issue under consideration from the d-th viewpoint, and is replaced with the current view (x^d_i).

4.3.5. Rules and Implementation of SNS Algorithm

As illustrated in [35], the method is produced by various moods, where each user's viewpoint is altered, and fresh views are utilized based on their merit. If the new idea is superior to the existing one, it will be approved. As a result, the value of a new concept may be determined by the objective function of X_{inew}, which can be calculated analytically and compared to the value of an existing thought (X_i) as follows:

$$X_i = \begin{cases} X_i, & f(X_i) < f(X_{inew}) \\ X_{inew}, & f(X_{inew}) \geq f(X_i) \end{cases} \tag{28}$$

The implementation of the Social Network Search (SNS) algorithm unfolds across three phases: initialization, increasing popularity, and checking terminating conditions.

During the initialization phase, the algorithm sets up the initial conditions and parameters, establishing a baseline from which the search begins. The increasing popularity phase involves the propagation of ideas or solutions. This phase is critical as it determines the direction and momentum of the search process. Finally, the checking terminating conditions phase evaluates whether the search has met the predefined criteria, which would signal the completion of the algorithm's execution. This structured approach ensures that the algorithm systematically explores the solution space, efficiently optimizing towards the best possible outcomes.

5. Case Analysis

5.1. Basic Data

This section validates the effectiveness of the TOU pricing optimization model using typical daily load data from a specific period in the northern region of the State Grid. The renewable energy output data is presented in Table 2. The average utilization rate of renewable energy is 95.08%, with renewable energy generation accounting for 15.90%.

Table 2. Output and consumption of renewable energy in a power grid area of China.

Time	Renewable Energy Output/MW	Renewable Energy Consuming Load/MW	Renewable Energy Usage Rate	Renewable Energy Proportion
00:00	3492.29	3275.90	93.80%	14.66%
01:00	3283.07	3065.97	93.39%	13.93%
02:00	3230.80	3094.89	95.79%	14.15%
03:00	2952.94	2801.40	94.87%	13.03%
04:00	2792.09	2645.10	94.74%	12.06%
05:00	2882.21	2716.75	94.26%	11.91%
06:00	2782.50	2657.42	95.50%	11.34%
07:00	2894.47	2762.11	95.43%	11.37%
08:00	3172.81	2984.25	94.06%	12.23%
09:00	3953.16	3792.74	95.94%	15.74%
10:00	5332.17	5007.10	93.90%	20.94%

Table 2. *Cont.*

Time	Renewable Energy Output/MW	Renewable Energy Consuming Load/MW	Renewable Energy Usage Rate	Renewable Energy Proportion
11:00	6060.23	5701.89	94.09%	24.84%
12:00	6088.68	5730.08	94.11%	24.82%
13:00	5897.45	5600.63	94.97%	23.94%
14:00	5535.37	5220.15	94.31%	22.75%
15:00	4410.08	4236.63	96.07%	17.83%
16:00	2809.71	2683.14	95.50%	10.53%
17:00	2818.42	2715.48	96.35%	10.53%
18:00	3129.57	3005.72	96.04%	12.09%
19:00	3344.11	3170.38	94.80%	12.59%
20:00	3653.51	3536.35	96.79%	14.30%
21:00	4009.13	3845.02	95.91%	15.86%
22:00	4634.98	4516.13	97.44%	19.23%
23:00	5308.70	5056.85	95.26%	22.52%

5.2. Results

5.2.1. Time Period Division Results Based on Equivalent Load

The equivalent load is computed based on Equation (4). The traditional division based on typical loads includes 3 h in the sharp period from 16:00 to 18:00 and 19:00 to 20:00, 6 h in the peak period, 7 h in the flat period, and 8 h in the valley period. Keeping the cumulative duration of sharp, peak, flat, and valley periods unchanged, the division is recomputed using the hierarchical clustering method based on the equivalent load. As shown in Table 3, the results of the time period division between 05:00 and 06:00 changed from valley to flat, while they changed from flat to valley between 11:00 and 12:00, as indicated in bold.

Table 3. Typical load and equivalent load and corresponding time period division.

Time	Typical Load /MW	Equivalent Load /MW	Time Period Based on Typical Load	Time Period Based on Equivalent Load
00:00–01:00	22,345.87	22,687.40	valley	valley
01:00–02:00	22,002.30	22,457.81	valley	valley
02:00–03:00	21,874.76	22,350.26	valley	valley
03:00–04:00	21,507.32	22,119.14	valley	valley
04:00–05:00	21,934.15	22,491.49	valley	valley
05:00–06:00	**22,818.01**	**23,179.97**	**valley**	**flat**
06:00–07:00	23,438.28	23,686.03	flat	flat
07:00–08:00	24,299.29	24,349.42	peak	peak
08:00–09:00	24,410.55	24,391.57	peak	peak
09:00–10:00	24,090.94	23,968.30	peak	peak
10:00–11:00	23,916.54	23,575.81	flat	flat
11:00–12:00	**22,950.37**	**22,661.71**	**flat**	**valley**
12:00–13:00	23,088.40	22,765.67	flat	flat
13:00–14:00	23,394.45	23,036.29	flat	flat
14:00–15:00	22,942.89	22,756.39	valley	valley
15:00–16:00	23,762.03	23,613.79	flat	flat
16:00–17:00	25,479.33	25,305.09	sharp	sharp
17:00–18:00	25,791.04	25,546.42	sharp	sharp
18:00–19:00	24,863.28	24,747.40	peak	peak
19:00–20:00	25,181.11	24,965.96	sharp	sharp
20:00–21:00	24,721.92	24,524.04	peak	peak
21:00–22:00	24,237.13	24,073.72	peak	peak
22:00–23:00	23,489.37	23,338.40	flat	flat
23:00–00:00	22,454.81	22,402.05	valley	Valley

Rows with changed period division are indicated in bold.

5.2.2. Comparative Analysis of Solution Algorithms

The Social Network Search (SNS) algorithm is implemented to solve the problem described in Section 4. In order to evaluate the performance of the SNS algorithm, we performed a comparative analysis against two other prominent optimization algorithms: Genetic Algorithm (GA) and Particle Swarm Optimization (PSO). This analysis spanned 100 iterations. Figure 8 illustrates the comparative results of these algorithms.

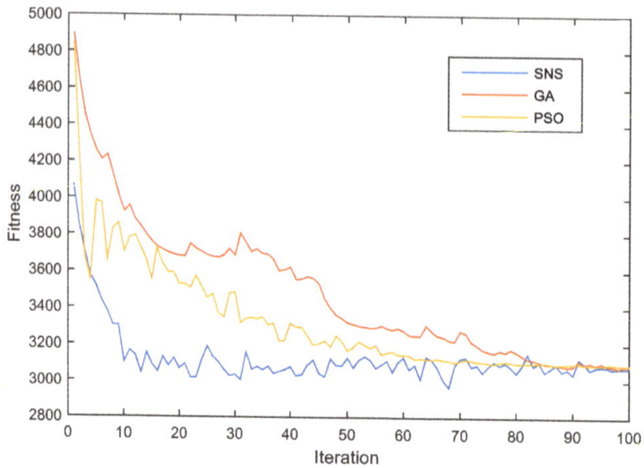

Figure 8. Comparison of optimization algorithm performance.

The performance comparison based on the Figure 8 is outlined as follows:

(1) Initial Performance

SNS starts at the lowest value, indicating the most effective initial condition among the three algorithms in minimizing the load difference. PSO and GA begin at a higher value than SNS, suggesting a less effective initial performance.

(2) Rate of Convergence

SNS shows a rapid improvement in the initial iterations, quickly reducing the load difference, which suggests a strong initial convergence towards an optimal solution. PSO decreases steadily but at a slower rate compared to SNS, indicating a moderate rate of convergence. GA also shows a decrease but remains higher than SNS throughout the iterations, indicating a slower convergence compared to SNS.

(3) Stability and Final Performance

All three algorithms begin to stabilize after about 30 iterations, with gradual improvements as iterations continue. SNS maintains the lowest values throughout the process, indicating that it consistently finds solutions with the smallest load differences, suggesting the best overall optimization performance.

(4) Final Convergence

Towards the final iterations (around 80 to 100), all algorithms show minimal changes, indicating convergence. SNS and PSO appear to converge at a similar level, which is better than GA.

In summary, SNS appears to be the most effective algorithm, offering the best optimization performance with the most stable convergence.

5.2.3. TOU Pricing Optimization Results

Before the Time of Use (TOU) pricing optimization, the electricity prices for each period in the region were as follows: 0.9699 CNY for sharp, 0.8082 CNY for peak, 0.5388 CNY for flat, and 0.2694 CNY for valley. However, due to changes in the characteristics of the power system load, it became necessary to adjust these TOU prices for optimization.

The equivalent load method was utilized, beginning with the calculation of the optimized equivalent load curve as defined by Equation (4). Subsequently, considering the consumption of renewable energy, the TOU pricing optimization model was solved using the SNS algorithm. As previously discussed in Section 2.1, Time of Use (TOU) pricing can be improved through optimization tailored to various grid load curves. To assess the effectiveness of the TOU pricing optimization method based on equivalent load, we performed a comparative analysis of TOU electricity pricing before and after optimization using different load models: typical load, net load, and equivalent load. This analysis is presented in Table 4, which displays the electricity prices for four distinct time periods—sharp, peak, flat, and valley—across four different scenarios.

Table 4. TOU pricing design based on typical load, net load and equivalent load.

Price/CNY	Before Optimization	Based on Typical Load	Based on Net Load	Based on Equivalent Load
Sharp price	0.9699	1.2279	1.2324	1.2313
Peak price	0.8082	0.8186	0.8216	0.8208
Flat price	0.5388	0.5388	0.5388	0.5388
Valley price	0.2694	0.1500	0.1500	0.1500
Sharp-valley price difference	0.7000	1.0779	1.0824	1.0813

Initially, the sharp price was 0.9699 CNY, which increased across all models after optimization, with the highest being 1.2324 CNY for the net load and a slightly lower optimized equivalent load price of 1.2313 CNY. The peak price saw a modest increase from the original 0.8082 CNY to 0.8208 CNY in the equivalent load model. The flat price remained constant at 0.5388 CNY across all scenarios. The valley price, however, saw a significant reduction from 0.2694 CNY to 0.1500 CNY in all optimized scenarios, reflecting a strategic decrease to encourage off-peak consumption.

The sharp–valley price difference before optimization was 0.7000 CNY, which increased notably in all scenarios post-optimization, with the equivalent load model showing a difference of 1.0813 CNY. The increased sharp–valley price difference post-optimization is a strategic move to enhance demand response. By widening the cost gap between the highest and lowest demand times, the TOU pricing encourages consumers to shift their usage to off-peak times, thus aiding in grid stability and efficient energy use.

Table 5 provides a detailed analysis of the effects of TOU pricing optimization on various key metrics, comparing the values before and after optimization using three different load models.

Table 5. Impacts of TOU pricing optimization based on typical load, net load and equivalent load.

Items	Before Optimization	Based on Typical Load		Based on Net Load		Based on Equivalent Load	
		Value	Increased	Value	Increased	Value	Increased
Cost of power generation/10,000 CNY	21,504.56	21,502.50	−2.06	21,502.19	−2.37	21,502.07	−2.49
Renewable energy consumption/MWh	89,822.08	91,422.55	1600.47	91,658.80	1836.72	91,757.64	1935.56
Utilization rate of renewable energy/%	95.08%	96.78%	1.69%	97.03%	1.94%	97.13%	2.05%

Initially, the cost of power generation was 21,504.56 × 10,000 CNY. After optimization, the costs were slightly reduced across all models. The equivalent load model achieved the lowest cost at 21,502.07 × 10,000 CNY, showing a decrease of 2.49 × 10,000 CNY. These reductions indicate that the equivalent load model effectively lowers the cost of power generation.

Regarding renewable energy consumption, it was initially 89,822.08 MWh. Post-optimization, the equivalent load model observed the highest increase to 91,757.64 MWh, up by 1935.56 MWh. This metric shows that TOU pricing optimization not only reduces costs but also significantly boosts renewable energy consumption, with the greatest increase achieved with the equivalent load model.

The utilization rate of renewable energy was 95.08% before optimization. After optimization, the equivalent load model reached the highest at 97.13%, an increase of 2.05%. The equivalent load model again shows the most substantial improvement, aligning with the increases in renewable energy consumption and reductions in generation costs.

5.3. *Impacts Analysis*

5.3.1. Impacts on Consumer Side

(1) Division Reflects the Output Level of Renewable Energy

Based on the division results presented in Table 3, a time period change graph is plotted in Figure 9. The division, which is based on the equivalent load curve, generally aligns with the division based on typical load. However, there are some variations during periods of low renewable energy output (5:00–6:00) and high output (11:00–12:00).

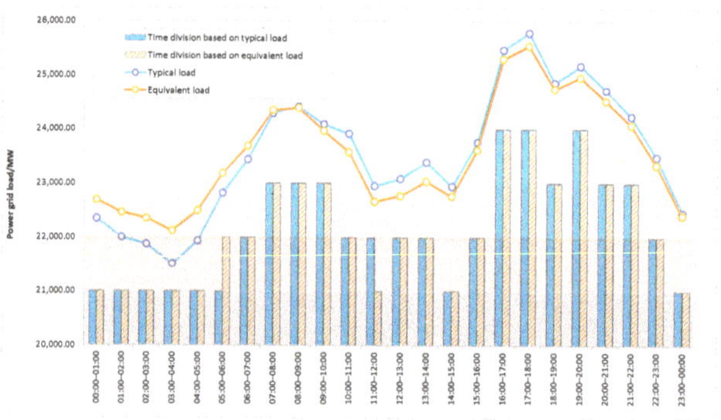

Figure 9. Time period division based on traditional method and equivalent load.

During the period of low renewable energy output (5:00–6:00), the equivalent load is higher, causing this period to shift from the valley to the flat period. Conversely, during the period of high renewable energy output (11:00–12:00), the equivalent load is lower, causing this period to shift from the flat to the valley period. Although the typical load during the period of high renewable energy output (11:00–12:00) is higher than during the period of low output (5:00–6:00), the equivalent load during the period of high output is lower. This results in users being charged valley prices during the period of high output, which helps to release demand and promote the consumption of renewable energy.

(2) Further Widening of Sharp–Valley Price Difference

The initial sharp–valley price difference was 0.7 CNY, with a sharp–valley ratio of 2.6. Following the optimization process, which utilized the equivalent load, net load, and typical load methods, prices during sharp and peak periods experienced a significant increase, while prices during the valley period decreased substantially. Figure 10 illustrates that the sharp–valley price difference achieved through the equivalent load method is 1.0813 CNY, with a sharp–valley ratio of 8.2. This represents a notable 3.6 times increase compared to the pre-optimization state, thereby enhancing price adjustment flexibility and strengthening the demand response from consumers.

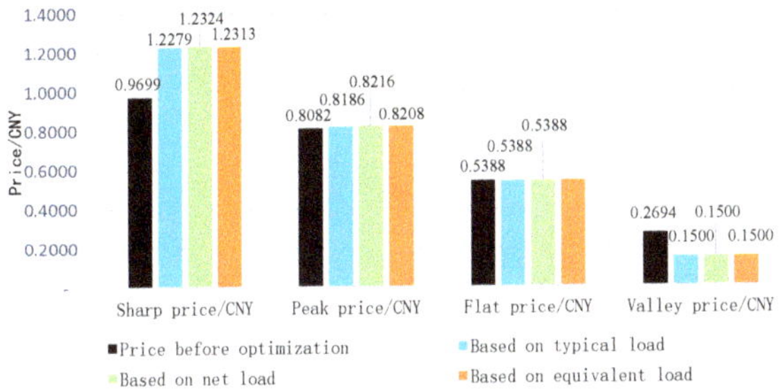

Figure 10. TOU pricing design based on typical load, net load and equivalent load.

5.3.2. Impacts on Supply Side

Figure 11 presents the load changes on the supply side following the optimization of the Time of Use electricity price based on typical load, net load, and equivalent load. The results demonstrate substantial peak-cutting and valley-filling effects on the load on the supply side, as detailed below:

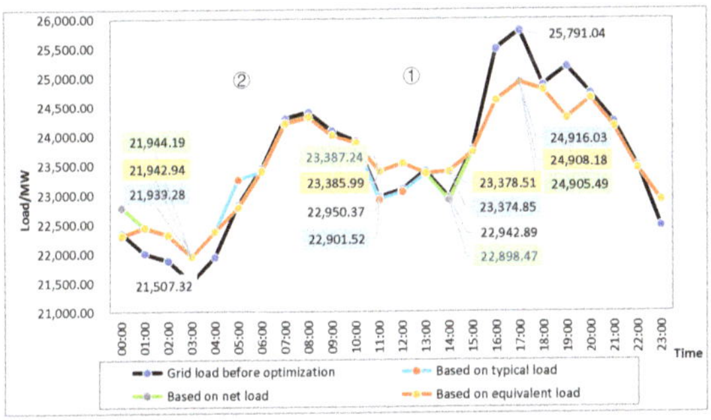

Figure 11. Daily load curve before and after TOU pricing optimization.

(1) Reduction in Peak Load

In Figure 11, the black line represents the typical load curve before optimization, the blue line represents the power grid load curve after optimization using the typical load method, and the green line represents the power grid load curve after optimization based on the net load. After optimizing the equivalent load curve, the new curve remains the equivalent load, which needs to be restored to the power grid load curve, represented by the orange curve in Figure 11. It is evident that all three optimization methods effectively reduce the highest load of the power grid. The highest load of the power grid is reduced from 25,791.04 MW to 24,916.03 MW, resulting in a peak reduction of 875.01 MW using the typical load method. The net load optimization reduces the highest load to 24,905.49 MW, achieving a peak reduction of 885.85 MW. After optimization based on the equivalent load, the highest load is further reduced to 24,908.18 MW, achieving a peak reduction of 882.86 MW. The peak-cutting effects of the three methods are relatively similar.

(2) Decrease in Sharp–Valley Load Difference

Table 6 provide a comprehensive analysis of the effects of TOU pricing optimization on sharp–valley load difference related to the power supply side.

The sharp–valley load difference was initially 4283.72 MW. After optimization, it decreased to 2976.75 MW with the typical load model (a reduction of 1306.97 MW), to 2961.30 MW with the net load model (a reduction of 1322.42 MW), and to 2965.24 MW with the equivalent load model (a reduction of 1318.48 MW). These significant reductions indicate that TOU pricing optimization effectively smooths out the load curve, reducing the disparity between the highest and lowest loads, which can lead to more efficient grid operation and less need for rapid ramping of power generation resources.

Table 6. Impacts at power supply side of TOU pricing optimization based on typical load, net load and equivalent load.

Items	Before Optimization	Based on Typical Load		Based on Net Load		Based on Equivalent Load	
		Value	Increased	Value	Increased	Value	Increased
Maximum load of grid/MW	25,791.04	24,916.03	−875.01	24,905.49	−885.55	24,908.18	−882.86
Minimum load of grid/MW	21,507.32	21,939.28	431.96	21,944.19	436.87	21,942.94	435.62
Sharp-valley load difference/MW	4283.72	2976.75	−1306.97	2961.30	−1322.42	2965.24	−1318.48

It is worth noting that during periods with more renewable energy output (area ① in Figure 11), only the grid supply load after optimization by the equivalent load method is higher and more stable, indicating that the output structure of the power source side has effectively been transmitted to the supply side, which can promote the power system to transition from "source follows load" to "source–load interaction".

The sharp–valley load difference is further presented in Figure 12, which illustrates that the TOU pricing optimization, particularly when based on the equivalent load model, effectively manages the power supply side by reducing peak loads, increasing minimum loads, and smoothing the load differences, thereby enhancing grid stability and operational efficiency.

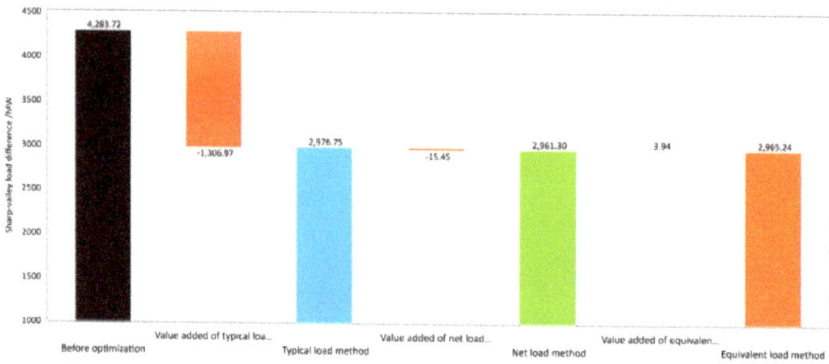

Figure 12. Effects of TOU pricing optimization on peak valley load differences.

5.3.3. Impacts on Generation Side

Figure 13 visually illustrates the impact of Time of Use (TOU) pricing optimization on renewable energy consumption before and after applying three different optimization methods: typical load, net load, and equivalent load. This bar chart clearly shows the incremental increases in renewable energy consumption resulting from each method, providing a quantitative comparison of their effectiveness.

The baseline scenario is represented by a black bar, showing the renewable energy consumption at 89,822.08 MWh before any optimization. The subsequent bars in cyan, green and orange represent the renewable energy consumption after optimization using the typical load, net load, and equivalent load methods, respectively.

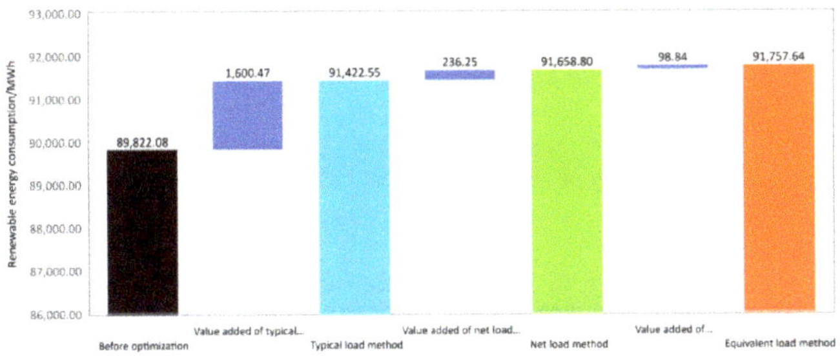

Figure 13. Renewable energy consumption changes before and after TOU pricing optimization.

The cyan bar for the typical load method shows an increase in renewable energy consumption to 91,422.55 MWh, which is an increase of 1600.47 MWh from the baseline. The green bar for the net load method indicates a further increase to 91,658.80 MWh. The most significant increase is shown by the orange bar for the equivalent load method, with renewable energy consumption rising to 91,757.64 MWh. This is an increase of 1935.56 MWh from the baseline, marking the highest improvement among the three methods.

In summary, the optimization of Time of Use (TOU) pricing through methods based on typical load, net load, and equivalent load all yield benefits such as peak shaving, valley filling, reduced peak–valley load difference, lower generation-side costs, and increased consumption of renewable energy. Notably, the net load and equivalent load methods outperform the traditional typical load method. The net load method slightly outperforms in terms of peak shaving and valley filling. However, the equivalent load method effectively aligns the output structure from the power generation side to the power supply side, resulting in a significant reduction in generation side costs and a more pronounced promotion of renewable energy consumption.

6. Conclusions

This paper introduces an innovative concept of equivalent load and proposes an optimized Time of Use (TOU) pricing optimization model from a demand response perspective, validated using power load data from a northern region of the national power grid of China. The analysis comprehensively assesses the impacts across the electricity consumer side, supply side, and generation side, revealing significant benefits.

The findings indicate that optimizing TOU pricing by widening the peak-to-valley price difference on the consumer side enhances price adjustment flexibility. On the supply side, the equivalent load method effectively reduces the maximum grid load and narrows the peak-to-valley load difference, contributing to a more stable grid load. Additionally, on the generation side, it lowers average generation costs and boosts the consumption of renewable energy.

The proposed TOU pricing optimization method, based on equivalent load, stands out from existing methods that rely on typical grid load and net load due to several distinctive features:

(1) Demand-Side and Generation-Side Linkage: The TOU electricity price based on equivalent load aligns demand-side user response with renewable energy consumption on the generation side. This promotes a transition in the power system from "source following load changes" to "source–load interaction," enhancing the dynamic balance between supply and demand.

(2) Enhanced Renewable Energy Utilization: By incorporating the power grid load, renewable energy responsibility weight, and renewable energy consumption, the equivalent load approach significantly enhances the utilization rate of renewable energy, especially in regions with high renewable output.

(3) Economic and Environmental Benefits: The equivalent load TOU pricing optimization method reduces generation side costs without increasing consumer costs. It supports peak shaving and valley filling, benefiting multiple stakeholders across the source and load sides. This contributes positively to the clean and low-carbon transformation of the power system, and supports the achievement of dual carbon goals.

Additionally, the implementation of the Social Network Search (SNS) algorithm in solving the TOU pricing optimization model based on equivalent load further enhances the method's effectiveness. The SNS algorithm, known for its robustness and efficiency in handling complex optimization problems, ensures that the pricing strategy is not only responsive to changes in demand and supply but also optimally aligned with the operational dynamics of the power grid.

Overall, the use of the equivalent load model, coupled with the SNS algorithm, demonstrates a sophisticated approach to integrating renewable energy metrics into pricing strategies, aiming to optimize both economic and environmental outcomes in the power sector. This method not only improves system efficiency and stability but also aligns with broader environmental objectives, marking a significant step forward in the sustainable evolution of power systems.

Author Contributions: Conceptualization, X.Z. and Y.W. (Yali Wang); methodology, X.Z.; validation, Z.H. and Y.W. (Yongfei Wu); formal analysis, X.Z.; investigation, X.Z. and Y.W. (Yongfei Wu); resources, X.Z. and Z.H.; data curation, X.Z. and Y.W. (Yali Wang); writing—original draft preparation, X.Z.; writing—review and editing, X.Z. and Y.W. (Yali Wang); visualization, X.Z. and A.L.; funding acquisition, X.Z. All authors have read and agreed to the published version of the manuscript.

Funding: This research was funded by National Social Science Foundation of China (Grant No. 21BGL176).

Data Availability Statement: The original contributions presented in the study are included in the article, further inquiries can be directed to the corresponding authors.

Conflicts of Interest: The authors declare no conflicts of interest.

References

1. Li, M.; Chen, G.; Dong, C.; Liang, Z.; Wang, W.; Fan, G. Research on Power Balance of High Proportion Renewable Energy System. *Power Syst. Technol.* **2019**, *43*, 3979–3986.
2. Yan, R.; Masood, N.A.; Saha, T.K.; Bai, F.; Gu, H. The Anatomy of the 2016 South Australia Blackout: A Catastrophic Event in a High Renewable Network. *IEEE Trans. Power Syst.* **2018**, *33*, 5374–5388. [CrossRef]
3. Yand, J.; Wang, X.; Xiao, D.; Zhao, J.; Liu, D. Research on the Transaction Mechanism and Benefit of Promoting New Energy Consumption. *Electr. Power* **2020**, *53*, 89–95.
4. Yilmaz, S.; Xu, X.; Cabrera, D.; Chanez, C.; Cuony, P.; Pate, M.K. Analysis of Demand-Side Response Preferences Regarding Electricity Tariffs and Direct Load Control: Key Findings from a Swiss Survey. *Energy* **2020**, *212*, 118712. [CrossRef]
5. Ahmed, E.M.; Rathinam, R.; Dayalan, S.; Fernandez, G.S.; Ali, Z.M.; Abdel Aleem, S.H.E.; Omar, A.I. A Comprehensive Analysis of Demand Response Pricing Strategies in a Smart Grid Environment Using Particle Swarm Optimization and the Strawberry Optimization Algorithm. *Mathematics* **2021**, *9*, 2338. [CrossRef]
6. Sun, Y.; Li, Y.; Wang, B.; Liu, X. Study on Operation Mode of Demand Response Accommodating the Utilization of Renewable Energy. *Power Demand Side Manag.* **2013**, *15*, 6–10.
7. Xu, H.; Meng, Z.; Wang, Y. Economic Dispatching of Microgrid Considering Renewable Energy Uncertainty and Demand Side Response. *Energy Rep.* **2020**, *6*, 196–204. [CrossRef]
8. Chen, Q.; Wang, Y.; Li, K. Research on Modeling and Scheduling of Virtual Power Plant with Dual Demand Response. *J. Syst. Simul.* **2023**, *35*, 822–832.
9. Dou, C.; Zhou, X.; Zhang, T.; Xu, S. Economic Optimization Dispatching Strategy of Microgrid for Promoting Photoelectric Consumption Considering Cogeneration and Demand Response. *J. Mod. Power Syst. Clean Energy* **2020**, *8*, 557–563. [CrossRef]
10. National Development and Reform Commission. Notice on Further Improving the Time of Use Price Mechanism (FGJ [2021]No.1093). Available online: http://www.gov.cn/zhengce/zhengceku/2021-07/29/content/5628297.htm (accessed on 26 July 2021).
11. Tan, X.D.; Chen, Y.C.; Li, Y.; Jing, J.B.; Jiang, N.; Wang, Z.J.; Shen, Y.W. Research on Optimization of TOU Considering Load Development and User Behavior. *Electr. Power* **2018**, *51*, 136–144.
12. Niu, W.; Wang, L.; Li, Y. Calculation Method and Application of Customer Baseline Load in Demand Response Project. *J. Southeast Univ. (Nat. Sci. Ed.)* **2014**, *44*, 556–560.

13. Fan, S.; Jia, K.; Wang, F.; He, G. Large-Scale Demand Response Based on Customer Directrix Load. Autom. *Electr. Power Syst.* **2020**, *44*, 19–27.
14. Fan, S.; Li, Z.; Yang, L.; He, G. Customer Directrix Load-Based Large-Scale Demand Response for Integrating Renewable Energy Sources. *Electr. Power Syst. Res.* **2020**, *181*, 106175. [CrossRef]
15. Ai, X.; Zhou, S.; Zhao, Y. Study on Time of Use Pricing of User Side Considering Wind Power Uncertainty. *Power Syst. Technol.* **2016**, *40*, 1529–1535.
16. Li, M.; Zhang, K. Research on TOU Pricing Model Taking Account of Distributed Photovoltaic Generation. *Power Syst. Clean Energy* **2018**, *34*, 74–78.
17. Ren, J.; Xue, C.; Ma, X.; Zhang, X.; Xiao, X.; Liu, Y. Research on User-Side Peak Shaving Mechanism to Promote the Consumption of New Energy. *Power Demand Side Manag.* **2021**, *23*, 58–62.
18. Xiu, X.; Tang, W.; Ma, J. Typical Load Curve Extraction Method for Energy Storage Capacity Configuration. *Acta Energiae Solaris Sin.* **2018**, *39*, 2234–2242.
19. Han, H.; Yang, Y.; Gao, N.; Ma, Q.; Zhao, J.; Yuan, T. Fitting Method of Typical Daily Load Based on Normal Distribution. *Distrib. Energy* **2020**, *5*, 69–73.
20. Wu, W.; Liao, W.; Miao, J.; Du, G. Using Gated Recurrent Unit Network to Forecast Short-Term Load Considering Impact of Electricity Price. *Energy Procedia* **2019**, *158*, 3369–3374. [CrossRef]
21. Chang, Z.; Zhang, Y.; Chen, W. Electricity Price Prediction Based on Hybrid Model of Adam Optimized LSTM Neural Network and Wavelet Transform. *Energy* **2019**, *187*, 115804. [CrossRef]
22. Yang, X.; Zhou, M.; Li, G. Survey on Demand Response Mechanism and Modeling in Smart Grid. *Power Syst. Technol.* **2016**, *40*, 220–226.
23. Aghaei, J.; Alizadeh, M.I. Demand Response in Smart Electricity Grids Equipped with Renewable Energy Sources: A Review. *Renew. Sustain. Energy Rev.* **2013**, *18*, 64–72. [CrossRef]
24. Fan, S.; Wei, Y.; He, G.; Li, Z. Discussion on Demand Response Mechanism for New Power Systems. *Autom. Electr. Power Syst.* **2022**, *46*, 1–12.
25. The National Development and Reform Commission. Reply to Reporters' Questions on the Notice on Further Improving the Time of Use Pricing Mechanism. Available online: http://www.gov.cn/zhengce/2021-08/03/content_5629171.htm (accessed on 3 August 2021).
26. Cheng, Y.; Zhai, N. Electricity Price Peak and Valley Periods Division Based on Customer Response. *Autom. Electr. Power Syst.* **2012**, *36*, 42–46+53.
27. Song, Z.; Zhang, J.; Niu, D.; Xiao, X. Green Time of Use Electricity Price Optimization Based on Fuzzy Density K-Medoids Algorithm and NSGA-II. *Smart Power* **2019**, *47*, 38–45.
28. Wang, W.; Wang, J.; Wang, K. Application of SOM Neural Network and C Means Method in Load Classification. *Proc. CSU-EPSA* **2011**, *23*, 36–39.
29. Xing, D.; Lei, X.; Li, J. Optimal Time Partition of TOU Price Based on Cost-Time Curve. *Power Demand Side Manag.* **2007**, *48*, 18–21.
30. Gao, Y.; Lyu, M.; Liang, H.; Zhang, J. Power Demand Price Elasticity Matrix Based on Discrete Attraction Model. Autom. *Electr. Power Syst.* **2014**, *38*, 103–107+144.
31. Wang, Y.; Shi, P.; Chen, G.; Wang, X.; Sun, X.; Ding, L.; Li, Y. Renewable Energy Consumption Mechanism Considering the Coordination of Inter-Provincial Transactions and Source-Load Interaction. *Proc. CSU-EPSA* **2022**, *34*, 16–22.
32. Ye, Z.; Wu, Y.; Zhang, X.; Liu, S.; He, J. Research on the Inclining Block Tariffs Scheme for Solving Cross-Subsidy Under Demand Response Based on the Perspective of Maximizing Social Welfare. *Chin. J. Manag. Sci.* **2019**, *27*, 149–159.
33. Jiang, H.; Liu, B.; Wang, Y.; Zheng, S. Multiobjective TOU Pricing Optimization Based on NSGA2. *J. Appl. Math.* **2014**, *2014*, 104518. [CrossRef]
34. Wang, Y.; Ye, Z.; Huang, J. Research on Economic Scheduling of Energy Storage Based on Dynamic Peak-Valley Time Division. *Electr. Power* **2022**, *55*, 64–72.
35. Talatahari, S.; Bayzidi, H.; Saraee, M. Social Network Search for Global Optimization. *IEEE Access* **2021**, *9*, 92815–92863. [CrossRef]

mathematics

Article

Energy–Logistics Cooperative Optimization for a Port-Integrated Energy System

Aiming Mo [1,2], Yan Zhang [2,*], Yiyong Xiong [3], Fan Ma [2] and Lin Sun [2]

[1] School of Electrical Engineering, Southeast University, Nanjing 210096, China; 220222775@seu.edu.cn
[2] National Key Laboratory of Electromagnetic Energy, Naval University of Engineering, Wuhan 430033, China; mafan0803@163.com (F.M.); sunlin_ee@163.com (L.S.)
[3] School of Electrical Engineering, Naval University of Engineering, Wuhan 430033, China; xiongyiyong1989@163.com
* Correspondence: zy331214534@126.com

Abstract: In order to achieve carbon peak and neutrality goals, many low-carbon operations are implemented in ports. Integrated energy systems that consist of port electricity and cooling loads, wind and PV energy devices, energy storage, and clean fuels are considered as a future technology. In addition, ports are important hubs for the global economy and trade; logistics optimization is also part of their objective, and most port facilities have complex logistics. This article proposes an energy–logistics collaborative optimization method to fully tap the potential of port-integrated energy systems. A logistics–energy system model is established by deeply examining the operational characteristics of logistics systems and their corresponding energy consumption patterns, considering ships' operational statuses, quay crane distribution constraints, and power balances. To better represent the ship–energy–logistics optimization problem, a hybrid system modeling technique is employed. The case of Shanghai Port is studied; the results show that costs can be reduced by 3.27% compared to the traditional optimization method, and a sensitivity analysis demonstrates the robustness of the proposed method.

Keywords: collaborative optimization; integrated energy system; energy–logistics coordination; port; renewable energy

MSC: 90c90

1. Introduction

A port comprises a logistics system and an energy system; the logistics system is the main area supplied by the energy system and consumes a considerable amount of energy [1]. Concurrently, ports have emerged as major contributors to air pollution [2]. Empirical data derived from ports situated within the Yangtze River Delta region indicate that approximately 64% of emissions can be attributed to berthed ships, while port machinery and the transportation infrastructure contribute to 16% of the emissions. Given these circumstances, energy conservation and emission reductions in ports are urgent.

From the energy consumption perspective, using a shore-based power supply to replace high-emission ship auxiliary engines during ship berthing [3–5] expands the connection between ships and ports from the logistics system to the energy system, achieving coupling between the two subsystems. A Combined Cooling, Heating, and Power (CCHP) system, as the primary energy supply equipment powered by fossil fuels, using natural gas as a fuel can not only generate electricity and heat energy, but can also cool when necessary. A CCHP system can be used to reduce energy consumption and control pollutant emissions with a very high energy efficiency of up to 75%, which is about 24% higher than traditional energy units [6]. Hydrogen, termed 'green hydrogen' when produced by renewable energies, is a versatile, potentially zero-emission fuel that can be used to power ships, as well as a range of port equipment and vehicles [7]. Giri and Roy [8,9] and Lei et al. [10] propose a renewable energy supply chain that utilizes power to hydrogen (P2H) and a methanation device (MR) as an energy supply. This not only achieves the consumption of renewable energy, but also achieves the goal of carbon reduction. Chavan et al. [11] propose fuel cell (FC) power generation, which is efficient and environmentally friendly. Combined with hydrogen production equipment based on electrolysis, it can help improve the consumption rate of renewable energy. Holder et al. [7], Kelmalis et al. [12], and Zhang et al. [13] propose the electrification of logistics equipment, which will also help to improve the consumption rate of renewable energy. From the perspective of energy production, ports utilize abundant renewable energy sources such as wind and light to generate electricity and integrate multiple forms of energy, combined with electrical coupling [14,15] and electric thermal coupling [16–19], to form an integrated energy supply system, which can effectively improve the energy efficiency and renewable energy consumption and reduce air pollution and carbon emissions [20,21].

From the perspective of improving the efficiency of logistics systems, Ren [22] established a mathematical model based on the principle of minimizing the ineffective operation time and analyzed the advantages and disadvantages of the "operation line" and "operation surface" scheduling modes for container trucks. Their experiment found that the "operation surface" scheduling mode shortened the average waiting time by 33% compared to the "operation line" scheduling mode. Borelli et al. [23] use the lowest cost of delay to minimize the total ship service time by considering berth productivity under a given berth schedule. Aljuaid et al. [24] adopt a mixed-integer linear programming model, aiming to minimize the waiting time of ships at ports and improve the efficiency of ship entry and exit. Song et al. [25] propose a joint berth allocation and dock crane allocation model. Kovač et al. [26] aim to minimize the total service time of fully electric ships and developed an optimal berth allocation model, which is solved using the particle swarm optimization method.

The above methods only consider the individual optimization of the port energy system and logistics system and do not consider the logistics system's impact on the energy system. As a matter of fact, the electricity consumption of the port logistics system accounts for more than 70% of the energy system, and there is a vast space for efficiency optimization. Different logistics scheduling schemes correspond to different energy consumption needs. A reasonable logistics scheduling scheme can effectively promote the operation optimization of the port energy system and improve the energy efficiency of the port [27,28].

More research is needed on the collaborative optimization of port logistics and energy systems. Shi et al. [29] propose a future port microgrid architecture that combines logistics and energy systems but does not provide a specific logistics–energy collaborative optimization method. A logistics and energy collaborative optimization strategy is constructed based on the demand response, and the results validate that the proposed strategy is effective for coordinating multi-energy and logistics scheduling and minimizing port operation cost [28]. Lassoued and Elloumi [30,31] investigate two crucial problems in ports, which are the berth allocation problem and the quay crane assignment problem. The optimization objective is to minimize the total service time of berthed vessels. Wang et al. [4] conduct in-depth research on the joint optimization of berth allocation and port energy supply and established an energy supply model for a port-integrated energy system (PIES) that considers multi-energy collaboration and berth optimization. In addition, traditional logistics systems mainly focus on the scheduling of berths, quay cranes, and ships to achieve optimal logistics costs without considering the energy usage of ships after connecting to shore power, resulting in the decoupling of logistics and energy systems [32,33]. At the same time, the lack of corresponding coordination and optimization methods has led to an increase in port operating costs and a decrease in energy efficiency.

Regarding modeling methods, the current optimization of port emission reductions mainly includes intelligent optimization algorithm-solving models, rule-based optimization models, mixed-integer programming models, etc. Wang [34] introduced the mutation operator from the differential evolution algorithm into the NSGA-II algorithm, obtaining a mixed differential NSGA-II algorithm, using this to obtain the optimal solution that minimizes the scheduling time of ships entering and exiting the port. An adaptive immune clone selection algorithm has been developed based on the mixed-integer programming model to minimize port operating costs to the greatest extent possible [4]. A distributed algorithm based on Benders decomposition embedded with an improved non-dominated sorting genetic (INSGA-II) algorithm is designed to realize the optimal collaboration of a PIES's energy outputs and port container logistic system energy demands in a port [35]. Shi et al. [29] use a mixed-integer linear programming model; numerical simulations were carried out verify that the proposed strategy can minimize the total cost of the integrated energy–logistics system and increase the utilization rate of renewable energy systems for green ports. Jiang et al. [36] innovatively propose a nonlinear mixed-integer programming formula to obtain the optimal mode of berth and quay bridge collaborative optimization in ports under uncertain conditions. Yu et al. [37] aim to minimize cranes' carbon emissions and operating costs. A hybrid non-inferior sorting genetic algorithm based on a simulated annealing algorithm is used to solve the yard crane scheduling problem, and the analytic hierarchy process is used to select an optimal solution. However, most coupling variables are simplified or not considered; for example, operation optimization of a PIES in the studies by Mao et al. [38], Yang et al. [39], and Zhen et al. [40] does not consider some coupling variables, such as the electrical load of quay cranes and moored ships. This research offers the following significant, novel contributions.

Abandoning the traditional operation mode of optimizing logistics and energy systems separately and introducing collaborative optimization between the two further improves the flexibility of port operation.

Adopting a hybrid system modeling method can decouple and finely describe coupling constraints by increasing the number of variables.

The model that has been suggested will bring considerable economic benefits to ports and has broad application prospects as proven by a case study on the collaborative optimization of logistics and energy systems in a port in Shanghai.

The structure of the paper is as follows: The related works that support the research in the proposed study are presented in Section 2. In Section 3, the port system is described. In Section 4, the problem statement and model formulation are discussed.

The objective function, balance, and model solution are shown in Section 5. Section 6 contains descriptions of the suggested model's comparative verification and sensitivity analysis. Section 7 presents the managerial ramifications of the proposed study. Finally, some limitations and future study directions are included in the concluding remarks found in Section 8.

2. Related Works

In this study, a summary of relevant studies is provided for three topics: (i) logistics system scheduling models, (ii) logistics system load models, and (iii) energy production models.

2.1. Logistics System Scheduling Model

This section mainly analyzes the composition of the port logistics system, including two parts: ships and quay cranes. Then, based on the scheduled arrival time of ships, the loading and unloading volumes of goods, and quay crane constraints, the logistics system model is constructed to obtain the ship-in-port state and quay crane operation state models.

2.2. Logistics System Load Model

This section introduces the load composition of the logistics system, including the electrical load caused by the operation of the shore bridge and the connection of the ship to the shore power. The operation status of the shore bridge is consistent with the port status of the ship, and the ship itself includes both a constant power load and a variable power load. The variable power load needs to reach its rated workload during the ship's berthing period.

2.3. Energy System Model

The energy system section introduces the energy facilities related to the port, covering power generation equipment and hydrogen production and storage equipment. The energy system provides the necessary electricity for the port logistics system.

2.4. Literature Analysis and Motivations

The literature review indicates that many studies have been conducted on ports from multiple perspectives such as berth optimization [23,24,30,31], logistics scheduling [36,38], and energy supply [5,6]. However, there is still relatively little research on the collaborative optimization of logistics and energy systems. There is still a lack of relevant sensitivity analyses for collaborative optimization systems of ports.

Motivation: To overcome this drawback and achieve optimal operating costs for the port, we construct a collaborative optimization model for logistics and energy systems and conduct relevant research and a sensitivity analysis using a port in Shanghai as an example. The results verify the effectiveness of the proposed optimization method in port energy conservation and emission reductions.

Although the published papers include the utilization of renewable energy, they have not achieved maximum use [7,9]. This is unfavorable for the development of green and low-carbon ports.

Motivation: To address this challenge, efforts should be made to promote the development of ports in a green and low-carbon direction. In this model, we introduce a renewable energy consumption system, and the intermittency of renewable energy leads to its low direct utilization rate. The introduction of P2H technology, MR, and hydrogen storage (HS) tanks absorbed some of the remaining renewable energy, thereby maximizing the consumption of renewable energy.

According to the related works in Section 1 and Table 1, we have learned about some optimization scheduling algorithms for PIESs. However, for situations with a large number of decision variables, their solving speed will become very slow, making it difficult to meet the needs of online scheduling.

Table 1. A comparison of the most relevant previous studies.

Study	DN	SO	RE	P2H	FP	SM
Lassoued and Elloumi [30]	M	LSO				bi-level programming model
Zhao et al. [28]	M	COLE	√		√	risk-aware stochastic method
Ji et al. [33]	S	LSO			√	enhanced non-dominated sorting genetic algorithm II
Shi et al. [29]	M	COLE	√	√		mixed-integer linear programming
Chang et al. [32]	M	LSO				genetic algorithm optimization approach
Wang et al. [4]	M	LSO			√	adaptive immune clone selection algorithm
Pu et al. [35]	M	COLE	√	√		distributed algorithm based on Benders decomposition
Jiang et al. [36]	M	LSO			√	nonlinear mixed-integer programming formulation
Lassoued and Elloumi [31]	M	LSO				bi-level programming model
Song et al. [25]	M	ESO	√			mixed-integer linear programming
Aljuaid et al. [24]	M	LSO				multi-objective optimization model based on goal programming
Kovač et al. [26]	S	LSO				hybrid metaheuristic model
Mao et al. [38]	M	COLE				Mixed-integer linear programming
Xu et al. [27]	M	LSO				a multi-objective berth allocation model
Proposed study	M	COLE	√	√	√	hybrid system modeling method

DN: design of network; M: multi-objective; S: single objective; SO: system optimization; LSO: logistics system optimization; ESO: energy system optimization; COLE: collaborative optimization of logistics and energy systems; RE: renewable energy; P2H: power to hydrogen; FP: flexible programming; SM: solution method.

Motivation: To overcome the problems of a slow model solving speed and a low solving accuracy, in this study, we construct a hybrid system modeling method that decouples and finely describes coupling constraints by increasing the number of variables, ultimately achieving fast and high-precision model solving. Compared with traditional modeling methods, this method leads to significant improvements in running speed and accuracy.

3. System Description

3.1. Description of the Port-Integrated Energy System

The PIES consists of a logistics system and an energy system, as shown in Figure 1. The concept of an integrated energy system, rooted in the energy hub (EH) model, includes the energy supply, energy conversion, and load sides. The logistics system not only performs logistics scheduling but also serves as a part of the load of the energy system. The two subsystems are coupled, forming a PIES that provides integrated logistics and energy services for ports and ships calling at ports. The energy supply side includes the main power grid, main gas grid, wind turbines (WTs), and photovoltaics (PV). The EH includes power grids, natural gas networks, heating networks, and various energy conversion equipment, ultimately achieving energy coupling and conversion. The inherent intermittency and peak–valley disparities associated with renewable energy generation, as identified within the scope of this discourse, present considerable challenges to traditional energy storage mechanisms which are only capable of partially mitigating these fluctuations. In light of this, the integration of hydrogen-based energy storage solutions is proposed, leveraging the expansive potential of hydrogen energy within ports. The load side includes port cooling and heating, civil electricity, and ship and quay crane loads. The dispatch center coordinates ships entering and leaving the port and the allocation of quay cranes, as well as the output of various energy equipment and the start and stop status of ship equipment, to ensure the coordinated and orderly operation of the port energy–logistics system. Among them, ships and quay cranes are the key to connecting the port logistics system and energy system. After berthing, the port operator arranges for the quay cranes to load and unload goods for ships immediately, and the corresponding quay cranes will stop operating after the ships leave the port. Based on this, we can achive logistics interaction between ships and ports. Meanwhile, shore-based power supply realizes energy interaction between ships and ports.

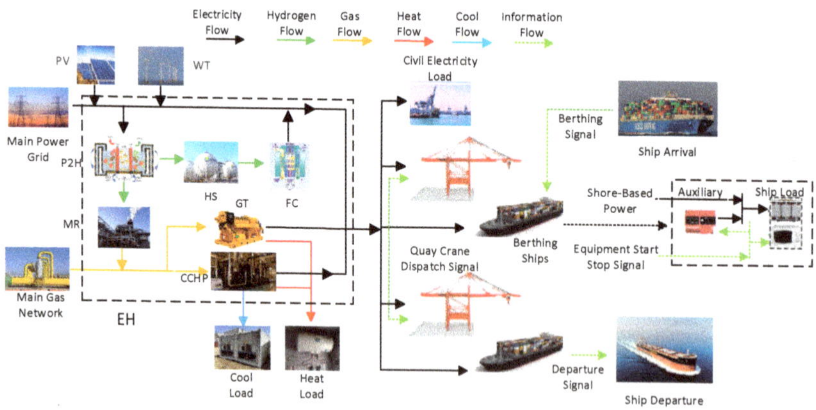

Figure 1. Port-integrated energy system.

The logistics system aims to minimize the waiting and berthing time of ships. By scheduling ships entering and leaving the port and allocating quantities of quay cranes, this goal is achieved, facilitating the prompt berthing of awaiting ships, ensuring the swift departure of docked ships, and improving the operational efficiency of the logistics system. The impact of ships berthing at port on the port energy system is as follows: after the ship and the port are connected through shore power, this directly brings the shore power load to the port power grid, and the distribution of the shore power load in time is determined by the ship's state in port. At the same time, by dispatching a certain number of quay cranes, ships berthing at the port indirectly increase the power load of the quay cranes, increasing the energy consumption of the logistics and energy systems and the overall operating cost of the system.

To decrease the energy consumption and operating cost, it is necessary to coordinate the operation of the energy system with the logistics system as the center. Based on fully considering the constraints of logistics scheduling through the reasonable scheduling of quay cranes and ships entering and leaving the port, and at the same time coordinating the output of various equipment in the energy system, the coordination and cooperation of the energy system with the logistics system can be realized, so that the ships and the quay cranes can flexibly adjust their loads based on completing logistics scheduling, at the same time allowing for the substitution of different types of energy, improving the flexibility and economy of system operation, promoting the consumption of renewable energy and reducing carbon dioxide emissions.

3.2. Description of the Modeling Method

The optimal scheduling of the PIES is a complex mixed-integer optimization problem, which contains real, integer and binary variables. Conventional optimization methodologies solve this problem but will encounter significant challenges in delivering rapid and precise solutions, particularly in instances characterized by a large number of decision variables inherent to the optimization and scheduling processes of PIESs. This complexity invariably results in diminished solution speeds, making it challenging to meet the solving needs of online scheduling. In light of these challenges, this article introduces the mixed logical dynamical (MLD) model to build a complex port framework. As first introduced by Bemporad and Morari [41], the MLD system modeling framework combines continuous and binary variables with logical relations in mixed-integer inequalities to express complex dynamic systems. It has been shown in work by Bemporad and Morari [41] and Heemels et al. [42] that such a framework can be used to model systems that have mixed continuous and discrete states and inputs, piece-wise affine and bilinear dynamics, finite state machines, qualitative outputs, and those with any combination of the former.

In addition, the optimization method based on Yalmip Toolbox was used by Liu et al. [43] and Xu et al. [44], which is adept at handling a plethora of standard optimization issues, including but not limited to linear programming, integer programming, nonlinear programming, mixed programming, and linear matrix inequalities (LMIs). Through its compatibility with CPLEX, various algorithms such as branch and bound and cutting plane algorithms are integrated, which can facilitate the efficient, rapid, and accurate derivation of solutions that align with the exigencies of online scheduling demands.

4. Energy–Logistics Integrated Systems Modeling

4.1. Logistics System Scheduling Model

Port logistics services are realized by dispatching a certain number of quay cranes to load and unload goods for ships berthing at the port, and the number of different quay cranes allocated is directly related to the time of ships in port, which in turn affects the status of ships in port. Therefore, establishing a relationship between the allocation quantity of quay cranes, the duration of ship berthing, and the ship's state in port is the basis for the optimal scheduling of the logistics system.

4.1.1. Ship Berthing Time Model

Ships will inform the port before they arrive so that the ships' arrival times are known. Ships do not dock immediately upon arrival at the port but wait in the waiting area for port dispatch. The relationship between the arrival time, the berth time, and the departure time of the ship is shown in Equation (1), where the departure time of the ship is determined by the port berth time, the loading and unloading volume of the ship and the number of allocated quay cranes, as shown in Equation (2):

$$t_0 \le t_1 \le t_{leave} \tag{1}$$

$$t_{leave} = t_1 + \frac{N_j}{\eta C_j} \tag{2}$$

Port dispatch requires ships to leave before the latest departure time, and the number of quay cranes that ships can carry limits the departure time of ships, keeping the departure time within a specific range, as shown in Equations (3) and (4):

$$t_{leave}^{\min} \le t_{leave} \le t_{leave}^{\max} \tag{3}$$

$$\begin{cases} t_{leave}^{\min} = t_1 + \frac{N_j}{\eta C_j^{\max}} \\ t_{leave}^{\max} = \min\left\{ t_1 + \frac{N_j}{\eta C_j^{\min}}, t_{leave}^{latest} \right\} \end{cases} \tag{4}$$

4.1.2. Ship-in-Port State Model

Equations (1)–(4) depict the relationship between ships' arrival, berthing, and departure times and the allocation quantity of quay cranes. At the same time, ships' berthing and departure times determine their states in port. A ship's state in port is not only the basis for logistics scheduling but also the basis for energy system load modeling. The state of ship j in port is $X_j(t)$, which is a variable of 0–1; the state in port before and after the ship docks at the port is 0, and the state in port during the port call is 1. In a single scheduling cycle, the ship's state in port is

$$X_j(t) = \begin{cases} 0, t \in [1, t_1] \\ 1, t \in [t_1, t_{leave}] \\ 0, t \in [t_{leave}, T] \end{cases} \tag{5}$$

From the beginning of the scheduling cycle to the end of the scheduling cycle, the total berthing time of the ship will be equal to the actual port call time:

$$\begin{cases} \sum_{t=1}^{T} X_j(t)\Delta t \ge \frac{N_j}{\eta C_j} \\ \sum_{t=1}^{T} X_j(t)\Delta t \le \frac{N_j}{\eta C_j} + \Delta t \end{cases} \tag{6}$$

The ship arrives at the port only once during the dispatch cycle and does not return after leaving the port:

$$X_j(t) \ge X_j(t+1), t \in [t_1, T-1] \tag{7}$$

4.1.3. Port Logistics Constraint Mode

The relationship between the ships' states in port and the number of quay cranes allocated constitutes the fundamental constraint for logistics system scheduling. In addition, due to limitations in ship length and loading and unloading capacity, the number of quay cranes that can be carried is limited, and the allocation of quay cranes cannot exceed the minimum and maximum quay crane demand limits of the ship, as shown in Equation (8); at the same time, due to the limited resources of the dock quay cranes, the total number of operating quay cranes at a particular time cannot exceed the total amount of quay cranes resources $C_{\max}$, as shown in Equation (9):

$$C_j^{\min} \le C_j \le C_j^{\max} \tag{8}$$

$$\sum_{j=1}^{n} X_j(t)C_j \leq C_{\max} \tag{9}$$

Based on Equations (1)–(9), the status of ships in port is adjusted by scheduling their berthing time and the number of quay cranes, and the coordination and interaction between quay cranes and ships at the logistics level are realized.

4.2. Logistics System Load Model

4.2.1. Quay Crane Load Model

Before the ship departs, the quay crane serves the same ship, and loading and unloading will not stop during the working period.

According to Equations (5)–(8), the number of quay crane operations during time *t* is obtained, and then the electrical load of the quay crane during time *t* is calculated.

$$P_{crane}(t) = \sum_{j=1}^{n} P_{crane}^{1} C_j X_j(t) \tag{10}$$

4.2.2. Ship Load Model

The ship load includes the propulsion, service, and loading and unloading. During berthing, the propulsion load is deactivated. Only the service and loading and unloading loads are operational, including lighting systems, kitchen equipment, air conditioning and refrigeration equipment, communication equipment, ventilation equipment, entertainment equipment, various pumps, other service equipment, and loading and unloading equipment such as cargo lifters. The equipment mentioned above is divided into two categories according to the operation characteristics: one category is equipment that operates continuously during the ship's berthing period, such as lighting equipment, air conditioning, and refrigeration equipment, which belongs to the constant power load and the other type is intermittent working equipment that controls the start and stop based on the energy demand of ships, such as water pumps, kitchen electrical equipment, etc., which belongs to the variable power load.

To mitigate the carbon emissions generated by ship power generation, after the ship docks, all the ship's load is supplied by shore power. The ship's total energy consumption bifurcates into constant and variable power loads. The constant power load, the ship's foundational energy requirement, remains stable throughout the docking period. Conversely, the variable power load is a combination of the energy consumption of assorted intermittent operational equipment onboard:

$$\begin{cases} L_{ship}(t) = L_{cons}(t) + L_{\text{var}}(t) \\ L_{\text{var}}(t) = \sum_{i=1}^{m} L_{\text{var},i}(t) \\ L_{cons}(t) = L_{base} X(t) \end{cases} \tag{11}$$

The 0–1 variable $s_i(t)$ is used to represent the start/stop states of intermittent working equipment *i*; $s_i(t) = 1$ indicates that the equipment is on and $s_i(t) = 0$ indicates that the equipment is off. Only considering the start and stop of intermittent work equipment during the ship's berthing period, each type of intermittent work equipment will complete its rated workload and will not exceed its power upper and lower limits during operation:

$$s_i(t) \leq X(t) \tag{12}$$

$$\sum_{t=t_1}^{t_{leave}} L_{\text{var},i}(t)\Delta t = W_{\text{var},i} \tag{13}$$

$$s_i L_{\text{var},i}^{\min} \leq L_{\text{var},i}(t) \leq s_i L_{\text{var},i}^{\max} \tag{14}$$

$$P_{ship}(t) = \sum_{j=1}^{n} [L_{cons,j}(t) + L_{\text{var},j}(t)] \quad (15)$$

The load model of the logistics system includes information on ships' states in port, a crucial variable reflecting port logistics scheduling. Therefore, this model can simultaneously reflect the operational characteristics of logistics and energy systems. Ships change their states in port by entering and leaving the port, bringing a certain amount of shore power load to the port at the same time. This affects the distribution quantity and load size of quay cranes, thereby changing the energy consumption and equipment output of the entire energy system and achieving interactive coupling between the logistics system and the energy system.

4.3. Energy System Model

4.3.1. Combined Cooling, Heating and Power

CCHP consists of a gas turbine (GT) and a lithium bromide absorption refrigeration machine (AC). The GT uses natural gas as a raw material for power generation while recovering high-temperature flue gas to generate heat. Its thermoelectric relationship is shown in Equations (16) and (17):

$$P^{e}_{CCHP,GT} = COP^{e}_{CCHP,GT} Q_{CCHP} \quad (16)$$

$$P^{h}_{CCHP,GT} = (1 - COP^{e}_{CCHP,GT} - COP^{h,loss}_{CCHP,GT}) COP^{h,recovery}_{CCHP,GT} COP^{h}_{CCHP,GT} Q_{CCHP} \quad (17)$$

The refrigeration power of AC is shown in Equation (18):

$$P^{c}_{CCHP} = COP^{c}_{AC}(P^{h}_{CCHP,GT} - P^{h}_{CCHP}) \quad (18)$$

4.3.2. Gas Turbine

When the capacity of the CCHP system cannot meet the heat demands of the port, the GT needs to be used for heating. The GT can produce a fixed proportion of electrical power while heating, and its electric heating model is as follows:

$$P^{e}_{GT} = COP^{e}_{GT} Q_{GT} \quad (19)$$

$$P^{h}_{GT} = COP^{h}_{GT} Q_{GT} \quad (20)$$

4.3.3. Fuel Cell

The FC uses hydrogen as a raw material, which is environmentally friendly. It can make up for electricity shortages at the port.

$$P_{FC} = M_{FC} COP_{FC} \quad (21)$$

4.3.4. Photovoltaics and Wind Turbine

PV and the WT, as clean energy sources, play a crucial role in energy conservation and emission reductions in ports [36]. In addition, they can also reduce port operating costs. Therefore, it is particularly important to fully utilize them.

4.3.5. Power to Hydrogen

Due to the high uncertainty of new energy generation, phenomena such as wind and solar power abandonment are often inevitable in the actual operation of port energy systems. P2H technology can be used in PIESs to convert wind power into hydrogen for storage and utilization.

$$M_{P2H} = COP_{P2H} P_{P2H} \quad (22)$$

4.3.6. Hydrogen Storage

HS can improve the utilization of energy over time and coordinate the imbalance between sources and loads. The HS device in this article can be used in conjunction with P2H to achieve the storage and utilization of hydrogen gas. By optimizing the storage behavior of hydrogen systems, better services can be provided to hydrogen equipment.

$$M_{HS,t} = M_{HS,t-1} + M_{HS,t}^{in} COP_{HS}^{in} - M_{HS,t}^{out} / COP_{HS}^{out}, \forall t \geq 1 \tag{23}$$

4.3.7. Methanation Device

The MR can be used to convert hydrogen produced by P2H into methane, providing fuel for natural gas power generation equipment in the PIES.

$$Q_{MR} = M_{MR} COP_{MR} \tag{24}$$

5. Energy–Logistics Optimization

5.1. Objective Functions

The optimization strategy proposed in this paper aims to minimize the operating cost of the energy–logistics coupling system and realize the economic operation of the port through the collaborative optimization of the logistics and energy systems. System operating costs include energy purchase costs (natural gas purchases and power purchases from the grid) C_{buy}, wind and solar curtailment penalties, C_{loss}, carbon emission costs, C_{co2}, and ship logistics costs, C_{ship}:

$$\min\left\{ C_{buy} + C_{loss} + C_{ship} + C_{co_2} \right\} \tag{25}$$

5.2. Balance Model

(1) Electrical power balance

$$P_{grid} + P_{WT} + P_{PV} + P_{FC} + P_{CCHP} + P_{GT} = P_{loss}^{WT} + P_{loss}^{PV} + P_{load} + P_{ship} + P_{crane} + P_{P2H} \tag{26}$$

where P_{grid}, P_{WT}, P_{PV}, P_{FC}, P_{CCHP}, P_{GT} and P_{loss}^{WT}, P_{loss}^{PV}, P_{load}, P_{ship}, P_{crane}, P_{P2H} are, respectively, the power of main power grid, wind turbine, photovoltaic, FC, CCHP, GT, and abandoned wind and photovoltaic power, civilian power load, ship shore power, quay crane load, and P2H power.

(2) Heat load balancing

$$H_{GT} + H_{CCHP} = H_{load} \tag{27}$$

(3) Cooling load balancing

$$L_{CCHP} = L_{load} \tag{28}$$

(4) Hydrogen balance

$$M_{P2H} = M_{HS}^{in} + M_{MR} \tag{29}$$

$$M_{HS}^{out} = M_{FC} \tag{30}$$

Equation (30) indicates that the hydrogen released from the hydrogen storage tank is supplied to the FC for power generation.

(5) Natural gas balance

$$Q_{gas} + Q_{MR} = Q_{CCHP} + Q_{GT} \tag{31}$$

5.3. Model Solving

Figure 2 shows the energy–logistics collaborative optimization scheduling mode of the PIES. The dispatch center coordinates the logistics and energy systems by issuing instructions. The logistics system dispatches the number of quay crane allocations and the ships' states in port, and inputs the energy demand of ships at shore and the quay crane load into the energy system. The energy system optimizes and schedules the output of each energy equipment based on power balance, equipment output, and ship load constraints, and it provides power support for the logistics system. Through the coupling interaction between the two systems, an optimal total operating cost is achieved, showcasing the efficacy of this integrated approach.

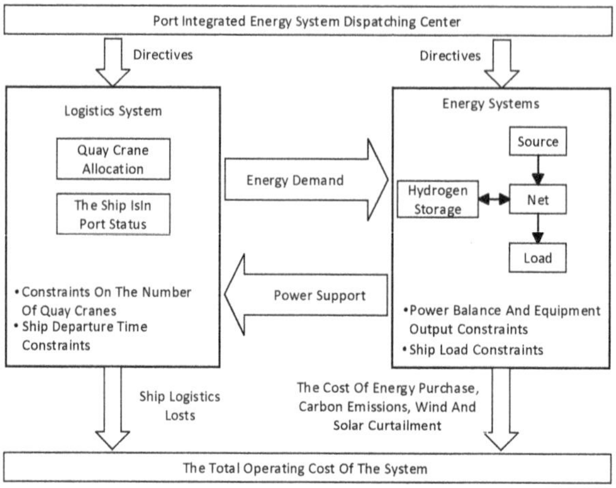

Figure 2. Port energy–logistics system collaborative optimal scheduling.

6. Case Verification

Taking a port in Shanghai as an example, the proposed method and model are verified. With a scheduling period of 48 h and a unit scheduling period of 1 h, the parameters of the port logistics and energy system are shown in Table 2 and the interaction parameters between ships and ports are shown in Table 3. The simulation was conducted on a 64-bit PC with a 2.40 GHZ CPU and 16 GB RAM, using MATLAB R2023a with a YALMIP solver.

Table 2. Parameters of the port logistics and energy system.

Parameter	Value	Parameter	Value	Parameter	Value
η (TEU/H)	35	COP^{e}_{Gt}	0.3	β (kg/kWh)	2.262
C_{max}	7	COP^{h}_{GT}	0.55	P_{gas} (USD/kWh)	0.0422
P^{1}_{crane} (kW)	320	COP_{FC}	0.65	P_{co2} (USD/kg)	0.0068
$COP^{e}_{CCHP,GT}$	0.3	COP_{P2H}	0.6	CO_2^{max} (kg/h)	35,000
$COP^{h,loss}_{CCHP,GT}$	0.15	COP^{in}_{HS}	0.98	$P_{abbandon}$ (USD/kWh)	0.0138
$COP^{h,recovery}_{CCHP,GT}$	0.3	COP^{out}_{HS}	0.98	a_1 (USD/kWh)	0.0651
$COP^{h}_{CCHP,GT}$	0.8	COP_{MR}	0.5	a_2 (USD/kWh)	0.1211
COP^{c}_{AC}	1.2	α (kg/kWh)	0.7129	a_3 (USD/kWh)	0.1514

Table 3. Parameters of ship and port interactions [45].

Ship Number	Time of Arrival/h	Latest Departure Time/h	Loading And Unloading /Box	Largest Quay Crane Demand/Unit	Minimal Quay Crane Demand/Unit
1	1	14	450	4	2
2	2	14	600	3	1
3	5	25	800	5	2
4	8	27	500	3	2
5	11	30	550	3	2
6	15	25	500	3	1
7	18	34	600	2	1
8	23	42	500	3	2
9	27	39	650	3	1
10	29	42	550	4	2
11	31	46	450	3	1
12	34	47	550	2	1
13	38	48	600	5	2
14	40	48	500	4	2

6.1. Results and Discussion

6.1.1. Energy–Logistics System Collaborative Optimization Analysis

To verify the economic feasibility of collaborative optimization between the port logistics system and the energy system, two comparative cases are set up as follows:

(1) Case A: Separate optimization of logistics and energy systems;
(2) Case B: Collaborative optimization of logistics and energy systems.

Specifically, the separate optimization of logistics and energy systems was carried out in two steps. The first step is to minimize the waiting and berthing time of ships and obtain the allocation quantity of quay cranes and the ships' states in port. The waiting and berthing time of ships is represented by the logistics cost of the ship.

After obtaining the number of quay cranes and the state of ships in port through minimizing C_{ship}, the second step is to substitute the number of quay cranes and the ships' states in port as known quantities into the integrated energy system for optimization and solution generation to obtain the output curve of each energy equipment and the operating cost of the system.

Table 4 presents the scheduling results of the two comparison cases, showing that the operation mode in case B brings superior economic advantages to the PIES and can effectively increase the renewable energy consumption rate and concurrently minimize carbon emissions. Conversely, in case A, the logistics and energy systems function in isolation. This segregation restricts the flexibility of both the ship and the quay crane in response to the energy system's parameters, resulting in a less economically efficient outcome compared to case B.

Table 4. Total cost of the two schemes.

Parameter	Case A	Case B
C_{buy}/USD	30,094.7	27,199
C_{co2}/USD	8896.5	9511.1
C_{loss}/USD	362.4	83.1
Abandoned wind and solar rate/%	10.32	2.37
C_{ship}/USD	10,926.7	11,894.9
Total cost/USD	50,280.3	48,688.1
Compare with case B	+3.27%	-

As shown in Figure 3, when the logistics and energy systems are co-optimized, the electrical load is consistent with the wind and solar output. It is jointly supplied by the main power grid, the GT, and CCHP. Notably, the FC plays a minimal role in the energy dispatch cycle, attributed to its comparatively lower efficiency and economic disadvantages. In the thermal schedule plan, the heat load is almost entirely supplied by the GT, and the CCHP system contributes marginally, engaging only during specific intervals. Due to the single piece of cooling equipment, the cooling load is only provided by CCHP. This configuration ensures the utilization of nearly all waste heat generated by CCHP for refrigeration purposes, with heating applications become a secondary priority when the demand for cooling subsides.

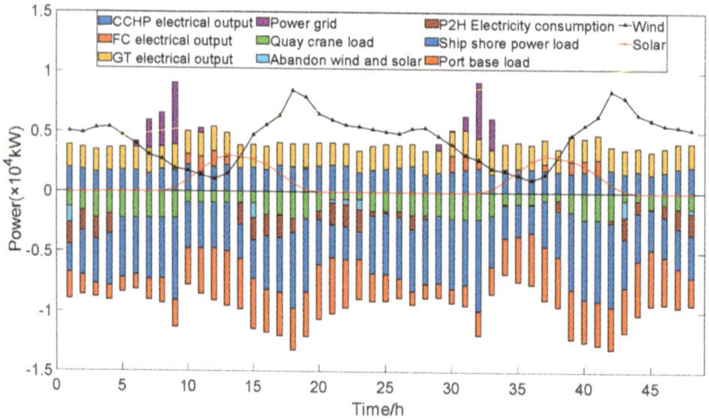

(**a**) Power schedule planning

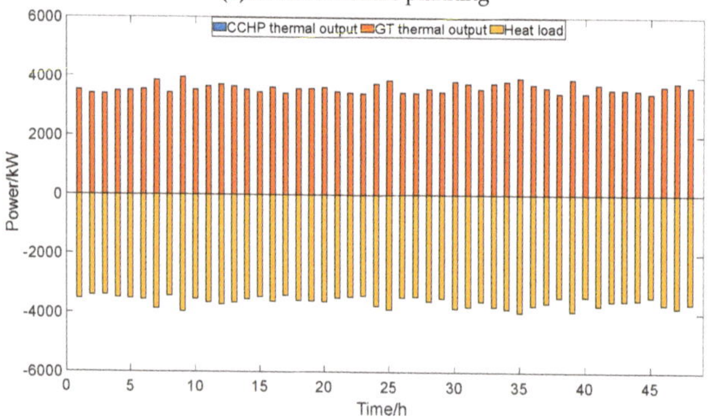

(**b**) Thermal schedule planning

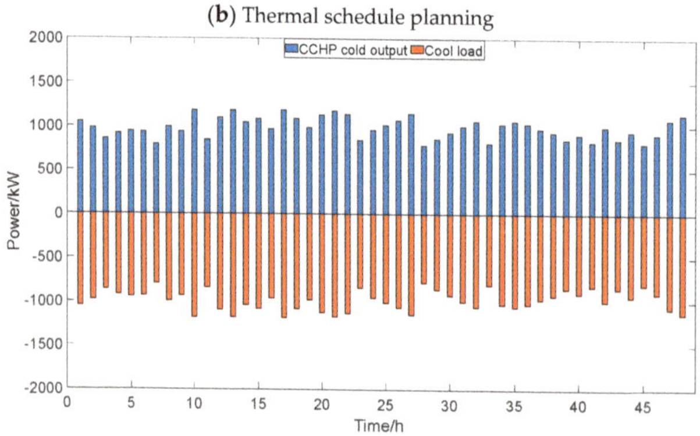

(**c**) Cooling schedule planning

Figure 3. Energy schedule in case B.

To quantitatively analyze the advantages of the optimization method proposed in this paper, the following is a detailed comparative analysis of case A and case B. Figure 4 illustrates the duration of the ship's stay in port for both cases, providing a visual representation to support the evaluation of the optimization method's efficacy.

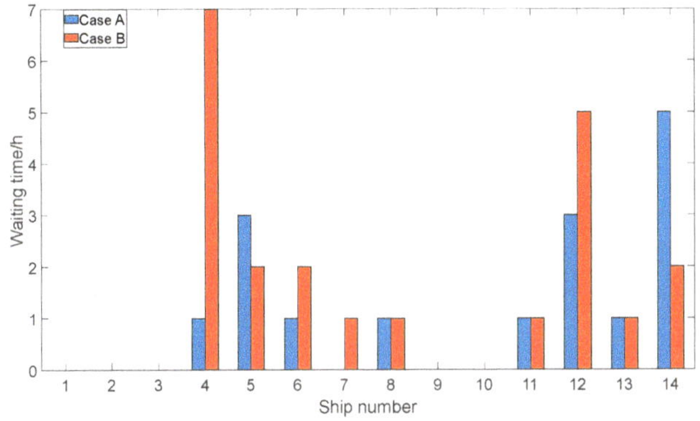

(**a**) The length of time the ship waits

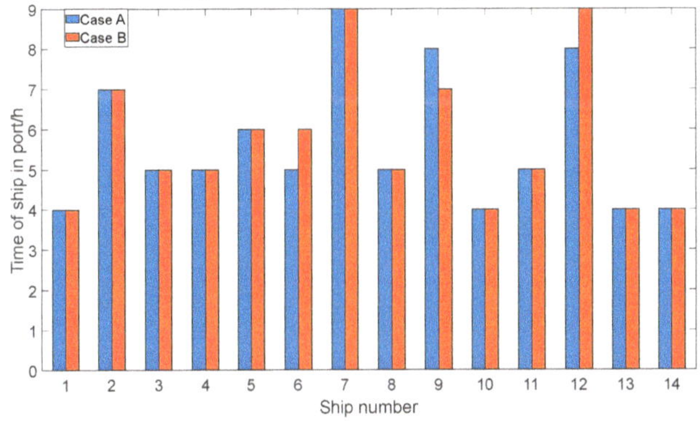

(**b**) The length of time the ship is in berth

Figure 4. Duration of ship in port.

Case A focuses on optimizing the scheduling of quay cranes and ships with the objective of minimizing the overall cost of the logistics system. Consequently, this approach prioritizes the reduction in berthing and waiting times, as rapid docking and departure of ships are seen as essential to lowering these specific costs. However, this strategy leads to an increase in energy expenditure, which paradoxically results in a higher total cost compared to case B. Although the logistics costs are elevated during collaborative optimization, this phase incorporates the consideration of the operating parameters of the energy system. As a result, despite the initial higher logistics expenditure, the comprehensive evaluation of energy parameters ensures that the aggregated cost of the system remains the lowest. This highlights the importance of holistic optimization strategies that account for both logistical efficiency and energy consumption in reducing the overall operational costs of the port.

In Figure 4, an elongated waiting duration for the ship in case B is observed, which suggests that an optimal berthing time has been selected by the shipping entity. This decision appears to be strategically made to achieve a balance between logistics and energy expenditures, ultimately aiming at cost minimization.

In Figure 5, a comparative analysis is presented between two distinct cases regarding the load management of ships. In case A, the distribution of ship load does not demonstrate a significant correlation with electricity pricing, attributing this outcome to the exclusive consideration of logistics costs. The energy consumption cost is reduced only by adjusting the variable power load in a fixed period, and the adjustment effect is not apparent because the variable power load is small. Conversely, case B illustrates a strategic approach where ships possess the flexibility to modify their port arrival timings and load statuses in response to fluctuations in electricity prices. This adaptability results in a more efficient load distribution, characterized by reduced ship loads during periods of elevated electricity prices and increased loads when electricity prices are lower. This approach facilitates a more harmonious integration with the energy system, distinguishing it markedly from the outcomes observed in case A.

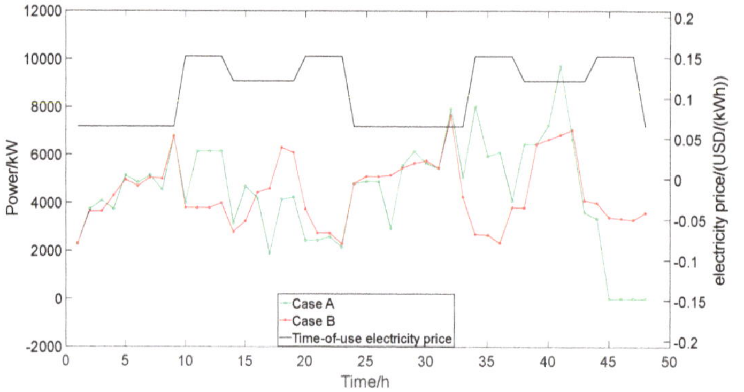

Figure 5. Comparison of ship load in cases A and B.

Figure 6 shows cases A and B's P2H power and wind–solar load curves. The P2H power of case A is relatively high. During 1:00–4:00, 14:00–16:00, 17:00–27:00, and 42:00–44:00, the combined output from wind and solar sources falls short of the total electricity load. Nevertheless, the electricity yielded by the gas equipment's combined heat and power generation results in an excess of wind and solar energy, prompting the P2H system to activate and subsequently reach its capacity limit during certain periods. This leads to the squandering of renewable energy resources. During the 17:00 and 45:00–48:00 periods, the output from wind and solar exceeds the total electrical load. However, constraints related to the P2H power capacity and the operational limits of gas-powered electrical equipment prevent the full utilization of wind and solar energy, culminating in a significant wind and solar curtailment rate of 10.32%. Case B's output from wind and solar is lower than the electrical load. The surplus wind and solar energy seldom breaches the P2H system's upper power threshold when considering the contribution of gas equipment, leading to a markedly reduced incidence of renewable energy wastage, quantified at a mere 2.37%. In Figure 6b, the maximum and minimum values of the electricity load in case B are 12,823 kW and 5788 kW, respectively. Compared to case A's 15,626 kW and 2347.7 kW, the electricity load curve in case B is more stable and the trend in changes is closer to the wind and solar power output, indicating that energy–logistics collaborative optimization enables ships to better synchronize with the available wind and solar energy. Based on meeting production demands, adjusting the temporal distribution of the load allows the logistics system to flexibly change according to the energy system, thus achieving interaction between the two systems.

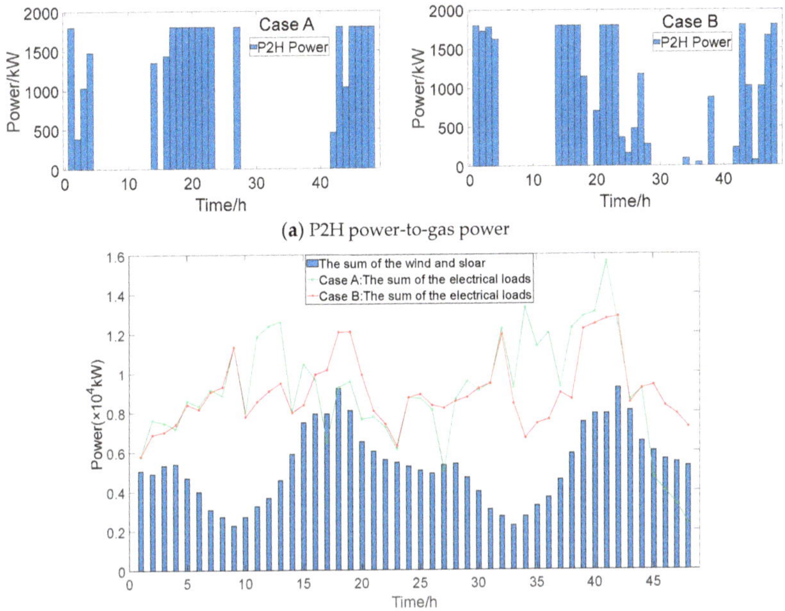

(**a**) P2H power-to-gas power

(**b**) Wind and solar load curves

Figure 6. Comparison of P2H power and wind–solar load curves in case A and case B.

6.1.2. Scheduling Analysis of Ships Waiting for Berth

Based on the collaborative optimization of logistics and energy systems, to further study the impact of ship scheduling on the system, the following comparative cases are studied.

Case C: Regardless of the scheduling of waiting ships, when the ship arrives at the port, it immediately berths. That is, the ship's arrival time is equal to the berthing time.

The cost comparison between case C and case B is shown in Table 5, and a comparison of ship load, P2H power, and wind–solar load curves is shown in Figures 7 and 8, respectively.

Table 5. Scheduling results of case B and case C.

Parameter	Case B	Case C
C_{buy}/USD	27,199	31,653.8
C_{co2}/USD	9511.1	9690
C_{loss}/USD	83.1	412.2
Abandon wind and solar rate/%	2.37	11.73
C_{ship}/USD	11,894.9	11,203.3
Total cost/USD	48,688.1	52,959.3
Compare with case B	-	+8.77%

Upon analyzing Tables 4 and 5, it is evident that even in scenarios where waiting costs are not considered, the logistics cost associated with case C remains higher than that of A, indicating that the port call time of the ship is relatively longer to distribute the load of the ship during the period when the electricity price is lower, or the wind and solar output is more extensive. In Table 5, compared with case C, case B achieves a more substantial reduction in cost by incorporating the scheduling of waiting ships. This finding suggests that the strategic scheduling of ships awaiting berth not only enhances the system's overall flexibility but also yields a more pronounced optimization effect than the strategies employed in cases A and C.

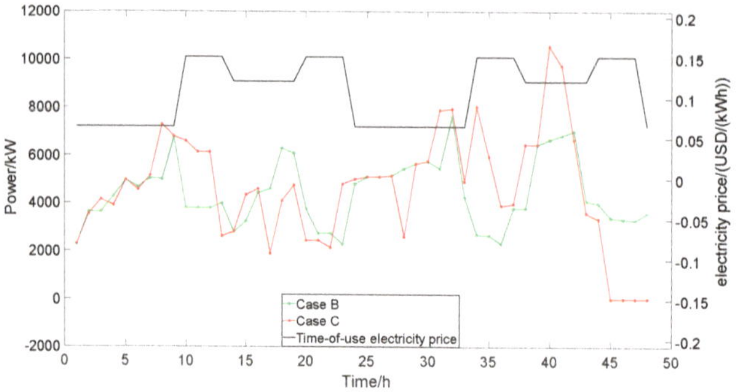

Figure 7. Comparison of ship load in case B and case C.

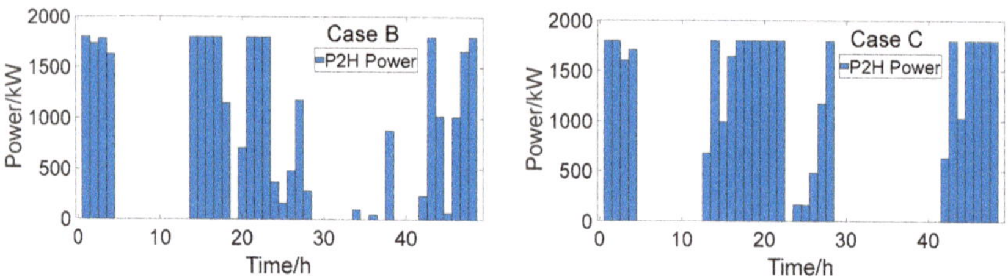

(**a**) P2H power-to-gas power

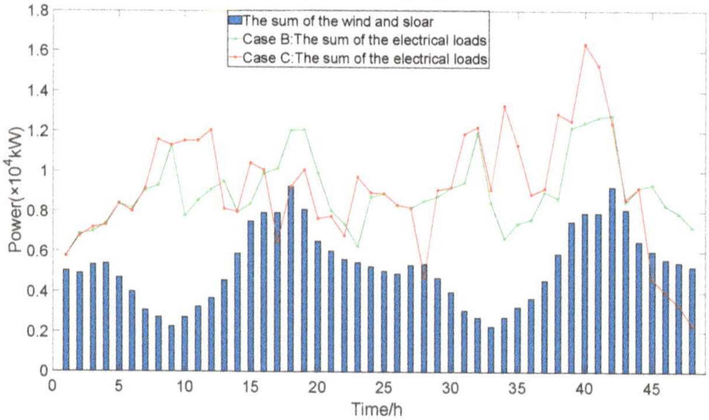

(**b**) Wind and solar load curves

Figure 8. Comparison of P2H power and wind–solar load curves in case B and case C.

In the analysis presented in Figure 7, although case C is a collaborative optimization of logistics and energy, this approach overlooks the crucial aspect of scheduling for waiting ships. This oversight leads to a suboptimal alignment between the demand load curve and the fluctuating electricity prices, consequently elevating the system's overall operational costs. Compared with Figures 5 and 7, the ship load curves and system operating costs of the two cases exhibit a notable similarity because the ships' waiting times in cases A and C are almost the same. During the period of 10:00–20:00 and 30:00–42:00, the load curves across the three studied cases are inversely correlated with the variations in electricity pricing. This phenomenon is primarily influenced by factors such as the ships' scheduled arrival times, production time requirements, and the availability of quay cranes. In the period of 31:00–41:00, the load attributed to ships in case B is markedly lower than those observed in cases A and C. This discrepancy underscores the potential for ships in case B to effectively adjust their operations in response to electricity pricing dynamics, highlighting strategic advantages in operational flexibility and cost efficiency. This indicates that when berth allocation is combined with a time-of-use pricing model, port operators can optimize the berthing sequence to schedule electricity demand, allowing docked ships' needs to be met at a lower total cost.

Figure 8 shows a comparison of P2H power and wind–solar load curves between case B and case C. Notably, case C exhibits a higher P2H power output relative to case B. During P2H operations, a recurrent observation is its operation at the power limit, rendering it incapable of fully integrating available renewable energy sources. This operational characteristic, in turn, contributes to an elevated rate of wind and solar curtailment in case C as compared to case B. Figure 8b shows that the maximum and minimum values of the electricity load in case C are 16,373 kW and 2347.7 kW, respectively. Compared with case B, the fluctuation in its electricity load is larger, and its fitting degree to wind and solar power output is poor. This in turn proves that the optimized scheduling of waiting vessels can improve the utilization rate of renewable energy.

In conclusion, the optimization strategy delineated within this paper demonstrates a significant reduction in operational costs for port systems by adjusting the ship's state in port and the state of the load operation, as well as the output of various energy equipment, based on fully considering the port's logistics scheduling. This approach offers dual benefits. Firstly, it enhances the efficiency and productivity of port operations, aligning with the operational paradigms and production management expectations of ship owners. Secondly, it embodies a commitment to economic viability and environmental protection, making it a holistic solution for contemporary maritime logistics challenges.

6.2. Sensitivity Analysis

Here, several sensitivity analyses are illustrated for different important parameters to validate the effectiveness of the developed model (Table 6).

Table 6. Sensitivity analysis of different parameters.

Parameter	Case B	P2H*2	Re*2	(P2H+Re)*2	Fixed Electricity Price	CO_2*2
C_{buy}/USD	27,119	27,072.7	24,992.9	24,340.4	27,690.3	26,968.7
C_{co2}/USD	9511.1	9503.4	9413.9	9418	9486.1	18,987.7
C_{loss}/USD	83.1	0	2568.5	1749.9	53	65.7
Abandon rate/%	2.37	0	36.56	24.91	1.51	1.87
C_{ship}/USD	11,894.9	11,894.9	11,203.3	11,065	12,309.8	12,171.5
Total cost/USD	48,688.1	48,471	48,178.6	46,573.3	49,539.2	58,193.6
Compared with case B	-	−0.45	−1.05	−4.34	+1.75	+19.52

P2H*2: P2H maximum power multiplied by two; Re*2: renewable energy generation multiplied by two; (P2H+Re)*2: P2H maximum power and renewable energy generation multiplied by two; CO_2*2: the price of carbon dioxide emissions multiplied by two.

(a) Through a data comparison, it is found that when the upper limit of P2H power increases, the consumption rate of renewable energy improves, indirectly reducing the purchasing power of the port, thereby reducing the operating costs of the port.

(b) When only renewable energy generation is increased, this will cause excessive waste, and the operating costs of ports will not significantly increase; when the upper limit of P2H power and the amount of renewable energy generation increase synchronously, the operating costs of the port will be further reduced. Therefore, when expanding, it is possible to consider binding the two together.

(c) When a fixed electricity price is used in ports instead of time-of-use electricity prices, the flexibility of berth scheduling is independent of electricity prices, which further reduces the performance of port collaborative optimization scheduling. Therefore, time-of-use electricity prices are an indispensable part of port collaborative optimization scheduling.

(d) When doubling the carbon emission price of the port, the carbon emission cost of the port also doubles and the operating cost increases significantly. Thus, it can be seen that carbon emission prices have a significant impact on port operating costs.

7. Managerial Implications

Here, we discuss some managerial implications of the suggested research.

(a) We should advocate for the coordinated optimization of port logistics and energy systems, which can reduce the operating costs of a port overall. This can promote the collaborative optimization of ports by implementing practical reward and punishment mechanisms for port operators and relevant stakeholders.
(b) Policy-makers can encourage port operators to install more PV and WTs, emphasizing the importance of renewable energy for green and low-carbon ports. This can not only promote energy conservation and emission reductions in ports, but also reduce dependence on fossil fuel power generation, thereby protecting the environment.
(c) Governments should encourage port operators to adopt P2H technology and related hydrogen equipment to reduce carbon dioxide emissions. This may include providing subsidies to ports that purchase equipment that helps reduce carbon dioxide emissions.
(d) Policy-makers should encourage learning and exchange between different countries and ports to share knowledge and learn about port operation strategies and carbon reduction methods. This can promote a global approach to reducing port operating costs and promoting the consumption of renewable energy.

8. Conclusions, Limitation and Future Research

In recent times, ports have become increasingly important hubs for international trade and engines for economic development in various countries, while their energy consumption has also increased sharply. To improve the economic and environmental efficiency of ports, this paper delves into the intricacies of PIESs, scrutinizing the interconnections and potential for optimization within logistics systems, ships, and diverse forms of energy. We propose a novel approach for collaborative optimization scheduling, specifically tailored for the energy–logistics nexus within port environments. The primary conclusions drawn from this study are systematically presented, highlighting the significant implications for enhancing the efficiency and sustainability of port operations.

(1) In contrast to the isolated optimization of logistics and energy systems, a collaborative optimization approach has been observed to decrease operational costs by 3.27%. The inclusion of ship waiting schedule optimization further enhances the system's flexibility. Moreover, the integrated optimization of both logistics and energy systems has been notably effective in minimizing the curtailment rates of wind and solar energies. This indicates that the proposed methodology not only considers economic and environmental sustainability but also significantly improves the overall energy utilization rate by seamlessly integrating port logistics with energy systems.

(2) Upon conducting a comprehensive analysis focused on the collaborative optimization of logistics and energy systems, it has been observed that the operational expenditures associated with the system were notably reduced. Concurrently, there was an absence of substantial alterations in the scheduling of ship itineraries. This outcome suggests that the methodology proposed herein is capable of effectively enhancing the interconnectivity between logistical and energy systems operating within a port. This enhancement has been accomplished without compromising the service expectations of ship owners regarding port production management. Consequently, this approach not only facilitates energy conservation and emission reductions but also promotes the economic viability of port operations.

Apart from the numerous benefits that the proposed model offers, this study has certain limitations that may be addressed in future research. The optimization approach proposed in this paper lacks consideration of other uncertainties and the interaction between port operators and ships. In addition, acquiring dependable, useful, and correct data is the most crucial task. The ambiguity resulting from human factors as well as the use of software cannot be ignored, even though the primary data sources for this study are peer-reviewed publications.

In the future, multi-scenario port energy management studies can be conducted to analyze the social benefits of optimal scheduling and flexible berth allocation while accounting for different types of uncertainties such as vessel arrivals, electricity prices, and fuel costs. Statistical or ambiguous logic-based techniques should be used to estimate the model's necessary data. This study contributes significantly to enhancing the energy efficiency and economic performance of PIESs, leveraging advanced methodologies and theoretical frameworks to explore innovative solutions for sustainable port infrastructure development.

Author Contributions: Conceptualization, A.M. and Y.Z.; methodology, A.M., Y.Z. and L.S.; software, A.M., Y.Z. and L.S.; validation, A.M., Y.Z., L.S. and Y.X.; formal analysis, F.M. and Y.X.; investigation, Y.Z. and F.M.; resources, Y.Z., F.M. and Y.X.; data curation, A.M.; writing—original draft preparation, A.M.; writing—review and editing, A.M. and Y.Z.; visualization, A.M., Y.Z. and L.S.; supervision, F.M. and Y.X.; project administration, Y.X. Thank you for the funding from Y.X. All authors have read and agreed to the published version of the manuscript.

Funding: This work was partly supported by the Logistics research funding program (No. BHJ22R047).

Data Availability Statement: Data are contained within the article.

Conflicts of Interest: The authors declare no conflicts of interest.

Nomenclature

Acronyms	
PIES	Port-Integrated Energy System.
CCHP	Combined Cooling, Heating, and Power.
GT	Gas turbine.
AC	Refrigeration machine.
P2H	Power to hydrogen.
PV	Photovoltaics.
WT	Wind turbine.
HS	Hydrogen storage.
EH	Energy hub.
MR	Methanation device.
FC	Fuel cell.
Indices	
n/j	Set/index of ships.
T,t	Set/index of operation periods.
m/i	Set/index of variable power equipment.
Parameters	
t_0/t_{leave}^{latest}	Estimated arrival/departure time of a ship.
N_j	Number of loading or unloading containers.
η	Loading and unloading efficiency of quay cranes.
C_j^{max}/C_j^{min}	Maximum and minimum number of quay cranes.
P_{crane}^1	Power consumption of a single quay crane.
Δt	Unit scheduling period.
$C_{\max}$	Total amount of quay crane resources.
$W_{var,i}$	Rated workload of the intermittent equipment.
$L_{var,i}^{min}/L_{var,i}^{max}$	Upper/lower limits of the intermittent equipment.
$COP_{CCHP,GT}^{e}$	Electrical efficiency of GT.
$COP_{CCHP,GT}^{h,loss}$	Heat loss rate of GT.
$COP_{CCHP,GT}^{h,recovery}$	Flue gas recovery rate of GT.
$COP_{CCHP,GT}^{h}$	Recovery rate of waste heat of GT.
COP_{AC}^{c}	Refrigeration coefficient of AC.

COP_{Gt}^{e}	Electrical efficiency of GT.
COP_{GT}^{h}	Thermal efficiency of GT.
COP_{FC}	Electrical efficiency of FC.
COP_{P2H}	Electrolytic efficiency of P2H.
COP_{HS}^{in}	Charging efficiency of HS.
COP_{HS}^{out}	Discharging efficiency of HS.
COP_{MR}	Conversion efficiency of MR.
H_{load}	Constant heat load of the port.
L_{load}	Constant cooling load of the port
α/β	Carbon emission coefficient of power/gas.
P_{gas}	Natural gas price.
P_{co2}	Carbon emission price.
CO_2^{max}	Maximum carbon emissions of ports.
$P_{abandon}$	Abandoned wind and solar punishment cost.
a_1	Valley price.
a_2	Ordinary price.
a_3	Peak price.
Variables	
t_1/t_{leave}	Berthing time/departure time of ship.
C_j	Allocation quantity of quay cranes.
$t_{leave}^{min}/t_{leave}^{max}$	Earliest/latest departure time of ship.
C_j^{max}/C_j^{min}	Maximum and minimum number of quay cranes.
$X_j(t)$	Ship in port state.
$P_{crane}(t)$	Power consumption of all quay cranes.
$L_{ship}(t)$	Total load power of the ship.
$L_{cons}(t)$	Constant power load of the ship.
$L_{var}(t)$	Variable power load of the ship.
$L_{var,i}(t)$	Size of variable power.
$s_i(t)$	Status of intermittent working equipment.
$P_{ship}(t)$	Sum of the shore power of all ships.
Q_{CCHP}	Gas consumption of CCHP.
$P_{CCHP,GT}^{e}$	Power generation of GT.
$P_{CCHP,GT}^{h}$	Recyclable heat power of GT exhaust gas.
$P_{CCHP,GT}^{h}$	Total thermal produced by CCHP.
P_{CCHP}^{c}	Cold power output by CCHP.
P_{CCHP}^{h}	Heat supplied to the port outputting by CCHP.
P_{GT}^{e}	Power generation of GT.
P_{GT}^{h}	Heat generation of GT.
Q_{GT}	Gas consumption of GT.
M_{FC}	Hydrogen consumption of FC.
P_{FC}	Power generated by FC.
P_{P2H}	Electrical power consumed by P2H.
M_{P2H}	Hydrogen production of P2H.
$M_{HS,t}$	Energy storage state value of HS.
$M_{HS,t}^{in}/M_{HS,t}^{out}$	Charging/discharging hydrogen power of HS.
M_{MR}	Hydrogen consumption of the MR.
Q_{MR}	Power of methane production of the MR.

References

1. Ezeh, C.I.; Richter, U.H.; Seufert, J.H.; Peng, C. Operational-Based Decarbonization of Container Ports: The Case of Ningbo-Zhoushan Port. *Int. J. Sustain. Transp.* **2024**, *18*, 34–45. [CrossRef]
2. Zhou, Y.; Zhou, H. The Emission Reduction Technology Decision of the Port Supply Chain. *Mathematics* **2024**, *12*, 848. [CrossRef]
3. Daniel, H.; Trovão, J.P.F.; Williams, D.; Boulon, L. Unlocking Shore Power in St. Lawrence and Great Lakes for Cargo Ships. *Transp. Res. Part D Transp. Environ.* **2024**, *131*, 104230. [CrossRef]
4. Wang, Z.; Hu, H.; Zhen, L. Berth and Quay Cranes Allocation Problem with On-Shore Power Supply Assignment in Container Terminals. *Comput. Ind. Eng.* **2024**, *188*, 109910. [CrossRef]
5. Karimi, S.; Zadeh, M.; Suul, J.A. Operation-Based Reliability Assessment of Shore-to-Ship Charging Systems Including On-Shore Batteries. *IEEE Trans. Ind. Appl.* **2023**, *59*, 4752–4763. [CrossRef]

6. Qi, P.; Gao, W. Study on Load Forecasting of Combined Cooling, Heat and Power System with Deep Learning Algorithm Based on Attention Mechanism. In Proceedings of the 2023 5th International Academic Exchange Conference on Science and Technology Innovation (IAECST), Guangzhou, China, 8–10 December 2023; pp. 1353–1358.
7. Holder, D.; Percy, S.D.; Yavari, A. A Review of Port Decarbonisation Options: Identified Opportunities for Deploying Hydrogen Technologies. *Sustainability* **2024**, *16*, 3299. [CrossRef]
8. Giri, B.K.; Roy, S.K.; Deveci, M. Fuzzy Robust Flexible Programming with Me Measure for Electric Sustainable Supply Chain. *Appl. Soft Comput.* **2023**, *145*, 110614. [CrossRef]
9. Giri, B.K.; Roy, S.K. Fuzzy-Random Robust Flexible Programming on Sustainable Closed-Loop Renewable Energy Supply Chain. *Appl. Energy* **2024**, *363*, 123044. [CrossRef]
10. Lei, J.; Zhang, H.; Pan, J.; Zhuo, Y.; Chen, A.; Chen, W.; Yang, Z.; Feng, K.; Li, L.; Wang, B.; et al. Techno-Economic Assessment of a Full-Chain Hydrogen Production by Offshore Wind Power. *Energies* **2024**, *17*, 2447. [CrossRef]
11. Chavan, H.R.; Knollmeyer, J.; Khan, S. A Study on the Potential of Hydrogen Fuel Cells for Maritime Transportation Applications. In Proceedings of the SoutheastCon 2023, Orlando, FL, USA, 1–16 April 2023; pp. 498–503.
12. Kelmalis, A.; Dimou, A.; Lekkas, D.F.; Vakalis, S. Cold Ironing and the Study of RES Utilization for Maritime Electrification on Lesvos Island Port. *Environments* **2024**, *11*, 84. [CrossRef]
13. Zhang, L.; Zeng, Q.; Wang, L. How to Achieve Comprehensive Carbon Emission Reduction in Ports? A Systematic Review. *J. Mar. Sci. Eng.* **2024**, *12*, 715. [CrossRef]
14. Sun, P.; Wang, L.; Yuan, T.; Ma, D.; Ma, L.; Li, L.; Guo, J.; Dong, X.; Gao, K. A Comprehensive Study on Electric Field Coupling Effects of Medium-Voltage SiC Power Module and Optimization Design. In Proceedings of the 2024 IEEE Applied Power Electronics Conference and Exposition (APEC), Long Beach, CA, USA, 25–29 February 2024; pp. 2556–2561.
15. He, W.; Feng, Y.; Wu, S.; Wang, W. Mechanical–Thermal–Electrical Coupling Modeling and Temperature Rise Characteristic of a Parallel Groove Clamp with Improved Representation of Contact Interactions. *IEEE Trans. Compon. Packag. Manuf. Technol.* **2023**, *13*, 356–364. [CrossRef]
16. Xu, Z.; Zhang, C.; Sun, B.; Liu, S. The Electric-Thermal Coupling Simulation and State Estimation of Lithium-Ion Battery. *J. Energy Storage* **2023**, *58*, 106431. [CrossRef]
17. Fu, L.; Li, H.; Deng, Y.; Tang, C. The Influence of Small Molecule Products on Natural Ester Impregnated Cellulose Insulation Paper under Electric-Thermal Coupling Field. *Colloids Surf. A Physicochem. Eng. Asp.* **2024**, *697*, 134426. [CrossRef]
18. Song, R.; Hamacher, T.; Terzija, V.; Perić, V.S. Potentials of Using Electric-Thermal Sector Coupling for Frequency Control: A Review. *Int. J. Electr. Power Energy Syst.* **2023**, *151*, 109194. [CrossRef]
19. Liu, W.; Teh, J.; Alharbi, B.; Yang, G.; Wang, B.; Meng, D.; Shi, J.; AlKassem, A.; Aljabr, A.; Alshammari, N. An Electric-Thermal Coupling Modeling Method for Lithium-Ion Battery Using the State of Charge Normalization Calculation Method. *J. Energy Storage* **2023**, *72*, 108724. [CrossRef]
20. Skowron, Ł.; Chygryn, O.; Gąsior, M.; Koibichuk, V.; Lyeonov, S.; Drozd, S.; Dluhopolskyi, O. Interconnection between the Dynamic of Growing Renewable Energy Production and the Level of CO_2 Emissions: A Multistage Approach for Modeling. *Sustainability* **2023**, *15*, 9473. [CrossRef]
21. Putranto, L.M.; Budi, R.F.S.; Novitasari, D. Generation Expansion Planning with a Renewable Energy Target and Interconnection Option: A Case Study of the Sulawesi Region, Indonesia. *Renew. Sustain. Energy Rev.* **2023**, *183*, 113489. [CrossRef]
22. Ren, Y. Research of AGV Scheduling in Container Terminal. Master's Thesis, Jimei University, Xiamen, China, 2014.
23. Borelli, D.; Devia, F.; Schenone, C.; Silenzi, F.; Tagliafico, L.A. Dynamic Modelling of LNG Powered Combined Energy Systems in Port Areas. *Energies* **2021**, *14*, 3640. [CrossRef]
24. Aljuaid, A.M.; Koubâa, M.; Ammar, M.H.; Kammoun, K.; Hachicha, W. Mathematical Programming Formulations for the Berth Allocation Problems in Container Seaport Terminals. *Logistics* **2024**, *8*, 50. [CrossRef]
25. Song, T.; Li, Y.; Zhang, X.-P.; Wu, C.; Li, J.; Guo, Y.; Gu, H. Integrated Port Energy System Considering Integrated Demand Response and Energy Interconnection. *Int. J. Electr. Power Energy Syst.* **2020**, *117*, 105654. [CrossRef]
26. Kovač, M.; Tadić, S.; Krstić, M.; Roso, V. Modelling Dry Port Systems in the Framework of Inland Waterway Container Terminals. *Comput. Model. Eng. Sci.* **2023**, *137*, 1019–1046. [CrossRef]
27. Xu, X.; Li, Z.; Jiang, X.; Huang, X.; Lu, Y.; Li, L. Port Berth Allocation and Microgrid Cluster Joint Optimization Scheduling Based on Master-Slave Game. *J. Clean. Prod.* **2024**, *452*, 142220. [CrossRef]
28. Zhao, W.; Ma, K.; Yang, J.; Guo, S. A Risk-Averse Logistics-Energy Coordination Optimization Strategy for Port Energy System Considering Demand Response Program. *Electr. Power Syst. Res.* **2024**, *231*, 110297. [CrossRef]
29. Shi, Z.; Fan, F.; Tai, N.; Qing, C.; Meng, Y.; Guo, R. An Optimal Operation Strategy for Integrated Energy-Logistics System in Green Port. In Proceedings of the 2022 IEEE/IAS Industrial and Commercial Power System Asia (I&CPS Asia), Shanghai, China, 8–11 July 2022; pp. 1592–1597.
30. Lassoued, R.; Elloumi, A. A Bi-Level Optimization Model for Solving the Berth and Quay Cranes Allocation Problems in Port Terminal. In Proceedings of the 2021 International Conference on Decision Aid Sciences and Application (DASA), Sakheer, Bahrain, 7–8 December 2021; pp. 981–985.
31. Lassoued, R.; Elloumi, A. Hierarchical Optimization for Solving the Integrated Berth and Quay Crane Assignment Problem in Port Terminal. In Proceedings of the 2022 8th International Conference on Control, Decision and Information Technologies (CoDIT), Istanbul, Turkey, 17–20 May 2022; Volume 1, pp. 1479–1483.

32. Chang, S.-C.; Lin, M.-H.; Tsai, J.-F. An Optimization Approach to Berth Allocation Problems. *Mathematics* **2024**, *12*, 753. [CrossRef]
33. Ji, B.; Huang, H.; Yu, S.S. An Enhanced NSGA-II for Solving Berth Allocation and Quay Crane Assignment Problem with Stochastic Arrival Times. *IEEE Trans. Intell. Transp. Syst.* **2023**, *24*, 459–473. [CrossRef]
34. Wang, Z. Optimization of Port Ship Collaborative Scheduling Based on Differential NSGA-II Algorithm. *China Water Transp.* **2023**, *23*, 19–21.
35. Pu, Y.; Liu, H.; Wang, J.; Hou, Y. Collaborative Scheduling of Port Integrated Energy and Container Logistics Considering Electric and Hydrogen-Powered Transport. *IEEE Trans. Smart Grid* **2023**, *14*, 4345–4359. [CrossRef]
36. Jiang, M.; Ma, F.; Zhang, Y.; Lv, S.; Pei, Z.; Wu, G. Collaborative Scheduling Optimization of Container Port Berths and Cranes under Low-Carbon Environment. *Sustainability* **2024**, *16*, 2985. [CrossRef]
37. Yu, M.; Lv, Y.; Li, W. Multi objective optimization of low-carbon global scheduling for field bridges. *Logist. Technol.* **2020**, *39*, 41–47.
38. Mao, A.; Yu, T.; Ding, Z.; Fang, S.; Guo, J.; Sheng, Q. Optimal Scheduling for Seaport Integrated Energy System Considering Flexible Berth Allocation. *Appl. Energy* **2022**, *308*, 118386. [CrossRef]
39. Yang, J.; Wang, J.; Ma, K.; Liu, H.; Dai, Y.; Li, C. A Multi-Energy Pricing Strategy for Port Integrated Energy System Based on Bayesian Stackelberg Game. *Sustain. Energy Grids Netw.* **2024**, *38*, 101264. [CrossRef]
40. Zhen, L.; Yang, Z.; Wang, S.; Hu, H.; Chew, E.P.; Fan, T. Integrated Planning Model for Two-Story Container Ports. *Transp. Res. Part C Emerg. Technol.* **2024**, *160*, 104535. [CrossRef]
41. Bemporad, A.; Morari, M. Control of Systems Integrating Logic, Dynamics, and Constraints. *Automatica* **1999**, *35*, 407–427. [CrossRef]
42. Heemels, W.P.M.H.; Schutter, B.D.; Bemporad, A. Equivalence of Hybrid Dynamical Models. *Automatica* **2001**, *37*, 1085–1091. [CrossRef]
43. Liu, Y.; Zhang, T.; Gao, Y.; Lv, L.; Song, X. A MATLAB GUI Toolbox for Surrogate-Based Design and Optimization. In Proceedings of the 2019 IEEE 9th Annual International Conference on CYBER Technology in Automation, Control, and Intelligent Systems (CYBER), Suzhou, China, 29 July–2 August 2019; pp. 103–106.
44. Xu, L.; Xu, X.; Tang, Y.; Ren, X.; Guo, Y. A Matlab Toolbox for Modelling Viscoelastic Constitutive Equation and Parameter Optimization. In Proceedings of the 2017 3rd IEEE International Conference on Computer and Communications (ICCC), Chengdu, China, 13–16 December 2017; pp. 2884–2888.
45. Huang, Y.; Huang, W.; Wei, W.; Tai, N.; Li, R. Logistics-energy Collaborative Optimization Scheduling Method for Large Seaport Integrated Energy System. *Chin. J. Electr. Eng.* **2022**, *42*, 6184–6196. [CrossRef]

mathematics

MDPI

Article

A New Hybrid Improved Arithmetic Optimization Algorithm for Solving Global and Engineering Optimization Problems

Yalong Zhang [1,2] and Lining Xing [1,*]

[1] Key Laboratory of Collaborative Intelligence Systems, Ministry of Education, Xidian University, Xi'an 710071, China; yalong52051@163.com
[2] School of Mechatronic Engineering and Automation, Foshan University, Foshan 528200, China
* Correspondence: lnxing@xidian.edu.cn

Abstract: The Arithmetic Optimization Algorithm (AOA) is a novel metaheuristic inspired by mathematical arithmetic operators. Due to its simple structure and flexible parameter adjustment, the AOA has been applied to solve various engineering problems. However, the AOA still faces challenges such as poor exploitation ability and a tendency to fall into local optima, especially in complex, high-dimensional problems. In this paper, we propose a Hybrid Improved Arithmetic Optimization Algorithm (HIAOA) to address the issues of susceptibility to local optima in AOAs. First, grey wolf optimization is incorporated into the AOAs, where the group hunting behavior of GWO allows multiple individuals to perform local searches at the same time, enabling the solution to be more finely tuned and avoiding over-concentration in a particular region, which can improve the exploitation capability of the AOA. Second, at the end of each AOA run, the follower mechanism and the Cauchy mutation operation of the Sparrow Search Algorithm are selected with the same probability and perturbed to enhance the ability of the AOA to escape from the local optimum. The overall performance of the improved algorithm is assessed by selecting 23 benchmark functions and using the Wilcoxon rank-sum test. The results of the HIAOA are compared with other intelligent optimization algorithms. Furthermore, the HIAOA can also solve three engineering design problems successfully, demonstrating its competitiveness. According to the experimental results, the HIAOA has better test results than the comparator.

Keywords: arithmetic optimization algorithm; grey wolf optimization algorithm; sparrow search algorithm; Cauchy variation; engineering design problems

MSC: 65K10

1. Introduction

People have always been pursuing improvements in production efficiency and reductions in costs, and every industrial revolution has brought huge social and economic benefits; however, with the rapid development of modern science and society, complex optimization problems with multi-objective and large-scale characteristics have emerged. These problems often affect social production efficiency and cause a waste of resources. The global optimization problems arise in various practical applications in the real world, including machine learning [1], resource scheduling [2,3], path planning [4], community detection [5], and resource allocation [6]. However, these problems often exhibit multi-objective, large-scale, uncertain, and complex analytical characteristics [7]. This makes it difficult for traditional optimization algorithms that rely on explicitly defining and describing the problem in mathematical form to solve it [8]. In this context, metaheuristic algorithms are characterized by their powerful global search capability and adaptability, while becoming an important tool for solving global optimization problems [9]. The metaheuristic algorithms are global optimization methods designed based on three categories:

natural evolution, physical phenomena, and swarm intelligence (SI) [10]. They have their own unique structure and can solve various optimization problems regardless of the type of problem.

In recent years, more optimization algorithms based on SI have been proposed and successfully applied to solve various problems in the real world [11–13]. These methods often search in swarm for the best solution to a problem. Therefore, the field of SI [14] has been studied by many researchers, and various swarm-based metaheuristic algorithms have been proposed, such as Particle Swarm Optimization (PSO) [15], Ant colony optimization [16], Grey Wolf Optimizer (GWO) [17], Sand Cat Swarm Optimization [18], Aquila Optimizer (AO) [19], Sea Horse Optimizer [20], Dung Beetle Optimizer (DBO) [21], the African Vultures Optimization Algorithm [22], Spider wasp Optimizer [23], and the Black Kite Algorithm (BKA) [24].

Although optimization algorithms are often regarded as black boxes that can flexibly solve various complex optimization problems, this does not guarantee that all the algorithms reported in the literature will obtain the global optimal solution to a variety of optimization problems [25]. Therefore, to better solve some problems or provide new solutions to these problems, many researchers modify existing algorithms or propose new algorithms. For example, Zhou et al. [26] proposed an Adaptive Differential Evolutionary Algorithm to solve the problem of assigning jobs to batches without breaking the machine capacity constraints, and then sequencing the batches to minimize the completion time. Yi et al. [27] proposed an improved version of the NSGA-III algorithm (INSGA-III) by introducing the concept of Stud and designing several improved crossover operators such as SBX, UC, and SI, which reduced the computational cost of the algorithm in solving large-scale optimization problems. Xing et al. [28] proposed a novel evolutionary approach (EA) called HHEA to study the multi-site capacity-constrained arc routing problem.

The Arithmetic Optimization Algorithm (AOA) [29] is an emerging swarm intelligence optimization method that aims to search the solution space of a problem using the distributional behavior of self-arithmetic operators including multiplication (M), division (D), subtraction (S), and addition (A). The AOA has a simple structure, flexible parameter settings, and a strong global search capability. However, the exploitation ability of the AOA is somewhat insufficient, and there are still some limitations in some complex high-dimensional and multi-peak problems, such as being prone to falling into local optimality and slow convergence [30]. The position update formula of the AOA lacks sufficient randomness for search agents, making it more prone to becoming trapped in local optima [31]. Moreover, the AOA's inadequate exploitation of the search space limits its ability to consistently achieve optimal parameter values when applied to PID controller optimization [32]. Therefore, the AOA requires further improvement. As of today, the number of pertinent citations in the literature is approaching 2000. The AOA has been successfully applied in many fields, such as engineering design [33], neural networks [34], energy storage grids [35], feature recognition [36], image segmentation [37], and data clustering [38]. Some variants of the AOA have also been used to solve multi-objective optimization problems [39]. The AOA is hybridized with the Aquila algorithm (AO-AOA) to solve optimal power flow problems [40]. A new hybrid approach (AOA-HGS) using Hunger Games Search (HGS) and the AOA is used to perform unconstrained and constrained problems. The method was evaluated for its performance using 23 test functions [41]. As an enhanced version of the AOA, the chaotic AOA was used to improve its convergence speed and escape from local extremes [42]. It is noteworthy that the AOA has also been used as a strategy to improve other metaheuristic algorithms. The exploration phase of the Improved Arithmetic Optimization Algorithm (IAOA) has been incorporated into the learning phase of the Growth Optimizer (GO), forming a new hybrid algorithm, the Improved Hybrid Growth Optimizer (IHGO). This integration enhances the GO's exploration capability while reducing unnecessary search efforts [43]. The IHGO has successfully solved four discrete optimization problems related to skeletal structures. The growing body of research on the AOA's improvements and applications indicates that the AOA is emerging as a promising algorithm with significant research potential. Many researchers are working on enhancing its performance and expanding its applications through various improvement strategies.

With the widespread application of optimization algorithms in solving complex engineering design problems, enhancing algorithm performance has become a focal point of research. As mentioned above, the AOA often faces challenges like local optima traps and slow convergence when dealing with global optimization problems. To address these issues, various improvement methods have been proposed by researchers.

Considering that the strengths of the GWO lie primarily in its flexible search mechanisms and multi-leader collaboration strategy, which are particularly effective during the exploitation phase of optimization problems, this study aims to explore whether integrating GWO with the AOA can significantly enhance the AOA's performance in solving global optimization problems. Moreover, the follower mechanism in the Sparrow Search Algorithm (SSA) simulates the behavior of followers tracking the leader sparrow. This mechanism facilitates deep exploitation in local areas, ensuring that the population does not prematurely converge to local optima. By enhancing the diversity of the search process, this mechanism improves the algorithm's global search ability, helping to escape local optima.

Cauchy mutation is an adaptive search strategy that allows the algorithm to make larger jumps, helping it escape local optima when the local search becomes stagnated. The Cauchy distribution has heavy tails, meaning it occasionally generates long-range moves, which assist in guiding the algorithm out of local optima traps, thus improving global search capability.

This paper will analyze the follower mechanism of the Sparrow Search Algorithm (SSA) and Cauchy Mutation to evaluate their role in avoiding local optima.

The hypotheses of this study are as follows:

- Integrating GWO into the AOA can enhance the algorithm's local search capability, thereby improving its overall performance.
- Incorporating the follower mechanism of the Sparrow Search Algorithm (SSA) and Cauchy Mutation helps reduce the risk of becoming trapped in local optima.
- The Hybrid Improved Arithmetic Optimization Algorithm (HIAOA), which combines these improvements, is expected to outperform existing optimization algorithms in both benchmark test functions and practical engineering problems.

To validate these hypotheses, this study will test the proposed HIAOA on 23 benchmark functions and apply it to several engineering design problems. The performance advantages of the HIAOA will be evaluated through comparisons with various existing optimization algorithms.

The remainder of this paper is organized as follows: Section 2 introduces the basic principles of AOAs and related work; Section 3 describes in detail the design and implementation of the improved algorithm; Section 4 analyzes the experimental results of the function test and performance evaluation and solves three practical engineering design cases by using the proposed algorithm; and Section 5 summarizes the work and suggests directions for future research.

2. Overview of AOA Theory

As a swarm-based metaheuristic algorithm, the AOA focuses on common simple operators such as addition, subtraction, multiplication, and division as a mathematical optimization method to determine the globally optimal solution from a set of candidate solutions [29]. The exploration phase of the algorithm is mainly determined by multiplication and division, while addition and subtraction dominate in the exploitation phase. The mathematical function, gas pedal (M_{OA}), is mainly used as a control parameter between exploration and exploitation to determine the exploitation of algorithms, as shown in Equation (1).

$$M_{OA}(t) = Min + t \times \left(\frac{Max - Min}{T}\right) \quad (1)$$

where, Min is the minimum value of the acceleration function, Max represents the maximum value of the acceleration function, T denotes the maximum number of iterations, and t is the current number of iterations.

2.1. Exploration Phase

The AOA uses multiplication and division to perform position updates in the exploration phase. The highly discrete values or decisions obtained by mathematical computation of multiplication and division operators, compared to addition and subtraction, tend to be highly decentralized when it comes to division, which helps the algorithm to explore the mechanism. In the exploration phase, the comparison of the random number r_1 and M_{OA} is used as the judgment condition. When $r_1 > M_{OA}$, the algorithm executes the exploration phase. The formula is as follows:

$$X_{(t+1)} = \begin{cases} X^*(t) \div (M_{OP} + \varepsilon) \times ((UB - LB) \times \mu + LB), & r_2 < 0.5 \\ X^*(t) \times M_{OP} \times ((UB - LB) \times \mu + LB), & otherwise \end{cases} \tag{2}$$

where $X_{(t+1)}$ is the next iteration particle position, $X^*(t)$ stands for the current optimal position, ε and μ are constants, UB and LB denote the upper and lower bounds of the boundary constraints, respectively, and r_2 generates a random number between 0 and 1. The division position update formula is the first formula in Equation (3), which is executed for $r_2 < 0.5$, otherwise the multiplication position update rule is executed. The mathematical optimization probability (M_{OP}) is given by Equation (3) as an exploratory scaling parameter in Equation (2), and α is a constant.

$$M_{op}(t) = 1 - \left(\frac{t}{T}\right)^{\frac{1}{\alpha}} \tag{3}$$

2.2. Exploitation Phase

As the development phase requires a high-density search around the possible solutions to find their global optimal solutions, the AOA mainly utilizes low-dispersion additive and subtractive search strategies to perform the development operation. The algorithm fulfils the development operation at $r_1 \leq M_{OA}$. The specific formula refers to Equation (4); r_3 is a random number between 0 and 1.

$$X_{(t+1)} = \begin{cases} X^*(t) - M_{OP} \times ((UB - LB) \times \mu + LB), & r_3 < 0.5 \\ X^*(t) + M_{OP} \times ((UB - LB) \times \mu + LB), & otherwise \end{cases} \tag{4}$$

The AOA pseudo-code flow is shown in Algorithm 1.

Algorithm 1: The pseudo-code for the AOA

```
Initialize the population size N, the maximum iteration T, the relevant parameters ε, μ, and α
Generate the positions of X_i (i = 1, 2, ··· , n) randomly
while (t < T)
    Estimate the fitness of each individual and update the best individual X*
    Update M_OA and M_OP by Equations (2) and (4), respectively
    Generate random values between [0, 1] (r1, r2, and r3)
    for i = 1:N
        if (r1 > M_OA)
            if (r2 < 0.5)
                Update the solution using division operation in Equation (3)
            else
                Update the solution using multiplication operation in Equation (3)
            end if
        else if (r3 < 0.5)
                Update the solution using subtraction operation in Equation (5)
```

Algorithm 1: *Cont.*

```
            else
            Update the solution using addition operation in Equation (5)
            end if
        end if
    end for
    t = t + 1
end while
Return the best solution
```

3. HIAOA

The AOA's main advantage is its ability to explore division and multiplication operators efficiently. However, due to its low convergence accuracy and easy fall into local minima, it needs to be improved [32]. Hybrid methods are often used for algorithm improvement to utilize the strengths and overcome the weaknesses of the algorithms [44]. In the present work, the efficiency of basic AOA development is improved by combining the development mechanisms of GWO, whose main advantages are different effective development mechanisms that improve the focus of searching for local regions and avoiding falling into local optima. Moreover, the follower mechanism and the Cauchy variation operator in SSA are introduced into the AOA as a perturbation mechanism, and a greedy strategy is used to ascertain whether to keep this perturbation or not, which further improves the convergence and accuracy of the algorithm.

3.1. GWO

GWO is a swarm-based metaheuristic algorithm for modeling grey wolf social hierarchies and hunting strategies [17]. It is unique in that it simulates the hierarchy of grey wolf groups and classifies wolves into four classes based on fitness values, namely alpha wolf (α), beta wolf (β), delta wolf (δ), and omega wolf (ω). The alpha wolf is considered the best wolf (solutions); the beta wolf (β) and delta wolf (δ) follow the alpha wolf in that order, and the remaining grey wolves are labeled omega wolves (ω). In GWO, the best three solutions (i.e., α, β, and δ) from each generation are largely used to guide the optimization process.

Grey wolves hunt in groups according to their social hierarchy. Under the leadership of the alpha wolf, the wolves mainly adopt the three behaviors of rounding up, chasing, and attacking prey for hunting. The behavior of rounding up prey can be described by the following equation:

$$D = |C \cdot X_p(t) - X(t)| \tag{5}$$

$$X(t+1) = X_p(t) - A \cdot D \tag{6}$$

$$A = 2a \cdot r_1 - a \tag{7}$$

$$C = 2 \cdot r_2 \tag{8}$$

$$a = 2 - \frac{2t}{T} \tag{9}$$

where t is the current number of iterations, $X(t)$ denotes the position of the grey wolf, $X_p(t)$ is the position of the prey, A and C are coefficient vectors, r_1 and r_2 are random numbers in the range of [0, 1], and a is a control parameter that decreases linearly from 2 to 0.

During the hunt, it can be assumed that the prey is near the positions of the α-wolf, β-wolf, and δ-wolf. The other wolves will update their positions based on the positions of these three lead wolves. The specific calculation process is as follows:

$$D_\alpha = |C_1 \cdot X_\alpha - X|,\ D_\beta = |C_1 \cdot X_\beta - X|,\ D_\delta = |C_1 \cdot X_\delta - X| \tag{10}$$

$$X_1 = |X_\alpha - A_1 \cdot D_\alpha|,\ X_2 = |X_\beta - A_2 \cdot D_\beta|,\ X_3 = |X_\delta - A_3 \cdot D_\delta| \tag{11}$$

$$X(t+1) = \frac{(X_1 + X_2 + X_3)}{3} \tag{12}$$

here X_α, X_β, and X_δ denote the positions of the α-wolf, β-wolf, and δ-wolf, respectively, and X is the current wolf position. The next position update of an individual grey wolf is affected by the positions of these three lead wolves.

3.2. SSA

The Sparrow Search Algorithm (SSA) simulates the foraging behavior and role division of sparrows, including discoverer and follower sparrows, as well as alert sparrows (warning agents) [45]. In the SSA, the discoverers have the best fitness, accounting for 10–20% of the group. They are mainly responsible for finding new food resources, and show higher search ability and randomness. Followers are responsible for following the leader and foraging nearby, mainly performing utilization behaviors.

To obtain food, followers will follow the leader and compete for food ($i \leq N/2$) or forage alone ($i > N/2$) to increase their own predation rate. This mechanism allows the SSA to focus on the local optimum while also trying to find a better position in the local area.

The follower position update is represented by Equation (13):

$$X_i(t+1) = \begin{cases} Q \cdot exp\left(\frac{X_w(t) - X_i(t)}{i^2}\right), i > N/2 \\ X_p(t+1) + \left|X_i(t) - X_p(t+1)\right| \cdot A^+ \cdot L, otherwise \end{cases} \tag{13}$$

where X_p is the optimal position occupied by the leader (discoverer) and X_w denotes the global worst position in the current iteration. A is a $1 \times d$ matrix with only one variable internal element and $A^+ = A^T\left(AA^T\right)^{-1}$.

3.3. Cauchy Mutation Operation

Mutation operators are adopted to enhance the diversity of algorithms in the search space [46]. For the AOA, mutation operators can better solve its shortcoming of being easily trapped in local extreme values. According to previous studies, Cauchy mutation (CM) and Gaussian mutation (GM) are two commonly used mutation operators and have been successfully used to improve a variety of metaheuristic algorithms [47–49].

Inspired by the literature [48,50], the CM often has better search capabilities than the GM. When the algorithm falls into an extreme value, the use of CM can better enable the algorithm to escape from the local optimum.

The probability density function of the CM is expressed by Equation (14):

$$f_{(0,g)}(\gamma) = \frac{g}{\pi(g^2 + \gamma^2)} \tag{14}$$

where the value of g is 1, *rand* is a random number between 0 and 1, and $\gamma = tan(\pi(rand - 0.5))$.

CM is used to perturb the algorithm with mutations, and CM operations are performed on the algorithm during its operation to enhance its exploration capability. Therefore, the position of the HIAOA using a CM mutation operator can be expressed as follows:

$$X_i' = X_i + X_i \cdot C(\gamma) \tag{15}$$

$$X_i(t+1) = \begin{cases} X_i', & F(X_i') < F(X_i) \\ X_i, & otherwise \end{cases} \tag{16}$$

where X_i' is the position after mutation, and $C(\gamma)$ denotes a random distribution number drawn from the Cauchy distribution. After each update, a greedy mechanism is used to determine whether to keep the mutation position.

3.4. The Proposed HIAOA Method

The proposed HIAOA is described in detail with corresponding pseudo-code and flowcharts. The enhancement of the AOA is mainly achieved by mixing GWO, SSA, and CM operators. The AOA has excellent exploration performance, but its exploitation capability is somewhat lacking. In the exploitation phase, the exploitation of algorithms of the AOA (Equation (4)) is replaced by the update mechanism of GWO algorithms (Equations (7)–(12)) to improve its convergence accuracy. To prevent falling into a local optimum, the SSA follower mechanism (Equation (13)) and CM operator (Equation (15)) are selected after each iteration with the same probability of mutation. Actually, for both mechanisms the operation makes a decision about them after each iteration using the greedy mechanism and selects the better current solution.

In Algorithm 2, the specific hybridization process of the HIAOA is described. Figure 1 shows the flowchart of the proposed HIAOA.

Algorithm 2: The pseudo-code for the HIAOA

Initialize the population size N, the maximum iteration T, the relevant parameters ε, μ, and α
Generate the positions of $X_i (i = 1, 2, \cdots, n)$ randomly
while $(t < T)$
    Estimate the fitness of each individual and update the best individual X^*
    Update M_{OA} and M_{OP} by Equations (2) and (4), respectively
    Generate random values between [0, 1] (r_1, r_2, and r_3)
    for i = 1: N
      if $(r_1 > M_{OA})$
        if $(r_2 < 0.5)$
          Update the solution using division operation in Equation (3)
          else
        Update the solution using multiplication operation in Equation (3)
          end if
        else
          Update the parameters a, A, C of GWO according to Equations (7)–(9)
          Update the position according to Equations (10)–(12)
        end if
        Update the current position and fitness of the individual
        if $(r_3 < 0.5)$
          Update the current fitness value of individual according to Equation (13)
        else
          Update the position of the current individual according to Equation (15)
        end if
        Calculate the fitness of each individual
        Update the best solution X^* if there is a better solution
  end for
  $t = t + 1$
end while
Return the best solution

Time complexity is a measure used to evaluate how an algorithm's running time increases with the size of the input. The time complexity of the improved HIAOA primarily depends on population initialization, fitness evaluation, population size N, maximum number of iterations T, and problem dimension D. The complexity of population initialization, similar to that of the AOA, is $O(N \cdot D)$. While fitness evaluation depends largely on the complexity of the specific optimization problem, the focus here is on the complexity of updating the solutions. The time complexity of the HIAOA is $O(N \cdot T \cdot D)$. Since each complete iteration includes the steps of the AOA, GWO, and SSA, the overall time complexity remains linear. In comparison to using a single algorithm, the overall computational complexity does not increase significantly.

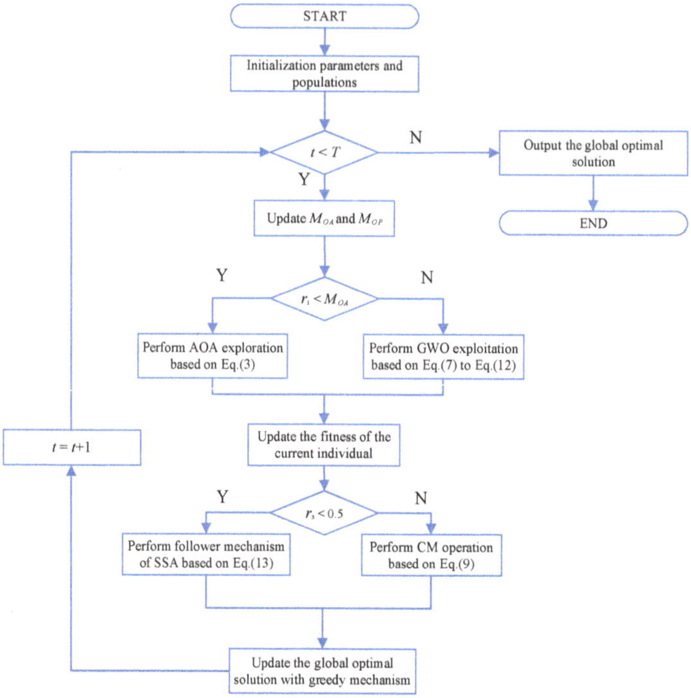

Figure 1. The flowchart for the proposed HIAOA.

The HIAOA generates random values, r_1, r_2, and r_3, and determines subsequent operations based on these values. Due to the uniform distribution of these random values, the algorithm achieves a balanced selection between different operations, ensuring the overall symmetry of its behavior. Over an extended runtime, all possible decision paths have an equal likelihood of being chosen, a mechanism that mathematically guarantees the algorithm's balance and impartiality, thereby avoiding excessive reliance on specific operations.

Specifically, the algorithm decides between the division and multiplication operations of the Arithmetic Optimization Algorithm (AOA) based on the values of r_1 and r_2. These operations are arithmetically symmetric, and they update the solution through different mathematical processes, ensuring that the algorithm does not favor one particular update method during long-term execution, thus enabling a balanced exploration of the solution space.

After completing the primary update steps, the HIAOA employs different additional strategies based on the value of r_3, including the follower mechanism from the Sparrow Search Algorithm and the Cauchy mutation operation. The selection of these strategies is also symmetric, ensuring their balanced application within the overall algorithm.

4. Experimental Results and Discussions

Some other optimization algorithms are selected for comparative experiments on 23 benchmark functions and to assess the performance of the proposed HIAOA on three engineering design problems. This paper compares algorithms and their parameter settings in Table 1. These parameters are the recommended values adopted by the proponents of each algorithm as first published.

Table 1. Parameter settings: comparator algorithms.

Algorithms	Parameters
GWO [17]	a decrease linearly from 2 to 0
SSA [45]	$sf = 30$; G_c = adaptive;
DBO [21]	$\alpha = rand(1); \theta \in [0, \pi]$;
PSO [15]	$c_1 = c_2 = 2$; $\omega_{max} = 0.9$; $\omega_{min} = 0.2$
GOOSE[51]	α ranges from 2 to 0
BKA [24]	$p = 0.9$;
AOA [29]; HIAOA	$\alpha = 5$; $\mu = 0.5$

4.1. Comparison and Analysis of Benchmark Results

There are three types of test functions selected in this paper: single-peak (F1–F7), multi-peak (F8–F13), and fixed-dimensional multi-peak (F14–F23). These functions are used to assess the algorithm's local search ability, global search ability, and the balance between the two, etc., according to their own characteristics. The specific function information [52] is expressed in detail. The names, domain value ranges, and optimal values of single-peak test function, multi-peak test function, and fixed-dimension multi-peak test function are given in Tables 2–4, respectively. To ensure the fairness of the experiment, the experimental algorithms are set to the same maximum number of iterations $T = 500$ and population size $N = 30$.

Table 2. Unimodal test function.

	Function Name	Domain Range	Dimension	Optimal Value
F1	Sphere	$[-100, 100]$	30	0
F2	Schwefel 2.22	$[-10, 10]$	30	0
F3	Schwefel 1.2	$[-100, 100]$	30	0
F4	Schwefel 2.21	$[-100, 100]$	30	0
F5	Rosenbrock	$[-30, 30]$	30	0
F6	Step	$[-100, 100]$	30	0
F7	Quartic	$[-1.28, 1.28]$	30	0

Table 3. Multimodal test function.

	Function Name	Domain Range	Dimension	Optimal Value
F8	Schwefel 2.26	$[-500, 500]$	$-418.9829 \times$ Dim	(−12,569.5)
F9	Rastrigin	$[-5.12, 5.12]$	30	0
F10	Ackley	$[-32, 32]$	30	0
F11	Griewank	$[-600, 600]$	30	0
F12	Penalized 1	$[-50, 50]$	30	0
F13	Penalized 2	$[-50, 50]$	30	0

Table 4. Fixed-dimensional multimodal functions.

	Function Name	Domain Range	Dimension	Optimal Value
F14	Foxholes	$[-65.536, 65.536]$	2	1
F15	Kowalik	$[-5, 5]$	4	0
F16	Humpback	$[-5, 5]$	2	−1.0316
F17	Branin	$[-5, 5]$	2	0.398
F18	Goldstein-Price	$[-2, 2]$	2	3
F19	Hartman's F1	$[0, 1]$	3	−3.8628
F20	Hartman's F2	$[0, 1]$	6	−3.3222
F21	Shekel's F1	$[0, 10]$	4	−10.4029
F22	Shekel's F2	$[0, 10]$	4	−10.1532
F23	Shekel's F3	$[0, 10]$	4	−10.5364

4.1.1. Sensitivity Analysis

To evaluate the search performance and accuracy of the HIAOA across various problem dimensions, the algorithm was applied to both unimodal and multimodal benchmark functions with dimensions of 30, 100, and 500. This was performed to assess the algorithm's sensitivity to changes in problem dimensions during benchmark testing. The appropriate problem dimension for further experimentation was determined based on the algorithm's computational time and the best-obtained solutions. The maximum number of iterations was uniformly set to $t = 500$, and the optimal dimension was selected for subsequent experiments. In the tables the bold values indicate the best-found solutions for each benchmark function when the population size is 30. The experimental results are presented in Table 5.

Table 5. Experimental testing of the HIAOA under different problem dimensions.

Func	Dim	Run Time/s	Algorithm Solution	Optimal Value
	30	$\mathbf{7.8725 \times 10^{-2}}$	**0**	
F1	100	1.2256×10^{-1}	0	0
	500	2.3971×10^{-1}	2.3179×10^{-99}	
	30	$\mathbf{6.4312 \times 10^{-2}}$	**0**	
F2	100	1.1546×10^{-1}	1.0358×10^{-223}	0
	500	2.4699×10^{-1}	3.7936×10^{-227}	
	30	$\mathbf{1.7324 \times 10^{-1}}$	**0**	
F3	100	4.5659×10^{-1}	0	0
	500	3.14453×10^{0}	0	
	30	$\mathbf{6.1452 \times 10^{-2}}$	2.7359×10^{-118}	
F4	100	1.1161×10^{-1}	1.0152×10^{-103}	0
	500	2.2119×10^{-1}	1.1476×10^{-108}	
	30	$\mathbf{1.2047 \times 10^{-1}}$	**0**	
F5	100	1.4307×10^{-1}	0	
	500	3.1637×10^{-1}	4.0726×10^{-5}	0
	30	$\mathbf{1.1063 \times 10^{-1}}$	**0**	
F6	100	1.2387×10^{-1}	0	0
	500	2.8327×10^{-1}	0	
	30	$\mathbf{2.2432 \times 10^{-1}}$	$\mathbf{4.2137 \times 10^{-6}}$	
F7	100	4.6771×10^{-1}	2.859×10^{-5}	0
	500	9.4901×10^{-1}	3.6927×10^{-5}	
	30	$\mathbf{1.2865 \times 10^{-1}}$	$\mathbf{-12{,}569.49 \times 10^{0}}$	
F8	100	1.8143×10^{-1}	$-41{,}898.29 \times 10^{0}$	−12,569.5
	500	6.3512×10^{-1}	$-209{,}491.4 \times 10^{0}$	
	30	$\mathbf{1.1403 \times 10^{-1}}$	**0**	
F9	100	1.3806×10^{-1}	0	0
	500	4.7295×10^{-1}	0	
	30	$\mathbf{1.0896 \times 10^{-1}}$	$\mathbf{8.8818 \times 10^{-16}}$	
F10	100	1.3952×10^{-1}	8.8818×10^{-16}	0
	500	4.5556×10^{-1}	8.8818×10^{-16}	
	30	$\mathbf{1.1935 \times 10^{-1}}$	**0**	
F11	100	1.7236×10^{-1}	0	0
	500	5.8136×10^{-1}	0	
	30	$\mathbf{3.5327 \times 10^{-1}}$	$\mathbf{7.7286 \times 10^{-11}}$	
F12	100	7.9541×10^{-1}	4.7116×10^{-8}	0
	500	4.27348×10^{0}	1.5655×10^{-3}	
	30	$\mathbf{3.1428 \times 10^{-1}}$	$\mathbf{5.3923 \times 10^{-12}}$	
F13	100	9.1459×10^{-1}	1.3498×10^{-11}	0
	500	4.45637×10^{0}	1.7041×10^{-7}	

As shown in Table 5, the MIWOA demonstrates higher solution accuracy and shorter running time when the problem dimension is 30. As the problem dimension increases, the difficulty of optimization for the HIAOA also increases, leading to longer running times and lower solution accuracy. Conversely, when the dimension is set to 30, the algorithm performs with shorter running times. Overall, considering both the algorithm's exploitation capability on unimodal functions and its global search ability and avoidance of local optima on multimodal functions, it is more reasonable to select a dimension of 30 for subsequent comparison experiments.

4.1.2. Performance Verification of Different Strategies to Improve the AOA

To validate the effectiveness of different improvement strategies in the HIAOA for enhancing the performance of the AOA, a comparative experiment was conducted between the hybrid algorithm that only integrates GWO into the AOA (GWOAOA), the AOA, and the HIAOA. The comparison was performed using the benchmark functions listed in Tables 2 and 3. The population size N, problem dimension D, and maximum number of t_{max} for all algorithms were set to 30, 30, and 500, respectively. Each algorithm was independently run 30 times, and the mean (Mean) and standard deviation (Std) of the results are provided in Table 6. The best solution obtained by each algorithm is highlighted in bold.

Table 6. Comparison results of different improvement strategies.

Func		AOA	GWOAOA	HIAOA
	Std	1.08×10^{-60}	**0**	**0**
F1	Mean	2.10×10^{-61}	4.80×10^{-113}	**0**
	Rank	3	2	**1**
	Std	7.95×10^{-41}	$\mathbf{1.00 \times 10^{-134}}$	2.42×10^{-123}
F2	Mean	1.82×10^{-41}	3.29×10^{-112}	$\mathbf{1.22 \times 10^{-123}}$
	Rank	3	2	**1**
	Std	4.48×10^{-5}	**0**	**0**
F3	Mean	1.41×10^{-5}	3.40×10^{-166}	**0**
	Rank	3	2	**1**
	Std	7.3×10^{-5}	1.62×10^{-86}	$\mathbf{2.05 \times 10^{-88}}$
F4	Mean	**0**	6.16×10^{-86}	**0**
	Rank	2	3	**1**
	Mean	3.22×10^{-5}	2.84×10^{-2}	**0**
F5	Std	8.88×10^{-5}	9.88×10^{-4}	$\mathbf{2.54 \times 10^{-5}}$
	Rank	2	3	**1**
	Std	$\mathbf{3.56 \times 10^{-6}}$	2.98×10^{-4}	4.46×10^{-6}
F6	Mean	1.07×10^{-6}	3.55×10^{-5}	**0**
	Rank	2	3	**1**
	Std	1.14×10^{-3}	7.41×10^{-5}	3.55×10^{-5}
F7	Mean	6.73×10^{-4}	9.32×10^{-6}	4.01×10^{-6}
	Rank	3	2	**1**
	Std	1.98×10^{3}	1.18×10^{3}	4.03×10^{0}
F8	Mean	−9940.9	−11,835.3	**−12,568.5**
	Rank	3	2	**1**
	Std	**0**	**0**	**0**
F9	Mean	**0**	**0**	**0**
	Rank	**1**	**1**	**1**
	Std	2.78×10^{-15}	3.26×10^{-15}	$\mathbf{8.88 \times 10^{-16}}$
F10	Mean	2.03×10^{-15}	1.70×10^{-15}	**0**
	Rank	3	2	**1**
	Std	**0**	**0**	**0**
F11	Mean	**0**	**0**	**0**
	Rank	**1**	**1**	**1**
	Std	8.71×10^{-8}	2.43×10^{-5}	$\mathbf{3.59 \times 10^{-9}}$
F12	Mean	2.79×10^{-8}	3.82×10^{-7}	$\mathbf{8.84 \times 10^{-10}}$
	Rank	2	3	**1**
	Std	$\mathbf{1.32 \times 10^{-8}}$	1.61×10^{-5}	2.22×10^{-7}
F13	Mean	7.32×10^{-7}	9.26×10^{-6}	$\mathbf{1.22 \times 10^{-8}}$
	Rank	2	3	**1**
	Mean Rank	2.07	2.07	**1**
	Final Rank	2	2	**1**

According to the performance index results in Table 6, the GWOAOA is on par with the AOA in the 13 benchmark function tests, but its ranking in functions F1–F3, F7, F8, and F10 is higher than that of the AOA. Both have their own characteristics. This shows that the improvement strategy of integrating GWO into the AOA is effective, but the scope of applicable problems is limited. The optimization effect of the HIAOA is significant, ranking 1 in all 13 test functions, and even reaching the theoretical optimality in the function optimization accuracy of F1, F3–F6, and F8–F10. Even if the optimization accuracy of the HIAOA does not reach the theoretical optimality in the remaining test functions, its convergence accuracy is not weaker than the AOA and GWOAOA. It proves that the HIAOA has better convergence and stability. The effectiveness of the HIAOA is verified.

4.1.3. Experimental Comparison and Analysis in Different Dimensions

According to previous research, the AOA achieved the best ranking in the evaluation of 30 dimensions [29]. In this section, we evaluate the selected optimization algorithms on the test functions (F1–F13) using 30, 50, and 100 dimensions, respectively, and run each algorithm independently 30 times in solving the test functions to validate the effectiveness of the proposed HIAOA improvement. The mean (Mean) and standard deviations (Std) of the solutions solved by each algorithm under 30, 50, and 100 dimensions are listed in Table 7, Table 8, and Table 9, respectively. The performance test results under a fixed-dimensional multi-peak function are also given in Table 6.

Table 7. Test results of each algorithm on F1–F13 and fixed-dimensional multi-peak functions (F14–F23) ($D = 30$).

Func		GWO	SSA	DBO	PSO	GOOSE	BKA	AOA	HIAOA
	Std	1.47×10^{-33}	6.66×10^{-58}	1.68×10^{-106}	6.24×10^{-4}	2.99×10^{2}	1.68×10^{-73}	6.97×10^{-12}	0
F1	Mean	6.98×10^{-34}	1.59×10^{-58}	3.1×10^{-107}	3.49×10^{-4}	9.24×10^{1}	3.07×10^{-74}	1.27×10^{-12}	0
	Rank	5	4	2	7	8	3	6	1
	Std	4.85×10^{-21}	3.88×10^{-28}	1.4×10^{-56}	2.31×10^{-02}	1.32×10^{3}	5.32×10^{-35}	0	0
F2	Mean	5.77×10^{-21}	7.35×10^{-29}	2.56×10^{-57}	2.27×10^{-2}	3.44×10^{2}	9.7×10^{-36}	0	0
	Rank	6	5	3	7	8	4	1	1
	Std	3.17×10^{-11}	4.64×10^{-23}	7.47×10^{-61}	4.07×10^{1}	2.86×10^{3}	2.24×10^{-93}	8.14×10^{-3}	0
F3	Mean	6.91×10^{-12}	8.49×10^{-24}	1.4×10^{-61}	9.21×10^{1}	5.97×10^{3}	4.17×10^{-94}	4.66×10^{-3}	0
	Rank	5	4	3	7	8	2	6	1
	Std	3.49×10^{-6}	6.16×10^{-28}	8.27×10^{-50}	2.11×10^{-1}	2.08×10^{1}	1.49×10^{-43}	1.94×10^{-2}	1.2×10^{-113}
F4	Mean	7.61×10^{-7}	1.96×10^{-28}	1.51×10^{-50}	1.07×10^{0}	1.64×10^{1}	2.74×10^{-44}	2.77×10^{-2}	2.7×10^{-114}
	Rank	5	4	2	7	8	3	6	1
	Std	7.21×10^{-1}	1.40×10^{-4}	2.68×10^{-1}	1.01×10^{2}	5.61×10^{2}	6.91×10^{-1}	3.20×10^{-1}	2.57×10^{-4}
F5	Mean	2.75×10^{1}	5.2×10^{-5}	2.57×10^{1}	1.21×10^{2}	3.18×10^{2}	2.81×10^{1}	2.83×10^{1}	1.23×10^{-4}
	Rank	4	1	3	7	8	5	6	2
	Std	5.06×10^{-1}	3.01×10^{-11}	9.34×10^{-3}	1.85×10^{-4}	1.28×10^{2}	9.60×10^{-1}	2.77×10^{-1}	4.27×10^{-6}
F6	Mean	2.09×10^{0}	1.10×10^{-11}	1.95×10^{-3}	1.16×10^{-4}	3.03×10^{1}	1.64×10^{0}	3.17×10^{0}	1.59×10^{-6}
	Rank	6	1	4	3	8	5	7	2
	Std	1.39×10^{-3}	1.23×10^{-3}	7.63×10^{-2}	8.83×10^{-2}	5.32×10^{-2}	2.25×10^{-4}	4.51×10^{-5}	3.71×10^{-5}
F7	Mean	2.05×10^{-3}	1.36×10^{-3}	1.01×10^{-3}	1.76×10^{-2}	1.34×10^{-1}	3.13×10^{-4}	4.74×10^{-5}	4.21×10^{-5}
	Rank	6	5	4	7	8	3	2	1
	Std	8.78×10^{2}	6.21×10^{2}	1.67×10^{3}	1.33×10^{3}	8.01×10^{2}	1.12×10^{3}	4.87×10^{2}	3.55×10^{2}
F8	Mean	-5.86×10^{3}	-8.61×10^{3}	-8.26×10^{3}	-5.53×10^{3}	-6.88×10^{3}	-8.93×10^{3}	-5.385×10^{3}	-1.25×10^{4}
	Rank	6	3	4	7	5	2	8	1
	Std	6.11×10^{0}	0	2.17×10^{0}	1.12×10^{1}	3.52×10^{1}	0	0	0
F9	Mean	4.61×10^{0}	0	3.97×10^{-1}	5.87×10^{1}	1.61×10^{2}	0	0	0
	Rank	3	1	2	4	5	1	1	1
	Std	5.35×10^{-15}	0	0	6.47×10^{-1}	9.16×10^{0}	0	0	0
F10	Mean	2.67×10^{-14}	8.88×10^{-16}	8.88×10^{-16}	3.43×10^{-1}	1.14×10^{1}	8.88×10^{-16}	8.88×10^{-16}	8.88×10^{-16}
	Rank	2	1	1	3	4	1	1	1
	Std	1.96×10^{-2}	0	2.65×10^{-8}	6.81×10^{-3}	2.09×10^{2}	0	1.71×10^{-1}	0
F11	Mean	1.46×10^{-2}	0	4.83×10^{-9}	7.24×10^{-3}	2.64×10^{2}	0	1.99×10^{-1}	0
	Rank	4	1	2	3	6	1	5	1
	Std	1.45×10^{-1}	6.41×10^{-12}	1.75×10^{-3}	4.51×10^{-2}	6.31×10^{0}	2.45×10^{-1}	4.42×10^{-2}	2.57×10^{-8}
F12	Mean	1.91×10^{-1}	1.86×10^{-12}	3.78×10^{-4}	1.38×10^{-2}	1.32×10^{0}	1.25×10^{-1}	5.12×10^{-1}	7.72×10^{-9}
	Rank	6	1	3	4	8	5	7	2

Table 7. *Cont.*

Func		GWO	SSA	DBO	PSO	GOOSE	BKA	AOA	HIAOA
	Std	2.75×10^{-1}	1.37×10^{-10}	4.33×10^{-1}	8.98×10^{-3}	8.91×10^{0}	5.26×10^{-1}	1.04×10^{-1}	1.91×10^{-7}
F13	Mean	1.62×10^{0}	3.69×10^{-11}	5.15×10^{-1}	5.55×10^{-3}	2.89×10^{0}	1.86×10^{0}	2.77×10^{0}	5.39×10^{-8}
	Rank	5	1	4	3	8	6	7	2
	Std	4.45×10^{0}	5.38×10^{0}	1.14×10^{0}	3.01×10^{0}	7.75×10^{0}	2.52×10^{-1}	4.55×10^{0}	4.52×10^{0}
F14	Mean	6.15×10^{0}	5.80×10^{0}	1.62×10^{0}	3.98×10^{0}	10.6×10^{0}	1.06×10^{0}	8.92×10^{0}	3.59×10^{0}
	Rank	6	5	2	4	8	1	7	3
	Std	1.29×10^{-2}	7.06×10^{-5}	3.11×10^{-4}	2.69×10^{-4}	8.66×10^{-3}	3.45×10^{-4}	2.09×10^{-2}	1.25×10^{-5}
F15	Mean	8.35×10^{-3}	3.32×10^{-4}	6.84×10^{-4}	8.42×10^{-4}	6.47×10^{-3}	4.72×10^{-4}	1.55×10^{-2}	3.21×10^{-4}
	Rank	7	2	4	5	6	3	8	1
	Std	1.58×10^{-8}	5.45×10^{-16}	6.18×10^{-16}	6.45×10^{-16}	8.18×10^{-1}	6.18×10^{-16}	1.96×10^{-7}	1.84×10^{-7}
F16	Mean	-1.03×10^{0}	-1.03×10^{0}	-1.03×10^{0}	-1.03×10^{0}	-6.86×10^{-1}	-1.03×10^{0}	-1.03×10^{0}	-1.03×10^{0}
	Rank	1	1	1	1	2	1	1	1
	Std	8.03×10^{-7}	0	0	0	8.47×10^{-10}	0	1.38×10^{-2}	3.26×10^{-6}
F17	Mean	3.97×10^{-1}	3.97×10^{-1}	3.97×10^{-1}	3.97×10^{-1}	3.97×10^{-1}	3.97×10^{-1}	4.11×10^{-1}	3.97×10^{-1}
	Rank	1	1	1	1	1	1	2	1
	Std	1.47×10^{1}	4.92×10^{0}	3.12×10^{-15}	1.68×10^{-15}	2.51×10^{1}	2.3×10^{-15}	1.02×10^{1}	2.08×10^{-7}
F18	Mean	5.70×10^{0}	3.9	3	3	12.9	3	7.51×10^{0}	3
	Rank	3	2	1	1	5	1	4	1
	Std	2.67×10^{-3}	1.41×10^{-1}	3.21×10^{-3}	2.63×10^{-15}	3.13×10^{-6}	2.35×10^{-15}	4.25×10^{-3}	9.48×10^{-5}
F19	Mean	−3.86118	−3.83701	−3.86121	−3.86278	−3.86278	−3.86278	−3.85246	−3.86278
	Rank	2	5	3	1	1	1	4	1
	Std	1.32×10^{-1}	6.03×10^{-2}	1.38×10^{-1}	5.71×10^{-2}	5.70×10^{-2}	5.89×10^{-2}	7.95×10^{-2}	4.83×10^{-2}
F20	Mean	-3.18×10^{0}	-3.26×10^{0}	-3.19×10^{0}	-3.28×10^{0}	-3.24×10^{0}	-3.31×10^{0}	-3.06×10^{0}	-3.30×10^{0}
	Rank	7	4	6	3	5	1	8	2
	Std	2.75×10^{0}	2.49×10^{0}	2.89×10^{0}	3.23×10^{0}	2.93×10^{0}	5.55×10^{-5}	1.53×10^{0}	1.41×10^{-2}
F21	Mean	-8.56×10^{0}	-8.28×10^{0}	-7.21×10^{0}	-6.88×10^{0}	-4.72×10^{0}	-10.15×10^{0}	-3.59×10^{0}	-10.15×10^{0}
	Rank	3	4	5	6	7	1	8	1
	Std	2.45×10^{0}	2.54×10^{0}	2.73×10^{0}	2.85×10^{0}	3.21×10^{0}	1.39×10^{0}	1.39×10^{0}	1.02×10^{2}
F22	Mean	-9.08×10^{0}	-8.63×10^{0}	-8.22×10^{0}	-8.87×10^{0}	-4.92×10^{0}	-10.14×10^{0}	-4.09×10^{0}	-10.4×10^{0}
	Rank	3	5	6	4	7	2	8	1
	Std	2.32×10^{0}	2.65×10^{0}	2.89×10^{0}	2.86×10^{0}	3.32×10^{0}	2.01×10^{0}	1.87×10^{0}	1.37×10^{0}
F23	Mean	-9.91×10^{0}	-9.27×10^{0}	-8.09×10^{0}	-10.16×10^{0}	-4.91×10^{0}	-10.54×10^{0}	-3.85×10^{0}	-10.54×10^{0}
	Rank	3	4	5	2	6	1	7	1
Mean Rank		4.30	2.82	3.08	3.91	6.08	2.34	4.91	1.30
Final Rank		6	3	4	5	8	2	7	1

Table 7 lists the experimental results of eight optimization algorithms on 23 test functions. The best results are marked and the performance of these algorithms is ranked. In Table 7, Rank denotes the algorithm performance ranking on individual test functions, Mean Rank is the overall average ranking, and Final Rank is the final one. The algorithm performance ranking in the subsequent tables will not explain the interpretation of Rank in this paper. The test results of the three groups of functions are analyzed as follows:

1. Single-peak test functions (F1–F7) are a type of test function commonly used in optimization algorithm evaluation. They are characterized by having only one global optimal solution and no complex valley and peak structures. Single-peak test functions are mainly employed to evaluate the local search (exploitation) ability of an algorithm. From the algorithm performance test results of single-peak functions, the proposed HIAOA has excellent overall performance compared with the comparison algorithms. In particular, the HIAOA achieved surprising results in terms of mean and standard deviation, and its optimization accuracy even reached the theoretical optimal value. The HIAOA also achieved excellent results. The SSA achieved the best results. Therefore, the results show that the proposed algorithm has better local development capabilities than the comparators assessed in the present work.
2. The main feature of multimodal test functions (F8–F13) is that they contain multiple local optimal points and one or more global optimal points. This type of function is used to evaluate the algorithm's global search ability and ability to avoid local optimal traps. In multimodal functions, the global optimal point may be hidden in a complex search space and difficult to find directly. From the test results, the HIAOA ranks first. The performances of the SSA, BKA, and AOA are similar to that of the HIAOA. Except for GWO, PSO, and GOOSE, the performance of the remaining algorithms is

comparable and ranks first. The SSA achieves the best results, evincing the strong competitive advantage of the HIAOA in global exploration ability and local escape ability.

3. Fixed-dimensional multimodal functions (F14–F23) are mainly used to evaluate the performance of algorithms in specific dimensions, especially the balance between exploration and development of algorithms. The test results show that the overall performance of the HIAOA remains good. Except for F16, F17, F18, and F19, which are not much different from the previous algorithm, the HIAOA performs better than the comparison algorithm in almost all the fixed-dimensional multimodal functions tested this time. BKA obtains the best results on F14, and performs similarly to the HIAOA on F20, F21, and F23. The test results also verify that the HIAOA has a good ability to balance algorithm exploration and development.

Table 8. Test results of each algorithm on F1–F13 (D = 50).

Func		GWO	SSA	DBO	PSO	GOOSE	BKA	AOA	HIAOA
F1	Std	8.25×10^{-25}	7.33×10^{-58}	3.5×10^{-122}	2.29×10^{-1}	1.96×10^{3}	2.13×10^{-81}	1.07×10^{-3}	0
	Mean	2.69×10^{-25}	1.35×10^{-58}	6.9×10^{-123}	2.17×10^{-1}	1.95×10^{3}	5.1×10^{-82}	4.18×10^{-4}	0
	Rank	5	4	2	7	8	3	6	1
F2	Std	4.91×10^{-16}	9.47×10^{-28}	8.96×10^{-52}	7.04×10^{-1}	1.87×10^{10}	7.88×10^{-43}	0	0
	Mean	5.53×10^{-16}	2.29×10^{-28}	1.64×10^{-52}	1.47×10^{0}	3.53×10^{9}	1.57×10^{-43}	2.2×10^{-191}	0
	Rank	6	5	3	7	8	4	2	1
F3	Std	1.37×10^{-3}	9.48×10^{-25}	5.25×10^{-55}	4.16×10^{2}	8.11×10^{3}	5.37×10^{-78}	7.25×10^{-2}	0
	Mean	3.02×10^{-4}	2.42×10^{-25}	9.58×10^{-56}	1.46×10^{3}	2.11×10^{4}	9.94×10^{-79}	8.57×10^{-2}	0
	Rank	5	4	3	7	8	2	6	1
F4	Std	1.85×10^{0}	6.78×10^{-29}	5.38×10^{-50}	5.41×10^{-1}	2.71×10^{1}	2.28×10^{-40}	1.08×10^{-2}	2.8×10^{-101}
	Mean	6.81×10^{-1}	1.39×10^{-29}	9.95×10^{-51}	3.69×10^{0}	3.51×10^{1}	4.17×10^{-41}	5.07×10^{-2}	5.3×10^{-102}
	Rank	6	4	2	7	8	3	5	1
F5	Std	6.45×10^{-1}	1.37×10^{-3}	7.81×10^{-1}	1.55×10^{2}	6.26×10^{2}	5.11×10^{-1}	2.33×10^{1}	2.25×10^{-3}
	Mean	4.81×10^{1}	8.18×10^{-4}	4.62×10^{1}	3.49×10^{2}	5.22×10^{2}	4.84×10^{1}	4.86×10^{1}	6.21×10^{-4}
	Rank	4	2	3	7	8	5	6	1
F6	Std	6.66×10^{-1}	2.34×10^{-8}	2.04×10^{-1}	1.11×10^{-1}	1.62×10^{3}	1.71×10^{0}	3.59×10^{-1}	6.88×10^{-6}
	Mean	5.12×10^{0}	1.61×10^{-8}	3.24×10^{-1}	1.78×10^{-1}	8.88×10^{2}	5.62×10^{0}	7.17×10^{0}	1.95×10^{-6}
	Rank	5	1	4	3	8	6	7	2
F7	Std	2.11×10^{-3}	2.09×10^{-3}	1.02×10^{-3}	3.30×10^{0}	2.15×10^{-1}	6.08×10^{-4}	6.65×10^{-5}	3.59×10^{-5}
	Mean	2.58×10^{-3}	2.06×10^{-3}	1.64×10^{-3}	3.12×10^{0}	6.58×10^{-1}	4.23×10^{-4}	6.67×10^{-5}	4.19×10^{-5}
	Rank	6	5	4	8	7	3	2	1
F8	Std	1.03×10^{3}	7.51×10^{2}	2.69×10^{3}	2.10×10^{3}	5.64×10^{2}	2.80×10^{3}	5.47×10^{2}	1.63×10^{-11}
	Mean	-8.46×10^{3}	-1.37×10^{4}	-1.32×10^{4}	-6.24×10^{3}	-1.11×10^{4}	-1.27×10^{4}	-6.89×10^{3}	-2.09×10^{4}
	Rank	6	2	3	8	5	4	7	1
F9	Std	1.15×10^{1}	0	2.04×10^{0}	1.98×10^{1}	5.03×10^{1}	0	0	0
	Mean	1.16×10^{1}	0	3.73×10^{-1}	1.41×10^{2}	3.05×10^{2}	0	0	0
	Rank	3	1	2	4	5	1	1	1
F10	Std	4.38×10^{-14}	0	0	4.26×10^{-1}	7.88×10^{0}	0	0	0
	Mean	1.39×10^{-13}	8.88×10^{-16}	8.88×10^{-16}	1.60×10^{0}	1.46×10^{1}	8.88×10^{-16}	8.88×10^{-16}	8.88×10^{-16}
	Rank	2	1	1	3	4	1	1	1
F11	Std	1.07×10^{-2}	0	0	1.11×10^{-2}	3.97×10^{2}	0	1.48×10^{0}	0
	Mean	6.34×10^{-3}	0	0	1.54×10^{-2}	4.75×10^{2}	0	1.32×10^{0}	0
	Rank	2	1	1	3	5	1	4	1
F12	Std	1.21×10^{-1}	5.93×10^{-9}	4.11×10^{-3}	1.44×10^{-1}	6.41×10^{-0}	2.37×10^{-1}	3.36×10^{-2}	2.13×10^{-7}
	Mean	3.13×10^{-1}	3.04×10^{-9}	4.54×10^{-3}	1.02×10^{-1}	1.51×10^{1}	2.36×10^{-1}	7.28×10^{-1}	4.52×10^{-8}
	Rank	7	1	3	4	5	6	8	2
F13	Std	2.81×10^{-1}	7.41×10^{-8}	8.69×10^{-1}	1.92×10^{-1}	3.14×10^{1}	6.77×10^{-1}	9.03×10^{-2}	1.74×10^{-6}
	Mean	2.97×10^{0}	2.88×10^{-8}	3.40×10^{0}	2.23×10^{-1}	3.40×10^{1}	3.49×10^{0}	4.85×10^{0}	5.28×10^{-7}
	Rank	4	1	5	3	8	6	7	2
Mean Rank		4.69	2.46	2.76	5.46	6.61	3.46	4.77	1.23
Final Rank		5	2	3	7	8	4	6	1

Table 9. Test results of each algorithm on F1–F13 (D = 100).

Func		GWO	SSA	DBO	PSO	GOOSE	BKA	AOA	HIAOA
	Std	2.71×10^{-17}	7.69×10^{-55}	3.91×10^{-120}	5.88×10^{0}	1.80×10^{4}	7.07×10^{-89}	8.52×10^{-3}	0
F1	Mean	2.95×10^{-17}	1.41×10^{-55}	1.11×10^{-120}	2.01×10^{1}	1.63×10^{4}	1.4×10^{-89}	2.61×10^{-2}	1.91×10^{-282}
	Rank	5	4	2	7	8	3	6	1
	Std	1.13×10^{-11}	1.08×10^{-26}	9.21×10^{-58}	8.38×10^{0}	7.11×10^{29}	1.01×10^{-38}	1.37×10^{-62}	0
F2	Mean	2.61×10^{-11}	2.43×10^{-27}	1.68×10^{-58}	3.53×10^{1}	1.31×10^{29}	1.84×10^{-39}	2.51×10^{-63}	0
	Rank	6	5	3	7	8	4	2	1
	Std	2.39×10^{2}	2.02×10^{-21}	2.21×10^{-6}	4.45×10^{3}	1.71×10^{4}	5.37×10^{-76}	5.95×10^{-1}	0
F3	Mean	1.12×10^{2}	5.25×10^{-22}	4.04×10^{-7}	1.68×10^{4}	9.97×10^{4}	9.81×10^{-77}	8.31×10^{-1}	6.91×10^{-297}
	Rank	6	3	4	7	8	2	5	1
	Std	1.41×10^{1}	3.17×10^{-30}	1.37×10^{-50}	1.25×10^{0}	3.27×10^{1}	3.16×10^{-37}	1.02×10^{2}	1.45×10^{-91}
F4	Mean	5.11×10^{1}	6.86×10^{-31}	2.54×10^{-51}	1.18×10^{1}	4.87×10^{1}	6.01×10^{-38}	9.17×10^{-2}	2.81×10^{-92}
	Rank	8	4	2	6	7	3	5	1
	Std	5.24×10^{-1}	3.40×10^{-3}	6.62×10^{-1}	8.38×10^{3}	7.41×10^{2}	2.81×10^{-1}	1.61×10^{-1}	5.43×10^{-5}
F5	Mean	9.82×10^{1}	1.98×10^{-3}	9.72×10^{1}	1.57×10^{4}	1.49×10^{3}	9.85×10^{1}	9.88×10^{1}	1.67×10^{-5}
	Rank	4	2	3	8	7	5	6	1
	Std	8.49×10^{-1}	2.47×10^{-6}	6.36×10^{-1}	5.10×10^{0}	1.78×10^{4}	2.06×10^{0}	5.86×10^{-1}	6.3×10^{-7}
F6	Mean	1.47×10^{1}	1.15×10^{-6}	4.68×10^{0}	2.09×10^{1}	1.93×10^{4}	1.48×10^{1}	1.80×10^{1}	2.4×10^{-7}
	Rank	4	2	3	8	7	5	6	1
	Std	2.68×10^{-3}	1.21×10^{-3}	1.31×10^{-3}	2.76×10^{2}	4.35×10^{0}	1.57×10^{-4}	5.78×10^{-5}	2.88×10^{-5}
F7	Mean	6.88×10^{-3}	1.35×10^{-3}	1.38×10^{-3}	1.59×10^{3}	1.67×10^{1}	2.38×10^{-4}	6.39×10^{-5}	2.79×10^{-5}
	Rank	7	4	5	6	8	3	2	1
	Std	1.42×10^{3}	1.37×10^{3}	6.64×10^{3}	3.37×10^{3}	1.01×10^{3}	7.05×10^{3}	9.10×10^{2}	3.76×10^{3}
F8	Mean	-1.41×10^{4}	-2.61×10^{4}	-2.72×10^{4}	-1.01×10^{4}	-1.88×10^{4}	-2.35×10^{4}	-1.01×10^{4}	-4.09×10^{4}
	Rank	6	3	2	7	5	4	7	1
	Std	1.61×10^{1}	0	0	8.02×10^{1}	8.05×10^{1}	0	0	0
F9	Mean	1.45×10^{1}	0	0	5.92×10^{2}	8.78×10^{1}	0	0	0
	Rank	2	1	1	3	4	1	1	1
	Std	2.78×10^{-8}	0	0	3.33×10^{-1}	7.74×10^{0}	0	1.27×10^{-3}	0
F10	Mean	5.49×10^{-9}	8.88×10^{-16}	8.88×10^{-16}	3.63×10^{0}	1.38×10^{1}	8.88×10^{-16}	7.6×10^{-4}	8.88×10^{-16}
	Rank	2	1	1	4	5	1	3	1
	Std	1.21×10^{-2}	0	0	6.88×10^{-2}	8.73×10^{2}	0	1.71×10^{2}	0
F11	Mean	6.56×10^{-3}	0	0	3.97×10^{-1}	1.41×10^{3}	0	6.51×10^{2}	0
	Rank	2	1	1	3	5	1	4	1
	Std	7.20×10^{-2}	9.01×10^{-8}	4.95×10^{-2}	1.78×10^{0}	9.57×10^{0}	2.44×10^{-1}	3.34×10^{-2}	6.87×10^{-8}
F12	Mean	5.36×10^{-1}	3.43×10^{-8}	7.06×10^{-2}	5.03×10^{0}	2.01×10^{1}	4.66×10^{-1}	9.05×10^{-1}	2.23×10^{-8}
	Rank	5	2	3	7	8	4	6	1
	Std	3.05×10^{-1}	4.35×10^{-6}	1.13×10^{0}	2.12×10^{1}	6.42×10^{1}	7.76×10^{-1}	5.81×10^{-2}	1.57×10^{-5}
F13	Mean	8.33×10^{0}	2.16×10^{-6}	8.41×10^{0}	6.28×10^{1}	1.26×10^{2}	8.24×10^{0}	9.96×10^{0}	3.33×10^{-6}
	Rank	4	1	6	7	8	3	5	2
Mean Rank		4.69	2.53	2.76	6.15	6.76	3.00	4.46	1.07
Final Rank		6	2	3	7	8	4	5	1

To visualize the difference between the convergence speed and accuracy of different algorithms and the HIAOA, the convergence curves of the best fitness values of the benchmark test functions (F1–F13) solved by different algorithms are given in Figure 2. From Figure 2, the proposed HIAOA has faster convergence speed and optimization accuracy, and can find the theoretical optimal value of the objective function with fewer iterations on some of the functions. The performance of the HIAOA, when compared to the other seven optimization algorithms on the test functions, mostly generates the best result. The main reason for this is that the HIAOA has excellent exploration and development capabilities, thanks to its combination of the advantages of GWO and SSA to compensate for its lack of development capabilities.

The performance of the HIAOA and the comparison algorithms in different dimensions is further assessed. Under the conditions of dimension 50 (Table 8) and 100 (Table 9), the HIAOA still shows strong competitiveness, and its comprehensive performance rankings are all located in first place, especially in the single-peak function; although its accuracy gradually decreases as the dimension increases, it maintains a high convergence accuracy relative to the comparison algorithm proposed herein. The results in Table 8 show that the HIAOA ranks first in the performance of the remaining single-peak functions except F6; however, the average value of the solution is similar to that of the first-ranked SSA in terms of F6. The results in Table 8 are summarized as follows: among the multi-peak functions, the SSA, BKA, AOA, and HIAOA have comparable performances for the SSA on

F9, F10, and F11. The SSA gives the best results for the multi-peak functions F22 and F23. The results are presented in Table 8.

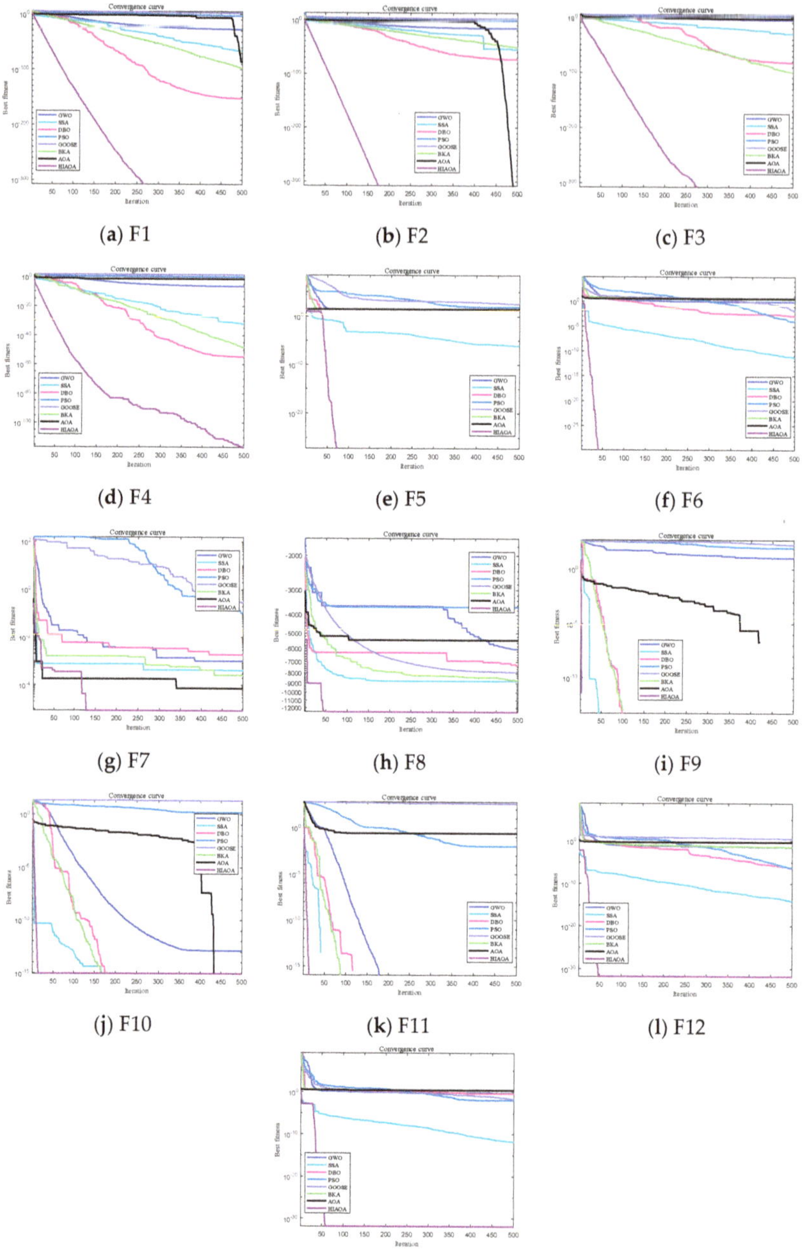

(**a**) F1 (**b**) F2 (**c**) F3

(**d**) F4 (**e**) F5 (**f**) F6

(**g**) F7 (**h**) F8 (**i**) F9

(**j**) F10 (**k**) F11 (**l**) F12

(**m**) F13

Figure 2. Convergence of eight algorithms from F1 to F13. The convergence curves represent the situations where the algorithms find the best fitness in the same number of iterations. The iterative convergence curves of each algorithm for unimodal function are (**a**–**g**), and the iterative convergence curves of each algorithm for multimodal function are (**h**–**m**).

Likewise, according to the results in Table 9 we also find that the HIAOA obtains the best results on both F1 to F12. The proposed algorithm performs very well in comparison to the remaining algorithms. The data results show that the proposed algorithm is competitive and the proposed improvement strategy is effective. It is noteworthy that the optimal value of a function is affected by its dimension. Therefore, the optimal values found in different dimensions are not the same, which we need to take into account.

4.1.4. Convergence Analysis

Whether the optimization algorithm can find the global optimal solution in a reasonable time is an important indication of its convergence degree. At the early stage of solving the problem, the HIAOA finds preliminary feasible solutions in the search space as much as possible with the help of the powerful exploration mechanism of the AOA. Since the HIAOA conducts a local search (perturbation variant) in the vicinity of the explored points after each exploration and adopts the greedy mechanism to keep the optimal solution found this time, it does not miss the opportunity to update the globally optimal solution. We select unimodal functions F1 and F3, and multimodal function F8, respectively. When the dimension D is 30, the search history, average fitness, search trajectory curve, and corresponding function graph of the HIAOA are illustrated in Figure 3, Figure 4, and Figure 5, respectively.

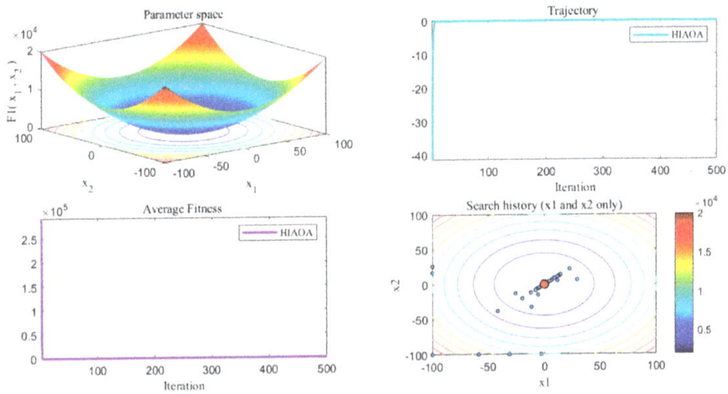

Figure 3. HIAOA search history, trajectory, and average fitness on F1.

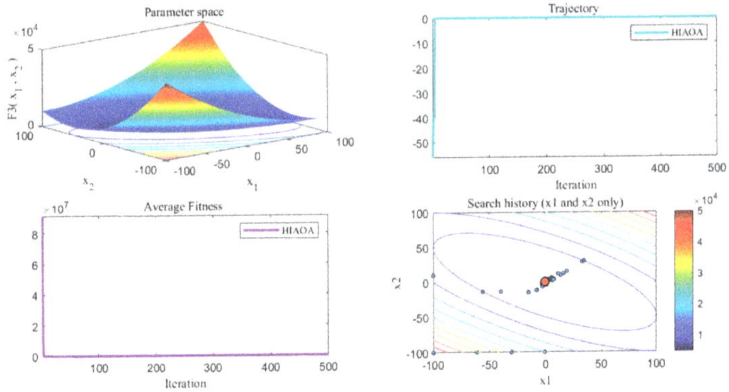

Figure 4. HIAOA search history, trajectory, and average fitness on F3.

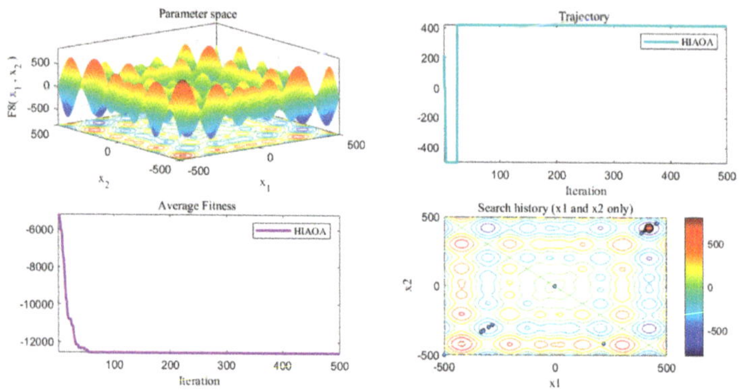

Figure 5. HIAOA search history, trajectory, and average fitness on F8.

The single-peak function is free of peaks and valleys and can be adequately employed to evaluate the local exploitation of the algorithm. As shown in Figures 3 and 4, the local exploitation ability of the HIAOA is competitive, with most particles quickly converging to the global optimum point. The multi-peak test function mainly contains multiple local extreme values and one or more global optimal points, which is helpful for evaluating the algorithm's global search ability and ability to stay away from local optimal traps. Figure 5 demonstrates that the HIAOA stagnates at the local extremes early on, and quickly jumps out of the local optimum and eventually converges to the global optimum point due to its excellent local escaping ability. This further verifies that the improvement strategy proposed in this paper effectively enhances the performance of the AOA.

4.1.5. Analysis of Significance

Besides evaluating the algorithm's performance across the previously mentioned dimensions, we also utilized the Wilcoxon rank-sum test to assess its significance. This non-parametric statistical test is used to compare the distributions of two independent samples [53]. The HIAOA is compared with each of the other algorithms pairwise to determine if there is a significant difference between them, based on a preset significance level of $p = 0.05$. When $p < 0.05$, it indicates a significant difference in the performance of the two algorithms; otherwise, it suggests there is no significant difference between them. The results of the rank-sum test for the statistical test functions F1–F13 in 30 dimensions and the fixed-dimension functions F14–F23 are listed in Table 9. The symbols + and − indicate that the optimization search results of the HIAOA differ significantly and are not significantly different from those of the comparator algorithms, respectively.

As displayed in Table 10, except for functions F9–F11 where the SSA, BKA, AOA, and HIAOA show no significant difference in optimization results, the p-values for most tested functions are less than 0.05. This indicates that the optimization results of the HIAOA on most of the functions are significantly different from those of the comparator algorithms.

Table 10. Wilcoxon rank-sum test results.

Func	GWO	SSA	DBO	PSO	GOOSE	BKA	AOA
F1	1.21×10^{-12}	1.21×10^{-12}	1.21×10^{-12}	1.21×10^{-12}	1.21×10^{-12}	1.21×10^{-12}	1.21×10^{-12}
F2	1.21×10^{-12}	1.21×10^{-12}	1.21×10^{-12}	1.21×10^{-12}	1.21×10^{-12}	1.21×10^{-12}	1
F3	1.21×10^{-12}	1.21×10^{-12}	1.21×10^{-12}	1.21×10^{-12}	1.21×10^{-12}	1.21×10^{-12}	1.21×10^{-12}
F4	3.02×10^{-11}	3.02×10^{-11}	3.02×10^{-11}	3.02×10^{-11}	3.02×10^{-11}	3.02×10^{-11}	3.02×10^{-11}
F5	2.11×10^{-11}	8.79×10^{-2}	2.11×10^{-11}	2.11×10^{-11}	2.11×10^{-11}	2.11×10^{-11}	2.11×10^{-11}
F6	4.11×10^{-12}	2.94×10^{-8}	5.11×10^{-12}	7.88×10^{-12}	4.11×10^{-12}	4.11×10^{-12}	4.11×10^{-12}
F7	3.02×10^{-11}	3.02×10^{-11}	3.02×10^{-11}	3.02×10^{-11}	3.02×10^{-11}	1.56×10^{-8}	2.06×10^{-1}

Table 10. *Cont.*

Func	GWO	SSA	DBO	PSO	GOOSE	BKA	AOA
F8	1.99×10^{-11}	1.99×10^{-11}	3.00×10^{-11}	1.99×10^{-11}	1.99×10^{-11}	3.67×10^{-11}	1.99×10^{-11}
F9	5.74×10^{-11}	1	3.33×10^{-1}	1.21×10^{-12}	1.21×10^{-12}	1	1
F10	8.55×10^{-13}	1	1	1.21×10^{-12}	1.21×10^{-12}	1	1
F11	1.31×10^{-7}	1	3.33×10^{-1}	1.21×10^{-12}	1.21×10^{-12}	1	1.21×10^{-12}
F12	3.16×10^{-12}	2.48×10^{-8}	3.53×10^{-12}	6.81×10^{-12}	3.16×10^{-12}	3.16×10^{-12}	3.16×10^{-12}
F13	7.88×10^{-12}	5.17×10^{-6}	7.88×10^{-12}	4.19×10^{-11}	7.88×10^{-12}	7.88×10^{-12}	7.88×10^{-12}
F14	3.03×10^{-3}	7.44×10^{-2}	8.76×10^{-8}	2.89×10^{-1}	5.59×10^{-7}	4.12×10^{-8}	1.73×10^{-6}
F15	4.84×10^{-2}	1.86×10^{-6}	8.88×10^{-6}	3.02×10^{-11}	3.34×10^{-11}	1.19×10^{-6}	8.15×10^{-11}
F16	1.12×10^{-2}	6.32×10^{-12}	1.45×10^{-11}	5.14×10^{-12}	4.08×10^{-5}	1.34×10^{-11}	7.71×10^{-4}
F17	4.22×10^{-3}	1.21×10^{-12}	1.21×10^{-12}	1.21×10^{-12}	3.34×10^{-11}	1.21×10^{-12}	3.02×10^{-11}
F18	8.99×10^{-11}	5.05×10^{-10}	2.91×10^{-11}	2.03×10^{-11}	4.73×10^{-1}	2.91×10^{-11}	2.71×10^{-1}
F19	3.31×10^{-3}	1.08×10^{-11}	6.69×10^{-6}	8.87×10^{-12}	9.92×10^{-11}	1.54×10^{-11}	3.02×10^{-11}
F20	1.09×10^{-5}	1.59×10^{-2}	1.29×10^{-1}	4.08×10^{-4}	5.69×10^{-4}	2.78×10^{-7}	5.49×10^{-11}
F21	3.77×10^{-5}	1.71×10^{-3}	1.76×10^{-3}	6.61×10^{-1}	2.68×10^{-6}	7.36×10^{-10}	3.01×10^{-11}
F22	1.37×10^{-1}	2.54×10^{-2}	4.11×10^{-1}	2.62×10^{-9}	7.59×10^{-3}	3.78×10^{-10}	2.98×10^{-11}
F23	1.86×10^{-5}	7.48×10^{-2}	5.68×10^{-2}	3.49×10^{-4}	9.39×10^{-6}	6.93×10^{-7}	2.93×10^{-11}
+/−	22/1	18/5	19/4	21/2	22/1	20/3	20/3

4.2. HIAOA for Solving Engineering Problems

The proposed algorithm is used to solve three engineering design problems to verify the capability of the HIAOA in solving real-world problems. Each problem is solved by subjecting the HIAOA to the same maximum number of iterations, $T = 500$, and population size, $N = 30$, and run independently for 30 times, as in the function test. The obtained results are compared with the solutions provided by other algorithms in the literature. The following subsections demonstrate the comparison of the results of the proposed HIAOA with others.

4.2.1. Pressure Vessel Design Problems

The pressure vessel design problem is a prevalent issue that many researchers have used in their studies to validate the effectiveness of their new optimization algorithms [54]. The problem involves four main variables: shell thickness T_s, head thickness T_h, inner radius R, and vessel length L. The objective is to minimize the total cost of designing the pressure vessel, which is an optimization problem, and the specific information related to this problem and the meaning of the constraints represented by the variables is given elsewhere [55].

Objective function:

$$min f(x) = 0.6224x_1x_3x_4 + 1.7781x_2x_3^2 + 3.1661x_1^2x_4 + 19.84x_1^2x_3 \tag{17}$$

Decision variables:

$$x = [x_1, x_2, x_3, x_4] = [T_s, T_h, R, L]. \tag{18}$$

Constraints:

$$\begin{gathered} g_1(x) = -x_1 + 0.0193x_3 \leq 0, \\ g_2(x) = -x_2 + 0.00954x_3 \leq 0, \\ g_3(x) = -\pi x_3^2 - \tfrac{4}{3}\pi x_3^3 + 129600 \leq 0, \\ g_4(x) = x_4 - 240 \leq 0, \\ 0 \leq x_1 \leq 100,\ 0 \leq x_2 \leq 100,\ 10 \leq x_3 \leq 100,\ 10 \leq x_4 \leq 100. \end{gathered} \tag{19}$$

Table 11 lists the results of comparisons of the proposed algorithm (HIAOA) with other algorithms proposed in the literature for solving the pressure vessel problem. The results in Table 11 imply that the HIAOA finds almost better results than the comparison algorithms and can find a lower total cost.

Table 11. Comparison of results of different algorithms for solving pressure vessel design problems.

	$minf(x)$	T_s	T_h	R	L
HIAOA	**5885.3328**	0.7781686	0.3846492	40.31962	200
BKA [24]	5887.36492	0.778433	0.384690	40.319619	200
AOA [29]	6048.7844	0.8303737	0.4162057	42.75127	169.3454
SMA [56]	5994.1857	0.7931	0.3932	40.6711	196.2178
WOA [57]	6393.731	0.896181	0.507493	46.16543	132.0086
GWO [17]	6051.5639	0.812500	0.434500	42.089181	176.758731
AVOA [17]	5886.67659	0.778954	0.3850347	40.360312	199.434299
AO [17]	5949.2258	1.0540	0.182806	59.6219	38.8050
AEO [58]	5994.50695	0.8374205	0.413937	43.3898597	161.268592

4.2.2. Welded Beam Design Problems

The main objective of the welded beam design problem is primarily to minimize the overall fabrication cost of the welded beam while satisfying all specified constraints. The problem includes four primary variables: weld height (h), weld length (l), beam height (t), and beam width (b). The specific constraint variables and their meanings in this problem are described elsewhere [59]. The mathematical model is as follows:

Objective function:

$$minf(x) = 1.10471x_1^2x_2 + 0.04811x_3x_4 \cdot (14 + x_2) \tag{20}$$

Decision variables:

$$x = [x_1, x_2, x_3, x_4] = [h, l, t, b]. \tag{21}$$

Constraints:

$$\begin{gathered} g_1(x) = \tau(x) - \tau_{max} \leq 0, \\ g_2(x) = \sigma(x) - \sigma_{max} \leq 0, \\ g_3(x) = \delta(x) - \delta_{max} \leq 0, \\ g_4(x) = x_1 - x_4 \leq 0, \\ g_5(x) = P - P_c(x) \leq 0, \\ g_6(x) = 0.125 - x_1 \leq 0, \\ g_7(x) = 1.10471x_1^2 + 0.04811x_3x_4 \cdot (14 + x_2) - 5 \leq 0, \\ 0.1 \leq x_1 \leq 2,\ 0.1 \leq x_2 \leq 10,\ 0.1 \leq x_3 \leq 10,\ 0.1 \leq x_4 \leq 2. \end{gathered} \tag{22}$$

in which

$$\tau(x) = \sqrt{(\tau')^2 + 2\tau'\tau''\frac{x_2}{2R} + (\tau'')^2}, \tag{23}$$

$$\tau' = \frac{P}{\sqrt{2}x_1x_2},\ \tau'' = \frac{MR}{J},\ M = P\left(L + \frac{x_2}{2}\right), \tag{24}$$

$$R = \sqrt{\frac{x_2^2 + (x_1 + x_3)^2}{4}}, \tag{25}$$

$$J = 2\left\{\sqrt{2}x_1x_2\left[\frac{x_2^2}{12} + \frac{(x_1 + x_3)^2}{4}\right]\right\},\ \sigma(x) = \frac{6PL}{x_4x_3^2}, \tag{26}$$

$$\delta(x) = \frac{4PL^3}{Ex_3^3x_4},\ P_c(x) = \frac{4.013E\sqrt{\frac{x_3^2x_4^6}{36}}}{6L^2}\left(1 - \frac{x_3}{2L}\sqrt{\frac{E}{4G}}\right). \tag{27}$$

where σ_{max} = 30,000 psi, P = 6000 lb, L = 14 in, E = 30e6 psi, G = 12e6 psi, δ_{max} = 0.25 in, τ_{max} = 13,000 psi.

Table 12 presents the comparative results of applying the HIAOA and other algorithms from the literature to solve the welded beam design problem. The results indicate that the HIAOA achieves superior solutions for the welded beam design problem compared to other optimization algorithms.

Table 12. Comparison of results of different algorithms for solving the welded beam design problem.

	minf(x)	h	l	t	b
HIAOA	**1.7068**	0.20134	3.372	9.0478	0.22286
BKA [24]	1.724853	0.205730	3.470488	9.036622	0.205730
AOA [29]	1.7164	0.194475	2.57092	10.000	0.201827
MPA [60]	1.824853	0.205728	3.470509	9.036624	0.205730
WOA [57]	1.730499	0.205396	3.484293	9.037426	0.206276
GWO [17]	1.72624	0.205676	3.478377	9.03681	0.205778
AVOA [22]	1.724852	0.205730	3.470474	9.036621	0.205730
AO [19]	1.749188	0.200517	3.654022	9.057898	0.206271
SHO [20]	1.7259	0.20585	3.46946	9.03276	0.20591

4.2.3. Three-Bar Truss Design Problem

The three-bar truss is usually a simple plane truss structure consisting of three bars forming a triangle. Its design variables usually include the cross-sectional area or size of the bars, and the goal is to minimize the total mass of the three-bar truss. The total mass is expressed as the sum of the masses of each bar, while satisfying stress and geometric constraints. The specific constraint variables and their meanings in this problem can be found elsewhere [61]. This problem is described by the following mathematical model:

Objective function:

$$minf(x) = \left(2\sqrt{2}x_1 + x_2\right) \cdot l \tag{28}$$

Decision variables:

$$x = [x_1, x_2] = [A_1, A_2]. \tag{29}$$

Constraints:

$$\begin{aligned} g_1(x) &= \frac{\sqrt{2}x_1 + x_2}{\sqrt{2}x_1^2 + 2x_1x_2} P - \sigma \le 0, \\ g_2(x) &= \frac{x_2}{\sqrt{2}x_1^2 + 2x_1x_2} P - \sigma \le 0, \\ g_3(x) &= \frac{1}{\sqrt{2}x_2 + x_1} P - \sigma \le 0, \\ &0 \le x_1 \le 1,\ 0 \le x_2 \le 1. \end{aligned} \tag{30}$$

where $l = 1000$ mm, $P = 2\ \text{kN/cm}^2$, $\sigma = 2\ \text{kN/cm}^2$.

Table 13 lists the comparative results of applying the HIAOA and other algorithms from the literature to solve the three-bar truss design problem. The outcomes demonstrate that the HIAOA can generate superior solutions for this problem compared to other optimization algorithms.

Table 13. Comparison of results of different algorithms for solving the three-bar truss design problem.

	minf(x)	A_1	A_2
HIAOA	**263.895774**	0.78856	0.40825
BKA [24]	263.895843	0.788675	0.408248
AOA [29]	263.9154	0.79369	0.39426
MFO [62]	263.8959797	0.788444771	0.4094669
GOA [63]	263.89588149	0.78889755	0.40761957
CS [64]	263.9716	0.78867	0.40902
MVO [65]	263.895849	0.788602	0.408453
MBA [66]	263.8958522	0.788565	0.4085597

5. Conclusions and Potential Future Research

An HIAOA is proposed to address the drawbacks of AOAs, such as poor exploitation and tendency to fall into local optima. We embed the exploitation mechanism of GWO into an AOA, and after each optimization, the follower mechanism of SSA and Cauchy mutation operation with equal probability are used to perturb it. Finally, the greedy mechanism is used to select the optimal solution.

The proposed HIAOA algorithm was compared with the GWOAOA and AOA using different improvement strategies on 13 benchmark test functions. The experimental results demonstrate that the GWOAOA outperforms the AOA in solving certain optimization problems, indicating the effectiveness of the GWOAOA modification. However, the data also reveal that the HIAOA significantly surpasses both the GWOAOA and AOA in terms of performance and stability. This validates the positive impact of incorporating the SSA mechanism and Cauchy mutation in escaping local optima. Afterwards, the HIAOA is also used to conduct experimental comparisons with seven other intelligent optimization algorithms on 23 benchmark test functions to analyze the competitiveness of the HIAOA in local search and global exploration. Afterwards, the Wilcoxon rank-sum test is employed to estimate the statistical differences between the HIAOA and other algorithms to confirm that the improvement strategy proposed herein represents an improvement on the AOA. The experimental results demonstrate that the HIAOA exhibits superior convergence accuracy and stability, and the convergence curve also verifies that the HIAOA allows faster convergence. Finally, the HIAOA is utilized to address three engineering design problems. The results demonstrate that the HIAOA achieves superior solutions compared to algorithms proposed in the literature for these engineering problems, indicating its potential as a novel and effective method for practical problem-solving.

Although this study attempts to integrate parts of the development and exploration mechanisms from GWO and SSA into the Arithmetic Optimization Algorithm (AOA), the experimental results demonstrate that the proposed improvement strategies effectively enhance the performance of the AOA. However, there are still some limitations. For instance, the HIAOA incorporates additional mechanisms such as GWO, the SSA's follower mechanism, and Cauchy mutation, which may increase computational complexity. In practical applications, particularly for large-scale problems, this added computational cost could impact the algorithm's efficiency. Future research could explore ways to reduce the computational overhead while maintaining performance, such as optimizing the algorithm's implementation or adopting more efficient computational strategies.

Additionally, the performance of HIAOA is sensitive to parameter settings, which may affect the stability and robustness of the algorithm across different problem instances. Further studies should conduct a comprehensive sensitivity analysis of the algorithm's parameters and explore adaptive parameter-tuning methods to improve its stability and generalization capabilities. Furthermore, while this study evaluated the HIAOA using 23 benchmark functions and several engineering design problems, these tests may not fully cover all real-world scenarios. Future work will expand the experimental scope to assess the HIAOA's performance in a broader range of application areas and diverse real-world problems to further verify its effectiveness and applicability.

In the present research, we integrate some of the mechanisms of GWO and SSA into the AOA, and the experimental results demonstrate that this enhancement strategy effectively enhances the AOA's performance. In the subsequent research, the search strategy of arithmetic optimization will continue to be improved and optimized to enhance the stability and balance of the algorithm. Furthermore, based on the fact that the mathematical function gas pedal M_{OA} of AOAs is a simple linear structure, we will explore more effective parameter tuning and self-adaptive strategies, and pull to adjust the focus of the algorithms on exploration and exploitation of algorithms at different stages, to improve the applicability and robustness of the algorithms to different problems. Finally, we will further expand the range of application of the AOA in various fields, such as feature selection, power model parameter optimization, deep learning, and other practical problems, to promote the wider application of the algorithm in practice.

Author Contributions: Conceptualization, Y.Z. and L.X.; Funding acquisition, L.X.; Investigation, Y.Z.; Methodology, Y.Z. and L.X.; Resources, L.X.; Supervision, L.X.; Validation, Y.Z.; Visualization, Y.Z.; Writing—original draft, Y.Z.; Writing—review and editing, Y.Z. and L.X. All authors have read and agreed to the published version of the manuscript.

Funding: This research was funded by the Science and Technology Innovation Team of Shaanxi Province, grant number 2023-CX-TD-07; the Key R&D Program Projects in Shaanxi Province, grant number 2024GH-ZDXM-48; the National Natural Science Foundation of China, grant number 61773120; the Special Projects in Key Fields of Universities in Guangdong, grant number 2021ZDZX1019; and the Natural Science Foundation Project of Hunan Province, grant number 2024JJ5109 and 2024JJ7098.

Data Availability Statement: Data are contained within the article.

Conflicts of Interest: The authors declare no conflicts of interest.

References

1. Wu, X.; Feng, Z.; Chen, H.; Qin, Y.; Zheng, S.; Wang, L.; Liu, Y.; Skibniewski, M.J. Intelligent Optimization Framework of near Zero Energy Consumption Building Performance Based on a Hybrid Machine Learning Algorithm. *Renew. Sustain. Energy Rev.* **2022**, *167*, 112703. [CrossRef]
2. Song, Y.; Ou, J.; Pedrycz, W.; Suganthan, P.N.; Wang, X.; Xing, L.; Zhang, Y. Generalized Model and Deep Reinforcement Learning-Based Evolutionary Method for Multitype Satellite Observation Scheduling. *IEEE Trans. Syst. Man Cybern. Syst.* **2024**, *54*, 2576–2589. [CrossRef]
3. Yao, F.; Du, Y.; Li, L.; Xing, L.; Chen, Y. General Modeling and Optimization Technique for Real-World Earth Observation Satellite Scheduling. *Front. Eng. Manag.* **2023**, *10*, 695–709. [CrossRef]
4. Yan, Z.; Yan, J.; Wu, Y.; Cai, S.; Wang, H. A Novel Reinforcement Learning Based Tuna Swarm Optimization Algorithm for Autonomous Underwater Vehicle Path Planning. *Math. Comput. Simul.* **2023**, *209*, 55–86. [CrossRef]
5. Gharehchopogh, F.S. An Improved Harris Hawks Optimization Algorithm with Multi-Strategy for Community Detection in Social Network. *J. Bionic Eng.* **2023**, *20*, 1175–1197. [CrossRef]
6. Teekaraman, Y.; Manoharan, H.; Basha, A.R.; Manoharan, A. Hybrid Optimization Algorithms for Resource Allocation in Heterogeneous Cognitive Radio Networks. *Neural Process. Lett.* **2023**, *55*, 3813–3826. [CrossRef]
7. Wan, M.; Ye, C.; Peng, D. Multi-Period Dynamic Multi-Objective Emergency Material Distribution Model under Uncertain Demand. *Eng. Appl. Artif. Intell.* **2023**, *117*, 105530. [CrossRef]
8. Kumar, P.; Govindaraj, V.; Erturk, V.S.; Nisar, K.S.; Inc, M. Fractional Mathematical Modeling of the Stuxnet Virus Along with an Optimal Control Problem. *Ain Shams Eng. J.* **2023**, *14*, 102004. [CrossRef]
9. Huang, J.; Hu, H. Hybrid Beluga Whale Optimization Algorithm with Multi-Strategy for Functions and Engineering Optimization Problems. *J. Big Data* **2024**, *11*, 3. [CrossRef]
10. Wang, G.-G. Moth Search Algorithm: A Bio-Inspired Metaheuristic Algorithm for Global Optimization Problems. *Memetic Comput.* **2018**, *10*, 151–164. [CrossRef]
11. Shams, M.Y.; El-Kenawy, E.-S.M.; Ibrahim, A.; Elshewey, A.M. A Hybrid Dipper Throated Optimization Algorithm and Particle Swarm Optimization (Dtpso) Model for Hepatocellular Carcinoma (Hcc) Prediction. *Biomed. Signal Process. Control* **2023**, *85*, 104908. [CrossRef]
12. Li, W.; Jing, J.; Chen, Y.; Chen, X.; Moshayedi, A.J. Evolutionary Experience-Driven Particle Swarm Optimization with Dynamic Searching. *Complex Syst. Model. Simul.* **2023**, *3*, 307–326. [CrossRef]
13. Xing, L.-N.; Rohlfshagen, P.; Chen, Y.-W.; Yao, X. A Hybrid Ant Colony Optimization Algorithm for the Extended Capacitated Arc Routing Problem. *IEEE Trans. Syst. Man Cybern. Part B (Cybern.)* **2011**, *41*, 1110–1123. [CrossRef]
14. Beni, G.; Wang, J. Swarm Intelligence in Cellular Robotic Systems. In *Robots and Biological Systems: Towards a New Bionics?* Springer: Berlin/Heidelberg, Germany, 1993; pp. 703–712.
15. Kennedy, J.; Eberhart, R. Particle Swarm Optimization. In Proceedings of the ICNN'95-International Conference on Neural Networks, Perth, Australia, 27 November–1 December 1995; Volume 4, pp. 1942–1948. [CrossRef]
16. Dorigo, M.; Birattari, M.; Stutzle, T. Ant Colony Optimization. *IEEE Comput. Intell. Mag.* **2006**, *1*, 28–39. [CrossRef]
17. Mirjalili, S.; Mirjalili, S.M.; Lewis, A. Grey Wolf Optimizer. *Adv. Eng. Softw.* **2014**, *69*, 46–61. [CrossRef]
18. Seyyedabbasi, A.; Kiani, F. Sand Cat Swarm Optimization: A Nature-Inspired Algorithm to Solve Global Optimization Problems. *Eng. Comput.* **2023**, *39*, 2627–2651. [CrossRef]
19. Abualigah, L.; Yousri, D.; Elaziz, M.A.; Ewees, A.A.; Al-Qaness, M.A.; Gandomi, A.H. Aquila Optimizer: A Novel Meta-Heuristic Optimization Algorithm. *Comput. Ind. Eng.* **2021**, *157*, 107250. [CrossRef]

20. Zhao, S.; Zhang, T.; Ma, S.; Wang, M. Sea-Horse Optimizer: A Novel Nature-Inspired Meta-Heuristic for Global Optimization Problems. *Appl. Intell.* **2023**, *53*, 11833–11860. [CrossRef]
21. Xue, J.; Shen, B. Dung Beetle Optimizer: A New Meta-Heuristic Algorithm for Global Optimization. *J. Supercomput.* **2023**, *79*, 7305–7336. [CrossRef]
22. Abdollahzadeh, B.; Gharehchopogh, F.S.; Mirjalili, S. African Vultures Optimization Algorithm: A New Nature-Inspired Metaheuristic Algorithm for Global Optimization Problems. *Comput. Ind. Eng.* **2021**, *158*, 107408. [CrossRef]
23. Abdel-Basset, M.; Mohamed, R.; Jameel, M.; Abouhawwash, M. Spider Wasp Optimizer: A Novel Meta-Heuristic Optimization Algorithm. *Artif. Intell. Rev.* **2023**, *56*, 11675–11738. [CrossRef]
24. Wang, J.; Wang, W.-C.; Hu, X.-X.; Qiu, L.; Zang, H.-F. Black-Winged Kite Algorithm: A Nature-Inspired Meta-Heuristic for Solving Benchmark Functions and Engineering Problems. *Artif. Intell. Rev.* **2024**, *57*, 98. [CrossRef]
25. Braik, M.; Sheta, A.; Al-Hiary, H. A Novel Meta-Heuristic Search Algorithm for Solving Optimization Problems: Capuchin Search Algorithm. *Neural Comput. Appl.* **2021**, *33*, 2515–2547. [CrossRef]
26. Zhou, S.; Xing, L.; Zheng, X.; Du, N.; Wang, L.; Zhang, Q. A Self-Adaptive Differential Evolution Algorithm for Scheduling a Single Batch-Processing Machine with Arbitrary Job Sizes and Release Times. *IEEE Trans. Cybern.* **2021**, *51*, 1430–1442. [CrossRef] [PubMed]
27. Yi, J.-H.; Xing, L.-N.; Wang, G.-G.; Dong, J.; Vasilakos, A.V.; Alavi, A.H.; Wang, L. Behavior of Crossover Operators in Nsga-Iii for Large-Scale Optimization Problems. *Inf. Sci.* **2020**, *509*, 470–487. [CrossRef]
28. Xing, L.; Rohlfshagen, P.; Chen, Y.; Yao, X. An Evolutionary Approach to the Multidepot Capacitated Arc Routing Problem. *IEEE Trans. Evol. Comput.* **2010**, *14*, 356–374. [CrossRef]
29. Abualigah, L.; Diabat, A.; Mirjalili, S.; Elaziz, M.A.; Gandomi, A.H. The Arithmetic Optimization Algorithm. *Comput. Methods Appl. Mech. Eng.* **2021**, *376*, 113609. [CrossRef]
30. Kaveh, A.; Hamedani, K.B. Improved Arithmetic Optimization Algorithm and Its Application to Discrete Structural Optimization. *Structures* **2022**, *35*, 748–764. [CrossRef]
31. Zheng, R.; Jia, H.; Abualigah, L.; Liu, Q.; Wang, S. An Improved Arithmetic Optimization Algorithm with Forced Switching Mechanism for Global Optimization Problems. *Math. Biosci. Eng.* **2022**, *19*, 473–512. [CrossRef]
32. Issa, M. Enhanced Arithmetic Optimization Algorithm for Parameter Estimation of Pid Controller. *Arab. J. Sci. Eng.* **2023**, *48*, 2191–2205. [CrossRef]
33. Hu, G.; Zhong, J.; Du, B.; Wei, G. An Enhanced Hybrid Arithmetic Optimization Algorithm for Engineering Applications. *Comput. Methods Appl. Mech. Eng.* **2022**, *394*, 114901. [CrossRef]
34. Khatir, S.; Tiachacht, S.; Le Thanh, C.; Ghandourah, E.; Mirjalili, S.; Wahab, M.A. An Improved Artificial Neural Network Using Arithmetic Optimization Algorithm for Damage Assessment in Fgm Composite Plates. *Compos. Struct.* **2021**, *273*, 114287. [CrossRef]
35. Kharrich, M.; Abualigah, L.; Kamel, S.; AbdEl-Sattar, H.; Tostado-Véliz, M. An Improved Arithmetic Optimization Algorithm for Design of a Microgrid with Energy Storage System: Case Study of El Kharga Oasis, Egypt. *J. Energy Storage* **2022**, *51*, 104343. [CrossRef]
36. Dahou, A.; Al-Qaness, M.A.; Elaziz, M.A.; Helmi, A. Human Activity Recognition in Ioht Applications Using Arithmetic Optimization Algorithm and Deep Learning. *Measurement* **2022**, *199*, 111445. [CrossRef]
37. Otair, M.; Abualigah, L.; Tawfiq, S.; Alshinwan, M.; Ezugwu, A.E.; Abu Zitar, R.; Sumari, P. Adapted Arithmetic Optimization Algorithm for Multi-Level Thresholding Image Segmentation: A Case Study of Chest X-Ray Images. *Multimed. Tools Appl.* **2024**, *83*, 41051–41081. [CrossRef]
38. Abualigah, L.; Altalhi, M. A Novel Generalized Normal Distribution Arithmetic Optimization Algorithm for Global Optimization and Data Clustering Problems. *J. Ambient. Intell. Humaniz. Comput.* **2024**, *15*, 389–417. [CrossRef]
39. Barua, S.; Merabet, A. Lévy Arithmetic Algorithm: An Enhanced Metaheuristic Algorithm and Its Application to Engineering Optimization. *Expert Syst. Appl.* **2024**, *241*, 122335. [CrossRef]
40. Ahmadipour, M.; Othman, M.M.; Bo, R.; Javadi, M.S.; Ridha, H.M.; Alrifaey, M. Optimal Power Flow Using a Hybridization Algorithm of Arithmetic Optimization and Aquila Optimizer. *Expert Syst. Appl.* **2024**, *235*, 121212. [CrossRef]
41. Mahajan, S.; Abualigah, L.; Pandit, A.K. Hybrid Arithmetic Optimization Algorithm with Hunger Games Search for Global Optimization. *Multimed. Tools Appl.* **2022**, *81*, 28755–28778. [CrossRef]
42. Aydemir, S.B. A Novel Arithmetic Optimization Algorithm Based on Chaotic Maps for Global Optimization. *Evol. Intell.* **2023**, *16*, 981–996. [CrossRef]
43. Kaveh, A.; Hamedani, K.B. A Hybridization of Growth Optimizer and Improved Arithmetic Optimization Algorithm and Its Application to Discrete Structural Optimization. *Comput. Struct.* **2024**, *303*, 107496. [CrossRef]
44. Yu, X.; Xu, W.; Li, C. Opposition-Based Learning Grey Wolf Optimizer for Global Optimization. *Knowl.-Based Syst.* **2021**, *226*, 107139. [CrossRef]
45. Xue, J.; Shen, B. A Novel Swarm Intelligence Optimization Approach: Sparrow Search Algorithm. *Syst. Sci. Control. Eng.* **2020**, *8*, 22–34. [CrossRef]
46. Li, K.; Li, S.; Huang, Z.; Zhang, M.; Xu, Z. Grey Wolf Optimization Algorithm Based on Cauchy-Gaussian Mutation and Improved Search Strategy. *Sci. Rep.* **2022**, *12*, 18961. [CrossRef]

47. Shan, W.; He, X.; Liu, H.; Heidari, A.A.; Wang, M.; Cai, Z.; Chen, H. Cauchy Mutation Boosted Harris Hawk Algorithm: Optimal Performance Design and Engineering Applications. *J. Comput. Des. Eng.* **2023**, *10*, 503–526. [CrossRef]
48. Salgotra, R.; Singh, U. Application of Mutation Operators to Flower Pollination Algorithm. *Expert Syst. Appl.* **2017**, *79*, 112–129. [CrossRef]
49. Zhang, X.; Xu, Y.; Yu, C.; Heidari, A.A.; Li, S.; Chen, H.; Li, C. Gaussian Mutational Chaotic Fruit Fly-Built Optimization and Feature Selection. *Expert Syst. Appl.* **2020**, *141*, 112976. [CrossRef]
50. Sapre, S.; Mini, S. Opposition-Based Moth Flame Optimization with Cauchy Mutation and Evolutionary Boundary Constraint Handling for Global Optimization. *Soft Comput.* **2019**, *23*, 6023–6041. [CrossRef]
51. Hamad, R.K.; Rashid, T.A. Goose Algorithm: A Powerful Optimization Tool for Real-World Engineering Challenges and Beyond. *Evol. Syst.* **2024**, *15*, 1249–1274. [CrossRef]
52. Suganthan, P.N.; Hansen, N.; Liang, J.J.; Deb, K.; Chen, Y.P.; Auger, A.; Tiwari, S. Problem Definitions and Evaluation Criteria for the Cec 2005 Special Session on Real-Parameter Optimization. *Nat. Comput.* **2005**, *341–357*, 341–357.
53. Noroozi, M.; Mohammadi, H.; Efatinasab, E.; Lashgari, A.; Eslami, M.; Khan, B. Golden Search Optimization Algorithm. *IEEE Access* **2022**, *10*, 37515–37532. [CrossRef]
54. Wang, H.; Li, C.; Liu, Y.; Zeng, S. A Hybrid Particle Swarm Algorithm with Cauchy Mutation. In Proceedings of the 2007 IEEE Swarm Intelligence Symposium, Honolulu, HI, USA, 1–5 April 2007; pp. 356–360. [CrossRef]
55. Che, Y.; He, D. An Enhanced Seagull Optimization Algorithm for Solving Engineering Optimization Problems. *Appl. Intell.* **2022**, *52*, 13043–13081. [CrossRef]
56. Li, S.; Chen, H.; Wang, M.; Heidari, A.A.; Mirjalili, S. Slime Mould Algorithm: A New Method for Stochastic Optimization. *Future Gener. Comput. Syst.* **2020**, *111*, 300–323. [CrossRef]
57. Mirjalili, S.; Lewis, A. The Whale Optimization Algorithm. *Adv. Eng. Softw.* **2016**, *95*, 51–67. [CrossRef]
58. Zhao, W.; Wang, L.; Zhang, Z. Artificial Ecosystem-Based Optimization: A Novel Nature-Inspired Meta-Heuristic Algorithm. *Neural Comput. Appl.* **2020**, *32*, 9383–9425. [CrossRef]
59. Yildiz, A.R. Comparison of Evolutionary-Based Optimization Algorithms for Structural Design Optimization. *Eng. Appl. Artif. Intell.* **2013**, *26*, 327–333. [CrossRef]
60. Faramarzi, A.; Heidarinejad, M.; Mirjalili, S.; Gandomi, A.H. Marine Predators Algorithm: A Nature-Inspired Metaheuristic. *Expert Syst. Appl.* **2020**, *152*, 113377. [CrossRef]
61. Yildirim, A.E.; Karci, A. Application of Three Bar Truss Problem among Engineering Design Optimization Problems Using Artificial Atom Algorithm. In Proceedings of the 2018 International Conference on Artificial Intelligence and Data Processing (IDAP), Malatya, Turkey, 28–30 September 2018; pp. 1–5. [CrossRef]
62. Mirjalili, S. Moth-Flame Optimization Algorithm: A Novel Nature-Inspired Heuristic Paradigm. *Knowl.-Based Syst.* **2015**, *89*, 228–249. [CrossRef]
63. Saremi, S.; Mirjalili, S.; Lewis, A. Grasshopper Optimisation Algorithm: Theory and Application. *Adv. Eng. Softw.* **2017**, *105*, 30–47. [CrossRef]
64. Bhargava, V.; Fateen, S.; Bonilla-Petriciolet, A. Cuckoo Search: A New Nature-Inspired Optimization Method for Phase Equilibrium Calculations. *Fluid Phase Equilibria* **2013**, *337*, 191–200. [CrossRef]
65. Mirjalili, S.; Mirjalili, S.M.; Hatamlou, A. Multi-Verse Optimizer: A Nature-Inspired Algorithm for Global Optimization. *Neural Comput. Appl.* **2016**, *27*, 495–513. [CrossRef]
66. Sadollah, A.; Bahreininejad, A.; Eskandar, H.; Hamdi, M. Mine Blast Algorithm: A New Population Based Algorithm for Solving Constrained Engineering Optimization Problems. *Appl. Soft Comput.* **2013**, *13*, 2592–2612. [CrossRef]

mathematics

MDPI

Article

Determination of Sequential Well Placements Using a Multi-Modal Convolutional Neural Network Integrated with Evolutionary Optimization

Seoyoon Kwon [1], Minsoo Ji [1,2], Min Kim [3], Juliana Y. Leung [4] and Baehyun Min [1,*]

1 Department of Climate and Energy Systems Engineering, Ewha Womans University, 52, Ewhayeodae-gil, Seodaemun-gu, Seoul 03760, Republic of Korea; sykwon024@ewhain.net (S.K.); msji048@ewhain.net (M.J.)
2 POSCO International, 165, Convensia-daero, Yeonsu-gu, Incheon 21998, Republic of Korea
3 Global E&P Technology Center, Korea National Oil Corporation, 305 Jongga-ro, Jung-gu, Ulsan 44538, Republic of Korea; m.kim@knoc.co.kr
4 Department of Civil and Environmental Engineering, University of Alberta, Edmonton, AB T6G 1H9, Canada; juliana2@ualberta.ca
* Correspondence: bhmin01@ewha.ac.kr

Abstract: In geoenergy science and engineering, well placement optimization is the process of determining optimal well locations and configurations to maximize economic value while considering geological, engineering, economic, and environmental constraints. This complex multi-million-dollar problem involves optimizing multiple parameters using computationally intensive reservoir simulations, often employing advanced algorithms such as optimization algorithms and machine/deep learning techniques to find near-optimal solutions efficiently while accounting for uncertainties and risks. This study proposes a hybrid workflow for determining the locations of production wells during primary oil recovery using a multi-modal convolutional neural network (M-CNN) integrated with an evolutionary optimization algorithm. The particle swarm optimization algorithm provides the M-CNN with full-physics reservoir simulation results as learning data correlating an arbitrary well location and its cumulative oil production. The M-CNN learns the correlation between near-wellbore spatial properties (e.g., porosity, permeability, pressure, and saturation) and cumulative oil production as inputs and output, respectively. The learned M-CNN predicts oil productivity at every candidate well location and selects qualified well placement scenarios. The prediction performance of the M-CNN for hydrocarbon-prolific regions is improved by adding qualified scenarios to the learning data and re-training the M-CNN. This iterative learning scheme enhances the suitability of the proxy for solving the problem of maximizing oil productivity. The validity of the proxy is tested with a benchmark model, UNISIM-I-D, in which four oil production wells are sequentially drilled. The M-CNN approach demonstrates remarkable consistency and alignment with full-physics reservoir simulation results. It achieves prediction accuracy within a 3% relative error margin, while significantly reducing computational costs to just 11.18% of those associated with full-physics reservoir simulations. Moreover, the M-CNN-optimized well placement strategy yields a substantial 47.40% improvement in field cumulative oil production compared to the original configuration. These findings underscore the M-CNN's effectiveness in sequential well placement optimization, striking an optimal balance between predictive accuracy and computational efficiency. The method's ability to dramatically reduce processing time while maintaining high accuracy makes it a valuable tool for enhancing oil field productivity and streamlining reservoir management decisions.

Keywords: well placement; multi-modal convolutional neural network; evolutionary optimization; UNISIM-I-D

MSC: 68T20

1. Introduction

In the field of geoenergy science and engineering (e.g., petroleum engineering, carbon capture and storage, and geothermal engineering), well placement optimization refers to the process of determining the optimal locations and configurations for wells in a reservoir to maximize economic value (e.g., cumulative oil production, cumulative CO_2 storage, cumulative heat energy extraction, and net present value) while considering various constraints [1–8]. These constraints include geological factors (e.g., reservoir properties, faults, and barriers), engineering limitations (e.g., well spacing, bottom-hole pressures, and flow rates), economic considerations (e.g., drilling costs, operational expenses, oil prices, and CO_2 prices), and environmental regulations. The process relies on reservoir simulation models that capture complex fluid flow involving thermal, hydrological, mechanical, and chemical interactions. This multi-million-dollar problem involves determining several key parameters: the number and type of wells (e.g., producers, injectors, and observation wells), well locations (e.g., x, y, and z coordinates), well types (e.g., vertical, horizontal, directional, and multilateral), well trajectories and completions, and operational parameters (e.g., flow rates, bottom-hole pressures, and injection/production schedules). The challenge lies in the complex, nonlinear relationships between variables, the computational intensity of reservoir simulations required for each evaluation, and the need to account for uncertainties in geological models and future economic scenarios. Therefore, the practical goal of well placement optimization is to develop efficient algorithms, often incorporating machine learning and artificial intelligence techniques, to find near-optimal solutions with minimal function evaluations while considering the inherent uncertainties and risks associated with subsurface operations.

Well placement optimization is essential to maximize the economic profits of oil and gas field development. Various optimization methods integrated with full-physics reservoir simulation (RS) have been used to determine well placement. For example, gradient-based algorithms, such as the adjoint-based method [1], simultaneous perturbation stochastic approximation [2], and stochastic simplest approximate gradient [9], have been integrated with RS to optimize various field development and operating plans. Non-gradient-based evolutionary optimization algorithms, such as particle swarm optimization (PSO) [3–5,10] and genetic algorithms (GA) [6–8], have also been widely employed because of their extensive population-based search capabilities. To find the global optimum, these population-based methods are considered powerful for generating high-quality solutions with stable convergence at affordable computational costs [11,12]. The geoenergy industry, particularly oil and gas, has widely adopted these evolutionary algorithms as primary optimization tools. Notably, these algorithms have been implemented in commercial software packages such as SLB's MEPO (2020.01) [13] and CMG's CMOST-AI (2023.12) [14]. However, their high computational cost owing to exhaustive simulation runs for objective function evaluations has hindered their implementation [15]. In addition, the stagnation of search performance in later generations during the evolutionary process requires improvement [16].

To alleviate the cost of an exhaustive search, various proxies have been employed to enhance the computational efficiency of these algorithms, while reducing the number of RS runs [17–19]. Machine learning techniques have been used to solve reservoir optimization problems, such as support vector machines [20,21] and Extreme Gradient Boosting [22,23]. These machine learning techniques can distinguish superior solutions from those that violate constraints [15]. Recently, deep learning techniques such as artificial neural networks (ANNs) and convolutional neural networks (CNNs) have been demonstrated as partial or full substitutes for expensive reservoir simulators [24]. ANN has been actively adopted for well placement optimization [25–27]. However, ANNs cannot preserve the spatial features of large-scale problems because their input data are flattened into one-dimension [28]. Particularly, studies have demonstrated the excellent performance of CNNs in handling multi-dimensional data while preserving spatial features [28–30]. The multi-modal CNN (M-CNN), an enhanced CNN with multi-modal learning that functions by driving the fusion of input data from multiple sources [31], has been applied to predict cumulative oil production from near-wellbore static (e.g., permeability and porosity) and dynamic (e.g., pressure and saturation) properties [28,29].

Drawing inspiration from the M-CNN concept [29], this study seeks to enhance the solution quality of well placement problems by mitigating extrapolation effects and optimizing the learning data acquisition process. The performance of M-CNN is affected by the quantity and quality of learning data [32]. Considering the field development cost, the level of difficulty in applying the proxy has increased owing to the small ratio of the available data volume to the domain volume for well placement optimization problems [28]. To develop an efficient proxy, it is essential to balance accuracy and learning data acquisition costs. In the previous studies [28–30], generalization was achieved by randomly generating machine learning data, which increased the RS cost. For more efficiently managing the high computational cost of RSs associated with the acquisition of learning data, this study couples an M-CNN with an evolutionary algorithm (i.e., PSO). While PSO and GA are powerful for generating high-quality solutions, their high computational cost, resulting from exhaustive simulation runs, limits their practical application. In contrast, our approach integrates M-CNN with PSO and iterative learning, significantly reducing these costs while enhancing model accuracy. Another challenge in applying machine learning to well placement is the maximization problem that occurs when searching for the most productive region in a reservoir beyond the range of the learning data. Although features are captured well during machine learning interpolation, their predictability for extrapolation tends to deteriorate if the problem is nonlinear and complex [33–35]. We believe that the presence of PSO and iterative learning in the proposed framework enables the M-CNN to relieve the cost burden of RS. Constructing an M-CNN learned with PSO results and updating the proxy with iterative learning results are expected to allow the efficient selection of the optimal location with reasonable learning data volume for well placements. To the best of our knowledge, this is the first application of an evolutionary algorithm and iterative learning to obtain a dataset for a deep learning-based proxy model in the well placement optimization problem.

This study implements a hybrid workflow to sequentially determine locations that maximize hydrocarbon production. The proposed hybrid framework integrates M-CNN with PSO and iterative learning, addressing the high computational costs and accuracy limitations of traditional methods. This approach offers a more efficient and accurate solution for well placement optimization in dynamic, large-scale oil field developments. PSO was integrated to generate learning data within the framework of an M-CNN as a productivity estimator to determine the sequential placements of vertical oil production wells. Additionally, the concept of iterative learning was introduced to the M-CNN to mitigate the extrapolation problem. The M-CNN inputs spatial data (comprising static (e.g., permeability and porosity) and dynamic (e.g., pressure and oil saturation) reservoir properties) near a candidate well and outputs the oil productivity at that well location. Moreover, to consider the inter-well distance, auxiliary data (e.g., distances between the well and reservoir boundaries) are added as a 1D array to the full-connection stage of the

CNN. The M-CNN dataset was generated via a PSO-driven process by running the full-physics RSs of well-placing scenarios. The trained M-CNN is employed to evaluate the oil productivity at every candidate location. The results of the M-CNN are compared with the RS results for qualified (i.e., highly productive) well-placing scenarios to validate the model consistency. In addition, the M-CNN performance is compared with that of PSO to analyze the effect of using PSO to create datasets in the M-CNN. Expanding on the single vertical well placement optimization introduced by Kwon et al. [28], this study also enhances the methodology by enabling sequential well placement through a novel integration of the M-CNN with PSO and iterative learning techniques. This hybrid approach improves predictive accuracy and computational efficiency in dynamic reservoir scenarios, effectively addressing limitations identified in previous studies.

In brief, the key contributions of this study can be summarized as follows:

- Development of a Hybrid Optimization Framework:
  Introduced a novel hybrid framework integrating the M-CNN with PSO and iterative learning to optimize sequential well placement in reservoir management.
- Implementation of Iterative Learning for Enhanced Accuracy:
  Incorporated iterative learning to refine the training dataset, focusing on high-productivity scenarios to address extrapolation challenges and improve model generalization.
- Utilization of PSO for Efficient Data Generation:
  Leveraged PSO to generate learning data for the M-CNN, substantially reducing computational costs typically associated with full-physics reservoir simulations.
- Validation in Dynamic Reservoir Simulation Scenarios:
  Validated the proposed hybrid framework on the UNISIM-I-D benchmark model, demonstrating high predictive accuracy with reduced computational requirements.
- Pioneer Application of Integrated M-CNN Framework:
  To our knowledge, this study presents the first application of a hybrid M-CNN framework combined with PSO and iterative learning for dataset generation in sequential well placement optimization.

This paper is organized as follows: the literature review and scope of this study are introduced in Section 1; the methodology, including the theoretical background, structure of the M-CNN, and overall M-CNN workflow for sequential well placement optimization, is described in Section 2; the testing of the proposed methodology on a benchmark model UNISIM-I-D is presented in Section 3; and the conclusions based on the findings presented in Section 3 are summarized in Section 4.

2. Methodology

2.1. Well Placement Problem

Let $\mathbf{u} \in \mathbf{U}$ be a set of well locations in a given reservoir:

$$\mathbf{u} = [\mathrm{u}_1, \mathrm{u}_2, \cdots, \mathrm{u}_{N_w}] \tag{1}$$

where N_w is the number of wells, and $\mathrm{u}_i = (\mathrm{X}_i, \mathrm{Y}_i)$ is the coordinate in the Cartesian coordinate system. In this study, all wells in the reservoir were vertical and fully perforated. As a sequential well placement, u_i was drilled earlier than u_j where $1 \leq i \leq j \leq N_w$.

$Q_o(\mathbf{u})$ is the expected field cumulative oil production at $\mathbf{u}$:

$$Q_o(\mathbf{u}) = \int_0^T q_o^t(\mathbf{u})dt, \tag{2}$$

where T is the total production time, and q_o^t is the oil production rate at time t.

The well placement optimization problem aims to determine the optimal set of well locations $\mathbf{u}^*$ that can yield the highest oil productivity.

$$\mathbf{u}^* = \underset{\mathbf{u} \in \mathbf{U}}{\operatorname{argmax}}(Q_o(\mathbf{u})). \tag{3}$$

To determine $\mathbf{u}^*$ via a cost-efficient approach, this study implemented a hybrid of an evolutionary optimization algorithm and deep learning algorithm. Figure 1 shows the workflow of the hybrid proxy that consists of PSO (Module 1), M-CNN (Module 2), and iterative learning (Module 3) for solving a sequential well placement problem. To verify the proxy performance, the full-physics RS results (e.g., oil production rate, water cut, and bottomhle pressure) are used as references (i.e., answers) throughout this study.

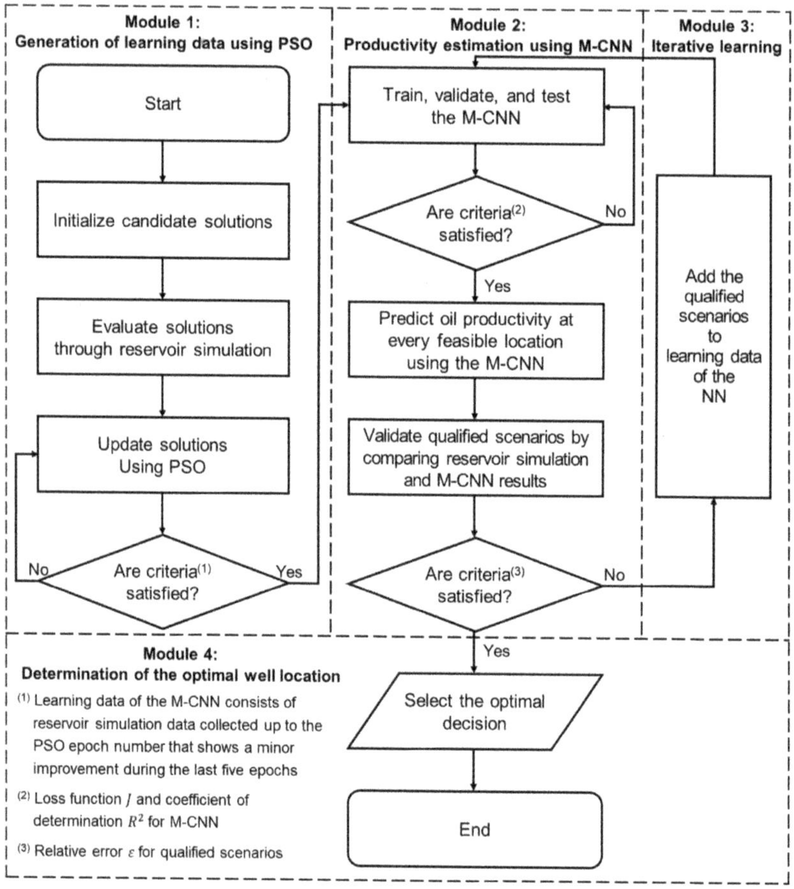

Figure 1. The flowchart of the proposed hybrid proxy to solve a sequential well placement problem. The optimum well locations are determined using the multi-modal convolutional neural network (M-CNN) incorporated with particle swarm optimization (PSO) and iterative learning.

2.2. Particle Swarm Optimization

PSO is a non-gradient population-based evolutionary optimization algorithm developed by Kennedy and Eberhart [10]. Figure 2a shows a schematic of the PSO. In PSO, the potential solutions are called particles, and a set of particles is referred to as a swarm [10]. Therefore, a swarm comprises the particles in the search space. The overall quality of the particles, as well as the swarm, evolves during the evolutionary process (i.e., epochs). In this study, PSO searches for the optimal well location that reveals the highest field cumulative oil production by running a full-physics RS at feasible well locations. That is, the swarm evolves in the direction of increasing $Q_o(\mathbf{u})$.

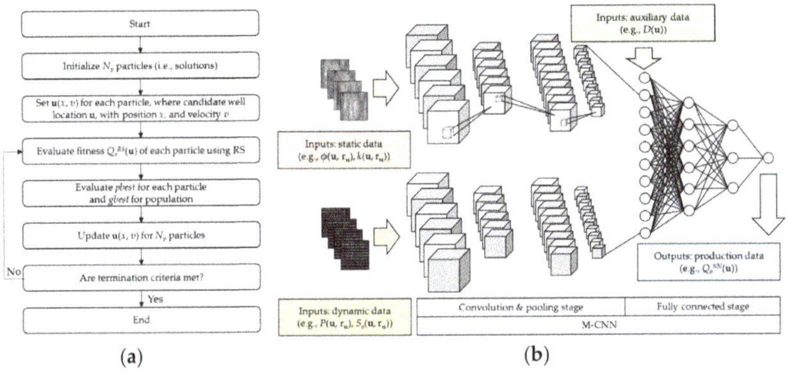

Figure 2. Schematic diagram of the PSO and M-CNN. (**a**) The PSO evolves solutions that are utilized as learning data of the M-CNN; (**b**) The M-CNN learns a pattern between inputs (i.e., petrophysical properties) and outputs (i.e., field cumulative oil production) extracted from the PSO solutions (modified from Chu et al. [29]).

Each particle corresponds to a candidate well location $\mathbf{u}$. A particle has velocity vector v and position vector x. The particle updates its v and x values based on the best individual and population solutions during each epoch.

v and x are updated as follows:

$$v_i^{k+1} = \omega v_i^k + c_1 r_1 \left(x_{i,pbest}^k - x_i^k \right) + c_2 r_2 \left(x_{i,gbest}^k - x_i^k \right), \tag{4}$$

$$x_i^{k+1} = x_i^k + v_i^{k+1}, \tag{5}$$

where v_i^k and x_i^k are the velocity and position vector of the i-th $\left(1 \le i \le N_p\right)$ particle in the k-th $(1 \le k \le N_e)$ epoch, respectively. N_p and N_e are the population size (i.e., swarm size) and maximum number of epochs, respectively. ω, c_1, and c_2 are the inertia, cognitive, and social weight components, respectively. r_1 and r_2 are uniformly distributed random numbers sampled from [0.0, 1.0]. *pbest* is the historical best solution of the particle and *gbest* is the population historical best solution. Typically, ω is set in [0.4, 0.9]; c_1 and c_2 are in [1.0, 2.0] with reference to [10]. With reference to [36], the weight components are set as ω = 0.730 and c_1 = c_2 = 1.496 throughout this study. PSO solves this well placement problem as an unconstrained problem in terms of the minimum inter-well distance because the M-CNN needs to learn that a short inter-well distance would yield poor oil production. During the optimization, the M-CNN learned well; thus, most solutions have sufficient inter-well distances. The use of PSO in this study is rooted in the desire to ensure the stability and reliability of the hybrid workflow. As this is the first attempt to integrate PSO with M-CNN and iterative learning, we chose to start with a well-established and proven optimization method. This approach minimizes the risks associated with using more complex or newer algorithms, providing a solid foundation for the workflow's performance and validation.

The proposed proxy employs PSO for two purposes. The first purpose is to generate learning data for the M-CNN. Specifically, the RS results obtained using PSO are used as learning data for the M-CNN: ($\mathbf{u}$, $Q_o^{RS}(\mathbf{u})$), where the superscript RS refers to the full-physics reservoir simulation. This ensures the collection of learning data from more hydrocarbon-prolific regions during the evolutionary process. Once the evolutionary process is complete, the best solution in the last epoch is considered as the optimal solution $\mathbf{u}^*$. Here, two stopping criteria for the evolutionary process are employed: N_e and the last epoch N_{es} with early stopping (ES) activation ($N_{es} \leq N_e$). The evolutionary process terminates early in the N_{es}-th epoch if the swarm quality improvement stagnates for the last five epochs. This early stopping criterion helps to reduce data acquisition costs, considering the high computational cost involved in field-scale RS. The second purpose of PSO in this study is to serve as a competitor for the developed proxy. In brief, the proxy results are compared with the PSO results with ES paying $N_p \times N_{es}$ RS runs, and with the simultaneous optimization of the field cumulative oil production $Q_o(\mathbf{u})$ and total computational cost.

2.3. Multi-Modal Convolutional Neural Network with Iterative Learning

Figure 2b illustrates the structure of the M-CNN developed for the sequential determination of well placements. This M-CNN inputs near-wellbore spatial properties (two static and two dynamic) and outputs the field cumulative oil production $Q_o^{NN}(\mathbf{u})$ at an arbitrary well location $\mathbf{u}$, where the superscript NN refers to a neural network (e.g., M-CNN in this study). Here, the spatial properties are porosity $\phi(\mathbf{u}, r_\mathbf{u})$, permeability $k(\mathbf{u}, r_\mathbf{u})$, pressure $P(\mathbf{u}, r_\mathbf{u})$, and oil saturation $S_o(\mathbf{u}, r_\mathbf{u})$, where $r_\mathbf{u}$ is the effective range from well $\mathbf{u}$ to an arbitrary reservoir location for determining the size of the 3D array data. Each location is assumed to be fully perforated. As sequential well placement enables the extraction of dynamic properties at each installation time, this study adopts multi-modal learning to input those properties. The features from the four spatial properties are extracted and upscaled during the convolutional and pooling stages. After convolution and pooling, the features are flattened and imported into the full-connection stage. In addition, the distance data $D(\mathbf{u})$ are also imported into the full-connection stage because they are scalar. $D(\mathbf{u})$ comprises the distance between the new well and reservoir boundaries and the distance between the new and existing wells.

The PSO results ($\mathbf{u}, Q_o^{RS}(\mathbf{u})$) are utilized as learning data for M-CNN. These learning data are split into training, validation, and test datasets for the efficient design and construction of the M-CNN. For each dataset, the performance of the M-CNN is assessed in terms of two indicators: loss function J and coefficient of determination R^2. Favored learning results are indicated by J values approaching zero from the right and R^2 values nearing one, signifying better model performance and fit.

The loss function J is designed to optimize the neural network's performance by balancing predictive accuracy with model generalizability, incorporating a regularization term that penalizes large weights to mitigate overfitting [32].

$$J = \text{RMSE} + L(\text{W}) = \sqrt{\frac{1}{N_d}\sum_{i=1}^{N_d}\left(Q_o^{RS}(\mathbf{u}_i) - Q_o^{NN}(\mathbf{u}_i)\right)^2} + \frac{\alpha}{2}\|\text{W}\|^2, \tag{6}$$

where RMSE is the root mean squared error, $L(\text{W})$ is the L2 regulation term for weight array W, N_d is the number of data points, and α is the regularization coefficient. This study used a regularization coefficient of α = 0.01, based on our previous work [28] where this value effectively balanced under- and over-regularization.

The predictive accuracy of the M-CNN is quantified using R^2, where values close to 1 indicate strong agreement between predicted values Q_o^{NN} and reference values Q_o^{RS}. In other words, the high R^2 values demonstrate the M-CNN's capability to accurately predict cumulative oil production at well locations. These results highlight the effectiveness of iterative learning, and the quality of the dataset generated by PSO, which successfully captured representative scenarios for productive well placements.

$$R^2 = \frac{\left\{N_d\left(\sum_{i=1}^{N_d} Q_o^{RS}(\mathbf{u}_i)Q_o^{NN}(\mathbf{u}_i)\right) - \left(\sum_{i=1}^{N_d} Q_o^{RS}(\mathbf{u}_i)\right)\left(\sum_{i=1}^{N_d} Q_o^{NN}(\mathbf{u}_i)\right)\right\}^2}{\left\{N_d\sum_{i=1}^{N_d} (Q_o^{RS}(\mathbf{u}_i))^2 - \left(\sum_{i=1}^{N_d} Q_o^{RS}(\mathbf{u}_i)\right)^2\right\}\left\{N_d\sum_{i=1}^{N_d} (Q_o^{NN}(\mathbf{u}_i))^2 - \left(\sum_{i=1}^{N_d} Q_o^{NN}(\mathbf{u}_i)\right)^2\right\}}, \tag{7}$$

Also, the threshold for R^2, denoted as θ_{R^2}, is employed to judge the acceptance of the learning performance of the M-CNN. The learning results are accepted if all R^2 for training, validation, and test datasets are greater than θ_{R^2}.

The cumulative field oil production at every feasible well location (i.e., the active grid block in the reservoir model) $\mathbf{u} \in \mathbf{U}$ was rapidly estimated using the trained M-CNN. This rapid approximation of oil estimates for the entire reservoir domain generates a hydrocarbon productivity map similar to a quality map [2,26,37]. In the descending order of $Q_o^{NN}(\mathbf{u})$, the most highly productive N_{qual} grid blocks are nominated as qualified locations. To re-validate the robustness of the M-CNN, full-physics RS is performed for every qualified location to assess the similarity between the simulation and proxy results in terms of the relative error ε:

$$\varepsilon(\mathbf{u}) = \frac{\left|Q_o^{RS}(\mathbf{u}) - Q_o^{NN}(\mathbf{u})\right|}{Q_o^{RS}(\mathbf{u})} \times 100(\%), \tag{8}$$

$$\varepsilon_{avg} = \frac{1}{N_{qual}}\sum_{i=1}^{N_{qual}} \varepsilon(\mathbf{u}_i), \tag{9}$$

The grid block with the highest Q_o^{RS} is selected as the optimal well location, $\mathbf{u}^*$, if the average relative error, ε_{avg}, is acceptable. If ε_{avg} > threshold θ_ε, ($\mathbf{u}$, $Q_o^{RS}(\mathbf{u})$) results of N_{qual} scenarios are added to the learning data, which are further split into training, validation, and test datasets, as shown in the flow chart (Figure 1). Subsequently, the M-CNN re-learns and yields an updated hydrocarbon productivity map. This iterative learning is performed until $\varepsilon_{avg} \leq \theta_\varepsilon$ is met.

Our hybrid approach synergistically combines the strengths of PSO and the M-CNN to address the limitations of standalone methods. PSO efficiently generates diverse, high-quality data, while M-CNN excels at preserving spatial features in high-dimensional datasets. The iterative learning process progressively refines the neural network model, enhancing its accuracy and robustness. This combination yields a more efficient and precise method for well placement optimization, overcoming the constraints of traditional techniques. By integrating these complementary approaches, our hybrid workflow mitigates common issues such as extrapolation errors and overfitting, which often plague standalone machine learning models or static optimization methods. Continuous dataset refinement through iterative learning ensures the model remains adaptive and increasingly accurate, leading to superior computational efficiency and predictive accuracy compared to conventional methods.

3. Results and Discussion

3.1. Field Description

An iterative learning-based proxy was applied to determine the locations of four vertical oil production wells for the UNISIM-I-D oil reservoir model at a primary production stage [38]. The original UNISIM-I-D is a benchmark reservoir model that encompasses the structural, facies, and petrophysical characteristics of the Namorado Field in Campos Basin, Brazil [39–41]. Table 1 summarizes the rock and fluid properties of UNISIM-I-

D. Further details of the model properties are available in the original study [38]. This benchmark reservoir model was initially introduced to create a field development plan for waterflooding, using 11 water injectors and 14 oil producers [42]. In this plan, waterflooding follows a four-year primary oil recovery (i.e., natural pressure drawdown) from four vertical oil wells installed at a four-month interval in a year, as designed in the original model [38]. Our analysis revealed that some of the primary production wells of the original model were installed in less prolific regions with low permeability, thus inspiring our motivation for well placement optimization for primary production. The optimization of the waterflooding plan will be investigated in future studies.

Table 1. Summary of the reservoir properties of the UNISIM-I-D used in this study.

Property	Value
Number of total grid blocks (X × Y × Z)	93,960 = 81 × 58 × 20
Number of active grid blocks	36,403
Grid block size (X × Y × Z), m × m × m	100 × 100 × 8
Depth of top layer, m	3000
Initial reservoir pressure, kg/cm^2	327.0
Porosity ($\mu \pm \sigma$), fraction	0.13 ± 0.08
Permeability ($\mu \pm \sigma$), mD	132.53 ± 184.95
Oil saturation ($\mu \pm \sigma$), fraction	0.56 ± 0.38

Figures 3–7 visualize 3D (Figure 3) and 2D distribution maps (Figures 4–7) of the top, middle, and bottom layers of the reservoir model for porosity, permeability, pressure, and oil saturation. The numbers of grid blocks in the X-, Y-, and Z-directions are 81, 58, and 20, respectively, for a total of 93,960 grid blocks in the UNISIM-I-D model. The number of active grid blocks is 36,403, which is the sum of the 2282, 2331, 2296, 802, 20, 2276, 2259, 2258, 2084, 2312, 2285, 2310, 1945, 16, 2308, 2200, 2221, 2250, 1883, and 65 active grid blocks from the top (1st) to the bottom (20th) layers. The inactive grid blocks are colored white.

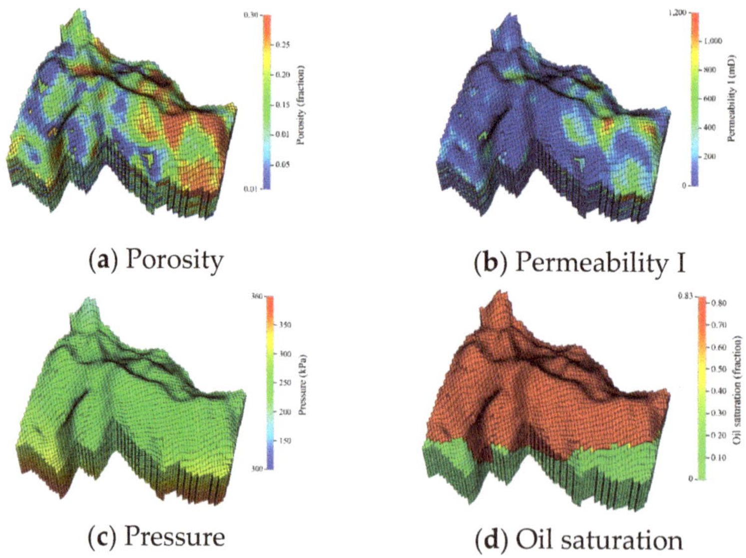

Figure 3. Three-dimensional distributions of petrophysical properties of the UNISIM-I-D. (**a**) Porosity; (**b**) permeability I; (**c**) pressure; (**d**) oil saturation. The total number of grid blocks is 93,960, with 36,403 of those being active.

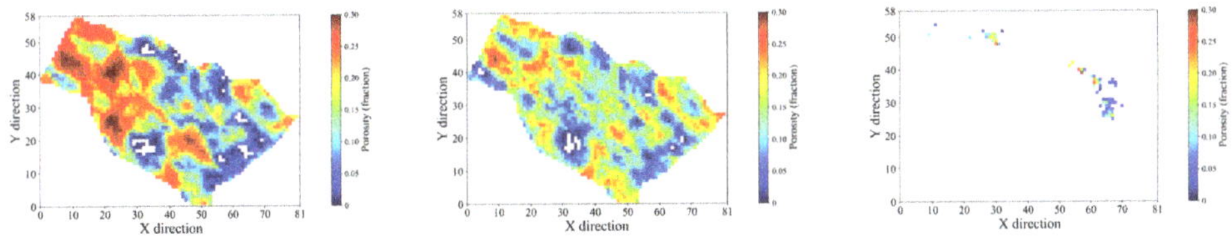

(**a**) 1st layer (**b**) 10th layer (**c**) 20th layer

Figure 4. Two-dimensional porosity distribution maps of the UNISIM-I-D. (**a**) The 1st layer (2282 active grid blocks); (**b**) 10th layer (2312 active grid blocks); (**c**) 20th layer (65 active grid blocks).

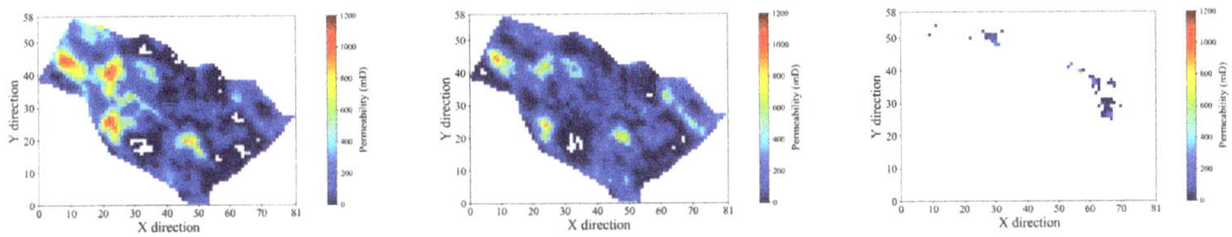

(**a**) 1st layer (**b**) 10th layer (**c**) 20th layer

Figure 5. Two-dimensional permeability distribution maps of the UNISIM-I-D. (**a**) The 1st layer (2282 active grid blocks); (**b**) 10th layer (2312 active grid blocks); (**c**) 20th layer (65 active grid blocks).

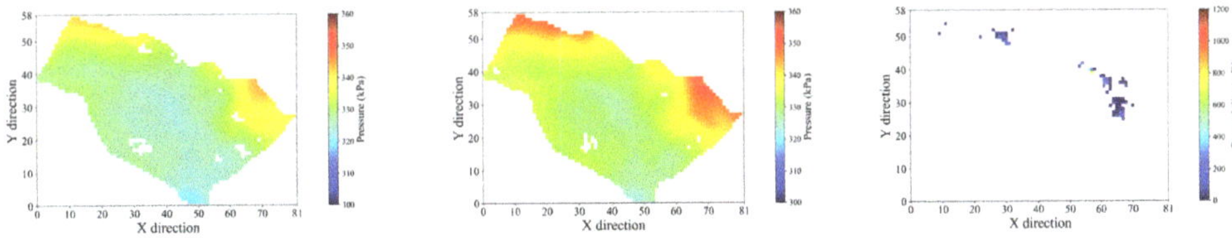

(**a**) 1st layer (**b**) 10th layer (**c**) 20th layer

Figure 6. Two-dimensional pressure distribution maps of the UNISIM-I-D. (**a**) The 1st layer (2282 active grid blocks); (**b**) 10th layer (2312 active grid blocks); (**c**) 20th layer (65 active grid blocks).

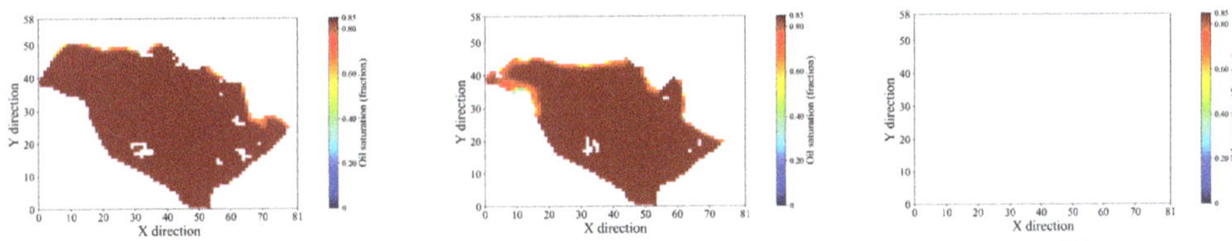

(**a**) 1st layer (**b**) 10th layer (**c**) 20th layer

Figure 7. Two-dimensional oil saturation distribution maps of the UNISIM-I-D. (**a**) The 1st layer (2282 active grid blocks); (**b**) 10th layer (2312 active grid blocks); (**c**) 20th layer (65 active grid blocks).

To maximize the four-year (T = 4) primary recovery, we initialized the well setting: all wells were removed from the reservoir model. This study focused on exploitation strategy during the four-year primary recovery period. Thereafter, this case study focuses on determining the locations of four primary production wells installed sequentially at the same four-month interval. Each vertical oil production well was fully perforated, except for the 4th, 5th, 14th, and 20th layers, where most of the grid blocks were inactive. The number of candidate well placement scenarios is equal to the number of active grid blocks in the top layer of the model. The numbers of candidates from the first to fourth production well placement problems are 2282, 2281, 2280, and 2279, respectively. In addition, the operating condition of each production well is a maximum surface liquid rate of 2000 m^3/day with a constraint of a minimum bottom-hole pressure of 150 kg/cm^2.

3.2. Generation of Learning Data Using Particle Swarm Optimization

Table 2 lists the experimental settings of PSO used for training the M-CNN (N_p = 20 and N_e = 20). The PSO algorithm parameters listed in Table 2 were adopted based on the settings referenced from the studies by Kennedy and Eberhart [10] and Clerc and Kennedy [36]. In this study, the PSO was performed using CMG's CMOST-AI (2023.12) [14]. Notably, the M-CNN learned the solutions (i.e., reservoir simulation results) accrued during the last five epochs, which exhibited a minor improvement in swarm quality. The early stopped epochs, N_{es}, were the 14th, 15th, 14th, and 6th epochs from the first to the fourth well placement problems, respectively. For example, Figure 8 shows box plots depicting the evolution of well placement scenarios for the first well placement. The overall quality of the learning data for the M-CNN improved progressively from the first generation to the last generation in the PSO process. Throughout the epochs, the highest value within the swarm increased, while its dispersion decreased. However, evolution stagnation was observed; the (near-) optima derived using PSO were identified in the 10th epoch, after which the evolution plateaued. Consequently, a total of 280 reservoir simulation results were accumulated up to the 14th epoch. Another limitation of the PSO is its redundancy. Up to the 14th epoch, 104 of the 280 results were duplicate well placement scenarios, indicating that the number of actual learning data obtained using the PSO (N_d) was 176 (=280 − 104). This redundancy occurred because the well coordinates were integer-type variables. Implementing an optimization algorithm to address redundancy in the solution set is expected to streamline learning data preparation for a machine learning technique.

Table 2. Experimental setting of the particle swarm optimization (PSO) algorithm used for training the M-CNN.

Parameter	Value
Population size, N_p	20
Maximum number of epochs, N_e	20
Inertia weight component, ω	0.730
Cognitive weight component, c_1	1.496
Social weight component, c_2	1.496

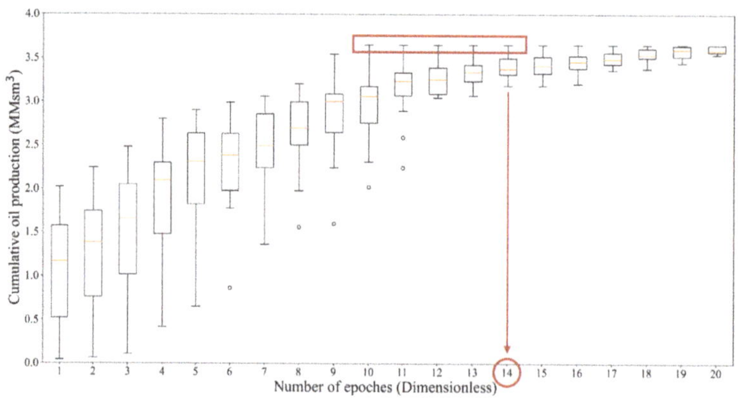

Figure 8. The box plots to show the evolution of well placement scenarios for the 1st well through PSO. Note that this study acquired the learning data for M-CNN through PSO. The PSO process initially improved solution quality, with increasing highest values and decreasing dispersion, but stagnated after the 10th epoch when (near-)optimal solutions were identified, concluding with 280 reservoir simulation results after 14 epochs. Small circles indicate outliers of the box plots.

3.3. Design of Multi-Modal Convolutional Neural Network

Table 3 summarizes the structure of the M-CNN used in the case study. As the initial reservoir model had homogeneous pressure and saturation, the first well placement case adopted a dual-modal M-CNN that inputs $\phi(\mathbf{u}, r_\mathbf{u})$ and $k(\mathbf{u}, r_\mathbf{u})$. For subsequent well placement cases, a quadmodal CNN with $\phi(\mathbf{u}, r_\mathbf{u})$, $k(\mathbf{u}, r_\mathbf{u})$, $P(\mathbf{u}, r_\mathbf{u})$, and $S_o(\mathbf{u}, r_\mathbf{u})$ was adopted. Here, $r_\mathbf{u}$ = 12; thus, the 3D array size for each spatial property data was 25 × 25 × 20.

Table 3. Structure of the M-CNN.

Parameter	Value
Number of input types	4
Type of inputs	Porosity ϕ, permeability k, pressure P, oil saturation S_o
Number of convolutional layers	2
Order of convolutional stage	Conv3D, BatchNormalization, AveragePooling3D
Number of hidden layers	3
Number of outputs	1
Type of outputs	Field cumulative oil production Q_o
Optimizer	Adam
Activation function	ReLU
Ratio of learning data splitting	Training 60%, validation 20%, test 20%

Each M-CNN comprises convolutional and fully connected stages. The convolutional stage consisted of two convolutional layers, two batch normalization layers, and two activation layers with ReLU [43]. Every element in each spatial input data array was normalized to [0.0,1.0]. Hyperparameters (e.g., the number of nodes in layers, convolutional filter, size of each filter, and type of pooling) were tuned to enhance the neural network performance. The learning stopping criteria during training and validation were early stopping and the maximum number of epochs. The patience in early stopping and maximum epoch number were 20 and 300, respectively. A threshold, θ_{R^2} = 0.75, was used to evaluate the training, validation, and test performances, ensuring sufficient predictive accuracy before proceeding to subsequent steps. For iterative learning, N_{qual} = 10 was adopted from Kwon et al. [28], where it was a sufficient number to select representative scenarios. Additionally, θ_ε of 5% was set as the relative error tolerance considering Chu et al. [29], where their CNN model yielded an average relative error of 4.27%, with the higher threshold accounting for variability and ensuring robustness.

In this study, every M-CNN was built using the Keras deep learning library and its back-end engine TensorFlow in Python 3.11 environments, as in our previous studies [28,29]. All computations were executed using the following computer hardware specifications: Intel (R) Core (TM) i7–10700 CPU @ 2.9 GHz with 64.0 GB RAM and NVIDIA GeForce RTX 3060 Ti 8 GB.

3.4. Determination of the Well Locations and Performan ce Evaluation

For each sequential well placement, its learning data were divided into training (60%), validation (20%), and test (20%) sets, a commonly used ratio in machine learning [44]. A similar ratio was also employed in the previous studies [28–30], where it proved to be both reliable and effective in training proxy models for well placement optimization. Then, oil productivity at all feasible locations was evaluated using the learned proxy. Thereafter, the top ten qualified scenarios were selected in descending order of field cumulative oil production estimated using the proxy Q_o^{NN}. Table 4 summarizes the performance of the proxy for the learning data and the ε_{avg} values of the top ten qualified scenarios. All R^2 values exceed an θ_{R^2} of 0.75, confirming satisfactory learning performance. In addition, three cases (excluding the fourth well) were sufficiently trained using iterative learning. The relatively low R^2 value for the 1st well was attributed to the limited dataset available for training during its evaluation. As the iterative process progresses and more wells were included, the dataset expanded, enabling the model to better generalize and reduce prediction uncertainty. This results in higher R^2 values for subsequent wells, reflecting improved predictive accuracy.

Table 4. Iterative learning performance of the M-CNN for the sequential well placement problem of the UNISIM-I-D.

Well	Number of Iterative Learning	Number of Feasible Well Locations	Number of Learning Data	R^2		ε_{avg} (%) for Ten Qualified Scenarios
				Training Data	Test Data	
1st well	Basecase	2282	176	0.93	0.87	13.34
	1st		186	0.85	0.77	7.13
	2nd (final)		196	0.89	0.84	2.64
2nd well	Basecase	2281	209	0.95	0.93	5.31
	1st (final)		219	0.94	0.90	1.66
3rd well	Basecase	2280	180	0.91	0.87	21.53
	1st (final)		190	0.96	0.94	0.68
4th well	Basecase (final)	2279	80	0.94	0.86	2.23

Second, compared with previous studies in which learning data are collected randomly, the preparation of learning data based on evolution was more efficient. This ensured the specialization of the constructed machine learning model for evaluating highly prolific regions. The number of learning data for each well placement was approximately 200, which was smaller than that reported by [26–28] (i.e., 504, 2000, and 400, respectively), although their target reservoirs were different from each other. The reduction in the cost of learning data preparation was further highlighted when the proposed approach was applied to field-scale simulations.

Third, the M-CNN with iterative learning exhibited reduced ε_{avg} compared to that without iterative learning owing to adding more high-productivity regions in its learning data. This contributes to the search for an optimal well location. The performance of the M-CNN in high-productivity regions increased with an increase in the number of iterative learning attempts if the computational cost was available. The behavior of the model within the ranges spanned by the learning data barely affects its generalization performance as a high-productivity region (i.e., N_{qual}) outside the learning data [45]. These results support the ability of iterative learning to overcome the intrinsic limitation of the extrapolation of neural networks by adding high Q_o^{NN} scenarios to the learning dataset for the next proxy implementation. Completing the iteration process implies that the extrapolation problem (i.e., the maximization problem) is almost entirely converted into an interpolation problem.

Figures 9–12 show the scatter plots used to compare the reference and predicted production for the test data scenarios and the top ten qualified scenarios for each well placement problem. In each subfigure, the red dots represent the Q_o^{RS} and Q_o^{NN} pairs for the test data. Similarly, the black dots represent pairs of the top ten scenarios. For the basecases, the proxies tended to overestimate the oil productivity for the top ten scenarios. As previously mentioned, this overestimation reveals the intrinsic limitation of machine learning prediction for extrapolation. This limitation could be overcome by implementing iterative learning. Based on these results, it is recommended to conduct iterative learning up to a level at which the improvement in evaluation performance becomes insignificant when applying machine learning for extrapolation, such as in well placement problems. Because the production wells were installed sequentially, the number of iterative learning applications decreased. In particular, the fourth well obtained high-quality results without iterative learning (Figure 12) because the M-CNN had already learned the input data with sufficient information.

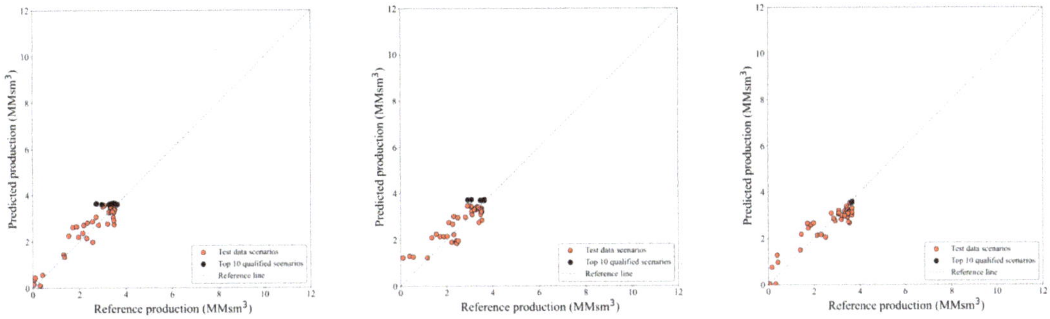

(**a**) Basecase (**b**) 1st iterative learning (**c**) 2nd iterative learning

Figure 9. Scatter plots to compare the reference and predicted production for test data scenarios and top ten qualified scenarios for the 1st well placement problem. (**a**) Basecase ($R^2 = 0.87$, $\varepsilon_{avg} = 13.34\%$); (**b**) 1st iterative learning ($R^2 = 0.77$, $\varepsilon_{avg} = 7.13\%$); (**c**) 2nd iterative learning ($R^2 = 0.84$, $\varepsilon_{avg} = 2.64\%$).

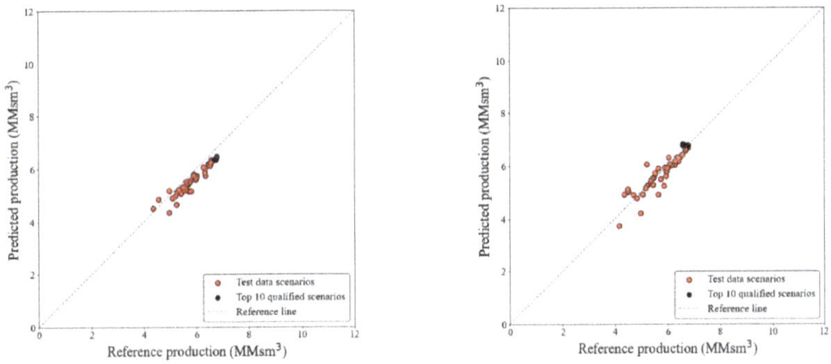

(**a**) Basecase (**b**) 1st iterative learning

Figure 10. Scatter plots to compare reference and predicted production for test data scenarios and top ten qualified scenarios for the 2nd well placement problem. (**a**) Basecase ($R^2 = 0.93$, $\varepsilon_{avg} = 5.31\%$); (**b**) 1st iterative learning ($R^2 = 0.90$, $\varepsilon_{avg} = 1.66\%$).

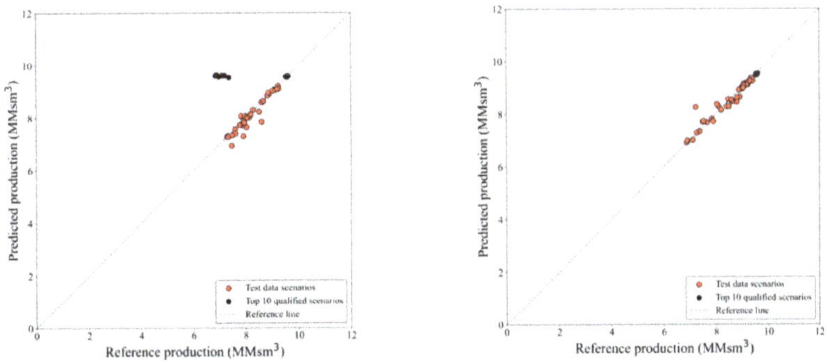

(**a**) Basecase (**b**) 1st iterative learning

Figure 11. Scatter plots to compare reference and predicted production for test data scenarios and top ten qualified scenarios for the 3rd well placement problem. (**a**) Basecase ($R^2 = 0.87$, $\varepsilon_{avg} = 21.53\%$); (**b**) 1st iterative learning ($R^2 = 0.94$, $\varepsilon_{avg} = 0.68\%$).

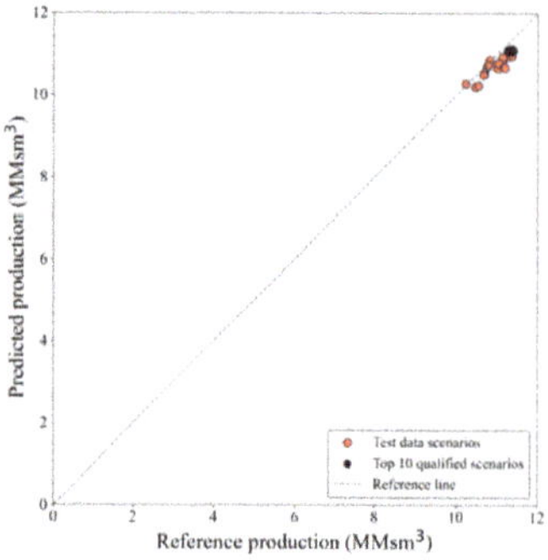

Figure 12. Scatter plots to compare reference and predicted production for test data scenarios and top ten qualified scenarios for the basecase of the 4th well placement problem ($R^2 = 0.86$, $\varepsilon_{avg} = 2.23\%$).

Figure 13 shows the oil productivity maps of the field cumulative oil production (i.e., Q_o^{NN} and Q_o^{RS} maps) obtained using M-CNN and RS. For quantitative comparison, relative error maps (i.e., ε maps) were drawn using Equation (8) (Figure 13c,f,i,l): In Figure 13, the black dots indicate the location of the well selected using the proposed approach. For most real-world problems, the acquisition of Q_o^{RS} maps is extremely difficult because of high computational costs (Figure 13b,e,h,k). By contrast, acquiring Q_o^{NN} maps is affordable and reliable, provided that reasonable accuracy is guaranteed for the test data and final solutions (Figure 13a,d,g,j). Overall, the Q_o^{NN} maps are similar to the corresponding Q_o^{RS} maps, particularly in highly prolific regions. Some large ε values were obtained along the reservoir boundary because of the low-proliferation regions, where the Q_o^{RS} values were significantly smaller than the Q_o^{NN} values. Owing to this overestimation of Q_o^{NN}, ε was higher than 20% because Q_o^{RS} is the denominator of Equation (8). Nevertheless, these low-proliferation regions were not the targets of this study. Instead, this study focused on the search for highly prolific regions. To achieve this, masking is useful in excluding lowly productive regions based on expert knowledge, either a priori or a posteriori [29]. Furthermore, the overall quality improved during the sequential well placement problem, as shown in Figure 13c,f,i,l.

Figures 14–16 show the production profiles at the four well locations selected using the M-CNN, PSO with ES, and the original study [38], respectively. To maintain the oil production rate close to the maximum surface liquid rate of 2000 m^3/day for as long as possible, the most significant factor affecting oil production was a minimum bottom-hole pressure of 150 kg/cm^2. Compared with the bottom-hole pressure, the water production was relatively insignificant in every well during primary production.

Table 5 compares the final well locations and corresponding field cumulative oil production: the production results of the original study [38], PSO results with ES, M-CNN results, and PSO for simultaneous well placement. These four methods yielded different well locations and drilling sequences, thereby yielding different four-year field cumulative productions. Both PSO and M-CNN recommended grid block coordinates (64, 22) as the drilling location of the third production well, indicating that both PSO and the proxy are useful in the optimal search. The proposed proxy exhibited 47.40% in field cumulative production compared with the original study [38]. Comparing the PSO with ES and PSO for simultaneous optimization, the improvement of the field cumulative oil production obtained using the M-CNN was 0.092 $MMsm^3$ (0.81%) and 0.033 $MMsm^3$ (0.29%), yielding an additional profit of 57.87 MMUSD and 20.75 MMUSD when the oil price is USD 100/STB, respectively. In summary, the accuracy of the developed proxy integrating PSO, M-CNN, and iterative learning in the decision making of well placement problems was validated.

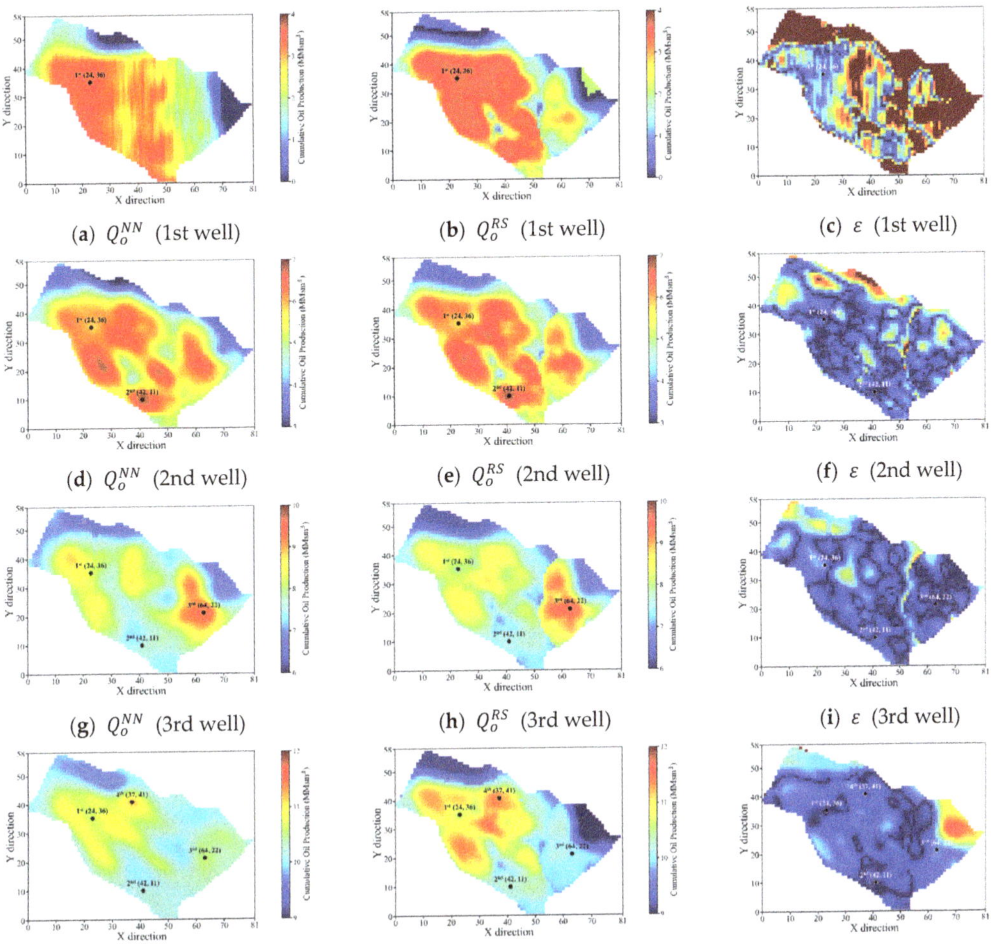

(**a**) Q_o^{NN} (1st well) (**b**) Q_o^{RS} (1st well) (**c**) ε (1st well)

(**d**) Q_o^{NN} (2nd well) (**e**) Q_o^{RS} (2nd well) (**f**) ε (2nd well)

(**g**) Q_o^{NN} (3rd well) (**h**) Q_o^{RS} (3rd well) (**i**) ε (3rd well)

(**j**) Q_o^{NN} (4th well) (**k**) Q_o^{RS}(4th well) (**l**) ε (4th well)

Figure 13. Oil productivity and relative error (ε) maps obtained using M-CNN and reservoir simulation (RS). (**a**) Q_o^{NN} (1st well); (**b**) Q_o^{RS} (1st well); (**c**) ε (1st well); (**d**) Q_o^{NN} (2nd well); (**e**) Q_o^{RS} (2nd well); (**f**) ε (2nd well); (**g**) Q_o^{NN} (3rd well); (**h**) Q_o^{RS} (3rd well); (**i**) ε (3rd well); (**j**) Q_o^{NN} (4th well); (**k**) Q_o^{RS} (4th well); (**l**) ε (4th well).

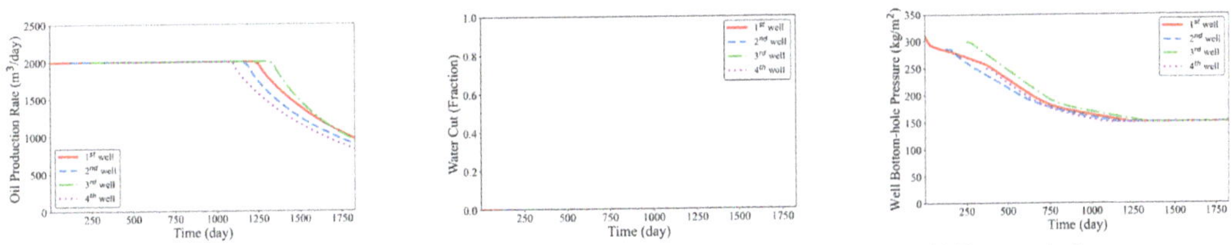

(**a**) Oil production (**b**) Water cut (**c**) Bottom-hole pressure

Figure 14. Well production profiles at the selected four well locations based on the M-CNN results. (**a**) Oil production; (**b**) water cut; (**c**) bottom-hole pressure.

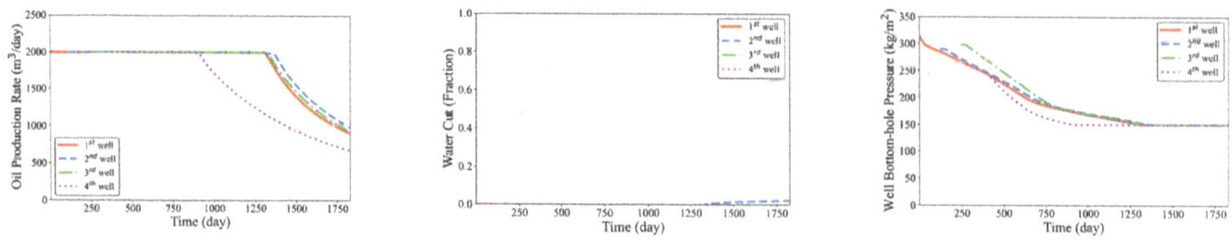

(**a**) Oil production (**b**) Water cut (**c**) Bottom-hole pressure

Figure 15. Well production profiles at the selected four well locations based on the PSO with early stopping (ES) results. (**a**) Oil production; (**b**) water cut; (**c**) bottom-hole pressure.

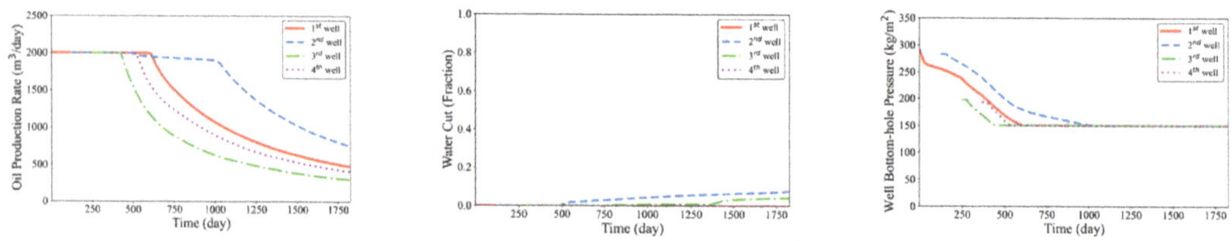

(**a**) Oil production (**b**) Water cut (**c**) Bottom-hole pressure

Figure 16. Well production profiles at the four original well locations in the original study from the original study [38]. (**a**) Oil production; (**b**) water cut; (**c**) bottom-hole pressure.

Table 5. Comparison of the oil productivity with four well locations and their field cumulative oil production: the results of the original study [38], PSO results with early stopping (ES), M-CNN results, and PSO without ES for simultaneous well placement. Note that M-CNN was designed based on the PSO results with ES for an efficient generation of learning data. Also, PSO for simultaneous well placement failed to activate ES in this study.

Method		**Final Well Location (X, Y)**				**Field Cumulative Oil Production (MMsm³)**
		1st Well	**2nd Well**	**3rd Well**	**4th Well**	
Original well placement [38]		(38, 36)	(21, 36)	(44, 43)	(31, 27)	7.742
Sequential well placement	PSO w/ES	(25, 24)	(24, 41)	(64, 22)	(46, 10)	11.320
	M-CNN	(24, 36)	(42, 11)	(64, 22)	(37, 41)	11.412
Simultaneous well placement	PSO w/o ES	(43, 13)	(63, 23)	(34, 34)	(14, 43)	11.379

Table 6 presents a comparison of computational costs based on the number of RS runs. The RS was compared for all feasible scenarios: PSO with ES, M-CNN, and PSO for simultaneous well placement. For sequential well placement, the PSO results with ES were obtained from $N_{pop} \times N_{es}$ RS runs. The cost of the M-CNN was the sum of the PSO with ES cost $N_{pop} \times N_{es}$ and the number of additional RS for iterative learning $N_{iter} \times N_{qual}$, where N_{iter} refers to the number of iterations. In the case of the PSO used for simultaneous optimization, the experimental settings were N_{pop} = 40 and N_e = 40, with early stopping. The ES was not activated in this case study because the particles maintained the evolution slowly. Thus, the number of RS runs reached 1600. Evidently, the M-CNN proxy exhibited the advantage of computational efficiency over the full search using the full-physics RS. The ratio of the computational cost of the proxy to that of the full search using the RS was 11.18% (=1020/9122 × 100%). Compared with the PSO with ES results, the M-CNN delivered a superior solution by increasing the computational cost by 4.08% (=(1020−980)/980 × 100%). The M-CNN results showed a decrease in computational cost of 36.25% (=(1600−1020)/1600 × 100%) compared with PSO with ES and simultaneous well placement. Similarly to Table 6, Table 7 summarizes the total time required for all computations. The computational cost to execute the M-CNN was 541.5 (=271.0 + 129.2 + 101.8 + 39.5) seconds, which is only 1.6% (=541.5/(9957 + 10,288.9 + 9625.1 +3982.8) × 100%) of the PSO with ES cost.

Table 6. Comparison of the computational cost (the number of full-physics reservoir simulation (RS) runs): RS runs for all feasible scenarios, PSO with ES, M-CNN, and PSO without ES for simultaneous well placement.

Method		**Number of RS Runs**				
		1st Well (A)	**2nd Well (B)**	**3rd Well (C)**	**4th Well (D)**	**Total (E = A + B + C + D)**
RS for all feasible scenarios	Full search	2282	2281	2280	2279	9122
Sequential placement	PSO w/ES	280	300	280	120	980
	M-CNN	300	310	290	120	1020
Simultaneous placement	PSO w/o ES	1600				1600

Table 7. Comparison of the computational cost (time): RS runs for all feasible scenarios, PSO with ES, M-CNN, and PSO without ES for simultaneous well placement.

Method		**Computational Cost for RS Runs (s)**				**Computational Cost for M-CNN (s)**				**Total Computational Cost (s)**
		1st Well	**2nd Well**	**3rd Well**	**4th Well**	**1st Well**	**2nd Well**	**3rd Well**	**4th Well**	
RS for all feasible scenarios	Full search	75,739.6	75,706.4	75,673.2	75,640.0	-	-	-	-	302,759.2
Sequential placement	PSO w/ES	9293.2	9957.0	9293.2	3982.8	-	-	-	-	32,526.2
	M-CNN	9957.0	10,288.9	9625.1	3982.8	271.0	129.2	101.8	39.5	34,395.3
Simultaneous placement	PSO w/o ES	65,097.0				-	-	-	-	65,097.0

3.5. Discussion

Based on these numerical results, this study demonstrated that the integration of evolutionary optimization, machine learning, and iterative learning produced effective solutions for well placement optimization problems at a reasonable computational cost. While our focus was on optimizing well locations within a sequential well placement framework, future research aims to extend the methodology to incorporate well operating conditions (e.g., water injection rates during waterflooding, CO_2 injection rates for enhanced oil recovery or geological carbon storage). This expansion will enable optimization of both the spatial arrangement of wells and operational parameters, potentially enhancing overall field development strategies. For the sake of clarity and scope management, the current study primarily validated the performance of the proposed methodology for well location optimization. Subsequent research will address rate optimization and other operational considerations, building upon this foundational work. Furthermore, the framework can be applied to solve a variety of geoenergy engineering problems such as history matching [46,47], pipeline management [48,49], and reservoir-well-surface facility-integrated system design [50].

While this study demonstrates promising results, there are several avenues for improvement. Although PSO has proven effective and computationally efficient for well placement optimization, more advanced algorithms, such as the Artificial Hummingbird Algorithm (AHA), could yield superior convergence speed and accuracy [51]. Future work will explore integrating these advanced algorithms into our hybrid framework to enhance optimization processes and performance in large-scale applications. Despite PSO's ability to reduce computational costs compared to exhaustive simulations, its role in dataset generation can become a bottleneck in large-scale optimization problems, particularly with heterogeneous or complex reservoir models. In such scenarios, PSO's initial population and convergence speed can significantly impact efficiency, potentially leading to extended computation times.

Furthermore, in large-scale reservoir models with numerous candidate well placements and high spatial resolution, the iterative learning process can become computationally intensive, especially when coupled with full-physics reservoir simulations. As the number of wells increases, so does the computational burden, making optimizing the balance between accuracy and efficiency crucial. Consequently, additional research is necessary to address scalability challenges in large field-scale applications. Our future studies will investigate the practicability of the algorithm for various complex problems, including enhanced oil recovery and CO_2 sequestration. These investigations will further refine our approach and extend its applicability to a broader range of reservoir management scenarios.

4. Conclusions

This study designed an M-CNN, learning the PSO results, and enhanced its performance with iterative learning to solve the sequential well placement problem in UNISIM-I-D. After running the RS, the qualified locations selected using the M-CNN integrated with PSO and iterative learning for the four wells were validated. In addition, the performance of the M-CNN was compared with that of PSO. The M-CNN constructed with the learning dataset obtained using an evolutionary algorithm (i.e., PSO) exhibited increased accuracy and reduced computational cost. Iterative learning enabled the intensive search of high-oil-potential regions, thereby overcoming the limitations of neural networks in an extrapolation problem. Using the developed hybrid method, the computational cost spent to evaluate all feasible well location cases was approximately 11.18% of the cost required for exhaustive evaluation through RS. Despite the constraints of limited training data, the M-CNN model, when integrated with PSO and iterative learning, demonstrated superior performance compared to PSO alone. This hybrid approach achieved remarkable accuracy with a relative error of less than 3% and significantly boosted cumulative oil production by 47.40% relative to the original well placement strategy. Notably, the M-CNN's predictive capabilities rivaled those of the exhaustive RS-based search, underscoring its efficiency and effectiveness. This achievement highlights the robustness of the M-CNN framework in optimizing well placement, even under data scarcity, and its potential to revolutionize reservoir management practices by combining high accuracy with computational efficiency. Another advantage of the proposed approach was its ability to swiftly test every candidate location, thereby providing a detailed quality map for further examination. These results demonstrate the efficacy of M-CNN for the multi-well placement optimization problem, as it achieved a balance between accuracy and computational cost savings. This rapid and precise approach can enhance decision making for well placement in multi-million-dollar geoenergy projects.

Author Contributions: Conceptualization, S.K. and B.M.; methodology, S.K. and B.M.; software, S.K., M.J., M.K., J.Y.L. and B.M.; validation, S.K., M.K., J.Y.L. and B.M.; formal analysis, S.K. and B.M.; investigation, S.K., M.J. and B.M.; resources, S.K. and B.M.; data curation, S.K. and B.M.; writing—original draft preparation, S.K.; writing—review and editing, M.J., M.K., J.Y.L. and B.M.; visualization, S.K. and B.M.; supervision, B.M.; project administration, B.M.; funding acquisition, B.M. All authors have read and agreed to the published version of the manuscript.

Funding: This work was supported by the National Research Foundation of Korea (NRF) funded by the Ministry of Education (No. 2018R1A6A1A08025520) and the Ministry of Science and ICT (No. RS-2023-00208297). Additionally, this work was supported by the Korea Agency for Infrastructure Technology Advancement (KAIA) grant funded by the Ministry of Land, Infrastructure and Transport (No. RS-2022-00143644).

Data Availability Statement: The data presented in this study are available on request from the corresponding author.

Acknowledgments: We appreciate Computer Modelling Group Ltd. (CMG) for providing their reservoir simulation software package. Baehyun Min and Minsoo Ji also express our gratitude to the Weather and Climate Data Convergence Analysis Specialized Graduate School supported by the Korea Meteorological Institute.

Conflicts of Interest: Author Minsoo Ji is currently employed by the company POSCO International. The remaining author declare that the research was conducted in the absence of any commercial or financial relationships that could be construed as a potential conflict of interest.

References

1. Zandvliet, M.J.; Handels, M.; van Essen, G.M.; Brouwer, D.R.; Jansen, J.D. Adjoint-based well placement optimization under production constraints. *SPE J.* **2008**, *13*, 392–399. [CrossRef]
2. Pouladi, B.; Karkevandi-Talkhooncheh, A.; Sharifi, M.; Gerami, S.; Nourmohammad, A.; VahidiLi, A. Enhancement of SPSA algorithm performance using reservoir quality maps: Application to coupled well placement and control optimization problems. *J. Petrol. Sci. Eng.* **2020**, *189*, 106984. [CrossRef]
3. Boah, A.E.; Kondo, O.K.S.; Borsah, A.A.; Brantson, E.T. Critical evaluation of infill well placement and optimization of well spacing using the particle swarm algorithm. *J. Pet. Explor. Prod. Technol.* **2019**, *9*, 3113–3133. [CrossRef]
4. Ding, S.; Lu, R.; Xi, Y.; Liu, G.; Ma, J. Efficient well placement optimization coupling hybrid objective function with particle swarm optimization algorithm. *Appl. Soft Comput.* **2020**, *95*, 106511. [CrossRef]
5. Wang, X.; Haynes, R.D.; Feng, Q. Well control optimization using derivative-free algorithms and a multiscale approach. *Comput. Chem. Eng.* **2019**, *123*, 12–33. [CrossRef]
6. Bertini, J.R., Jr.; Funcia, M.A.; Santos, A.A.; Schiozer, D.J. A comparison of machine learning algorithms as surrogate model for net present value prediction from wells arrangement data. In Proceedings of the International Joint Conference on Neural Networks, Budapest, Hungary, 14–19 July 2019.
7. Lu, R.; Reynolds, A.C. Joint optimization of well locations, types, drilling order and controls given a set of potential drilling paths. In Proceedings of the SPE Reservoir Simulation Conference, Galveston, TX, USA, 10–11 April 2019.
8. Wang, N.; Chang, H.; Zhang, D.; Xue, L.; Chen, Y. Efficient well placement optimization based on theory-guided convolutional neural network. *J. Petrol. Sci. Eng.* **2022**, *208*, 109545. [CrossRef]
9. Fonseca, R.R.-M.; Chen, B.; Jansen, J.D.; Reynolds, A. A stochastic simplex approximate gradient for optimization under uncertainty. *Int. J. Numer. Meth. Eng.* **2017**, *109*, 1756–1776. [CrossRef]
10. Kennedy, J.; Eberhart, R.C. A new optimizer using particle swarm theory. In Proceedings of the 6th International Symposium on Micro Machine and Human Science, Nagoya, Japan, 4–6 October 1995.
11. Lee, K.Y.; Park, J.B. Application of particle swarm optimization to economic dispatch problem: Advantages and disadvantages. In Proceedings of the 2006 IEEE PES Pewer Systems Conference and Esposition, Atlanta, GA, USA, 7 February 2006.
12. Lee, S.; Min, B.; Wheeler, M.F. Optimal design of hydraulic fracturing in porous media using the phase field fracture model coupled with genetic algorithm. *Comput. Geosci.* **2018**, *22*, 833–849. [CrossRef]
13. Schlumberger. *MEPO User Guide (Version 2020.01)*; Schlumberger: Houston, TX, USA, 2020.
14. CMG. *CMOST-AI User Guide (Version 2021.10)*; Computer Modeling Group LTD: Calgary, AB, Canada, 2021.
15. Salehian, M.; Haghighat, M.; Muradov, K. Multi-solution well placement optimization using ensemble learning of surrogate models. *J. Petrol. Sci. Eng.* **2022**, *210*, 110076. [CrossRef]
16. Min, B.; Sun, A.Y.; Wheeler, M.F.; Jeong, H. Utilization of multiobjective optimization for pulse testing dataset from a CO_2-EOR/sequestration field. *J. Petrol. Sci. Eng.* **2018**, *170*, 244–266. [CrossRef]
17. Guo, Z.; Reynolds, A.C.; Zhao, H. Waterflooding optimization with the INISIM-FT data-driven model. *Comput. Geosci.* **2018**, *22*, 745–761. [CrossRef]
18. de Brito, D.U.; Durlofsky, L.J. Well control optimization using a two-step surrogate treatment. *J. Petrol. Sci. Eng.* **2020**, *187*, 106565. [CrossRef]

19. Kuang, L.; Liu, H.; Ren, Y.; Luo, K.; Shi, M.; Su, J.; Li, X. Application and development trend of artificial intelligence in petroleum exploration and development. *Petrol. Explor. Dev.* **2021**, *48*, 1–14. [CrossRef]
20. Ali Ahmadi, M.; Bahadori, A. A LSSVM approach for determining well placement and conning phenomena in horizontal wells. *Fuel* **2015**, *153*, 276–283. [CrossRef]
21. Panja, P.; Velasco, R.; Pathak, M.; Deo, M. Application of artificial intelligence to forecast hydrocarbon production from shales. *Petroleum* **2018**, *4*, 75–89. [CrossRef]
22. Nwachukwu, A.; Jeong, H.; Pyrcz, M.; Lake, L.W. Fast evaluation of well placements in heterogeneous reservoir models using machine learning. *J. Petrol. Sci. Eng.* **2018**, *163*, 463–475. [CrossRef]
23. Wang, M.; Hui, G.; Pang, Y.; Wang, S.; Chen, S. Optimization of machine learning approaches for shale gas production forecast. *Geoenergy Sci. Eng.* **2023**, *226*, 211719. [CrossRef]
24. Zhu, Q.; Lin, B.; Yang, G.; Wang, L.; Chen, M. Intelligent production optimization method for a low pressure and low productivity shale gas well. *Petrol. Explor. Dev.* **2022**, *49*, 886–894. [CrossRef]
25. Centilmen, A.; Ertekin, T.; Grader, A.S. Applications of neural networks in multiwell field development. In Proceedings of the SPE Annual Technical Conference and Exhibition, Houston, TX, USA, 3–6 October 1999.
26. Min, B.; Park, C.; Kang, J.M.; Park, H.J.; Jang, I.S. Optimal well placement based on artificial neural network incorporating the productivity potential. *Energy Sources* **2011**, *33*, 1726–1738. [CrossRef]
27. Jang, I.S.; Oh, S.E.; Kim, Y.; Park, C.; Kang, H. Well-placement optimisation using sequential artificial neural networks. *Energy Explor. Exploit.* **2018**, *36*, 433–449. [CrossRef]
28. Kwon, S.; Park, G.; Jang, Y.; Cho, J.; Chu, M.; Min, B. Determination of oil well placement using convolutional neural network coupled with robust optimization under geological uncertainty. *J. Petrol. Sci. Eng.* **2021**, *201*, 108118. [CrossRef]
29. Chu M -g Min, B.; Kwon, S.; Park, G.; Kim, S.; Huy, N.X. Determination of an infill well placement using a data-driven multi-modal convolutional neural network. *J. Petrol. Sci. Eng.* **2020**, *195*, 106805.
30. Kim, J.; Lee, K.; Choe, J. Efficient and robust optimization for well patterns using a PSO algorithm with a CNN-based proxy model. *J. Petrol. Sci. Eng.* **2021**, *207*, 109088. [CrossRef]
31. Atrey, P.; Hossain, A.; El Saddik, A.; Kankanhalli, M. Multi-modal fusion for multimedia analysis: A survey. *Multimed. Syst.* **2010**, *16*, 345–379. [CrossRef]
32. Dodge, S.; Karam, L. Understanding how image quality affects deep neural networks. In Proceedings of the 8th International Conference on Quality of Multimedia Experience, Lisbon, Portugal, 6–8 June 2016.
33. Busemeyer, J.R.; Byun, E.; Delosh, E.L.; McDaniel, M.A. *Learning Functional Relations Based on Experience with Input-Output Pairs by Humans and Artificial Neural Networks*; The MIT Press: Cambridge, MA, USA, 1997.
34. Delosh, E.L.; Busemeyer, J.R.; McDaniel, M.A. Extrapolation: The sine qua non for abstraction in function learning. *J. Exp. Psychol. Learn. Mem. Cogn.* **1997**, *23*, 968–986. [CrossRef] [PubMed]
35. McDaniel, M.A.; Busemeyer, J.R. The conceptual basis of function learning and extrapolation: Comparison of rule-based and associative-based models. *Psychon. Bull. Rev.* **2005**, *12*, 24–42. [CrossRef] [PubMed]
36. Clerc, M.; Kennedy, J. The particle swarm-explosion, stability, and convergence in a multidimensional complex space. *IEEE Trans. Evol. Comput.* **2002**, *6*, 58–73. [CrossRef]
37. da Cruz, P.S.; Horne, R.N.; Deutsch, C.V. The quality map: A tool for reservoir uncertainty quantification and decision making. *SPE Reserv. Eval. Eng.* **1999**, *7*, 6–14. [CrossRef]
38. Gaspar, A.T.F.S.; Avansi, G.D.; Santos, A.D.S.; Hohendorff Filho, J.C.V.; Schiozer, D.J. UNISIM-I-D: Benchmark studies for oil field development and production strategy selection. *Int. J. Model. Simul. Pet. Ind.* **2015**, *9*, 47–55.
39. Almeida, F.; Davolio, A.; Schiozer, D.J. Reducing uncertainties of reservoir properties in an automatized process coupled with geological modeling considering scalar and spatial uncertain attributes. *J. Petrol. Sci. Eng.* **2020**, *189*, 106993. [CrossRef]
40. Gaspar, A.T.F.S.; Santos, S.M.G.; Ferreira, C.J.; Davolio, A.; Schiozer, D.J. Estimation of the chance of success of a four-dimensional seismic project for a developed oil field. *Comput. Geosci.* **2022**, *26*, 463–475. [CrossRef]
41. Negash, B.M.; Tufa, L.D.; Ramasamy, M.; Awang, M.B. System identification-based proxy model of a reservoir under water injection. *Model. Simul. Eng.* **2017**, *2017*, 7645470. [CrossRef]
42. Avansi, G.D.; Schiozer, D.J. UNISIM-I: Synthetic model for reservoir development and management applications. *J. Model. Simul. Petrol. Ind.* **2015**, *9*, 21–30.
43. Glorot, X.; Bordes, A.; Bengio, Y. Deep sparse rectifier neural networks. In Proceedings of the 14th International Conference on Artificial Intelligence and Statistics, Fort Lauderdale, FL, USA, 11–13 April 2011.
44. Gómez, D.; Rojas, A. An empirical overview of the no free lunch theorem and its effect on real-world machine learning classification. *Neural Comput.* **2016**, *28*, 216–228. [CrossRef] [PubMed]
45. Balestriero, R.; Pesenti, J.; LeCun, Y. Learning in high dimension always amount to extrapolation. *arXiv* **2021**, arXiv:2100.09485.
46. Jo, S.; Jeong, H.; Min, B.; Park, C.; Kim, Y.; Kwon, S.; Sun, A. Efficient deep-learning-based history matching for fluvial channel reservoirs. *J. Petrol. Sci. Eng.* **2022**, *208 Pt E*, 109247. [CrossRef]

47. Al-Mudhafar, W.J.; Vo, T.H.; Wood, D.A.; Min, B. Stochastic lithofacies and petrophysical property modeling for fast history matching in heterogeneous clastic reservoir applications. *Sci. Rep.* **2024**, *14*, 22. [CrossRef] [PubMed]
48. Shaik, N.B.; Jongkittinarukorn, K.; Benjapolakul, W.; Bingi, K. A novel neural network-based framework to estimate oil and gas pipelines life with missing input parameters. *Sci. Rep.* **2024**, *14*, 4511. [CrossRef]
49. Shaik, N.B.; Benjapolakul, W.; Pedapati, S.R.; Bingi, K.; Le, N.T.; Asdornwised, W.; Chaitusaney, S. Recurrent neural network-based model for estimating the life condition of a dry gas pipeline. *Process Saf. Environ.* **2022**, *164*, 639–650. [CrossRef]
50. Choi, S.; Kim, T.-W.; Choi, B.; Min, B. Design of integrated CO_2 transportation-injection-storage system based on multi-objective optimization. *J. Korean Inst. Min. Energy Resour. Eng.* **2024**, *61*, 347–362. [CrossRef]
51. Zhao, W.; Wang, L.; Mirjalili, S. Artificial hummingbird algorithm: A new bio-inspired optimizer with its engineering applications. *Comput. Methods Appl. Mech. Eng.* **2022**, *388*, 114194. [CrossRef]

mathematics

Article

An Improved Pareto Local Search-Based Evolutionary Algorithm for Multi-Objective Shortest-Path Network Counter-Interdiction Problem

Chenghui Mao [1], Ronghuan Gao [1], Qizhang Luo [2,*] and Guohua Wu [2]

[1] School of Traffic and Transportation Engineering, Central South University, Changsha 410075, China; mchh99@csu.edu.cn (C.M.); 234212142@csu.edu.cn (R.G.)
[2] School of Automation, Central South University, Changsha 410083, China; guohuawu@csu.edu.cn
* Correspondence: qz_luo@csu.edu.cn

Abstract

Most existing studies on the Shortest-Path Network Interdiction Problem (SPIP) adopt the attacker's perspective, often overlooking the critical role of defender-oriented strategies. To support proactive defense, this paper introduces a novel problem named the Multi-Objective Shortest-Path Counter-Interdiction Problem (MO-SPCIP). The problem incorporates a backup-based defense strategy from the defender's viewpoint and addresses the inherent trade-offs among minimizing the shortest path length, minimizing backup resource consumption, and maximizing the attacker's resource usage. To solve this complex problem, we propose an Improved Pareto Local Search-based Evolutionary Algorithm (IPLSEA). The algorithm integrates several problem-specific components, including a tailored initial solution generation method, a customized solution representation, and specialized genetic operators. In addition, an improved Pareto Local Search (IPLS) is incorporated into the algorithm framework, allowing an adaptive and selective search. To further enhance local refinement, three problem-specific neighborhood search operations are designed and embedded within the Pareto Local Search. The experimental results demonstrate that IPLSEA significantly outperforms state-of-the-art algorithms in terms of its convergence quality and solution diversity, enabling a more robust performance in network counter-interdiction scenarios.

Keywords: network counter-interdiction; backup strategy; multi-objective optimization; evolutionary algorithm

MSC: 90C29

1. Introduction

Research on the Shortest-Path Network Interdiction Problem (SPIP) has achieved significant progress over time, particularly in modeling and algorithmic approaches from the attacker's perspective [1]. Traditional SPIP assumes that an attacker seeks to maximize the shortest path length between designated nodes by disrupting critical network links or nodes under limited resources [2]. This attacker-centric viewpoint has found extensive applications in domains such as electrical grid analysis [3,4] and military affairs [5,6]. Notably, it serves as a valuable tool for assessing critical infrastructure vulnerability and evaluating a system's resilience against potential disruptions.

However, a major limitation of existing SPIP studies lies in treating the network as a passive entity, overlooking the active defense strategies that are available to network defenders in real-world scenarios. In practice, network administrators possess both resources and technical capabilities to mitigate such attacks through methods like protecting key parts [7], backing up components [8–10], and repairing components [11]. This highlights the need for research focused on defender-oriented strategies, which offer both theoretical innovation and tangible operational benefits for real-world system protection.

This paper considers a backup-based defense strategy to mitigate the impacts of network interdiction, wherein backup links are activated to restore the shortest path connectivity following an attack. From the defender's perspective, this involves navigating multiple competing objectives, including ensuring service availability via acceptable path lengths, minimizing the cost of deploying backup links, and maximizing the attacker's resource expenditure by redirecting attacks toward less critical components. These objectives often conflict. For example, improving the path efficiency may demand greater resource investment, while cost reduction could compromise the performance. Moreover, effective attacker diversion requires strategic redundancy planning. These inherent trade-offs motivate our extension of the traditional SPIP into a multi-objective problem, i.e., Multi-Objective Shortest-Path Counter-Interdiction Problem (MO-SPCIP).

To solve multi-objective optimization problems like MO-SPCIP, two main kinds of approaches exist. The first kind of method is the weighted aggregation-based algorithms [12], which transform the problem into a single-objective formulation via weighted aggregation. However, the weighted aggregation-based algorithms require predefined preferences, often unavailable or uncertain in real-world settings. Another kind of method is the multi-objective evolutionary algorithms (MOEAs), which leverage Pareto dominance to generate a set of non-dominated solutions in a single run, making it more suitable for scenarios with unclear or evolving objective priorities [13]. In this paper, we adopt MOEAs due to their ability to provide a set of solutions to network administrators for flexible decisions without predefined preferences, which is more suitable for real-world applications.

Nevertheless, applying MOEAs to MO-SPCIP presents specific challenges. Particularly, MOEAs, as a class of metaheuristic algorithms, require problem-specific design adaptations to perform effectively [14]. Without such customizations, existing algorithms often struggle to generate high-quality solutions for real-world problems such as the proposed problem. On the other hand, it is still an open challenge for striking a balance between diversity and convergence during the multi-objective optimization process [15]. Ensuring the sufficient exploration of the solution space while maintaining convergence toward the Pareto front requires a carefully designed search mechanism. Therefore, we propose an enhanced MOEA named the Improved Pareto Local Search-based Evolutionary Algorithm (IPLSEA), which incorporates several problem-specific features, including tailored initial solution generation, customized solution representation, and specialized genetic operators. In addition, the algorithm integrates an Improved Pareto Local Search (IPLS) component into the framework to enhance local exploitation while maintaining global diversity.

The main contributions of this paper are as follows:

(i) We propose a novel multi-objective optimization problem named MO-SPCIP. Different from most previous studies that focus on the attacker's perspective, the proposed problem addresses the practical needs of network defense. By shifting the analytical focus to the defender's perspective, the proposed problem simultaneously aims to minimize the post-attack shortest path length, reduce the consumption of defense resources, and maximize the attacker's resource expenditure. Further, we present the mathematical model of MO-SPCIP.

(ii) We develop an enhanced MOEA named the IPLSEA. Problem-specific components, including a tailored initial solution generation method, a customized solution representation, and specialized genetic operators, as well as an IPLS, are reasonably incorporated into the multi-objective evolutionary algorithm framework. In particular, different from the traditional Pareto Local Search (PLS) that exhaustively explores all individuals on the Pareto front, we propose an adaptive mechanism and three neighborhood search operations to make the Pareto Local Search more selective and effective.

(iii) We conduct comprehensive experiments to evaluate the performance of the IPLSEA. The results demonstrate that the IPLSEA outperforms state-of-the-art algorithms in terms of its convergence quality, solution diversity, and approximation to the true Pareto front. Furthermore, the algorithm enables more effective backup planning strategies and significantly enhances network resilience in the face of attacks.

The rest of this paper is organized as follows: Section 2 reviews related work, Section 3 presents the model of MO-SPCIP, Section 4 details the IPLSEA, Section 5 reports the computational results, and Section 6 concludes the paper.

2. Related Works

The network interdiction problem focuses on disrupting critical network components to degrade the system performance or functionality. This research area has garnered considerable attention due to its relevance in diverse domains such as military operations [16], infectious disease containment [17], border security [18], hazardous materials transportation [19], and critical infrastructure protection in supply chains [20], power grids [4], and aviation systems [21]. Existing research primarily focuses on fundamental objectives such as shortest-path interdiction [22], maximum flow reduction [23], and connectivity degradation [24], resulting in a wide range of optimization models and algorithmic solutions.

Particularly, in the SPIP, an attacker aims to increase the shortest path length between designated source and target nodes by strategically removing or degrading links or nodes. Recent research has significantly advanced both the modeling and solution techniques for this problem. Key modeling extensions incorporate uncertainty [25], incomplete information [26], and temporal dynamics [27]. For instance, Holzmann et al. [25] developed a random attack strategy where defenders only possess probabilistic knowledge of potential attacks. Yang et al. [26] proposed a randomized feedback-based greedy strategy for sequential shortest-path interdiction under conditions of limited feedback and incomplete cost information. Bochkarev et al. [27] integrated temporal dynamics into their interdiction model. Ho et al. [28] applied a Monte Carlo Tree Search (MCTS) to optimize the balance between exploration and exploitation in strategy evaluation. Huang et al. [29] introduced a reinforcement learning framework incorporating pointer networks to manage variable-sized outputs. Ma et al. [30] developed an innovative algorithm that reformulates the SPIP as a generalized iterative set cover problem and employed an adaptive mechanism to enhance both the computational speed and solution accuracy.

While attackers dominate the focus of much of the literature, defenders of networks are rarely concerned. In the limited studies that consider the defender's perspective, the defenders usually have access to resources and technical capabilities that enable the implementation of protective measures such as protecting key parts [7], backup components [8–10], and repair components [11] to mitigate the impact of attacks. For instance, Xu [7] et al. identified critical nodes to strengthen the protection of key areas, and the study demonstrates that safeguarding these nodes significantly enhances the model robustness. Banner and Orda [10] proposed the use of dedicated backup networks to protect against single-link failures, allowing for quick recovery without excessive resource allocation. Johnston et al. [8] extended this approach to handle multiple random failures. These efforts underscore the need to examine defense strategies from the defender's perspective, especially those that incorporate pre-deployed link backups for rapid path restoration after an attack, as is the approach that this paper adopts. He and Oki [9] proposed a novel resource allocation model which provides probabilistic protection against multiple physical device failures while minimizing the required backup capacity. Moshiri et al. [11] combined hyperbolic geometry with link prediction techniques and developed a recovery strategy for complex networks to protect the network functionality and overall robustness.

Furthermore, in designing defense strategies, defenders often face competing objectives. For example, Royset [31] considered minimizing both the total interdiction cost and maximum flow in the maximum-flow network-interdiction problem, addressing this multi-objective optimization problem by decomposing it into a series of single-objective subproblems. Ramírez-Márquez et al. [32] introduced the network recovery time as a third objective and applied a probability-driven evolutionary algorithm to solve the problem. These conflicting objectives present significant challenges for the solution methods. In particular, when the number of objectives increases to three or more, the performance of traditional MOEAs often degrades due to difficulties in maintaining convergence and diversity. Many studies have been carried out to solve this issue [33–37]. For instance, Agrawal et al. [37] proposed a two-stage evolutionary algorithm that combines nearest neighbor and 2-opt heuristics with NSGA-II through a hybrid local search approach (HLS-EA), first generating Pareto frontier corner solutions via single-objective optimization and then using them as seeds in SHLS-EA to effectively solve multi-objective Euclidean TSP problems. Li et al. [36] proposed a Pareto front (PF) model-based local search method that first constructed a predicted PF model to identify sparse regions for targeted exploration, then integrated surrogate model optima to accelerate extreme point discovery, ultimately enhancing a surrogate-assisted multi-objective evolutionary algorithm's convergence toward the true PF. Luo et al. [35] proposed an innovative hybrid multi-objective genetic algorithm that integrated a Pareto Local Search with greedy-based heuristic initialization and adaptive strategies to optimize truck–drone collaborative routing while balancing cost and customer satisfaction. Lv and Shen [34] developed an improved genetic algorithm with specialized local search and problem-specific operators to better optimize production and inventory scheduling for the maintenance of spare parts across three key objectives. Kolaee et al. [33] developed a novel genetic algorithm with a local search that optimized both the cost and attractiveness for medical tourism trips while considering patient preferences and time constraints.

In summary, most existing research has predominantly focused on the attacker's perspective, with limited attention given to the defender's viewpoint. Only a few recent studies have considered multiple optimization objectives despite their importance for addressing real-world defense scenarios. Moreover, current multi-objective optimization algorithms often struggle to balance the solution diversity and convergence, which hampers their effectiveness. To address these challenges, this paper introduces a novel multi-objective shortest-path counter-interdiction problem that simultaneously aims to minimize the post-attack shortest path length, reduce defense resource consumption, and maximize the attacker's resource expenditure. To solve this problem, we develop a hybrid evolutionary algorithm that integrates problem-specific components with an improved Pareto Local Search. The hybrid strategy could help balance the diversity and convergence of solutions during the optimization process.

3. Problem Definition and Formulation

In this paper, we consider a backup-based defense strategy to mitigate the impacts of network interdictions. Particularly, the defender will preconfigure backup links that can be activated once an attack has occurred during the network deployment phase. After an attack, the primary network is integrated with the backup network, allowing the defender to recompute the shortest path between a source node and a target node. These backup links are treated as protected resources, meaning they are immune to attack. This also reflects real-world protection mechanisms, such as physical isolation and redundant path hardening, which are commonly used to ensure the resilience and reliability of critical communication infrastructure.

By leveraging backup links, the defender can substantially reduce the shortest path length after an attack. This concept is illustrated with a simple example below. Consider the network shown in Figure 1, where the defender attempts to transmit a message from node s to node t. Each link is labeled with its transmission delay, and the defender's objective is to minimize the message delivery time. Parenthetical values indicate the increased delays for traversing links when the links are attacked. The attacker's goal is to maximize the shortest message delivery time. Before any attack, the shortest transmission path of the network is $s \to 3 \to t$ (shown as a green solid line), with a total delay of nine. Then, as shown in Figure 2, when the attacker is allowed to interdict up to three links, the optimal attack strategy (marked by red solid lines) intercepts links $(s, 1)$, $(s, 3)$, and (s, t). In this context, the defender's shortest available path becomes $s \to 1 \to t$, resulting in a total delay of 14. Suppose the defender has preconfigured a protected backup link $(s, 2)$ with a transmission delay of four, as shown in Figure 3. Since this link cannot be attacked, the attacker's best strategy shifts to targeting $(2, t)$. Consequently, the defender's new shortest path becomes $s \to 2 \to t$, with a total delay of 7, demonstrating how backup links can halve the post-attack delay from 14 to 7.

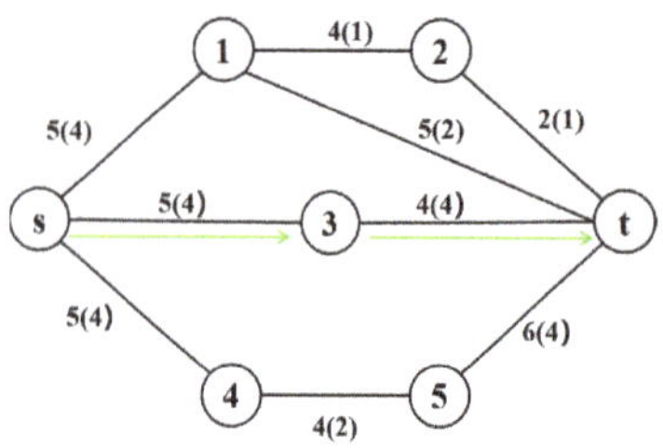

Figure 1. Example network.

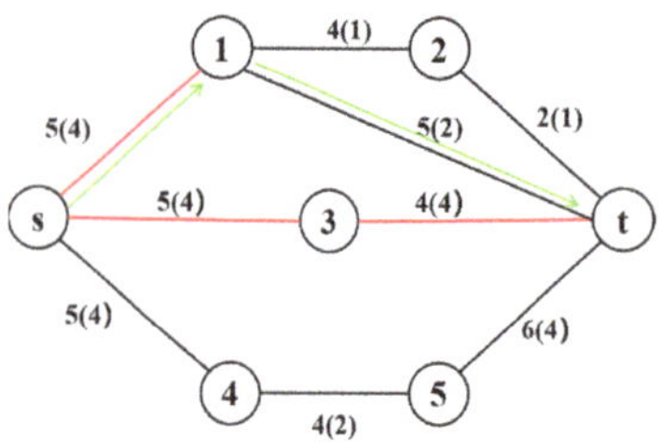

Figure 2. Network after being interdicted by an attacker.

However, the practical deployment of backup links involves critical trade-offs, including ensuring acceptable path lengths after an attack to maintain service continuity, managing the cost of deploying and maintaining backup resources, and maximizing the attacker's resource expenditure to divert attacks from vital components. These considerations motivate the formulation of the Multi-Objective Shortest-Path Counter-Interdiction Problem (MO-SPCIP), which aims to minimize the post-attack shortest path length, minimize the defender's backup resource usage, and maximize the attacker's resource consumption, simultaneously. The notations used for the formulation are detailed in Table 1.

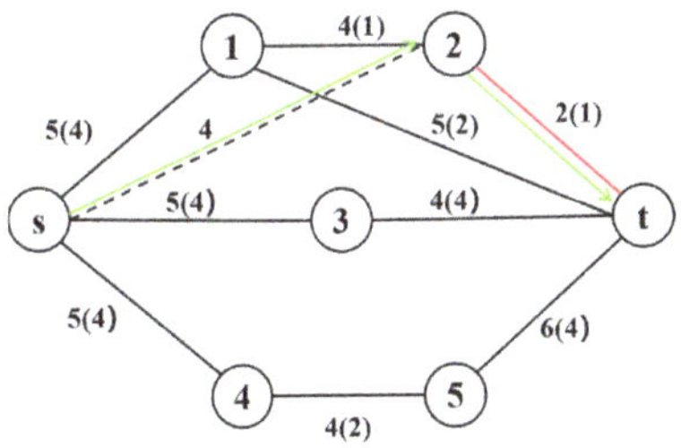

Figure 3. Interdicted network with pre-deployed backup resources.

Table 1. Notation description.

Notation	Description
G	Initial network without backup and attack
N	Set of nodes in G
L	Set of links in G
A	Set of all links constituted by the nodes in N
B	Set of backup links, $B \subset A$
r_k	Cost required to interdict link k, $k \in L$
c_k	Delay of passing through link k, $k \in A$
d_k	Increased delay of passing through link k after it is interdicted, $k \in L$
q_k	Resources required to backup link k, $k \in B$
$FS(i)$	Forward set of node i, $i \in N$
$RS(i)$	Backward set of node i, $i \in N$
R	Total affordable cost of interdiction
M	Total available amount of backup resources
s	Source node of the shortest path
t	Target node of the shortest path
x_k	$x_k = 1$ if link k is interdicted by the attacker, 0 otherwise, $k \in L$
y_k	$y_k = 1$ if link k is chosen by the defender, 0 otherwise, $k \in A$
z_k	$z_k = 1$ if link k is backed up, 0 otherwise, $k \in B$

In addition, to facilitate the modeling, some assumptions are provided as follows:

(i) All problem data are fully known to both the attacker and the defender.

(ii) The attacker acts first, selecting which links to interdict. Afterward, the defender applies the backup strategy.

(iii) The interaction is modeled as a zero-sum game between attacker and defender.

(iv) The game is played in a single round with no repetitions or learning.

Assumption (i) means that the network information is fully known to the attacker and the defender. This assumption is valid in domains such as smart grids and critical infrastructure, where attackers and defenders can theoretically access complete network information through monitoring or topological analysis [38]. Assumption (ii) reflects scenarios where interdiction events occur before defensive rerouting is possible, such as the coordinated sabotage of transportation or communication links, or targeted cyberattacks that disrupt network edges before rerouting protocols activate. This ordering is consistent with Stackelberg-type leader–follower dynamics commonly used in interdiction planning models [39]. Assumption (iii) simplifies the strategy analysis and makes it easier to derive Nash or optimal response solutions. In certain sudden attacks, such as a node injection causing the entire CPS chain to fail, attacks and defenses often end in a single interaction without the need for multiple rounds of adjustments [40]. Assumption (iv) allows for a focus on immediate strategic trade-offs without the complexity of iterative learning.

Although the above assumptions enhance the traceability of the problem model, we have to admit that these assumptions may inevitably reduce the fidelity to certain operational contexts. For instance, network interdiction and defense often occur over multiple stages, with both sides adapting to observed actions. Assumption (iv) may limit the model's applicability in environments with ongoing attacks or evolving defensive strategies. More realistic assumptions could be considered in further extensions of the proposed model.

The model of MO-SPCIP is shown below:

$$\text{MIN } f_1 = \max_{x_k} \min_{y_k, z_k} \sum_{k \in A} (c_k + x_k d_k) y_k \tag{1}$$

$$\text{MIN } f_2 = \sum\nolimits_{k \in B} q_k z_k \tag{2}$$

$$\text{MAX } f_3 = \sum_{k \in L} r_k x_k \tag{3}$$

$$\text{s.t. } \sum\nolimits_{k \in FS(i)} y_k - \sum\nolimits_{k \in RS(i)} y_k = \begin{cases} 1 \; for \; i = s \\ 0 \; \forall i \in N\{s,t\} \\ -1 \; for \; i = t \end{cases} \tag{4}$$

$$y_k \le z_k, \forall k \in A \tag{5}$$

$$\sum_{k \in B} q_k z_k \le M \tag{6}$$

$$\sum_{k \in L} r_k x_k \le R \tag{7}$$

$$x_k \in \{0,1\}, \forall k \in L \tag{8}$$

$$x_k = 0, \forall k \in B \tag{9}$$

$$y_k \in \{0,1\}, \forall k \in A \tag{10}$$

$$z_k = 1, \; \forall k \in L \tag{11}$$

$$z_k \in \{0,1\}, \; \forall k \in \text{B} \tag{12}$$

Objective (1) aims to minimize the shortest path between the designated source and target nodes after the network has been attacked. Objective (2) represents minimizing the backup resource consumption by the defender, while Objective (3) focuses on maximizing the resource consumption by the attacker. Constraint (4) denotes the complete path constraint. Constraint (5) enforces that the defender cannot traverse links that are not backed up. Constraint (6) imposes a limit on the total amount of backup resources that can be deployed. Constraint (7) represents the attacker's interdiction resource consumption limitation, restricting the number of links that can be interdicted. Constraints (8) and (9) ensure that the attacker can only interdict links in L, because the backup links deployed by the defender cannot be interdicted. This corresponds to the protection mechanism for backups in reality. Constraint (10) defines the range of variables y_k. By setting z_k in the original network to one through Constraints (11), we correspond with Constraint (5) so that all links in the original network can be selected for the passage. Constraint (12) indicates that defenders can choose to backup all links except those in the initial network, which corresponds to the backup strategy in reality.

4. Solution Approach

To address the proposed MO-SPCIP, this paper proposes a Pareto Local Search-Enhanced Evolutionary Algorithm (IPLSEA) to enhance both the convergence precision and distributional diversity of solutions. The framework and important components of IPLSEA are detailed in the following.

4.1. Framework of IPLSEA

Algorithm 1 outlines the procedure of the IPLSEA. The inputs of the algorithm include the target network G, population size N, maximum iteration count T, crossover rate c_r, and mutation rate m_r. The output is an approximate Pareto optimal solution set PF^*.

At the initialization stage, the algorithm will generate a set of the initial population based on the initial method detailed in Section 4.2 (line 1). Following the initialization, the evolutionary process iterates until reaching the maximum iteration count T (lines 3–19). In each iteration, the offspring population Q_t is generated using problem-specific genetic operators detailed in Section 4.3 (line 4). Then, by combining the parent population P_t and offspring population Q_t with the candidate population R_t, the algorithm selects a new population P_{t+1} from the candidate population R_t via nondominated sorting and crowding distance computation (lines 8–18). The nondominated sorting and crowding distance computation are commonly used techniques in multi-objective optimization algorithms such as NSGA-II, which could refer to [41], and the specific process of nondominated sorting can be seen in Section 4.3. When a set of solutions is added to the first Pareto front, an Improved Pareto Local Search (IPLS) is triggered with a probability *prob* to refine PF^*, further enhancing the local convergence (line 12). The IPLS is an extension of the conventional Pareto Local Search (PLS) proposed in this study, which will be detailed in Section 4.5. The probability *prob* increases linearly by $1/T$ per generation. This adaptive mechanism creates a dynamic exploration–exploitation balance where early phases emphasize a global search through a lower trigger probability while later phases prioritize local refinement with a higher trigger probability of an IPLS.

Algorithm 1: Framework of IPLSEA

Input: Network G, population size N, generations T, crossover rate c_r, mutation rate m_r.
Output: Pareto front solutions PF^*.
1: **Initialize**: $P_1 \leftarrow$ Initialize Population (G, N), $PF^* \leftarrow$ Nondominated sorting $(P_1)[0]$, $prob \leftarrow 0$
2: $t \leftarrow 1$
3: **while** $t \leq T$ **do**
4: $Q_t \leftarrow$ Genetic operation (P_t)
5: $R_t \leftarrow Q_t \cup P_t$
6: Nondominated sorting (R_t)
7: $P_{t+1} \leftarrow \varnothing, i \leftarrow 1$
8: **while** $|P_{t+1}| + |F_i| \leq N$ **do**
9: **if** $i = 1$ **then**
10: $PF^* \leftarrow$ Update (PF^*, F_1)
11: **if** $rand < prob$ **then**
12: $PF^* \leftarrow$ IPLS (PF^*)
13: $F_1 \leftarrow PF^*$
14: Crowding distance (F_i)
15: $P_{t+1} \leftarrow P_{t+1} \cup F_i$
16: $i \leftarrow i + 1$
17: Sort $(F_i, \prec N)$
18: $P_{t+1} \leftarrow P_{t+1} \cup F_i[1 : N - |P_{t+1}|]$
19: $t \leftarrow t + 1$, $prob \leftarrow prob + 1/T$

4.2. Initial Solution Generation

The strategy for generating initial solutions plays a critical role in obtaining high-quality outcomes. To balance the population diversity with algorithmic efficiency, we design a problem-specific initial solution generation method. In this approach, half of the initial population is generated randomly, while the other half is constructed based on key path information.

Particularly, for the random generation process, a subset of candidate backup links is randomly selected and designated as backup links. This promotes diversity in the initial population. We define a parameter $\rho \epsilon [0, 1]$ to control the proportion of candidate backup links to be selected as backup links. For the path-based generation, we define candidate backup links that are connected to either the source node or the target node as key links. These links are likely to have a higher impact on path recovery. During the construction of each individual in this part of the population, a random number of key links is selected. This process continues until half of the initial population is generated using this strategy. Figure 4 illustrates the concept of key links, in which solid black lines represent the original network, dashed lines represent candidate backup links, and red dashed lines indicate key links used during the initial solution generation process. Furthermore, during initial solution generation, the total resource consumption of the selected backup links must not exceed the available resource constraint, ensuring that each solution is feasible with respect to the resource limits.

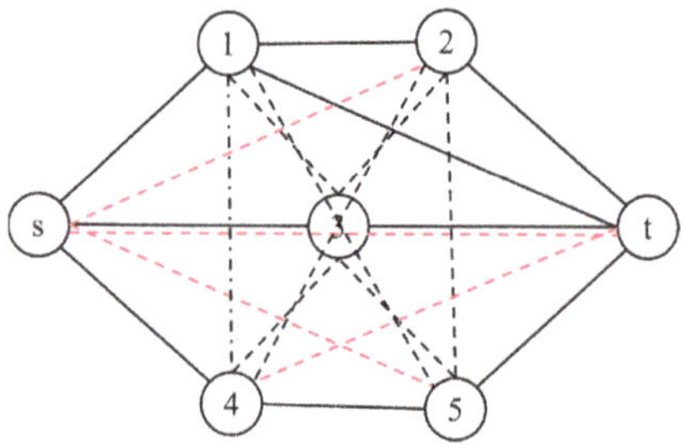

Figure 4. Diagram of key links.

To facilitate computation, the solution is represented using a binary encoding scheme, where the length of the binary vector corresponds to the number of candidate backup links. Each bit in the vector indicates whether a backup link is selected (marked by 1) or not selected (marked by 0). In the example shown in Figure 5, the solution includes 10 candidate backup links, with selected links marked by 1 and non-selected links by 0.

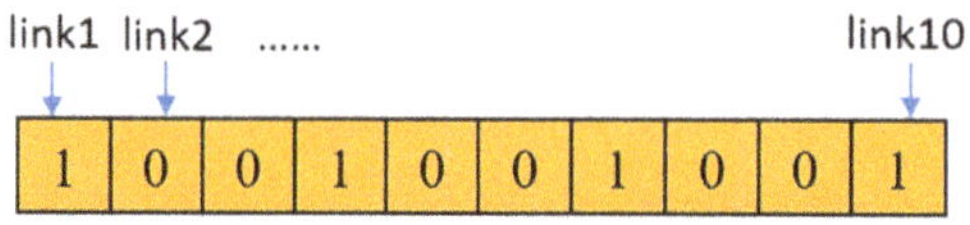

Figure 5. Representation of the solution structure.

4.3. Nondominated Sorting

Algorithm 2 introduces the procedure of nondominated sorting. The input of the algorithm is a set of individuals P where each individual has m objectives. The output is a set of Pareto fronts F sorted by their nondomination level. First, two data structures are initialized for each individual in the population. One is the dominance set S_i, which keeps track of all solutions dominated by individual p_i. The other is the $domCount[i]$, which records how many individuals dominate p_i. Both structures start as empty or zero (lines 1–3). Then, the algorithm compares every pair of individuals to determine dominance based on the multi-objective rule. Specifically, if an individual p_i is not worse than individual p_j in all objectives and strictly better in at least one, p_i is said to dominate p_j. In this case, p_j is added to S_i and $domCount[i]$ is increased by one. If p_j dominates p_i instead, the dominance set and domination count are updated accordingly (lines 4–10). After pairwise comparisons, the algorithm identifies the first Pareto front by selecting solutions with zero *domCount* (lines 11–14). Next, the algorithm builds subsequent fronts iteratively. For each individual in the current front, the *domCount* of every solution in its dominance set is decreased by one. Whenever an individual's *domCount* reaches zero, it is assigned to the next Pareto front. This process repeats until every individual is assigned to a front (lines 15–24).

Algorithm 2: Nondominated sorting

Input: Population $P = \{p_1, p_2, \ldots p_n\}$ with m objectives.
Output: Set of Pareto fronts $F = [F_1, F_2, \ldots]$ sorted by nondomination level.
1: **for** each p_i in P **do**
2: $\quad S_i \leftarrow \emptyset$
3: $\quad domCount[i] \leftarrow 0$
4: **for** each pair (p_i, p_j) with $i \neq j$ **do**
5: $\quad$ **if** $p_i \prec p_j$ **then**
6: $\quad\quad S_i \leftarrow S_i \cup \{p_j\}$
7: $\quad\quad domCount[j] \leftarrow domCount[j] + 1$
8: $\quad$ **else if** $p_j \prec p_i$ **then**
9: $\quad\quad S_j \leftarrow S_j \cup \{p_i\}$
10: $\quad\quad domCount[i] \leftarrow domCount[i] + 1$
11: $F_1 \leftarrow \varnothing$
12: **for** each p_i in P **do**
13: $\quad$ **if** $domCount[i] = 0$ **then**
14: $\quad\quad$ add(p_i) *to* F_1
15: $t \leftarrow 1$
16: **while** $F_t \neq \varnothing$ **do**
17: $\quad Q \leftarrow \varnothing$
18: $\quad$ **for** each $p_i \in F_t$ **do**
19: $\quad\quad$ **for** each $p_j \in S_i$ **do**
20: $\quad\quad\quad domCount[j] \leftarrow domCount[j] - 1$
21: $\quad\quad\quad$ **if** $\boldsymbol{domCount}[j] = 0$ **then**
22: $\quad\quad\quad\quad$ add(p_j) *to* Q
23: $\quad t \leftarrow t + 1$
24: $\quad F_t \leftarrow Q$
25: **return** F

4.4. Genetic Operations

Through crossover and mutation operators, the algorithm could perform genetic recombination and local perturbation on individuals in the current population. Based on the solution structure introduced above, this section describes tailored crossover and mutation operations for the proposed algorithm.

(i) Crossover
The algorithm will randomly select two parent individuals from the current population and perform the crossover operation based on these two parents. A preset crossover

probability (c_r) is used to decide whether to perform the crossover operation. If the execution condition is satisfied, a uniform crossover is performed on the parent individuals. Otherwise, the two parent individuals will be directly copied as offspring individuals. An example of the crossover operation is in Figure 6. For each bit of the individual's genes (i.e., the selection state of each link), the values of the corresponding bits are exchanged between Parent 1 and Parent 2 with a probability of 0.5 to construct two child individuals.

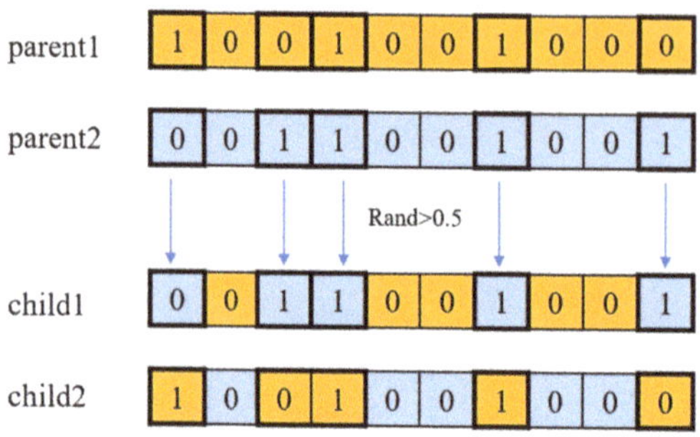

Figure 6. Schematic diagram of the crossover operator.

(ii) Mutation

To further increase the diversity of the population, we propose three kinds of mutation operations, including add_backup, remove_backup, and random_flip. The algorithm will randomly select one of the mutation operations each time during offspring generation. The illustrations of the three mutation operations are shown in Figure 7.

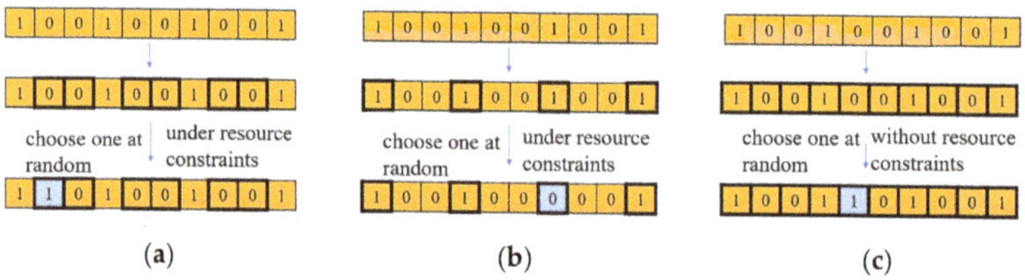

Figure 7. Schematic diagram of the mutation operations: (**a**) add_backup, (**b**) remove_backup, and (**c**) random_flip.

a. add_backup

This operation randomly selects a link that is not currently backed up and attempts to add a backup to the current solution, while ensuring that the total resource constraint is not violated. Specifically, the operation traverses the set of non-backed-up links and filters out those candidate links that would still satisfy the resource constraints if included. A link from the filtered set is then randomly selected and added as a backup. This mutation operation could enhance the solution diversity and introduce local perturbations without violating the feasibility.

b. remove_backup

This operation randomly selects a currently backed-up link and reverses its status, removing the backup designation. It is a deterministic and computationally efficient operation. By recovering potentially over-allocated resources, it helps maintain solution feasibility and creates more space for subsequent optimization. This operator is particularly useful for escaping local optima by freeing up resources for more promising backup configurations.

c. random_flip

This operation creates a neighborhood solution by randomly selecting a link index in the solution structure and flipping its binary state (e.g., changing a 0 to 1 or a 1 to 0). Unlike the other two operations, this one does not check resource constraints, which allows it to introduce greater diversity into the population. It is especially effective during the early stages of the algorithm, when global exploration is critical for covering a diverse regions of the search space.

4.5. Improved Pareto Local Search

To maintain a balance between convergence and diversity, we propose an Improved Pareto Local Search (IPLS). Unlike traditional a Pareto Local Search [42], which exhaustively explores all individuals on the Pareto front, IPLS introduces a more selective and efficient mechanism. It is adaptively triggered during the optimization process based on a generation-dependent probability and operates exclusively on previously unexplored solutions within the current non-dominated set. Furthermore, we design three problem-specific neighborhood search operations, i.e., heuristic_add, greedy_remove, and swap_backup, to guide the local search effectively, as shown in Figure 8. For each newly examined solution, the algorithm sequentially applies these three operations to generate neighborhood solutions. The IPLS could ensure the systematic exploration of the solution space without redundant computational overhead. The three designed neighborhood search operations are introduced as follows.

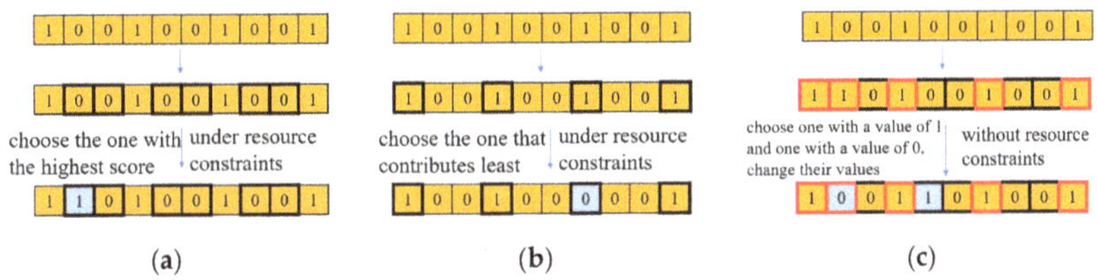

Figure 8. Schematic diagram of neighborhood search operations: (**a**) heuristic_add, (**b**) greedy_remove, and (**c**) swap_backup.

a. heuristic_add

The heuristic_add operation leverages network topology information to guide the selection of backup links. It will add a key link that satisfies resource constraints to the current solution each time. To determine a reasonable key link, we define a scoring metric, as shown in Equation (13), where $Degree(node1)$ and $Degree(node2)$ are node degrees of the two nodes and r_{edge} is the resource cost of a feasible and non-backed-up key link. The degree of a node indicates the number of other nodes it is connected to (i.e., its connectivity). The key link with a higher degree will be preferred. The rationale behind this metric is that high-degree nodes often serve as critical network hubs intersecting multiple shortest paths, making their connecting links highly valuable for structural resilience. By accounting for both structural significance and resource efficiency, this operation aims to maximize the structural benefit per unit of resource, thereby improving the efficiency of the backup configuration.

$$score = \frac{Degree(node1) + Degree(node2)}{1 + r_{edge}} \tag{13}$$

b. greedy_remove

The operation employs a greedy strategy to remove an existing backup link that contributes least to the network performance from a solution. Particularly, this operation will evaluate the impact of removing each existing backup link, where the impact is measured by the resulting increase in the shortest path length. Then, the link with minimal negative impact will be removed. This operation allows for the recovery of redundant resources while preserving the overall quality of the solution, creating space for further optimization.

c. swap_backup

The swap_backup operation performs a state exchange by randomly selecting one backed-up link and one non-backed-up link, and swapping their backup statuses. This operation does not perform feasibility verification, but it ensures that total resource consumption remains constant. By exploring different resource configurations under a fixed resource budget, this operator enables the search to uncover better-performing solutions while preserving the underlying structure of the solution space, thereby introducing diversity without violating feasibility constraints.

The framework of the IPLS is displayed in Algorithm 3. The inputs of the algorithm include Pareto front solutions PF^*, maximum iterations $plsIter$, and three specific neighborhood search operators $neighOps$. The output is an improved Pareto front PF^*. Initially, the algorithm will identify the solutions new to PF^*. Following the initialization, the search process iterates until reaching the maximum iteration count or no new solutions (lines 3–19). In each iteration, the algorithm performs the search operator in $neighOps$ one by one on each new solution in PF^*_{new} (lines 4–6). If the obtained new solution is not dominated by any solutions in PF^*, it will be considered to be a potential and added to $nextNew$ and PF^* for the next iteration. Meanwhile, the solutions in PF^* dominated by the new solution will be eliminated.

Algorithm 3: IPLS

Input: Pareto front solutions PF^*, maximum iterations $plsIter$,
neighborhood operators $neighOps$
Output: Improved Pareto front PF^*.
1: **Initialize**: $iter \leftarrow 1$, $PF^*_{new} \leftarrow$ Find solutions new to PF^*
2: **while** $PF^*_{new} \neq \emptyset$ and $iter < plsIter$ **do**
3: $nextNew \leftarrow \emptyset$
4: **for** each s in PF^*_{new} **do**
5: **for** each $op \in neighOps$ **do**
6: $s' \leftarrow op(s)$
7: $isDom \leftarrow$ False
8: **for** each $e \in PF^*$ **do**
9: **if** dominates (e, s') **then**
10: $isDom \leftarrow$ True
11: **break**
12: **if** $\neg isDom$ **then**
13: **for** each $e \in PF^*$ **do**
14: **if** dominates (s', e) **then**
15: $PF^* \leftarrow PF^* \setminus \{e\}$
16: $PF^* \leftarrow PF^* \cup \{s'\}$
17: $nextNew \leftarrow nextNew \cup \{s'\}$
18: $PF^*_{new} \leftarrow nextNew$
19: $iter \leftarrow iter + 1$
20: **return** PF^*

5. Computational Experiments

In this section, we design various typical undirected network topologies as experimental scenarios to verify the effectiveness and superiority of the proposed IPLSEA in solving MO-SPCIP through comparison experiments, ablation experiments, and parameter sensitivity analysis experiments.

5.1. Experimental Design

(i) Instances

This study employs four characteristic undirected network topologies as experimental scenarios, as shown in Table 2.

Table 2. Structural information of the networks.

Network	Number of Nodes	Number of Original Links	Number of Backupable Links
ER1	8	12	16
ER2	20	152	38
BA1	8	12	16
BA2	20	30	160
WS1	8	21	7
WS2	20	80	110
Sioux Falls	23	38	215
Eastern Massachusetts	74	129	2572

a. Erdős–Rényi Random Network (ER)

The Erdős–Rényi (ER) network [43] is generated by connecting each pair of nodes with a uniform probability, resulting in a random graph where the degree distribution approximately follows a Poisson distribution. In this study, two ER network instances are constructed. The first instance, ER1, consists of 8 nodes with a connection probability of 0.5. The second instance, ER2, contains 20 nodes, also with a connection probability of 0.5. These random topologies provide a baseline for testing the algorithm performance in uniformly connected environments.

b. Barabási–Albert Scale-Free Network (BA)

The Barabási–Albert (BA) network [44] is built using a preferential attachment mechanism, where new nodes are more likely to connect to existing nodes with higher degrees. This results in a scale-free topology characterized by a power-law degree distribution. Two test instances are created for this study. In BA1, the network begins with a 3-node star, and 5 nodes are added sequentially, each forming 3 connections ($m = 3$). In BA2, the network starts with a 5-node star (node 0 as the hub), and 12 nodes are added with 2 to 4 connections per node ($m \approx 3$ on average). These networks model real-world systems where hubs naturally emerge.

c. Watts–Strogatz Small-World Network (WS)

The Watts–Strogatz (WS) network [45] is constructed from a regular ring lattice, where each node is connected to its k_ws nearest neighbors, and a fraction of the links is randomly rewired with probability p_ws. This results in a small-world topology that combines high clustering with short average path lengths. Two instances are used. WS1 is a 7-node torus where each node connects to 4 neighbors ($k\_ws = 4$) with a rewiring probability of 0.3. WS2 is a 20-node torus with $k\_ws = 8$ and $p\_ws = 0.3$.

These instances are used to evaluate the algorithm performance in networks with both local and global connectivity features.

d. Real-World Network

The real-world networks used in this study are derived from the standard Sioux Falls transportation network dataset and a highway subnetwork extracted from the entire Eastern Massachusetts network dataset (EMS) [46]. These networks preserve the original node–link structure and realistic link weights. They serve as practical benchmarks to evaluate the algorithm's effectiveness under real-world topological and operational constraints, offering valuable insights into its applicability beyond synthetic network models.

The initial and backup link weights of all networks are uniformly set to random integers between 1 and 12. In terms of the resource allocation, the interdicting resources and backup resources are configured in proportion according to the link weight at a ratio of 5:12 units. The incremental length after a link is interdicted is set to a random value between 1 and 5. For each instance, the total amount of backup resources is set to 30.

(ii) Performance Metrics

Two principal metrics are employed to evaluate the algorithm performance from complementary perspectives: the inverted generational distance (IGD) [47] for convergence assessment and hypervolume (HV) [48] for diversity measurement.

a. IGD

The IGD quantifies the average minimum Euclidean distance between points on the true Pareto front (P) and solutions in the obtained set (Q):

$$IGD(P,Q) = \frac{1}{|P|}\sum_{v \in p} d(v,Q), \tag{14}$$

where $d(v,Q)$ calculates the Euclidean distance between points. Smaller IGD values indicate better convergence. For small networks (ER1, BA1, and WS1), the true Pareto front is obtained via a brute-force search. For larger networks, we construct an approximate front by combining all algorithm results and performing non-dominated sorting.

b. HV

The HV measures the volume of the objective space dominated by the solution set with respect to a reference point z^*:

$$HV = \delta\left(\bigcup_{i=1}^{|S|} v_i\right) \tag{15}$$

where δ denotes the Lebesgue measure, S is the non-dominated solution set, and each v_i represents a solution vector. Larger HV values indicate better diversity and convergence. The reference point z^* is determined by identifying the maximum value in each objective dimension across all normalized solutions and adding a 0.1 offset to ensure strict domination. This offset guarantees all solutions lie within the measurable hypervolume.

(iii) Comparison Algorithms and Parameter Settings

The comparison algorithms used in this study include three classical multi-objective evolutionary algorithms, i.e., NSGA-II [41], NSGA-III [49], and SPEA2 [50], and two state-of-the-art algorithms, i.e., the Hybrid Multi-Objective Modified-NSGA-II

Variable Neighborhood Search (MO-NSGA-VNS) [14] and Dual-Population-based Constrained MOEAs (DPCPRA) [51].

Based on preliminary experiments presented in Section 5.4, the parameters for each algorithm are set as shown in Table 3 for a fair comparison, where ρ is the proportion of candidate backup links selected during initial solution generation, $plsIter$ is the maximum number of iterations in the improved Pareto Local Search, c_r is the crossover rate in genetic operations, and m_r is the mutation rate in genetic operations. In addition, for all algorithms, the number of populations was 200, and the number of generations was 50. All computations were conducted on a 64-bit Windows operating system with Intel(R) Core (TM) i7-10700K, 3.8 GHz, and 64 GB RAM.

Table 3. Parameter settings.

Algorithm	ρ	$plsIter$	c_r	m_r
NSGA-II	/	/	0.8	0.3
NSGA-III	/	/	0.8	0.3
SPEA2	/	/	0.8	0.3
DPCPRA	/	/	0.8	0.3
MO-NSGA-VNS	/	/	0.8	0.3
IPLSEA	0.1	3	0.8	0.3

5.2. Comparison Experiments

Each algorithm was run independently 30 times in 8 experimental scenarios and the results obtained are shown in Tables 4 and 5, respectively.

Table 4. IGD results of six algorithms (lower is better).

Network	NSGA-II		NSGA-III		SPEA2		DPCPRA		MO-NSGA-VNS		IPLSEA	
	Mean	Std	Mean	Std	Mean	Std	Mean	Std	Mean	Std	Mean	Std
ER1	0.0178	0.0145	0.0059	0.0061	0.0013	0.0049	0.0012	0.0039	**0.0000**	0.0000	**0.0000**	0.0000
ER2	0.0811	0.0482	0.0711	0.0700	0.1236	0.0558	0.0760	0.0646	0.0575	0.0546	**0.0350**	0.0414
BA2	0.0898	0.0274	0.1341	0.0257	0.081	0.0243	0.079	0.0232	0.074	0.0163	**0.0249**	0.002
WS1	0.0172	0.0243	0.0256	0.0582	0.0384	0.0677	0.0222	0.0581	**0.0000**	0.0000	**0.0000**	0.0000
WS2	0.1542	0.0152	0.1212	0.0226	0.1097	0.0416	0.1021	0.0384	0.0874	0.0187	**0.0725**	0.0075
Sioux Falls	0.1200	0.0133	0.1401	0.0037	0.1209	0.0540	0.0853	0.0527	0.0507	0.0104	**0.0337**	0.0160
EMS	0.1978	0.0362	0.2055	0.0069	0.1492	0.0190	0.1607	0.0331	0.1378	0.0042	**0.1321**	0.0187

Bolded values indicate the bestresults in each case.

Table 5. HV results of six algorithms (higher is better).

Network	NSGA-II		NSGA-III		SPEA2		DPCPRA		MO-NSGA-VNS		IPLSEA	
	Mean	Std	Mean	Std	Mean	Std	Mean	Std	Mean	Std	Mean	Std
ER1	0.7385	0.0052	0.7411	0.0030	0.7445	0.0019	0.7447	0.0014	**0.7450**	0.0000	**0.7450**	0.0000
ER2	0.3136	0.0137	0.3047	0.0152	0.2936	0.0290	0.3042	0.0240	0.3070	0.0204	**0.3152**	0.0131
BA1	0.0756	0.0267	0.0746	0.0262	0.0795	0.0247	0.0814	0.0233	**0.0931**	0.0000	**0.0931**	0.0000
BA2	0.6820	0.0155	0.6738	0.0174	0.6928	0.0140	0.6934	0.0120	0.7000	0.0054	**0.7244**	0.0012
WS1	0.2553	0.0047	0.2516	0.0189	0.2480	0.0224	0.2522	0.0190	**0.2587**	0.0000	**0.2587**	0.0000
WS2	0.6803	0.0331	0.7230	0.0227	0.6911	0.0270	0.7135	0.0358	0.7484	0.0096	**0.7569**	0.0046
Sioux Falls	0.7643	0.0099	0.7270	0.0046	0.7669	0.0643	0.8054	0.0610	0.8429	0.0197	**0.8705**	0.0112
EMS	0.2423	0.0520	0.2358	0.0142	0.2669	0.0327	0.2706	0.0034	**0.3154**	0.0206	0.2967	0.0261

Bolded values indicate the best results in each case.

According to the results, the IPLSEA demonstrates consistent and significant performance advantages across most tested networks. In three small-scale networks (ER1, BA1, and WS1), the IPLSEA and MO-NSGA-VNS successfully identify an entire true Pareto front, achieving an identical and best performance in both the IGD and HV. For larger and more complex networks, IPLSEA maintains a good performance compared to benchmark and state-of-the-art algorithms. In terms of the IGD, it achieves the lowest mean values in ER2, BA2, WS2, Sioux Falls, and EMS. For instance, in BA2, it records 0.0249, significantly outperforming NSGA-II (0.0898) and SPEA2 (0.0790), demonstrating its ability to generate solution sets that better approximate the true Pareto frontier. The HV results further confirm this advantage, with the IPLSEA achieving the highest hypervolume values in all but one tested network. In addition, the IPLSEA exhibits better robustness, with minimal standard deviations across different networks. For example, in BA2, the HV standard deviation is only 0.0012 and the IGD standard deviation is 0.0020, highlighting its stable performance across multiple independent runs. These comprehensive results establish IPLSEA's dual advantage in both the solution quality and robustness, particularly for complex network optimization problems like MO-SPCIP.

For detailed analysis, BA2 serves as an illustrative example, containing 30 main links and 180 optional backup links, with attributes detailed in Table 6. The cost represents resources required to interdict the corresponding link and d represents the increased delay of passing through the corresponding link. With backup resource constraints set to 30 units and pivot nodes selected as 0 (source) and 19 (destination), the network's size precludes the exhaustive determination of true Pareto frontiers. Instead, this study constructs an approximate frontier through the non-dominated sorting of all algorithm results, yielding 41 solutions, as shown in Figure 9. The shortest path length is 9, which corresponds to backup resource 8 and interdicting resource 0, where the attacker does not interdict and, at this time, the backup path of the defender is (0, 19) and the shortest path is also (0, 19). The longest path length is 38, which corresponds to both the backup resource and interdicting resource 0 and 39, representing no backup, as shown in Figure 10, where the red solid line indicates the attacker's interdicting link and the green solid line indicates the defender's shortest path. The minimum value of the backup resource is 0 and the maximum value is 30. When the defense chooses to backup (7, 19), (10, 19), (3, 16), and (0, 16), all 30 backup resources are used up, as shown in Figure 11, and then the attacker interdicts the links (3, 10), (0, 2), (2, 10), and (7, 16) with 36 resources and the defender chooses (0, 16), (16, 7), and (7, 19) with the length of 17. The minimum value of interdicting resources is 0 and the maximum is 40.

Table 6. Attributes of BA2.

No.	Node to Node	Length	Cost	d	No.	Node to Node	Length	Cost	d
1	0, 1	11	5	1	16	4, 14	15	9	4
2	0, 2	8	8	1	17	5, 15	8	10	1
3	0, 3	11	9	1	18	6, 16	10	7	4
4	0, 4	13	5	4	19	7, 16	4	11	4
5	0, 5	6	6	2	20	8, 16	7	5	1
6	1, 6	8	7	3	21	9, 17	10	5	4
7	1, 7	4	8	4	22	10, 17	11	10	3
8	1, 8	9	8	3	23	11, 17	13	5	2
9	2, 8	13	10	3	24	12, 19	13	10	3
10	2, 9	7	6	1	25	13, 18	13	7	4
11	2, 10	6	6	4	26	14, 18	4	8	4
12	3, 10	5	11	4	27	15, 18	9	9	4
13	3, 11	12	9	4	28	16, 19	15	9	1
14	3, 12	7	5	4	29	17, 19	11	10	4
15	4, 13	8	9	3	30	18, 19	14	10	1

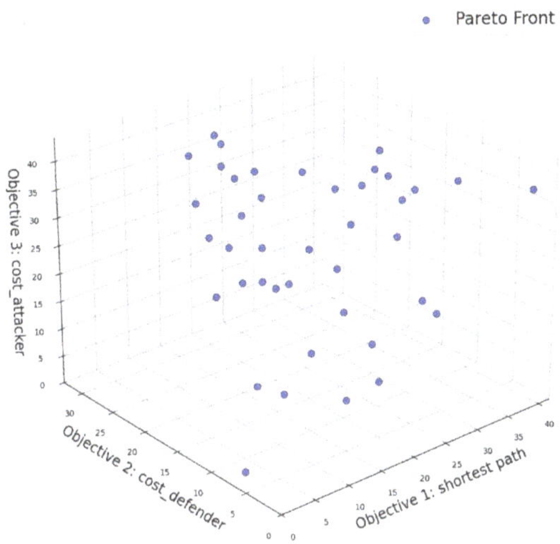

Figure 9. Approximate Pareto front of BA2.

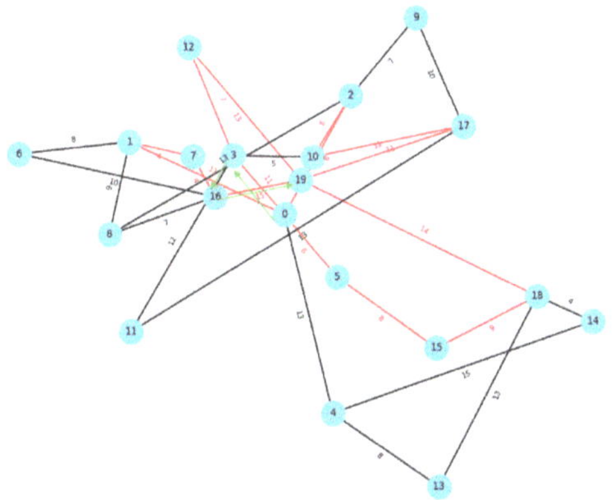

Figure 10. Decision result when there is no backup.

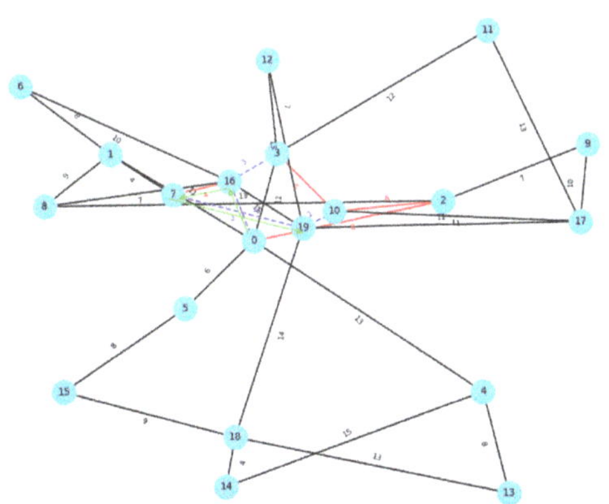

Figure 11. Decision result when backup resources are fully consumed.

The comparative results for the BA2 network are presented in Figure 12 and Tables 7 and 8, demonstrating IPLSEA's superior performance across both evaluation metrics. Regarding the IGD values, the IPLSEA achieves an optimal performance with a mean of 0.0249, significantly outperforming control algorithms such as the MO-NSGA-VNS (0.0740) and DPCPRA (0.070). This substantial advantage reflects IPLSEA's enhanced approximation capability to the true Pareto frontier.

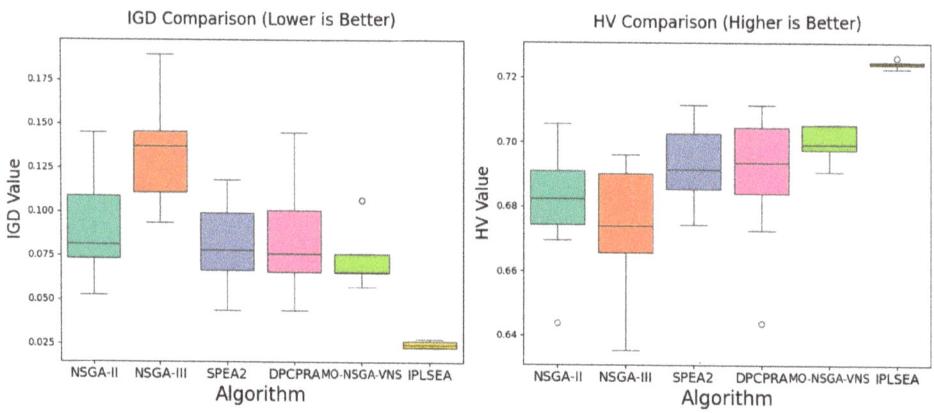

Figure 12. IGD and HV metrics results of all algorithms for the BA2 network.

Table 7. IGD results of BA2 (lower is better).

Algorithm	Mean	Std	Min	Max
NSGA-II	0.0898	0.0274	0.0527	0.1451
NSGA-III	0.1341	0.0257	0.0933	0.1896
SPEA2	0.0810	0.0232	0.0441	0.1181
DPCPRA	0.0790	0.0243	0.0441	0.1451
MO-NSGA-VNS	0.0740	0.0163	0.0573	0.1068
IPLSEA	0.0249	0.0020	0.0230	0.0276

Table 8. HV results of BA2 (higher is better).

Algorithm	Mean	Std	Min	Max
NSGA-II	0.6820	0.0155	0.6438	0.7056
NSGA-III	0.6738	0.0174	0.6355	0.6960
SPEA2	0.6928	0.0120	0.6744	0.7114
DPCPRA	0.6934	0.0140	0.6438	0.7114
MO-NSGA-VNS	0.7000	0.0054	0.6908	0.7053
IPLSEA	0.7244	0.0012	0.7228	0.7262

In HV metrics, the IPLSEA maintains its leading position with a mean value of 0.7244, the highest among all compared algorithms, coupled with exceptional stability evidenced by its minimal standard deviation (0.0012). This combination of a high hypervolume and low variability confirms the algorithm's robust solution quality and reliable performance. The MO-NSGA-VNS and DPCPRA show stable but inferior results. These comprehensive results underscore IPLSEA's dual advantage in both solution quality and algorithmic stability for multi-objective network optimization challenges.

We also provide the computational complexity analysis of the IPLSEA and its comparison algorithms. IPLSEA's complexity is mainly determined by nondominated sorting, with a single generation being approximately $O\left(MN^2\right)$ and the overall complexity being $O\left(TMN^2\right)$, where N is the population size, M is the number of objectives, and T is the number of iterations. In comparison, the classical NSGA-II and NSGA-III also have the same dominant complexity. NSGA-III adds reference point processing, but the overall complexity remains $O\left(TMN^2\right)$. SPEA2 calculates the distance matrix between individuals, with a complexity of $O\left(TMN^2\right)$. DPCPRA adopts a two-population structure, with a complexity approximately twice that of non-dominated sorting, still belonging to the $O\left(TMN^2\right)$ level. MO-NSGA-VNS introduces a neighborhood search, with a complexity approximately equal to $O\left(TMN^2 + NL\right)$, where the local search overhead L is typically smaller than the non-dominated sorting overhead. Overall, the IPLSEA has comparable complexity to these algorithms, and the addition of a local search helps improve the performance without significantly increasing the computational burden.

5.3. Ablation Experiments

The ablation experiments are designed to evaluate the effectiveness of key components within the IPLSEA by comparing the performance of three algorithmic variants. These include the RIA, which removes the initial solution construction module from the IPLSEA, RIPLS, which excludes the IPLS operator from the IPLSEA, and EA, which removes both components from the IPLSEA. Each variant is compared against the full IPLSEA, as well as two strong baseline methods: SPEA2 and MO-NSGA-VNS. All algorithms are evaluated on the Sioux Falls network through 15 independent runs, using IGD and HV metrics.

Figure 13's results demonstrate RIA's significant superiority over the RIPLSA and EA and RIPLSA's superiority over EA, confirming that both the structured initialization and IPLS operator enhance the algorithmic performance, with the IPLS operator showing particularly pronounced benefits. However, both variants underperform relative to the full IPLSEA, as evidenced by their degraded IGD and HV values. RIA's notably poorer results inversely validate the critical role of the proposed IPLS operator in maintaining solution quality. These findings collectively establish that the IPLSEA's synergistic integration of structured initialization and a targeted local search delivers an optimal performance for network optimization challenges.

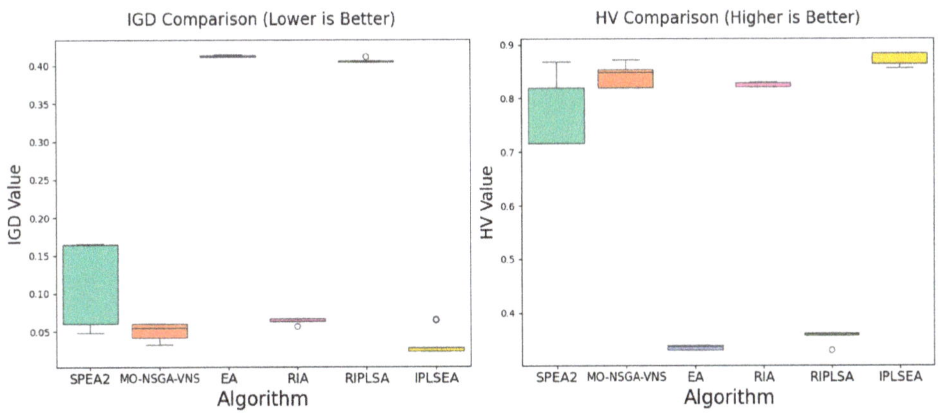

Figure 13. Comparison results chart of the ablation experiment.

5.4. Parameter Sensitivity Analysis

In order to find a suitable combination of algorithm parameters and analyze the impacts of the algorithm parameters, 10 combinations of algorithm parameters were designed based on practical experience and 30 independent experimental runs on the BA2 network were conducted. The algorithm parameters involved were as follows: ρ (the proportion of candidate backup links selected during initial solution generation), $plsIter$ (the maximum number of iterations in the improved Pareto Local Search), c_r (the crossover rate in genetic operations), and m_r (the mutation rate in genetic operations). The results corresponding to different parameter combinations are shown in Table 9.

Table 9. IGD results of BA2 with different combinations of algorithm parameters.

ρ	*plsIter*	c_r	m_r	**Average IGD Value**
0.1	1	0.8	0.3	0.0566
0.1	3	0.6	0.3	0.0570
0.1	3	0.8	0.1	0.0359
0.1	3	0.8	0.3	0.0255 ↓
0.1	3	0.8	0.5	0.0341
0.1	3	0.9	0.3	0.0277
0.1	5	0.8	0.3	0.0236 ↓
0.2	3	0.8	0.3	0.0368
0.3	3	0.8	0.3	0.0398
0.05	3	0.8	0.3	0.0297

The results indicate that setting the value of ρ to 0.1 yields a better solution set. As $plsIter$ increases from 1 to 5, the IGD values show an overall downward trend, but the improvement rate decreases significantly when $plsIter$ r exceeds 3, indicating diminishing marginal returns from additional iterations. c_r primarily affects the results at extreme values (e.g., 0.6 or 0.9), while the moderate value of 0.8 typically exhibits stable performance. m_r shows little variation within the range of 0.1–0.5, and 0.3 has a relatively balanced performance in most combinations. Overall, the parameter combination ($\rho = 0.1$, $plsIter = 3$, $c\_r = 0.8$, $m\_r = 0.3$) performs nearly as well as the optimal combination ($\rho = 0.1$, $plsIter = 5$, $c\_r = 0.8$, $m\_r = 0.3$) on the IGD, with only a minimal difference between the two. However, the former has a significant advantage in computational cost, so this combination was selected as the default configuration for experiments.

To investigate the impact of backup resource allocation on the algorithm performance, we conducted 30 independent experimental runs on the Sioux Falls network instance for each of the following backup resource levels: 5, 15, 25, 30, 35, 40, and 45 units. We identified optimal compromise solutions through a normalized distance metric relative to the ideal point [37] to analyze the effects systematically. This approach involves normalizing each objective value against the ideal point and selecting the Pareto-optimal solution with the minimal Euclidean distance as the best compromise.

Figure 14 shows the average results. Adding more backup resources can shorten the path length, but uses more backup resources. Both the path length and resource use eventually level off. The attacker's resource use stays about the same no matter how many backup resources are available.

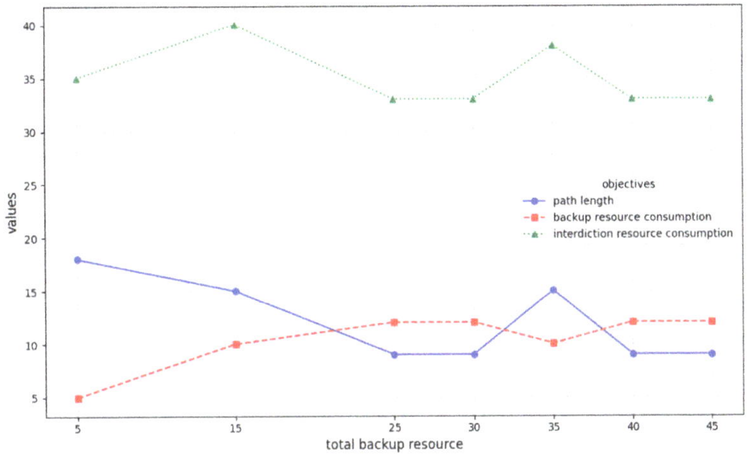

Figure 14. Change in optimal compromise solution with the change of total backup resources.

6. Conclusions

This paper addresses a multi-objective shortest-path interdiction problem under proactive defense strategies, where defenders pre-emptively configure backup links to mitigate attacks. The formulation simultaneously optimizes three objectives, including minimizing the post-attack shortest path length, minimizing backup resource consumption, and maximizing attacker resource utilization. To solve this challenging problem, we developed a specialized multi-objective evolutionary algorithm named the IPLSEA. The proposed algorithm features a problem-specific solution structure, initial population generation, and genetic operations. Furthermore, an IPLS based on an adaptive mechanism and multiple problem-specific neighborhood search operations is incorporated into the algorithm framework to further improve the performance of the algorithm.

A comprehensive experimental evaluation demonstrates the IPLSEA's superiority over state-of-the-art competitive algorithms, with a dominant performance in both the IGD and HV metrics. Ablation experiments confirm that both the initial solution generation method and IPLS significantly enhance the algorithm performance, with the IPLS contributing particularly substantial improvements. Sensitivity analysis experiments reveal that increased backup resources yield progressively shorter achievable path lengths until reaching a stabilization threshold, while attacker resource expenditure remains largely independent of backup availability.

Although the IPLSEA performs well in experiments, it still faces some challenges in practical applications. First, the network topology and link state data are often incomplete or noisy, which can affect the accuracy of defense strategies. Second, as the network scale and target numbers increase, the computational load of the algorithm also rises significantly, potentially failing to meet real-time response requirements, necessitating parallel computing or hardware acceleration to enhance the efficiency. Additionally, some real-world network environments change frequently, so the algorithm must have the ability to quickly adjust and adapt. Finally, there is often information asymmetry between attackers and defenders, which increases the difficulty of the strategy formulation. Future work could focus on optimizing the computational efficiency of the algorithm and designing defense mechanisms that can adapt to dynamic and asymmetric information environments to ensure that the algorithm can be better applied to real-world scenarios.

Author Contributions: Conceptualization, R.G., G.W. and C.M.; methodology, R.G. and Q.L.; validation, R.G.; formal analysis, R.G.; investigation, R.G.; resources, R.G.; data curation, R.G.; writing—original draft preparation, R.G.; writing—review and editing, G.W., Q.L. and C.M.; supervision, C.M.; project administration, Q.L.; funding acquisition, Q.L. All authors have read and agreed to the published version of the manuscript.

Funding: This research was jointly funded by the China Postdoctoral Science Foundation (Grant No. GZC20242042 and Grant No. 2024M763698) and the Natural Science Foundation of Hunan Province (Grant No. 2025JJ10007).

Data Availability Statement: Data are contained within this article.

Conflicts of Interest: The author declares no conflicts of interest.

Abbreviations

The following abbreviations are used in this manuscript:

SPIP	Shortest-Path Network Interdiction Problem
MO-SPCIP	Multi-Objective Shortest-Path Counter-Interdiction Problem
MOEAs	Multi-Objective Evolutionary Algorithms
IPLS	Improved Pareto Local Search
IPLSEA	Improved Pareto Local Search-based Evolutionary Algorithm
EMS	Eastern Massachusetts network dataset
MO-NSGA-VNS	Hybrid Multi-Objective Modified-NSGA-II Variable Neighborhood Search
DPCPRA	Dual-Population-based Constrained MOEAs

References

1. Smith, J.C.; Song, Y. A survey of network interdiction models and algorithms. *Eur. J. Oper. Res.* **2020**, *283*, 797–811. [CrossRef]
2. Israeli, E.; Wood, R.K. Shortest-path network interdiction. *Netw. Int. J.* **2002**, *40*, 97–111. [CrossRef]
3. López-Lezama, J.M.; Galeano, J.C.C.; Trujillo, E.R. Assessment of the electric grid interdiction problem considering different network models. *J. Appl. Sci. Eng.* **2020**, *20*, 175–183.
4. Sundar, K.; Mastin, A.; Garcia, M.; Bent, R.; Watson, J.-P. Exact and Heuristic Approaches for the Stochastic Nk Interdiction in Power Grids. In Proceedings of the 2024 18th International Conference on Probabilistic Methods Applied to Power Systems (PMAPS), Auckland, New Zealand, 24–26 June 2024; pp. 1–6.
5. Brown, G.G.; Carlyle, W.M.; Harney, R.C.; Skroch, E.M.; Wood, R.K. Interdicting a nuclear-weapons project. *Oper. Res.* **2009**, *57*, 866–877. [CrossRef]
6. Michalopoulos, D.P.; Morton, D.P.; Barnes, J.W. Prioritizing network interdiction of nuclear smuggling. In *Stochastic Programming: Applications in Finance, Energy, Planning and Logistics*; World Scientific: Singapore, 2013; pp. 313–346.
7. Xu, S.; Xia, Y.; Ouyang, M. Effect of resource allocation to the recovery of scale-free networks during cascading failures. *Phys. A Stat. Mech. Its Appl.* **2020**, *540*, 123157. [CrossRef]
8. Johnston, M.; Lee, H.-W.; Modiano, E. A robust optimization approach to backup network design with random failures. *IEEE/ACM Trans. Netw.* **2014**, *23*, 1216–1228. [CrossRef]
9. He, F.; Oki, E. Backup allocation model with probabilistic protection for virtual networks against multiple facility node failures. *IEEE Trans. Netw. Serv. Manag.* **2021**, *18*, 2943–2959. [CrossRef]
10. Banner, R.; Orda, A. *Designing Low-Capacity Backup Networks for Fast Restoration*; IEEE: Piscataway, NJ, USA, 2010.
11. Moshiri, M.; Safaei, F.; Samei, Z. A novel recovery strategy based on link prediction and hyperbolic geometry of complex networks. *J. Complex Netw.* **2021**, *9*, cnab007. [CrossRef]
12. Caramia, M.; Dell'Olmo, P.; Caramia, M.; Dell'Olmo, P. Multi-objective optimization. In *Multi-Objective Management in Freight Logistics: Increasing Capacity, Service Level, Sustainability, and Safety with Optimization Algorithms*; Springer: Cham, Switzerland, 2020; pp. 21–51.
13. Cheshmehgaz, H.R.; Haron, H.; Sharifi, A. The review of multiple evolutionary searches and multi-objective evolutionary algorithms. *Artif. Intell. Rev.* **2015**, *43*, 311–343. [CrossRef]
14. Granata, D.; Sgalambro, A. A hybrid modified-NSGA-II VNS algorithm for the multi-objective critical disruption Path Problem. *Comput. Oper. Res.* **2023**, *160*, 106363. [CrossRef]

15. Gao, X.; He, F.; Zhang, S.; Luo, J.; Fan, B. A fast nondominated sorting-based MOEA with convergence and diversity adjusted adaptively. *J. Supercomput.* **2024**, *80*, 1426–1463. [CrossRef]
16. Bailey, M.D.; Shechter, S.M.; Schaefer, A.J. SPAR: Stochastic programming with adversarial recourse. *Oper. Res. Lett.* **2006**, *34*, 307–315. [CrossRef]
17. Habboush, Y.; Yarrarapu, S.N.S.; Guzman, N. Infection control. In *StatPearls [Internet]*; StatPearls Publishing: Treasure Island, FL, USA, 2018.
18. Zhang, J.; Zhuang, J.; Behlendorf, B. Stochastic shortest path network interdiction with a case study of Arizona–Mexico border. *Reliab. Eng. Syst. Saf.* **2018**, *179*, 62–73. [CrossRef]
19. Kheirkhah, A.; Navidi, H.; Messi Bidgoli, M. A bi-level network interdiction model for solving the hazmat routing problem. *Int. J. Prod. Res.* **2016**, *54*, 459–471. [CrossRef]
20. Wein, L.M.; Liu, Y. Analyzing a bioterror attack on the food supply: The case of botulinum toxin in milk. *Proc. Natl. Acad. Sci. USA* **2005**, *102*, 9984–9989. [CrossRef]
21. Ghaffarinasab, N.; Atayi, R. An implicit enumeration algorithm for the hub interdiction median problem with fortification. *Eur. J. Oper. Res.* **2018**, *267*, 23–39. [CrossRef]
22. Borrero, J.S.; Sauré, D.; Trigo, N. Optimal sequential stochastic shortest path interdiction. *Eur. J. Oper. Res.* **2025**, *326*, 641–655. [CrossRef]
23. Bentoumi, I.; Furini, F.; Mahjoub, A.R.; Martin, S. Integer linear programming formulations for the maximum flow blocker problem. *Eur. J. Oper. Res.* **2025**, *324*, 742–758. [CrossRef]
24. Scaparra, M.P.; Church, R.L. A bilevel mixed-integer program for critical infrastructure protection planning. *Comput. Oper. Res.* **2008**, *35*, 1905–1923. [CrossRef]
25. Holzmann, T.; Smith, J.C. The shortest path interdiction problem with randomized interdiction strategies: Complexity and algorithms. *Oper. Res.* **2021**, *69*, 82–99. [CrossRef]
26. Yang, J.; Borrero, J.S.; Prokopyev, O.A.; Sauré, D. Sequential shortest path interdiction with incomplete information and limited feedback. *Decis. Anal.* **2021**, *18*, 218–244. [CrossRef]
27. Bochkarev, A.A.; Smith, J.C. Monte Carlo tree search for dynamic shortest-path interdiction. *Networks* **2024**, *84*, 398–419. [CrossRef]
28. Ho, Y.; Carbajal, A.; Escamilla, L.; Pinar, A. Neuromorphic Monte Carlo Tree Search Methods for Shortest Path Interdiction. In Proceedings of the 2024 International Conference on Neuromorphic Systems (ICONS), Arlington, VA, USA, 30 July–2 August 2024; pp. 307–311.
29. Huang, D.; Mao, Z.; Fang, K.; Chen, L. Solving the shortest path interdiction problem via reinforcement learning. *Int. J. Prod. Res.* **2023**, *61*, 31–48. [CrossRef]
30. Ma, C.; Zuo, T.; Zhang, H.-F. Network shortest path interdiction problem based on generalized set coverage. *IEEE Trans. Netw. Sci. Eng.* **2023**, *11*, 2191–2203. [CrossRef]
31. Royset, J.O.; Wood, R.K. Solving the bi-objective maximum-flow network-interdiction problem. *Inf. J. Comput.* **2007**, *19*, 175–184. [CrossRef]
32. Ramirez-Marquez, J.E. Bi and tri-objective optimization in the deterministic network interdiction problem. *Reliab. Eng. Syst. Saf.* **2010**, *95*, 887–896. [CrossRef]
33. Kolaee, M.H.; Al-e-Hashem, S.M.J.M.; Jabbarzadeh, A. A local search-based non-dominated sorting genetic algorithm for solving a multi-objective medical tourism trip design problem considering the attractiveness of trips. *Eng. Appl. Artif. Intell.* **2023**, *124*, 106630. [CrossRef]
34. Lv, L.; Shen, W. An improved NSGA-II with local search for multi-objective integrated production and inventory scheduling problem. *J. Manuf. Syst.* **2023**, *68*, 99–116. [CrossRef]
35. Luo, Q.; Wu, G.; Ji, B.; Wang, L.; Suganthan, P.N. Hybrid multi-objective optimization approach with Pareto local search for collaborative truck-drone routing problems considering flexible time windows. *IEEE Trans. Intell. Transp. Syst.* **2021**, *23*, 13011–13025. [CrossRef]
36. Li, F.; Gao, L.; Shen, W. Surrogate-assisted multi-objective evolutionary optimization with Pareto front model-based local search method. *IEEE Trans. Cybern.* **2022**, *54*, 173–186. [CrossRef]
37. Agrawal, A.; Ghune, N.; Prakash, S.; Ramteke, M. Evolutionary algorithm hybridized with local search and intelligent seeding for solving multi-objective Euclidian TSP. *Expert Syst. Appl.* **2021**, *181*, 115192. [CrossRef]
38. Shan, X.G.; Zhuang, J. A game-theoretic approach to modeling attacks and defenses of smart grids at three levels. *Reliab. Eng. Syst. Saf.* **2020**, *195*, 106683. [CrossRef]
39. Chen, L.; Wang, Z.; Li, F.; Guo, Y.; Geng, K. A stackelberg security game for adversarial outbreak detection in the internet of things. *Sensors* **2020**, *20*, 804. [CrossRef] [PubMed]

40. Liao, Z.; Shi, J.; Zhang, Y.; Wang, S.; Sun, Z. A survey of resilient coordination for cyber-physical systems against malicious attacks. *arXiv* **2024**, arXiv:2402.10505. [CrossRef]
41. Doerr, B.; Ivan, T.; Krejca, M.S. Speeding up the NSGA-II with a simple tie-breaking rule. In Proceedings of the AAAI Conference on Artificial Intelligence, Philadelphia, PA, USA, 25 February–4 March 2025; pp. 26964–26972.
42. Lust, T.; Teghem, J. Two-phase Pareto local search for the biobjective traveling salesman problem. *J. Heuristics* **2010**, *16*, 475–510. [CrossRef]
43. Mohandas, K.; Suchecki, K.; Hołyst, J.A. Paradise-disorder transition in structural balance dynamics on Erdös-Rényi graphs. *Phys. Rev. E* **2025**, *111*, 024310. [CrossRef]
44. Xie, F.; Zhao, Z.; Yang, P. Higher Order Preference on the Evolution of Cooperation on Barabási–Albert Scale-Free Network. In Proceedings of the International Conference on Natural Computation, Fuzzy Systems and Knowledge Discovery, Guiyang, China, 24–26 July 2021; pp. 137–149.
45. Alimohammadi, Y.; Işık, S.; Saberi, A. Local Limits of Small World Networks. *arXiv* **2025**, arXiv:2501.11226.
46. Transportation Networks for Research. Available online: https://github.com/bstabler/TransportationNetworks (accessed on 12 August 2024).
47. Deb, K.; Pratap, A.; Agarwal, S.; Meyarivan, T. A fast and elitist multiobjective genetic algorithm: NSGA-II. *IEEE Trans. Evol. Comput.* **2002**, *6*, 182–197. [CrossRef]
48. Lopes, G.; Klamroth, K.; Paquete, L. A greedy Hypervolume Polychotomic Scheme for multiobjective combinatorial optimization. *Comput. Oper. Res.* **2025**, *183*, 107140. [CrossRef]
49. Deb, K.; Jain, H. An evolutionary many-objective optimization algorithm using reference-point-based nondominated sorting approach, part I: Solving problems with box constraints. *IEEE Trans. Evol. Comput.* **2013**, *18*, 577–601. [CrossRef]
50. Zitzler, E.; Laumanns, M.; Thiele, L. SPEA2: Improving the strength Pareto evolutionary algorithm. *TIK Rep.* **2001**, *103*. [CrossRef]
51. Qiao, K.; Chen, Z.; Qu, B.; Yu, K.; Yue, C.; Chen, K.; Liang, J. A dual-population evolutionary algorithm based on dynamic constraint processing and resources allocation for constrained multi-objective optimization problems. *Expert Syst. Appl.* **2024**, *238*, 121707. [CrossRef]

MDPI AG
Grosspeteranlage 5
4052 Basel
Switzerland
Tel.: +41 61 683 77 34

Mathematics Editorial Office
E-mail: mathematics@mdpi.com
www.mdpi.com/journal/mathematics

www.ingramcontent.com/pod-product-compliance
Lightning Source LLC
Chambersburg PA
CBHW040813250926
51850CB00007BA/1157
* 9 7 8 3 7 2 5 8 5 5 0 9 4 *